FAIR USE AND FREE INQUIRY
Copyright Law and the New Media

COMMUNICATION AND
INFORMATION SCIENCE

A series of monographs,
treatises, and texts

Edited by
MELVIN J. VOIGT

University of California, San Diego

RHONDA J. CRANE • The Politics of International Standards: France and the Color
TV War
GLEN FISHER • American Communication in a Global Society
JOHN S. LAWRENCE AND BERNARD M. TIMBERG • Fair Use and Free Inquiry:
Copyright Law and the New Media
ROBERT G. MEADOW • Politics as Communication
VINCENT MOSCO • Broadcasting in the United States: Innovative Challenge and
Organizational Control
KAARLE NORDENSTRENG AND HERBERT I. SCHILLER • National Sovereignty and In-
ternational Communication: A Reader

In Preparation

HEWITT D. CRANE • The New Social Marketplace: Notes on Effecting Social
Change in America's Third Century
JOHN J. GEYER • Reading as Information Processing
BRADLEY S. GREENBERG • Life on Television: Content Analysis of U.S. TV Drama
MICHEL GUITE • Telecommunications Policy: The Canadian Model
ITHIEL DE SOLA POOL • Retrospective Technology Assessment of the Telephone
CLAIRE K. SCHULTZ • Computer History and Information Access

FAIR USE
AND FREE INQUIRY
Copyright Law and the New Media

JOHN SHELTON LAWRENCE
Morningside College

and

BERNARD TIMBERG
University of Nebraska, Omaha

Editors

Ablex Publishing Corporation
Norwood, New Jersey 07648

Printed in the United States of America.

Library of Congress Cataloging in Publication Data

Main entry under title:

Fair use and free inquiry.

  (Communication and information science)
  Bibliography: p.
  Includes index.
  1. Fair use (Copyright)—United States—Addresses,
essays, lectures. 2. Copyright—Broadcasting rights—
United States—Addresses, essays, lectures.
3. Freedom of information—United States—Addresses,
essays, lectures. 4. Fair use (Copyright)—Addresses,
essays, lectures. I. Lawrence, John Shelton.
II. Timberg, Bernard. III. Series.
ISBN 0-89391-028-7

ABLEX Publishing Corporation
355 Chestnut Street
Norwood, New Jersey 07648

To Nancy and Judy

CONTENTS

EDITORS' FOREWORD

This book is concerned with uses of the new mass media of the twentieth century—motion pictures, radio, comics, music recordings, and television—in teaching and in published scholarship.

Contemporary legal systems have developed a "fair use" principle to mediate between the exclusive rights of control granted to copyright owners and society's need to reexhibit, analyze, and criticize copyrighted creations. Fair use and its underlying philosophy is therefore the point of departure for almost every essay. Foreign legal scholars provide international perspective as they explain the working of the equivalent notions "fair dealing" (British Commonwealth), *l'usage loyal* (France), *Zitierfreiheit* (Germany), "fair practice" (Japan).

The United States Congress, in passing the Copyright Act of 1976, accorded "fair use" statutory recognition for the first time in American history. Congress understood, in fact purposely endorsed, the lack of precision in this "rule of reason." Its ambiguities are particularly troublesome in applications to the new media. Because of the unique problems presented by such applications, this volume largely excludes print-related issues, concentrating instead on the legal status of visual, audiovisual, and audio images.

In preparing this volume, we found several representatives of major trade associations and corporate litigators reluctant to write on acceptable interpretations of fair use. We also encountered hesitancy among a number of important "fair users" to participate. One book editor with a strong reputation for fair use publication of images responded to our invitation with these words:

> I honestly don't believe that I would want to make a public statement. It's not cowardice so much as a belief that if no one says anything about these matters, we can continue to proceed unimpeded for an indefinite period of time.

Other persons who are assembling new media archives of various kinds were similarly unwilling to call attention to their activities—even though they regarded their actions as lawful. There is then a lack of candor in both camps that hinders the development of a better-defined public policy of fair use.

We believe that this book, as a frank confrontation of some unique problems in copyright law and practice, helps to compensate for an unsatisfactory public silence. Although obviously oriented toward problems perceived by scholars and teachers, we believe that it does achieve a significant balance in expressing the contentions of differing factions. We also think that this volume will provide interested parties with a better understanding of fair use issues, if not of the workable resolutions for them. In some instances, these essays point toward significant changes in the law and its interpretation for the years ahead.

ACKNOWLEDGMENTS

Acknowledgments for assistance to the editors are embarrassingly extensive. Several persons deserve to be singled out for special recognition of their crucial roles: David Kunzle, Alan Latman, Harriet L. Oler—a model of the impartial assistance that the United States Office of Copyright can provide, Harry N. Rosenfield, Eleanor Ernst Timberg, and Sigmund Timberg. They steadily located contributors, transmitted documents, made suggestions, and provided encouragement.

Assistance through correspondence and telephone conversation was given by Erik Barnouw and Paul Spehr, at the Motion Picture, Broadcasting, and Sound Division of the Library of Congress; Dennis Bohnenkamp and Larry Carr, American Film Institute; Michael Cardozo, Attorney, Washington, D.C.; John Fell, San Francisco State University; Dave Geuelette, Northern Illinois University; Ivan Illich, Center for Intercultural Documentation, Cuernavaca; Sarah Lazin, *Rolling Stone* magazine; John Ohliger, Madison, Wisconsin; Marybeth Peters, Office of Copyright; Herbert Schiller, University of California, San Diego; Seth Siegelaub, International General Editions; Ellen Seeherman and Peter Weiss, Center for Constitutional Rights, New York City.

Institutions with which we have been associated provided a wealth of talent and helping hands: at Iowa State University, Ed Blinn, Linda

Busby, Dan Griffen, Jim Schwartz, Jack Shelley, George Wilson; at the University of Texas in Austin, William Buckner, Tom Cameron, Paul Dodson, David Hansard, James Kinneavy, Horace Newcomb, James Treece; at Morningside College, Joan Ayers, John Doohen, Delores Hibner, Orpha Jerman, Jane Lear, Kari Reimer, Frank Terry, Barrie Tritle, Bryan Watkins, Chris Zellmer, Inge Zibers, and especially Robert Jewett.

Conference advice and participation was provided for panels on fair use at the National Association of Broadcasters meeting in Washington by Robert Avery, Paul Spehr, Arthur Seidel, Eric Smith, George Wilson, and several contributors to the book; at the Speech Communication Association meeting in Minneapolis, by Stuart Bay, Don Roberts, and several contributors.

Our international contributors made unexpectedly generous exertions to provide manuscripts. They all deserve special acknowledgments.

Reflecting on the serendipitous origins of this volume, thanks must be extended to Professor Karl Acham and Die Gesellschaft für Soziologie at the University of Graz, Austria, who provided an occasion for John Lawrence to speak on related themes, and to Universitäts Dozent Dieter Prokop of J.W. Goethe Universität in Frankfurt, a Board Member of the Communication and Information Science Series, who provided initial suggestions for a book. The National Endowment for the Humanities provided research funding for John Lawrence during the period when this book began.

Our family members, Judy, Nancy, Eric, and Jennifer helped in all the ways that families can, especially in giving stylistic help and impromptu research assistance.

All these people, as well as others who are unacknowledged here, were relentlessly generous with their interest and time. Only through their gifts could a collective work of this kind appear.

JOHN SHELTON LAWRENCE
BERNARD TIMBERG

NOTES ON CONTRIBUTORS

Eugene N. Aleinikoff is an attorney who has served as broadcast counsel to the Corporation for Public Broadcasting. He has participated in several recent fair use conferences, including the Airlie Conference and the Information Futures Conference.

Marie-Laure Arié is Deputy Director for the promotion of scientific reviews in Groupe Maisons d'Edition Bordas/Dunod/Gauthier-Villars. She holds a doctorate in law from the University of Paris, where she presented her thesis, *La Reproduction Photographique et l'Edition Scientifique* (1975).

Carl Belz is Director of the Rose Museum of Art, Brandeis University. In addition to *The Story of Rock* (1969), he has written *Cezanne* (McGraw-Hill, 1975) and several dozen articles and reviews for professional art journals.

Harry S. Bloom is Senior Lecturer in Law at the University of Kent at Canterbury and Visiting Professor of Electronics at the University of Brunel near London. He is a specialist in the field of copyright for computer programs. He was assisted in the research for this article by his wife Sonia Bloom, a journalist.

R.B. Churchill is President of Churchill Films, an educational film production company in Los Angeles. His article was presented to the House Judiciary Subcommittee in 1975 and reprinted in the *Hearings* volumes.

John T. Curtin is Judge of the Western District Court of New York.

John Doohen (translator, Chapter 17) is Professor of French at Morningside College.

Jeanne Masson Douglas was Director of the Educational Resources Center at Reading Community College in Reading, Pennsylvania, when she wrote this article. It was presented in testimony during the House Judiciary hearings and reprinted in the *Hearings* volumes.

Leonard Feist is President of the National Music Publishers Association. He served as representative of his association in the negotiation of the fair use "Guidelines with Respect to Music" that accompanied the Copyright Act of 1976.

Billie Grace Herring is Associate Professor of Library Science in the Graduate School at the University of Texas in Austin. She writes, speaks and consults often on the new technologies for library use.

Douglas Kellner is Associate Professor of Philosophy at the University of Texas in Austin and has edited *Karl Korsch: Revolutionary Theory* (University of Texas Press, 1977). He produces a weekly, independent commentary program on Austin cable television.

A.A. (Frank) Keyes is Special Advisor to the Secretary of State Department, Government of Canada. He frequently represents Canada in international copyright conferences and is former Chairman of the Executive Committee of the Berne International Copyright Convention.

Cosette Kies is Associate Professor of·Library Science at the George Peabody School for Teachers in Nashville, an institution that shares the Vanderbilt News Archive resources. An earlier version of the essay in this volume appeared in the *Wilson Library Bulletin,* Vol. 50, 1975.

David Kunzle is Professor of Art History at UCLA. He was Lecturer at the National Gallery of Art in London when his study of the Hogarth piracies was carried out. In addition to translating *How to Read Donald Duck,* he has written *History of the Comic Strip, Vol. I . . . ca. 1450–1825* (University of California Press, 1973) and *Fashion and Fetishism,* whose publication has been delayed several years by permissions problems.

John Shelton Lawrence (*editor*) is Professor of Philosophy at Morningside College in Sioux City, Iowa. With Robert Jewett, he has written *The American Monomyth* (Anchor/Doubleday, 1977), which also appears in an Italian edition (Bompiani, 1980). He is the author of numerous articles in social philosophy, criticism of ideology, and popular culture interpretation. His training in philosophy was received at Stanford, Princeton, and the University of Texas in Austin.

Deborah Lulf (*bibliography*) is a law student at the University of South Dakota, Vermillion.

Gerald Mast is Professor of English and on the Committee of General Studies in the Humanities at the University of Chicago. His publications include *A Short History of the Movies* (Bobbs-Merrill, 1971), *The Comic Mind: Comedy and the Movies* (University of Chicago Press, 2d. ed., 1979), and *Film/Cinema/Movie: A Theory of Experience* (Harper & Row, 1977).

Jerome K. Miller is Assistant Professor in the Graduate School of Library Science at the University of Illinois at Urbana. His book-length publications are the edited *Copyright and the Teaching/Learning Process* (Information Futures, 1977), *Applying the New Copyright Law: A Guide for Educators and Librarians* (American Library Association, 1979), and *U.S. Copyright Documents, Selected, Annotated and Indexed for Use by Educators and Librarians* (Libraries Unlimited, forthcoming).

Hiroshi Minami is Professor of Social Psychology at Seijo University and President of the Japan Society of Image Arts and Sciences. His publications in English include *The Psychology of the Japanese People* (University of Tokyo Press, 1971; University of Toronto Press, 1972). He received his Ph.D. in psychology from Cornell University.

Demetrius Oekonomidis is Lawyer to the High Court in Athens and a research associate at the Max Planck Institut für Ausländische Internationales Patent-, Urheber-, und Wettbewerbsrecht in Munich.

Harriet L. Oler is Senior Attorney-Advisor in the United States Office of Copyright. She has written several articles for professional journals on issues related to copyright. She is an honors graduate of the University of Pennsylvania Law School and is a member of the Pennsylvania and District of Columbia Bars.

Harry N. Rosenfield is an attorney in Washington, D.C., who served for several years as Copyright Counsel to the National Education Association and was its representative to the Ad Hoc Committee on Copyright Law Revision. He has served as Chairperson of the American Bar Association Copyright Committee.

Rainer Sell (translator, Chapter 18) is Professor of Humanities at the University of Michigan-Dearborn.

William Stott is Associate Professor of American Studies at the University of Texas in Austin. In addition to *Documentary Expression and Thirties America* (Oxford, 1973) he has written with Jane Stott *On Broadway: Performance Photographs by Fred Fehl* (University of Texas Press, 1978).

Bernard Timberg (*editor*) is Assistant Professor of Communication at the University of Nebraska-Omaha. He received his education at the University of California, Berkeley, San Francisco State College, Iowa State University, and the University of Texas in Austin. He has produced films, television programs, and radio broadcasts. His field of specialization is film theory and criticism and popular culture. He is currently at work on a book dealing with the general theory of film and television. His previous essays include "E = mc² and the Birth of Film," *Texas Studies in Language and Literature* (Winter 1978–79); "Bob Dylan and Jimmy Carter: Ceremonies of National Revival," *Studies in Popular Culture* (Popular Culture Association in the South, 2, No. 1, 1979); and (with John Lawrence) "News and Mythic Selectivity: Entebbe, Mayaguez and Mogadishu," *Journal of American Culture*, Vol. 2, No. 2, 1979.

Sigmund Timberg is an attorney in Washington, D.C. specializing in industrial property law, antitrust, and international law. He has served as consultant on antitrust and patent law to the United Nations and the Organization of American States. He was delegate to the Universal Copyright Convention in 1952. His writings include edited volumes and several dozen articles. He has lectured at numerous universities in the United States and abroad, including the Georgetown Law School and the Parker School of Comparative Law at Columbia University. He delivered the Donald Brace Lecture on Copyright at Los Angeles in 1979.

I

ORIGINS

1

COPYRIGHT LAW, FAIR USE, AND THE ACADEMY: AN INTRODUCTION

JOHN SHELTON LAWRENCE

> Our copyright laws urgently need revision. They are imperfect in definition, confused and inconsistent in expression; they omit provision for many articles, which, under modern reproductive processes, are entitled to protection; they impose hardships upon the copyright proprietor which are not essential to the fair practices of the public; they are difficult for the courts to interpret and impossible for the Copyright Office to administer to the satisfaction of the public.
>
> Theodore Roosevelt, 1905[1]

Roosevelt's message has not been outdated either by the passage of time or by the enactment of new legislation. The U.S. Congress has struggled to enact satisfactory copyright statutes. Its most recent effort consumed some twenty-two years, culminating in the Copyright Act of 1976. During the act's gestation period from 1954 to 1976, thirty-five major studies were commissioned by the Office of Copyright. Testimony and affidavits were accepted from more than three hundred witnesses, their statements totalling more than 4,000 pages in the monumental volumes of hearings. The House Subcommittee of the Judiciary Committee met in executive session fifty-one times to produce a bill for congressional action.[2] Taking into consideration these circumstances of its passage, one would think that the Copyright Act of 1976 had fulfilled exemplary standards for procedural rationality and legislative success. Yet there remain uncertainties, confusions, and inconsistencies of the sort mentioned by Roosevelt.

Why did Congress fail to create more definitive legislation under nearly ideal conditions for legislative discussion? Although Congress can be faulted on detailed points of statutory definition and explanation of intent,[3] many copyright problems reflect the inherent complexities of this area for legislation. Such complexities arise from the conflicting interests to be compromised and from the relatively autonomous dynamic of technology itself. Thus new circumstances constantly surface to frustrate legislation. Commenting on the copyright issues in *Weems v. U.S.*, the Supreme Court stated:

> Time works changes, brings into being new conditions and purposes. Therefore a principle to be vital must be of wider application than the mischief which gave it birth.[4]

The history of copyright has been an interplay between "new conditions and purposes" and "mischievous" technology with law and social understanding repeatedly interacting in novel configurations.

Understanding copyright demands, therefore, that one examine the play of social forces at a particular historical moment, a task that requires us to look at the evolution of copyright legislation and its underlying philosophies. The brief remarks that follow provide a framework for the divergent approaches to copyright law and fair use practices that are assembled in this volume.

I. ORIGINS

Copyright, broadly conceived as a set of laws and practices restricting the right to reproduce or perform individual creations, has dual origins.

Monarchical Copyright

With Gutenberg's invention of movable type, the mass dissemination of written material became possible. When William Caxton established his press at Westminster in 1476, the British crown adopted the practice of granting exclusive licenses to print. Openly expressing the monarchy's fears of widespread political and theological heresy, the Star Chamber Decree of 1586 called for repressing the "greate enormities and abuses" of "dyvers contentyous and disorderlye persons professinge the arte or mystere of Pryntinge or sellinge of bookes. . . ."[5] And again in 1637 the Star Chamber decreed more pointedly:

> That no person or persons whatsouer shall presume to print, or cause to bee printed, either in the parts beyond the Seas, or in this Realme . . . any sediti-

ous, scismaticall, or offensive Bookes or Pamphlets, to the scandall of Reli-
gion, or the Church, or the Government, or Governours of the Church or
State. . . .[6]

Thus the administrative machinery of copyright in the English tradition
had its origins in requirements of royal censorship.

Bourgeois Copyright

A different strand in the origins of the copyright tradition
appeared almost as early as that of censorship. Presses multiplied in the
wake of Gutenberg's invention, and the demand for printed matter increased. A Stationers' Company was chartered in 1557 by Queen Mary;
one of its purposes was the registration of printed works, a function that
assisted in settling claims about literary priority and piracy.

When the English presses were liberated from royal control in
1695, wars of commercial plagiarism ensued. To end them, Parliament
passed the Copyright Act of 1710, the Statute of Anne, whose preamble
charged that printers and booksellers were in the habit of publishing
"books and other writings without the consent of the authors or proprietors of such books and writings, to their very great detriment, and
too often to the ruin of them and their families."[7] With this statute,
designed to remedy the "detriment" and "ruin" of piracy, came explicit
recognition of the new social roles of the Gutenberg era that required
protection—the writer and printer whose productions were threatened
by piratical theft. David Kunzle's essay on the Hogarth piracies and the
ensuing Engraver's Act of 1735 documents the emerging role of the
middle class graphic artist who was creating a new form of commodity
that required the protections accorded to real property.

It is safe to say that the American conception of copyright, at least
in its intent, derives more directly from the middle class property strand
rather than from the monarchical, censorship tradition. In 1789, the
Constitution provided for copyright with these words: "The Congress
shall have Power . . . To promote the Progress of Science and useful
Arts, by securing for limited Times to Authors and Inventors the exclusive Right to their respective Writings and Discoveries." (Art. I, sec. 8, cl.
8)Irwin Karp, Counsel for The Authors League of America, has
suggested that:

> . . . the instrument chosen by the Constitution to serve the public interest—
> i.e. the securing of literary and scientific works of lasting value—is an inde-
> pendent, entrepreneurial property-rights system of writing and publishing.
> The Copyright Act establishes the rights which prevent others from depriv-
> ing authors and publishers of the fruits of their labor.[8]

The scope of this property right and its relationship to other provisions of the Constitution is an issue of much debate among leading copyright authorities. Harry N. Rosenfield in this volume argues that the First Amendment has priority over the constitutional claims of intellectual property ownership.

II. CONCEPTIONS OF INTELLECTUAL PROPERTY

Since copyright has evolved into a form of property, we should expect that leading causes of change and conflict in the copyright tradition are differing conceptions of the importance and privileges of private property.

There are cultures in which almost no claims to private ownership of stories, images, songs, etc., are made; myths, historical knowledge, and artistic creation are the common possession of the community that is aware of them. Aubert J. Clark has described the communal tradition of the Middle Ages as follows:

> . . . books existed chiefly in single copies, almost like long letters from author to patron. . . . There were few lay writers and very little original writing. The ubiquitous monastic chronicler had renounced personal property, and even enterprising communities, which might have claimed some corporate right, were more interested in diffusion. Much of the work reproduced centered around the classics and long-dead Fathers and Doctors of the Church, and there was no one to dispute the freedom to copy. . . . Rabbinical authorities held the opinion that one was allowed to copy a manuscript without the consent of the author, and it was considered a blessing to permit scribes to make copies. Christian authorities heartily agreed. One synod went so far as to declare that the lending of books to be copied was one of the works of mercy.[9]

These sentiments may seem quaint to most contemporary Americans, though they occasionally surface again, as in a notation to J. Frank Dobie's revised edition of his Guide to *Life and Literature of the Southwest*:

> Not copyright in 1942
> Again not copyright in 1952
> Anyone is welcome to help himself to any
> of it in any way.[10]

Such sentiments are, of course, a vigorous component in the socialist tradition that extends back to Proudhon, who explicitly discussed copyright in the context of his dictum, "Property is theft."[11]

At the other end of the property spectrum, there has been an

attempt to define intellectual creation within the natural rights tradition
of John Locke and others, including the Founding Fathers, who saw the
copyrightable entity as a natural expression of ownership, conducive
to private exploitation and commerce. This tradition has pressed
for analogies that confer on intellectual creation the substantiality of
real estate or commodities. Writing within such a tradition during
the nineteenth century, Eaton S. Drone developed this notion as follows:

> The maker of a piece of cloth, a box, a wagon, or a house, has therein a title
> whose duration is not limited. His property is protected because it is a prod-
> uct of his labor. But time and money spent in producing a work of literature
> capable of doing good to men through all coming time, give to the producer
> no title beyond a brief term of years. . . . The law which puts an arbitrary
> terminus on the ownership of literary property is the same in principle with
> one that would abridge the farmer's right to his orchards and grainfields. If
> there were the remotest danger that this principle would ever be applied to
> material possessions, every English tongue would clamor for a new Magna
> Charta. . . . To take from one and give to all is not less communism in the case
> of literary property than it is in that of any other kind of property.[12]

Consistent with this "real estate model" of copyright, the legal encyclopedia *Corpus Juris Secundum* characterizes infringement as "a trespass on
a private domain owned and occupied by the owner of the copyright,
and therefore protected by law. . . ."[13] The existence of the "limited
times" specified in the Constitution notwithstanding, we are living in an
age that conceives of creation as property rather than in an age of "literary communism."

Although traditional notions of personal property remain central
in copyright discussion, their aptness has been eroded by the increasing
dominance of new corporate entities that produce and disseminate so
much copyrighted material. Although the small entrepreneur has survived in the age of corporate media giants, the metaphor of the painter
or engraver working alone—the philosophical equivalent of the small
landowner protecting his fields from trespass—has lost its cogency.
Using the services of thousands of hired employees, the new media
conglomerates command assets valued in the billions and produce works
through specialized assembly-line techniques.[14] In this regard our
French contributor, Marie-Laure Arié cites a provocative series of questions from Xavier Desjeux's essay, "Is the Law Attacking Education?"
Desjeux asks whether one can continue to speak of *originality* or *creativity*
in dealing with the enormous output of contemporary mass media even
if these concepts have traditionally been invoked as essential traits of the
protectible entity.

III. PROTECTION AND COMPENSATION FOR INTELLECTUAL PROPERTY

Once literary, artistic, and scientific creations were recognized as forms of property created by individual work, it followed that their producers were entitled to compensation and to protection from community exploitation. Hogarth's story is but one of many in the struggles that have been waged to allow an adequate return to creators and distributors. Walt Disney's early efforts, mentioned in my chapter on the administration of copyrighted material at Disney Productions, indicate the plight of the small, emerging entrepreneur. In almost every field of artistic creation during the modern period, piracy, counterfeiting, and bootlegging have threatened to destroy the incentive and economic base for production.

Several chapters in this volume throw light on the claims for compensation and protection that must be weighed against the arguments for limitations on exclusive rights of control. R.B. Churchill's essay evokes the marginal economics of the small, educational film producer, as does the preliminary injunction of the court in the BOCES case. The complaint in *Universal City Studios, et al. v. Sony Corporation of America*, discussed by Harriet L. Oler and Eugene Aleinikoff, contends that the spread of home recording technology is eroding the commercial value of copyrighted creations. And CBS contended—in its suit against Vanderbilt University, described by Cosette Kies—that the archival recording of its news programs could lead to widespread abuses. Such arguments for exclusive control have been given powerful formulations and they are heard often in the courts and at legislative hearings. Both Congress and the courts have been sympathetic to the claims for compensation and protection, though they have sometimes delayed for decades before providing statutory relief.[15] The histories of the sound recording industry generally and that of the movie sound track business in particular, provide good examples of the long periods of frustration that sometimes precede legislative action.

For such reasons, media interests place rather strict and literal interpretations upon the laws that confer protection. Media corporations may also litigate rather often, as does Walt Disney Productions, in order to insure that infringement or fair use practices do not, in effect, take their valuable materials into the public domain. The prospect of an expensive suit in court, initiated by a company that is prepared to litigate on a world-wide basis, can substantially magnify the protection of copyright statutes. Willingness to litigate, in conjunction with some properties of imagery that differentiate it qualitatively from print—discussed in the essays by Sigmund and Bernard Timberg—has resulted in almost monopolistic control over visual materials. Consequently visual images are far less accessible than printed materials for discussion and criticism. Yet our society has rarely been content with a complete monopoly in copyright because it clearly contradicts the requirements of discussion and analysis that must prevail in a democracy.

IV. COUNTERVAILING INTEREST IN FREE DISCUSSION: THE DOCTRINE OF FAIR USE

The U.S. Constitution's provision for copyright cites the aim of promoting "the progress of Science and the useful Arts." Harry N. Rosenfield and other students of the Constitution argue forcefully that the property rights secured by the copyright clause are *instrumental* to the public's interest in the progress of the sciences and the arts. "Limited times" were established precisely for the purpose of allowing material to pass rather quickly into the public domain. If the public interest has primacy, then copyright law may in fact conflict at times irreconcilably with rights of free speech. It has long been an axiom of democratic debate that one can cite the words of another without permission, even though the law may have granted an apparent monopoly to the copyright holder. Herein lies the basis for many of the conflicts that have arisen between the scholarly community and the copyright-owning community.

Long before the American Constitution, the perception of a need to balance public and private interests in the copyright arena had appeared in the writings of the English jurist, Lord Mansfield.

> We must take care to guard against two extremes, equally prejudicial; the one, that men of ability, who have employed their time in the service of the community, may not be deprived of their just merits, and the reward of their labor and ingenuity; the other, that the world may not be deprived of improvements, nor the progress of the arts retarded.[16]

Early attempts to balance these interests led a nineteenth century Supreme Court Justice, Joseph Story, to comment on "the metaphysics of the law" in this area, on the distinctions that are "very subtle and refined, and sometimes almost evanescent."[17]

The single concept through which the balancing of interests has been most often sought is that of "fair use." As early as 1843, Justice Story in *Folsom v. Marsh* had conceded some mitigation of property rights as "justifiable use" in cases of "fair abridgement" or "fair and reasonable" criticism. He articulated the principle that reproducing another's work might be excused or privileged when satisfactory answers could be given regarding "the nature and object of the selections, the quantity and value of the materials used, and the degree in which the use may prejudice the sale or diminish the profits, or supersede the objects of the original work."[18] Justice Story's factors have proved so durable that the U.S. Copyright Act of 1976, which gives fair use a statutory recognition for the first time in its long history, states the criteria of Justice Story in language that has altered only slightly. Section 107 reads as follows:

> §107. *Limitations on exclusive rights: Fair use*
>   Notwithstanding the provisions of section 106, the fair use of a copyrighted work, including such use by reproduction in copies or phonorecords or by any other means specified by that section, for purposes such as criticism, comment, news reporting, teaching (including multiple copies for classroom use), scholarship, or research, is not an infringement of copyright. In determining whether the use made of a work in any particular case is a fair use the factors to be considered shall include—
> (1) the purpose and character of the use, including whether such use is of a commercial nature or is for nonprofit educational purposes;
> (2) the nature of the copyrighted work;
> (3) the amount and substantiality of the portion used in relation to the copyrighted work as a whole; and
> (4) the effect of the use upon the potential market for or value of the copyrighted work.[19]

It is clear that this enumeration of factors, combined with a few examples of noninfringing activities, such as criticism and teaching, constitutes a set of criteria only in the sense of directing us to take certain features of an alleged infringement into consideration. As indicated by the congressional statement of legislative intent and by several authors in this volume, *fair use* is an equitable rule of reason, whose applicability in an individual case is dependent upon particular facts and their interrelationships.[20] Case law, or the body of decisions made by courts in considering allegations of copyright infringement and fair use defenses, provides important precedents that are discussed by contributors. But taken together, the cases provide no definitive specifications regarding the limits of fair use.

The conception of fair use as a somewhat indeterminate rule of reason is by no means unique among legal notions. Other areas of the law employ such expressions as "reasonable, prudent man" (torts), "due process" (constitutional), "unfair competition" (antitrust), and "equitable settlement" (divorce proceedings). A philosophical basis for such rules has been articulated by Benjamin Cardozo. In discussing the vagueness and flexibility of the law, he stated:

> No doubt the ideal system, if it were attainable, would be a code at once so flexible and so minute, as to supply in advance for every conceivable situation the just and fitting rule. But life is too complex to bring the attainment of this ideal within the compass of human powers.[21]

In a comparable spirit the 1976 copyright law acknowledges fair use in a manner that accords with the philosophical requirements for an "open concept." Judgments about the abridgement of the copyright holder's monopoly in particular cases are thus to vary with circumstances.

In addition to possessing an open character with respect to factual relationships, the concept of "fairness" is evaluative and will therefore vary in time with changing moral ideals. To consider a single, striking example, we can look at U.S. attitudes toward international piracy. The U.S. has possessed clear statutory protection for its literary writings from 1790 to the present. On the other hand, its 1831 legislation explicitly established that there should be "no prohibition to the printing, publication, importation, or sale of books, charts, dramatic or musical compositions, engravings, prints, written, composed or made *by anyone who is not a citizen or resident of the United States.*" (4 Stat. 436, 1831, Sec. 8; italics added) During most of the nineteenth century it seemed entirely fair that publishing houses, magazines, and newspapers should, in the case of foreign authors, circumvent the "formalities of permission to publish, purchase manuscripts, payment of royalties, and careful editing of authorized texts."[22] Charles Dickens, Sir Walter Scott, and dozens of other eminent English writers were pirated on a vast scale. Many Americans thought Charles Dickens had committed a major breach of etiquette when he brought up this subject during his first visit to America.[23] But after prolonged agitation, much of it by aggrieved American authors who found themselves undercut in their native market and reciprocally pirated abroad, an international copyright statute was adopted by the federal government in 1891. With its passage, a radically different conception of what was fair in the appropriation or reproduction of another's work had appeared.[24]

From this example, and from others that might be drawn from the history of attitudes toward copyright, we may conclude that future concepts of fair use are bound to be affected by the way in which contemporary social facts are perceived, by the emergence of new social ideals, and by reinterpretation of the Constitution's implications for discussion and research. In consequence, the notion of fair use demarcates a territory for debate among conflicting interests, rather than providing a ready means for resolving them.

V. NEW MEDIA AND NEW RESPONSIBILITIES
FOR THE ACADEMY

The new media have established themselves in the twentieth century as major economic powers. Companies that were once pygmies among the giants of steel, railroads, rubber, oil, and chemicals now control enormous capital. They can distribute their products on a worldwide basis, saturating the global environment with visual and auditory messages. Whether as radio, television, instructional or entertainment film, Muzak, or in myriad other forms, the new media have become a pulsing, flickering electronic wallpaper, forming an almost constant background for daily life. The academy has responded to these omnipresent new powers in several ways.

Participation

To a large extent, our educational system has participated in and celebrated the media revolution. Universities have always developed strong reciprocal relations to the central powers of society. In the emergence of the new media, they found another opportunity to serve the economic order; they have substantially helped it satisfy its enormous needs for writers, actors, directors, managers, market psychologists, designers, and other workers needed to operate the technologies of production and transmission. Departments of Television, Radio, Film, Marketing, Design, etc. were bound to appear in societies that had begun to find their central experiences and economic institutions in the worlds of film, radio, television, music, and in the advertising that linked them all.[25]

Assimilation

The academy at every level has assimilated technology from the new media and has adapted it straightforwardly for instruction. The film strip, the educational film, the slide show have become classroom commonplaces. The elementary schools in particular have oriented much of their formal and informal curriculum to the contents of television. Reading is sometimes approached through the distribution of television scripts for popular programs. The *Scholastic Magazine* publications distributed and sold through the public schools consist substantially of fan articles and books related to current television programs, blockbuster films, and their stars.[26]

Analysis and Criticism

Inevitably, anything as important as the new media would eventually become the subject for serious study and criticism. Gerald Mast describes the development of film history and analysis; Douglas Kellner gives survey information about the rise of television archives and study; and Bernard Timberg describes in his overview chapter the new forms of academic discourse and research made possible by new communication technologies.

To date, the universities have also provided the research base for serious media history and commentary. Erik Barnouw has written a substantial history of the rise of television and radio in *The Image Empire* and in shorter studies such as *The Sponsor: Notes on a Modern Potentate.*[27] Herbert Schiller has created a body of scholarship on the global aspects of American cultural diffusion through such works as *Mass Communication and American Empire.*[28] John Cawelti and Horace Newcomb, working with the concept of "formula," have made possible better psychological and critical appraisals of the new media.[29] Marshall McLuhan, Walter Ong, and Edumund Carpenter have suggested important cross-cultural and historical perspectives.[30] Major social histories of film, such as Garth Jowett's *Film: The Democratic Art*, have delineated relationships between media corporations, public expectations, and social science research.[31]

Among experimental social scientists, Albert Bandura has done extensive research on social learning and behavior modeling through the experience of television imagery.[32] Other psychologists—among them George Gerbner and Larry Gross,[33] who have studied media-induced violence—are carrying out long-term research on the cognitive, attitudinal, and behavioral effects of television on the adult population.

The intrinsic importance alone of the new media justifies these achievements of analysis and criticism, but there are other reasons for scholarly and critical attention. From their first appearance, the new media aroused public suspicions about their degenerative effects. Movements for regulation or censorship have been directed against the new media since the initial appearance of the peepshow "Dolorita in the Passion Dance" in 1894.[34] The interests promoting the new media responded in turn with claims about their civic virtue. Through its Motion

Picture Code of 1930, Hollywood asserted that films would morally improve their viewers. Movie producers

> ... though regarding motion pictures primarily as entertainment without any explicit purpose of teaching or propaganda ... know that the motion picture ... may be directly responsible for spiritual and moral progress, for higher types of social life, and for much correct thinking.[35]

The television networks, through their trade association, the National Association of Broadcasters, have also asserted high standards for their programming, promising to bring the viewer "toward informed adjustment to his society" and to "remind him of the responsibilities which a citizen has toward his society."[36]

Nor have media spokesmen limited their claims to the domestic scene, but have spoken of a "mission of entertainment" for the entire world—to use the phrase of Erik Johnson, former President of the Motion Picture Association of America. He suggested in 1957 that Hollywood films, "an agent for democracy, for the worth and dignity of man throughout the world," could save societies from their political and economic miseries.[37] The current MPAA president, Jack Valenti, has continued to affirm "The world needs American motion pictures," because conditions of life are changing for the world's people. . . . "The tooth and the tusk, the beak and the claw are no longer going to be the order of their lives."[38] Assertions of this kind are consistent with the "Miracle" decision (*Burstyn v. Wilson*) referred to by Gerald Mast, in which the Supreme Court held that "motion pictures are a significant medium for the expression of ideas."[39]

If scholarship takes seriously either the spokesmen for the media or the recurrent public concerns about them, then it has a substantial agenda that requires freedom of access for its discussions—even before it has begun to develop its independent interests. One may ask whether the new media's own claim to offer significant expression of democratic ideals is matched by the conditions under which society permits discussion of the media. This is the sort of fair use question toward which most of the contributions in this volume are directed.

The scholars writing in Part Two do not give a very encouraging report on the rates of exchange in the free marketplace of ideas. They suggest a kind of conspiracy of immunity, through which the several acts of timid publishers and universities combine with the uncooperativeness of copyright holders to frustrate the kinds of reproduction and performance that are essential to credibly documented discussion. In spite of a First Amendment logic that calls for the application of fair use in "criticism, comment, news reporting, teaching" (Section 107 of the 1976 statute), publishers have generally declined to print imagery, diagrams, and other nonverbal communication structures without obtaining permissions and paying fees. Even the Association of American University Presses extends no fair use waiver of permission to "maps, charts, tables, drawings or other illustrative materials, in whatever form they may be reproduced. . . ."[40] The consequences of such a policy are made evident in the stories of the scholars who were deprived of the opportunity to publish the documentation for their interpretations of the new media.

As regards off-air taping of television programs, universities have become similarly fearful of copyright interests. Even though Congress has made very clear its intent to apply the fair use provision to off-air taping, some universities and their media consortia have stopped all off-air taping not cleared by prior permission from the copyright holders.[41] Rather than asking themselves whether they have diminished their educational and critical functions, they seem to have quickly surrendered to the most restrictive of the commercial viewpoints, apparently thinking that staying out of court takes precedence over the risks inherent in the exercise of First Amendment and fair use rights of free inquiry.

VI. COPYRIGHT AS A SOCIAL ISSUE

The major questions posed by materials in this volume relate to education and the scholarship that sustains its vitality. Given the rich symbolic environments created by the new communications systems, democratic societies cannot avoid the problems of granting access for cultural historians, analysts, and critics. Do the procedural, economic, and legal restrictions of the sort discussed in this volume serve the interests of democracy? Can we find equitable means to bring the new media into the public forums and the open dialogue that their growing influence seems to require? The future of education and the processes of free inquiry that animate public debate rest upon the answers given to these questions.

NOTES

[1]Roosevelt's statement cited in testimony of John Lorenz, Acting Librarian of Congress, May 7, 1975. U.S., Congress, House, *Copyright Law Revision: Hearings before the Subcommittee on Courts, Civil Liberties and the Administration of Justice*, H.R., Serial 36, Part 1 (Washington, D.C.: U.S. Government Printing Office, 1976), p. 91.

[2]These details are provided in testimony by Barbara Ringer, *ibid.*, pp. 99–105.

[3]The most formidable and extensive of such critiques is Leon E. Seltzer, *Exemptions and Fair Use in Copyright: The Exclusive Rights Tensions in the 1976 Copyright Act* (Cambridge, Mass.: Harvard, 1978).

[4]Weems v. United States, 217 U.S. 349 (1910)

[5]Cited in Lyman Ray Patterson, *Copyright in Historical Perspective* (Nashville: Vanderbilt, 1968), pp. 235–36.

[6]*Ibid.*, p. 244.

[7]Cited in *Encyclopedia Britannica* (11 ed., 1910–11), "Copyright," p. 118. Also the source, along with Patterson, p. 244, n5, for other details about developments in English law.

[8]Testimony of Irwin Karp, *Hearings*, p. 221, n1. See the often cited Mazer v. Stein, 347 U.S. 201 (1954).

[9]Aubert J. Clark, *The Movement for International Copyright in Nineteenth Century America* (Washington, D.C.: Catholic University Press, 1960), pp. 1–2.

[10]Cited in Saul Cohen, "Duration," 24 *UCLA Law Review* 1230 (1977).

[11]Pierre Joseph Proudhon discusses copyright in *What is Property?: An Enquiry into the Principle of Right and of Government* (N.Y.: Howard Fertig, 1966), pp. 393–98.

[12]Drone cited in Cohen, 1182, n10.

[13]*Corpus Juris Secundum,* William Mack and Donald Kiser (Eds.), Brooklyn, N.Y.: American Book Co., 1939. 18 C.J.S. Copyright IX, Sect. 90, "Definition of Infringement or Piracy." So firmly rooted is the commodity concept that copyrighted works are often referred to as *properties*. In Max Wilk's novel, *The Moving Picture Boys* (N.Y.: W.W. Norton, 1978), a screen writer protests to his publicity agent about making a church appearance to stir interest in his script:

"I thought we were selling an honest story for a picture—and now you're turning it into some—goddamned medicine show!"

"Oh really now, Mr. Pure. . . . So tell me now, how do *you* think you hustle a property these days?" (p. 94)

[14]See Christopher H. Sterling and Timothy R. Haight (Eds.), *The Mass Media: Aspen Institute Guide to Communication Industry Trends* (N.Y.: Praeger, 1978), which provides statistical analyses of corporate ownership patterns. For a briefer, more popular treatment, see James Monaco (Ed.), *Media Culture: Television, Radio, Records, Books, Magazines, Newspapers, Movies* (N.Y.: Delta, 1978).

[15]See the excellent legal study of piracy by Ken Sutak, *The Great Motion Picture Sound Track Piracy: An Analysis of Copyright Protection* (N.Y.: Archon Books, 1976); James Monaco, "Stealing the Show: The Piracy Problem," *American Film* 3, No. 9 (1978) pp. 57–67.

[16]Cited in Louise Weinberg, "The Photocopying Revolution and the Copyright Crisis," *The Public Interest* No. 38 (1975): p. 107.

[17]Folsom v. Marsh, 9 Fed. Cas. 342, 344 (No. 4,091)

[18]*Ibid.*

[19]Public Law No. 94-553, Section 107.

[20]See H.R., *Report* No. 94-1476, Sept. 3, 1976, pp. 65 ff.

[21]Benjamin Cardozo, *The Nature of the Judicial Process* (New Haven: Yale, 1921), p. 143.

[22]Clark, pp. vii–viii, n9. The text of the 1831 legislation is from Clark, p. 27.

[23]See Edgar Johnson, *Charles Dickens, His Tragedy and Triumph* (N.Y.: Simon and Schuster, 1952), especially, "The American Dream," Vol. I, pp. 357*ff*.

[24]It is not clear that the notion of "fair use" ever entered this debate, since foreigners had no statutory protection whatsoever. The issue was discussed with a broader sense of fairness or justice, though the two senses are obviously related.

[25]See the international survey of media programs sponsored by UNESCO, May Katzen, *Mass communication: teaching and study at universities* (Paris: The Unesco Press, 1975) and the summary of academic media programs in Chapter 20.

[26]Typical books sold through the schools by *Scholastic Magazine* (through its Scholas-

tic Book Services of New York) in 1978 included Elliot Maggin, *Superman: Last Son of Krypton*; David Dachs, *Rock's Biggest Ten*; Margaret Ronan, *Superstars*; Barbara Rowes, *Rock Talk*; Bruce Weber, *All-Pro Basketball Stars 1979*.

[27]Erik Barnouw, *The Image Empire: A History of Broadcasting in the United States*, 3 vols. (N.Y.: Oxford, 1970); *The Sponsor: Notes on a Modern Potentate* (N.Y.: Oxford, 1978).

[28]Herbert I. Schiller, *Mass Communications and American Empire* (Boston: Beacon Press, 1971); *Communication and Cultural Domination* (N.Y.: International Arts and Sciences Press, 1976); K. Nordenstreng and Herbert I. Schiller, *National Sovereignty and International Communications* (Norwood, N.J.: Ablex Publishing Co., 1978).

[29]John G. Cawelti, *Adventure, Mystery and Romance: Formula Stories as Art and Popular Culture* (Chicago: Chicago, 1976); Horace Newcomb, *TV: The Most Popular Art* (N.Y.: Doubleday, 1974).

[30]Marshall McLuhan, *Understanding Media: The Extensions of Man* (N.Y.: McGraw-Hill, 1964); Walter J. Ong, *Interfaces of the Word: Studies in the Evolution of Consciousness and Culture* (Ithaca, N.Y.: Cornell, 1977); Edmund Carpenter, *Oh What a Blow That Phantom Gave Me* (N.Y.: Holt, Rinehart and Winston, 1973).

[31]Garth Jowett, *Film: The Democratic Art* (Boston: Little, Brown, 1976).

[32]Albert Bandura, *Aggression: A Social Learning Analysis* (Englewood Cliffs, N.J.: Prentice-Hall, 1973).

[33]George Gerbner and Larry Gross, *Trends in Network Drama and Viewer Conception of Social Reality, 1967–1973* (Violence Profile No. 6, Annenberg School of Communications, University of Pennsylvania, 1974).

[34]Cf. Terry Ramsaye, "The Rise and Place of the Motion Picture" in Wilbur Schramm, (Ed.), *Mass Communications* (Urbana, Ill.: University of Illinois Press, 2d ed., 1972), pp. 28–29.

[35]Cited in Jowett, p. 468, *n*31.

[36]From the "Television Code of the National Association of Broadcasters," in Schramm, p. 636, *n*34. See NAB Code, 1976 ed., for similar statements.

[37]Erik Johnson, "Hollywood: America's Traveling Salesman," *Vital Speeches*, July 1, 1957, p. 573.

[38]Jack Valenti, Press Release of the MPAA, Beverly Hills, CA, June 20, 1966.

[39]Cited in Jowett, p. 407, *n*31. Burstyn v. Wilson 303 N.Y. 242 (1951).

[40]From the AAUP "Resolution on Permissions," accepted by fifty-seven university presses in the U.S. and Canada.

[41]One major television consortium in the midwest, NETCHE (Nebraska Educational Television Consortium for Higher Education) has categorically urged its members to cease *all* unauthorized taping:

> "The new copyright law does not include audio or video recording rights . . . . It is illegal to make such recordings and the user and the person producing the recordings may be held liable. Specific penalties for infringement are stated. *Do not record without permission from the copyright holder.* It is recommended that all materials currently held in institutions' libraries be reviewed for possible infringement. Such materials should be immediately erased. [Emphasis in original.]

Undated memo from Lee Rockwell and Nancy Baer; received, December 1978, by the author's institution. That such a restrictive interpretation far surpasses the intent of the law is evident from Eugene Aleinikoff's discussion in Chapter 14.

Hogarth Piracies

In *The Image*, Daniel Boorstin discusses "the Graphic Revolution," a term that he applies to the contemporary "ability to make, preserve, transmit . . . precise images." (N.Y.: Harper & Row, 1964, p. 12) This revolution had impressive technological underpinnings that eventually permitted the movement from daguerrotype to color television within a century's span, but it also neeeded the legal protections that society gradually extended to the proliferating forms of artistic creation.

David Kunzle's essay on the Hogarth piracies describes one of the important legal steps in creating security for artists using mechanical tools for mass production. The piratical activities within the engraving trade eventually prompted—with the assistance of Hogarth's reputation and skillful lobbying—passage of the Engravers' Act of 1735 (reprinted in the Appendix). Similar struggles against piracy in other arts were waged during the eighteenth and nineteenth centuries, resulting in additional copyright laws and sanctions. A story with strong artistic and political similarities to Hogarth's involved the German composer, Johann Nepomuk Hummel; he mounted a legislative effort to secure uniform protection within his own country and against the foreign theft of his musical compositions in nations like Austria, whose entrepreneurs, like those of the U.S., were among the leading intellectual and artistic pirates of the nineteenth century. (Cf. Joel Sachs, "Hummel and the Pirates: The Struggle for Musical Copyright," *The Musical Quarterly*, LIX, No. 1, 1973)

Despite his sympathies for artists who suffer the crippling effects of piracy, Kunzle's final judgment on the evolution of artistic property represented by Hogarth's career is that the law eventually abetted pathological forms of artistic individualism; leading artists denied the communal sources of their art while quarreling about priority and theft.

Kunzle's essay is taken from the much longer "Plagiaries-by-Memory of the Rake's Progress and the Genesis of Hogarth's Second Picture Story" (*Journal of the Warburg and Courtaud Institutes*, XXIX, 1966) and is reprinted by their permission. The essay was revised slightly for this volume; the "Conclusion" was freshly written in 1978.

2

HOGARTH PIRACIES AND THE ORIGIN OF VISUAL COPYRIGHT

DAVID KUNZLE

It was in the later seventeenth century that consistent efforts were first made for the protection of literary property from the kind of piracy which had been characteristic of the English literary scene since Elizabethan times. This was a period of chaotic and ineffective manoeuvring, chiefly between the Stationers' Company and Parliament, in order to secure to the former some kind of copyright. Various petitions in the early years of the eighteenth century finally resulted in the Act for the Encouragment of Learning, 1710, which gave copyright for twenty-one or fourteen years either to the bookseller or to the author himself; but the act referred only to books and did not mention engraving.

This omission is odd because earlier statutes attempted much greater comprehensiveness in the control of printed matter. A Star Chamber decree of 1637 covered "books, ballads, charts, portraiture or any other thing or things" and forbade copying of "name, title, mark or vinnet." The latter term (vignette) may well have covered book illustrations in general, as well as the frontispiece in particular; it reappears (as "vinette") in the Act of 1662.[1] Perhaps it did not occur to the many creative literary men under Queen Anne that their more sterile colleagues in the graphic arts had need of such protection. In 1679, thirty years before the 1710 Act, a lawsuit could be opened over the rights to *A Pilgrim's Progress*; in 1732 Hogarth's *A Harlot's Progress* could be pirated with complete impunity.

In setting himself up as an independent engraver, the young Hogarth had at once to contend with this major enemy: the pirate of engravings. At the very beginning, he was obliged to sell his prints out-right to the print- and booksellers, who took a very large cut and were entitled to have cheap copies made, a system both financially and artisti-cally ruinous to the designer. One of the first independent productions of which Hogarth tried to retain control, *Masquerades and Operas*, was copied within a week of its publication, a piracy which can hardly have been offset by the very cheap (one penny) copies authorized by Hogarth himself afterwards. The album of *Hudibras* illustrations was sold only by the bookseller Philip Overton, who bought the original copperplates and advertised for subscribers. Priced as it was at fifteen shillings for twelve large prints, this first major series cannot have much profited the artist. Thereafter for a few years (1727–30) he avoided the tyrannical trade by concentrating on painting, but when he came to publish the first narra-tive sequence of his own invention, an object of particular pride (the *Harlot's Progress* of 1732), he found the pirates yet again at his throat. To cut himself free of that wretched intermediary, the printseller, it was not enough for Hogarth to place advertisements himself and sell from his own home by subscription, as he did with the *Harlot*. As soon as the original prints were in the hands of subscribers, and notwithstanding the cheap copies Hogarth immediately authorized (from G. King), the pi-rates attacked, seeking to kill the artist's postpublication sales, and con-fused the public as to the quality of the originals. The robber-chief of the *Harlot's Progress* was probably Elisha Kirkall, an engraver in league with several booksellers, who undersold the Hogarth originals with a vile set of full-sized copies in green mezzotint.[2] Other smaller unauthorized copies abounded, sometimes inserted among verse or prose which pur-ported to comment on Hogarth's story. Of these, the most relevant is that of J. Gay (pseudonym for Captain J.D. Breval) whose *Lure of Venus, or a Harlot's Progress, an heroical-comical poem in 6 Cantos* contains a preface dated November 30, 1732 (i.e., a fortnight after Kirkall started, or re-started advertising his green copies) ironically condemning plagiary in art as well as in literature: "Whenever a curious painting is finished, we are sure of a number of paltry copies."

RAKE'S PROGRESS AND THE ENGRAVERS' ACT OF 1735

Hogarth did not publish his next *Progress* series until 1735 and only then after resolving to secure greater protection for himself through legislation by Parliament. Hogarth first started to advertise for subscribers to his *Rake's Progress* at the end of the year 1733, stating that he would receive subscriptions at his house "where the pictures are to be seen." We may assume that the paintings were complete at the time[3] and

that the artist was in good faith when he promised delivery "at all convenient speed." But as he took up his engraving tools again after Christ-
mas, he must have reflected, first, how little he enjoyed the process, as
compared with the pleasures of drawing and painting (he had engraved
the *Harlot's Progress* himself only because he had been unable to find
professionals to his taste); and second, how likely the profits from this
hard labor were to pass into the pockets of the pirates. It must have
struck Hogarth overwhelmingly how this one major obstacle was frustrating his emancipation as a popular artist; so, for a mixture of motives,
economic, artistic, and social, he applied to the law for a copyright.

Joining with other "Artists and Designers of Paintings, Drawings
and Original Prints," after what must have been lengthy consultations,
Hogarth submitted a petition to the House in February 1735 claiming:

> That the Petitioners and others, have with great Industry and Expence, sev-
> erally invented, designed, or engraved, divers Sets of new Pictures and Prints,
> in hopes to have reaped the Benefit of their own Labour, and the Credit
> thereof; but that divers Printsellers, Printers, and other Persons, both here
> and abroad, have, of late, too frequently taken the liberty of copying, print-
> ing, and publishing, great quantities of base, imperfect, and mean, Copies
> and Imitations thereof; to the great detriment of the Petitioners, and other
> such Artists, and to the Discouragement of Arts and Sciences in this King-
> dom: And therefore praying, That Leave may be given for a Bill to be
> brought into the House, for preventing such Frauds and Abuses for the
> future, and securing the Properties of the Petitioners, as the Laws now in
> being have preserved the Properties of the Authors of Books; or in such
> other manner as by the House shall be thought fit.[4]

In stating its case, the petitioning pamphlet complained of "the Tyranny
of the Rich" and of "the Monopoly of the Rich." *The Rich* are identified,
not as "the Rich who are above them" nor as "the Rich of their own
Profession." The tyrannical rich are rather "the Rich of that very Trade
which cou'd not subsist without them."[5] These sellers of prints defraud
the original designers, engravers, and the unfortunate drudges who are
employed to make cheap copies. The latter are "Men who have all gone
through the same Distress in some degree or other; and are now kept
Night and Day at Work at miserable Prices, whilst the overgrown Shop-
keeper has the main profit of their Labour."[6]

As Ronald Paulson points out, the petitioners were concerned with
more than the unscrupulous sellers. "More important is the 'Improve-
ment of the Arts' in England, which can be brought about only if the
English artist can receive his just profits and spread his wares and fame
through good engravings (not shabby copies). Then the purchaser too
will have a greater choice of prints at a lower price, 'for when everyone is
secure in the Fruits of his own Labour, then the number of Artists will be
every Day increasing.' "[7]

Hogarth and his associates prevailed upon the House and obtained the legal relief that they sought. The text of the act (printed in full in the Appendix to this essay) opens as follows:

> Whereas divers Persons have by their own Genius, Industry, Pains, and expense, invented and engraved, or worked in Mezzotinto or Chiaro Oscuro, Sets of historical and other Prints, in hopes to have reaped the sole Benefit of their Labours: And whereas Printsellers, and other Persons, have of late, without the Consent of the Inventors, Designers and Proprietors of such Prints, frequently taken the Liberty of copying, engraving, and publishing, or causing to be copied, engraved, and published, base Copies of such Works, Designs, and Prints, to the very great Prejudice and Detriment of the Inventors, Designers and Proprietors thereof; for Remedy thereof, and for preventing such Practices for the future . . .[8]

Under the provisions of The Engravers' Act, a one-shilling fine was imposed for every impression of a pirated copy found in the possession of a printseller. The copyright was to last for fourteen years from the date—now of legal necessity inscribed on each print. The act circumvented the possibilities of evading the law through minor alterations by specifying that it would be an offense to "engrave, etch, or work . . . or in any other Manner copy and sell, or cause to be engraved, copied, or sold, in the Whole or in Part, by varying, adding to, or diminishing from the main Design . . . any such Print or Prints, or any Parts thereof, without the consent of the Proprietor or Proprietors. . . ."[9] Hogarth and his petitioning associates had obtained precisely the legislation that they had requested.

The effort required to lobby for The Engravers' Act took time. Hogarth so thoroughly devoted himself to building up his parliamentary pressure group, that he made no dated painting or engraving during the eighteen months (December 1733 to June 1735) which elapsed before the publication of the new act. He no doubt informed privately the few subscribers who had responded to his premature and quickly curtailed advertising campaign that a delay was expected. But he apparently did not find it necessary to inform the public at large until the end of the following year. By that time, Hogarth had presumably received assurance that the bill would be passed within months, so that he could start advertising again.

> In *The London Journal* for November 2, 1734, he announced: MR. HOGARTH *hereby gives Notice, That having found it necessary to introduce several additional Characters in his Paintings of the* Rake's Progress, *he could not get the Prints ready to deliver to his Subscribers at* Michaelmas *last (as he proposed.) But all the Pictures being now entirely finished, may be seen at his House, the* Golden-Head *in* Leicester-Fields, *where Subscriptions are taken; and the Prints being in great Forwardness, will be finished, with all possible Speed, and the Time of Delivery Advertised.*[10]

At this moment, Hogarth does not give the real reason for the delay, but mentions only the necessity for introducing "additional characters" into the paintings. He probably did touch up a few details, and the engravings were very likely in a state of "great Forwardness," as he says. With the publication of such advertisements, with the continued popularity of the first *Progress* in original engraving and copy as well as stage adaptations, and with the title of the next *Progress* known from the poem that began to circulate in 1732, and finally, with acquaintances and new subscribers presumably talking about the sensational new tale whose composition and legal protection Hogarth was preparing so sedulously—the air was surely full of rumor.

The gang of pirates, Henry Overton, John King, and Thomas and John Bowles,[11] must have strained their ears and licked their lips. On May 10, 1735, five days before the act received the Royal Assent, Hogarth announced the publication date, which was the same day the act came into force—June 25. He may have already suspected something, but refers only in general to the "scandalous and unjust custom . . . of vending base copies."[12] The pirates probably acted sometime during May; for when Hogarth revived his advertising campaign for the final three weeks before publication, he had reason to complain in more specifically bitter terms that the pirate printsellers had

> . . . in a clandestine Manner, procured mean necessitous Persons to come to Mr. William Hogarth's house, under the pretence of seeing his *Rake's Progress*, in order to pyrate the same, and publish base prints thereof before the Act commences, and even before Mr. Hogarth himself can publish the true ones. This Behavior, and men who are capable of a Practice so repugnant to Honesty, and destructive of Property, are humbly submitted to the Judgement of the Publick, on whose Justice the injured Person relies. N.B. The Prints of the *Rake's Progress*, designed and engraved by Mr. William Hogarth, will not be published till after the 24th day of June; and all prints thereof published will be an imposition on the Publick.[13]

The *modus operandi* for the "mean and necessitous Persons" must have been rather awkward. A series of agents was doubtless employed because a single person returning repeatedly would arouse suspicion; the memories of one visit even by more than one person would not have provided a good enough basis for so long a story. (One wonders whether the "visitors" attempted to allay suspicions, or atone a little for their crime by each subscribing on the spot.) The spies, moreover, could not have had any *known* connection with the trade, since any professional engraver or printseller would have been refused admittance.

As laymen in the arts, with minds untrained for feats of memory, the spies must have presented reports both garbled and contradictory. Collating the information, sorting out what was feasible and credible, and with bare notions of the placing of the main figures, the engravers had the unenviable task of working out the detailed composition for themselves while awaiting oral corrections from the spies. The work

Hogarth's "Tavern Scene," (above) the third engraving from his **Rake's Progress**, is richer in physical detail, psychological characterization and composition than the piracy opposite derived from the original painting. Yet, the feebler piracies substantially eliminated Hogarth's market for his own work.

must have been done at top speed, in order to appear before the act came into force. This strange form of collaboration had strange results. Some parts are fairly accurately remembered, others only vaguely so: a gesture, an attitude, an action, a character loses its way either to disappear altogether, or to reappear in another context. One can watch the engraver fumble and help himself out by reverting to a type provided either by an evident tradition, or by Hogarth himself in previously published work. The distortion of Hogarth is, on the whole, fairly constant; there is no composition which is obviously better or worse than the others, although some are more completely rendered than others. The spies were clearly struck by the number of figures and may have duplicated a character here and there in their reports, for it is remarkable that the world of the plagiarist is as a rule more heavily populated than Hogarth's.

Hogarth evidently expected these bastard progeny to appear before his originals, and in fact his timing was remarkably fortunate, for
another newspaper, the *Daily Advertiser* (June 3) simultaneously carried
an advertisement which the pirates themselves had the temerity to in-
sert:
"Now printing, and in a few days will be publishe'd, the Progress of
a Rake, exemplified in the Adventures of Ramble Gripe, Esq.; Son and
Heir of Sir Positive Gripe; curiously design'd and engrav'd by some of
the best Artists." This was printed for Henry Overton, John King, and
Thomas and John Bowles.
Hogarth thereafter repeated his complaint, together with the
straightforward advertisement, in the following two issues of his newspaper, the *London Evening Post*. He skipped an issue and then repeated
just the advertisement in the following four issues. In the last of these
(June 17–19) he added not only the old complaint, but details of his
countermeasures—his own cheap copies:

> Certain Printsellers intending not only to injure Mr. Hogarth in his Property,
> but also to impose their base Imitations of his *Rake's Progress* on the Publick,
> he, in order to prevent such scandalous Practices, and shew the *Rake's Progress*
> exactly (which the Imitators by Memory cannot pretend to) is oblig'd to
> permit his Original Prints to be closely copied, and the said Copies will be

> published in a few Days, and sold at 2s. 6d. each Set by Tho. Bakewell . . .
> N.B. . . . all Persons may safely sell the said Copies without incurring any
> Penalty for so doing . . .

The next issue of the *Post*, which covered the three days preceding
publication day (June 21–24), carried only Hogarth's advertisement; but
simultaneously, yet another newspaper, this time the *Whitehall Evening
Post* (June 21) announced that the Ramble Gripe piracies of Overton, *et
al.* were "just publish'd" at eight shillings.

Having at last seen with his own eyes the work of his robbers,
Hogarth was immediately (i.e., from the moment he was delivering his
own engravings) moved to repeat his complaint, in other newspapers
(e.g., the *London Daily Post* for June 27) and in a slightly recast form,
adding the phrase (after "carrying away by Memory from the Sight of his
Paintings") "have executed most wretchedly both in Design and Drawing. . . ." He then reminded the public that his own authorized copies
would be available "in a few days."[14] Now that he had finally sped the
original engravings into the hands of the subscribers, and warned the
public that these were not to be had any longer except at the increased
price of two guineas, his own copies were to cause the artist something of
a headache, with a six-week delay that left the field wide open to the
plagiaries. The actual date of publication could not be announced until
July 26 (*St. James Evening Post*), the copies to be published "*in ten days
without fail*" [original italics], the delay having been occasioned by the
illness of an engraver. Six plates were however already complete and the
prints visible at Bakewell's. Yet three days later, Hogarth was obliged to
announce a correction (in the *London Daily Post*), stating that the copies
would be published in nine days time, and that four (only) of the set of
eight prints were ready for inspection. This promise was kept; and the
Ramble Gripe copies advertised also appeared. The plagiarist responsible was Henry Overton's brother, Philip, who had earlier, when in
partnership with his brother, stolen the *Harlot's Progress*.

When finally passed, "Hogarth's Act," as the visual copyright law
came to be called, was apparently quite successful in stemming print
piracy. Hogarth himself was pleased with the results and commemorated
the passage of the act in the print *Crowns, Mitres, Maces, etc.* of 1754,
which is inscribed:

> In humble & grateful Acknowledgement of the Grace and Goodness of the
> *Legislature*, Manifested in the *Act of Parliament* for the Encouragement of the
> Arts of Designing, Engraving, etc. Obtained by the endeavours, and almost at
> the Sole expence, of the designer of this Print, in the year 1735; by which not
> only the Professors of those Arts were rescued from the Tyranny, Frauds &
> Piracies of Monopolising Dealers and Legally entitled to the Fruits of their
> own Labours; but Genius and Industry were also prompted by the most noble
> and generous Inducements to exert themselves.[15]

But the original duration of protection was too short to serve Hogarth's own long-term interests. However, he made no public complaints when *Rake's Progress* passed into the public domain in 1750 and even celebrated the act in the aforementioned print. But when Hogarth died, his widow was aware of the loss of sales through plagiaries. In 1767, the act was altered so as to grant twenty-eight years of protection. And for Mrs. Hogarth, the term was lengthened an additional twenty years.[16]

CONCLUSIONS: THE NEW ARTISTIC ROLE AND ITS NEW PROPERTY FORMS

With Hogarth, the essentially bourgeois concept of art object as publicly purchasable commodity, and artistic idea as legal property enters its first concrete phase. Before the eighteenth century in England, and up to the nineteenth century in most other European countries, writers and artists depended on private, usually aristocratic patronage. In the course of the eighteenth century, English writers were increasingly able to support themselves through the sale of books to a middle-class audience growing in numbers, disposable income, and cultural awareness. Hogarth was the first visual artist to tap systematically this broader market. He was followed in the nineteenth century by caricaturists and illustrators, such as Gillray and Cruikshank, and the mass distribution of prints derived from paintings became a preponderant economic factor in individual painters' careers. But it should be stressed that Hogarth, standing at the beginning of this development, saw his militance for economic independence in the print market in the same light as his other initiatives on the art-political scene, such as his participation in the Foundling Hospital. This, like his Copyright Act, was conducive not only to his economic self-interest, but also to the interest of English artists as a professional class generally, and, even more broadly, to that of the nascent "School of British Art" which he virtually founded.

During the nineteenth century, the emphasis in the history of copyright shifts to the efforts to secure an international copyright law. Many of Hogarth's successors in popular art and literature, such as Charles Dickens and Rodolphe Töpffer of Geneva, suffered from international piracy on an international scale, while their domestic market was protected. But this very protection seems to have stimulated a sense of intellectual property that extended now not merely to objects, but the very ideas underpinning those objects. The notion of an unconcretized artistic or literary *idea* as a commodity needing protection from piracy— if not by law, then at least by professional ethics—took on pathological forms in an age which honored individual competition even in cultural domains as a high and necessary element in the social struggle.

As an example of the pathology in claims to artistic paternity, we may cite the bitter and self-destructive complaint of George Cruikshank, who was hailed as the Hogarth of the early Victorian age, that Dickens "stole" the plot of *Oliver Twist* from him. This episode does little honor to Dickens, who emerged victorious and who could well have afforded to be more generous toward his erstwhile illustrator.[17] It occurred to neither of the parties involved in the dispute, nor to anyone else, that such an idea could be conceived simultaneously in different quarters, and that it might originate not only in an individual head, but also in the common ground of popular experience.

The concept of individual intellectual property, protected like material property by the law, tended in the nineteenth century to foster ungrounded accusations of plagiary and fears of artistic theft. This tendency is exacerbated today, when ideas and information are treated as commodities to be traded in corporate fashion by the mass media and fought over in the courts by individuals. But it must ultimately be recognized that all ideas and inventions, all aspects of advancing knowledge, have social rather than individual origins. As capitalism disappears, Hogarth's important initiative, although certainly progressive in its time, will be given its proper historical place, and all copyright laws will become historical curiosities.

NOTES

[1]See Harry Ransom, *The First Copyright Statute. An Essay on an Act for the Encouragment of Learning* (Austin: University of Texas Press, 1956), pp. 64, 77. Despite the attention paid today to copyright in the visual arts, there is as I know no study of artistic piracy in Europe during the sixteenth to eighteenth centuries, or of the distinction made (if any) between privilege or monopoly, and copyright in the modern sense; or of the conventions which engravers may have adopted more or less by mutual consent. In a well-known letter to Peiresc, Rubens, for instance, is "incensed and enraged" at the Parisian engraver who had done him "great prejudice and damage" by copying his engravings "notwithstanding that the privilege granted to him by His Most Majesty was renewed three years ago." The letter is cited in Jacob Burckhardt, *Recollections of Rubens* (London: Phaidon Editions, 1950), p. 237.

[2]The earliest advertisement for these found so far is of November 1732, i.e., six months after Hogarth's subscribers were handed their prints; but Kirkall would not have waited that long before putting them in the shops. Hogarth delivered his originals either on May 10, as he had promised, or on May 11, the last day when his advertisement (his thirtieth at least) appeared. By May 18, piracies were available, or were known to be imminent, for G. King in the *Daily Journal* warned the public to beware of "other copies" offered by hawkers or their accomplices.

[3]Ronald Paulson, *Hogarth's Graphic Works* (New Haven: Yale University Press, 1965), p. 158, thinks that "the paintings were not completed until the middle of 1734," on the grounds of an advertisement in the *London Journal* for November 2, 1734, which refers

to the introduction of "several additional characters." The additions were probably very minor, inflated for the purposes of the advertisement, which had to explain the delay without giving the real reason, that is, the Copyright Act.

[4]The petition is cited in Ronald Paulson, *Hogarth: His Life, Art and Times* (New Haven: Yale University Press, 1971), vol. I, p. 361.

[5]*Ibid.*, p. 360.

[6]*Idem.*

[7]*Ibid.*, p. 361.

[8]The entire text of the act, which appears in the Appendix, is printed in Paulson, *ibid.*, Vol. II, appendix F, pp. 489–90.

[9]*Ibid.*, p. 489.

[10]Paulson (1965), who first discovered this advertisement, transcribes it on p. 158.

[11]Not, apparently, Hogarth's former plagiarist-in-chief, Elisha Kirkall. Perhaps the painter had had a word with this engraver, who was quite well known and otherwise respectable (the "bounteous Kirkall" of Pope's *Dunciad*). The Overtons and John Bowles had already made cheap copies of Hogarth plates in their possession, as well as pirating designs of plates which they did not own, e.g., for the *Harlot's Progress*.

[12]See Paulson's (1965) complete transcription pp. 158–59.

[13]*London Evening Post*, June 17–19, 1735.

[14]The advertisement is fully transcribed in Paulson (1965), p. 159.

[15]Paulson (1965), p. 224.

[16]Paulson (1971), Vol. I, p. 361.

[17]Richard Vogler, "Cruikshank and Dickens: A Reassessment of the Role of the Artist and the Author," *Princeton University Library Chronicle* 35, (1973): 61–91, gives hitherto unknown evidence that Cruikshank conceived an *Oliver Twist*-related "Life of a Thief" before Dickens planned his novel. For Töpffer piracies and imitations, see David Kunzle, "Mr. Lambkin: Cruikshank's Strike for Independence," in the same journal.

APPENDIX: The Engravers' Act of 1735

THE ENGRAVERS' ACT*
Anno octavo Georgii II. Rigis

An Act for the Encouragement of the Arts of Designing, Engraving, and Etching historical and other Prints, by vesting the Properties thereof in the Inventors and Engravers, during the Time therein mentioned.

Whereas divers Persons have by their own Genius, Industry, Pains, and Expence, invented and engraved, or worked in *Mezzotinto*, or *Chiaro Oscuro*, Sets of historical and other Prints, in hopes to have reaped the sole Benefit of their Labours: And whereas Print-sellers, and other Persons, have of late, without the Consent of the Inventors, Designers, and Proprietors of such Prints, frequently taken the Liberty of copying, engraving, and publishing, or causing to be copied, engraved, and published, base Copies of such Works, Designs, and Prints, to the very great Prejudice and Detriment of the Inventors, Designers, and Proprietors thereof; for Remedy thereof, and for preventing such Practices for the future, may it please Your Majesty that it may be enacted, and be it enacted by the King's most Excellent Majesty, by and with the Advice and Consent of the Lords Spiritual and Temporal, and Commons, in this present Parliament assembled, and by the Authority of the same, That from and after the Twenty fourth Day of June, which shall be in the Year of our Lord One thousand seven hundred and thirty five, every Person who shall invent and design, engrave, etch, or work in *Mezzotinto* or *Chiaro Oscuro*, or, from his own Works and Invention, shall cause to be designed and engraved, etched, or worked in *Mezzotinto* or *Chiaro Oscuro*, any historical or other Print or Prints, shall have the sole Right and Liberty of Printing and Reprinting the same for the Term of Fourteen Years, to commence from the Day of the first Publishing thereof, which shall be truly engraved with the Name of the Proprietor on each Plate, and printed on every such Print or Prints; and that if any Print-seller, or other Person whatsoever, from and after the said Twenty fourth Day of June, One thousand seven hundred and thirty five, within the Time limited by this Act, shall engrave, etch, or work, as aforesaid, or in any other Manner copy and sell, or cause to be engraved, etched, or copied and sold, in the Whole or in Part, by varying, adding to, or diminishing from the main Design, or shall print, reprint, or import for Sale, or cause to be printed, reprinted, or imported for Sale, any such Print or Prints, or any Parts thereof, without the Consent of the Proprietor or Proprietors thereof first had and obtained in Writing, signed by him or them respectively, in the Presence of Two or more credible Witnesses, or, knowing the same to be so printed or reprinted without the Consent of the Proprietor or Proprietors, shall publish, sell, or expose to sale, or otherwise, or in any other Manner dispose of, or cause to be published, sold, or exposed to sale, or otherwise, or in any other Manner disposed of, any such Print or Prints without such Consent first had and obtained, as aforesaid, then such Offender or Offenders shall forfeit the Plate or Plates on which such Print or Prints are or shall be copied, and all and every Sheet or Sheets (being part of or whereon such Print or Prints are or shall be so copied or printed) to the Proprietor or Proprietors of such original Print or Prints, who shall forthwith destroy and damask the same; and further, that every such Offender or Offenders shall forfeit five Shillings for every Print which shall be found in his, her, or their Custody, either printed or published, and exposed to Sale, or otherwise disposed of contrary

---

*Reprinted from Ronald Paulson, *Hogarth: His Life, Art and Times* (New Haven: Yale University Press, 1971), by permission.

to the true Intent and Meaning of this Act, the One Moiety thereof to the King's most Excellent Majesty, His Heirs, and Successors, and the other Moiety thereof to any Person or Persons that shall sue for the same, to be recovered in any of His Majesty's Courts of Record at Westminster, by Action of Debt, Bill, Plaint, or Information, in which no Wager of Law, Essoign, Privilege, or Protection, or more than One Imparlance shall be allowed.

Provided nevertheless, That it shall and may be lawful for any Person or Persons, who shall hereafter purchase any Plate or Plates for printing, from the Original Proprietors thereof, to print and reprint from the said Plates, without incurring any of the Penalties in this Act mentioned.

And be it further enacted by the Authority aforesaid, That if any Action or Suit shall be commenced or brought against any Person or Persons whatsoever, for doing or causing to be done any Thing in pursuance of this Act, the same shall be brought within the Space of Three Months after so doing; and the Defendant and Defendants, in such Action or Suit, shall or may plead the General Issue, and give the special Matter in Evidence; and if upon such Action or Suit a Verdict shall be given for the Defendant or Defendants, or if the Plaintiff or Plaintiffs become nonsuited, or discontinue his, her, or their Action or Actions, then the Defendant or Defendants shall have and recover full Costs, for the Recovery whereof he shall have the same Remedy, as any other Defendant or Defendants in any other Case hath or have by Law.

Provided always, and be it further enacted by the Authority aforesaid, That if any Action or Suit shall be commenced or brought against any Person or Persons, for any Offence committed against this Act, the same shall be brought within the Space of Three Months after the Discovery of every such Offence, and not afterwards; any Thing in this Act contained to the contrary notwithstanding. . . .

And be it further enacted by the Authority aforesaid, That this Act shall be deemed, adjudged, and taken to be a Publick Act, and be judicially taken notice of as such by all Judges, Justices, and other Persons whatsoever, without specially pleading the same.

II
THE IMPACT OF COPYRIGHT LAW ON SCHOLARS AND PUBLISHERS

Unwriting *The Story of Rock*

In *The Times Atlas of World History* one finds "A World Chronology" section. Predictably, its entries for 1956 in diplomatic-military categories include the second Arab-Israeli War, the Suez Crisis, and the revolts in Hungary and Poland. The United States is excluded from mention during this year, except under the heading "Culture and Technology"—where "the beginning of rock and roll music" is credited as the sole major occurrence. (Geoffrey Barraclough, ed., Maplewood, N.J.: Hammond, 1978, p. 27)

Partisans of rock music, such as Charles Reich in *The Greening of America* and Theodore Roszak in *The Making of a Counterculture,* have suggested that rock should be seen as a major cultural force, helping to determine a new sensibility and way of life that will eventually change the politics of the industrialized world. The London *Times* entry, if not conceding such visionary importance, at least assigns to rock a substantial historical presence.

In the essay that follows, Carl Belz describes the difficulties he experienced in documenting his widely used book *The Story of Rock* (Oxford, 1969). Leonard Feist, President of the National Music Publishers Association—a trade group that represented composers' copyright interests during the most recent revision of the law—comments on Belz's essay.

3

UNWRITING THE STORY OF ROCK

CARL BELZ

By profession, I am an art historian and museum director. But a few years ago circumstances led me to write a book called *The Story of Rock*. The book has had two hardback editions at Oxford University Press and paperback edition at Harper and Row. Foreign editions have appeared in Italy and Japan; excerpts have been used in a German book on contemporary music. Because of its wide distribution and acceptance, the book's history and my experience of writing it—and then unwriting it in order to comply with copyright expectations—should be of interest to those concerned with writing about contemporary music as a branch of the new electronic, commercial media.

The idea for writing *The Story of Rock* arose in a casual way. During the summer of 1965, I was spending the summer with a friend who had just moved to the West Coast. During the summer, I discovered that my friend didn't know anything about popular, folk, or rock music. He did have an interest in music, however, and was very familiar with classical composers like Beethoven and Mozart. We spent a great deal of time that summer listening to the radio and I began to explain to him what I knew about various songs, artists, and dates of release as well as my own personal associations with the music. He, in turn, became quite interested and I found myself developing some broader ideas about popular music during my conversations with him.

By the end of the summer, it occurred to us that we might have the basis for a book in the developing ideas. .During the following summer, after a school year in which we accomplished little for our project, we did extensive research in *Billboard* magazine to build up an accurate set of dates, names of artists, and releases. We also began to research some of the sociological and economic aspects of the music, which were areas I had never really thought about previously—since I had confined my attention to musical content. Uncovering these new dimensions confirmed my belief that there really was a serious body of material to deal with. My friend, who had done much of the original research, eventually dropped out of the project, but I carried it forward myself. By the summer of 1967, I had written a rough draft of my manuscript.

As I wrote, I used many lyrics in my text, most of which I had picked up from the records. It seemed like a very natural thing to do. As an art historian and critic of art, it was automatic that one would have reproductions of the art under discussion. I quoted freely from Chuck Berry, the Beach Boys, and others as I made my observations about them. My conviction was that I had to allow the readers to see what I was talking about—to permit them to share my perception, or to reject it.

Fortunately, I found a literary agent who was interested in circulating my manuscript among publishers at a time when the market was being glutted with rock books by professional writers. I was extremely pleased when Oxford University Press expressed interest, because their scholarly standing implied a more serious book than the commercial competitors appearing at that time. Oxford initially offered an advance of $500 for the book, but my agent was able to secure a commitment for $1,500, which looked comfortable in relation to my anticipated expenses in providing the finished manuscript.

Oxford did mention something that came as a surprise to me. They explained that they would want permissions from the copyright holders for the quotations from lyrics that I had included in my text. I began to write to the persons controlling the rights for the songs that I had included and it rapidly became clear that I could not afford to publish the book that I had written. I wrote to fifteen or twenty publishers, only half of whom answered my inquiries. Those who did reply mentioned fees that totaled $5,000 to $6,000 of my own money. The big advance had shrunk to insignificant proportions.

Of all the music publishers that I wrote to, only one granted permission in a way that paralleled standard practice in literary permissions. The Beach Boys stated that they would be happy to have their material reproduced and they waived what must be a standard minimum fee of around $200 per lyric cited. All other answers stipulated fees from $200 to $300. Ten quotations from the Beatles would have cost $3,000. I had included several dozen songs in my text. The expense of the book could have been staggering.

I was so grateful to the Beach Boys that I included their acknowledgment on the page where the citation occurred. And the quotation itself almost appears to be a joke. The reader reaches page 100 of a book on rock without seeing a single lyric, encounters one, and then finishes the book without seeing a single additional lyric.

The oddity of the final manuscript was accounted for by the extensive "unwriting" that I had to undertake. Rewriting in order to eliminate lyric quotations was more than a merely stylistic problem. I really had to reconceive what I was doing in the book. Even in the original "naive" state of the manuscript, I was forced to describe the content of the song, which already abstracts one a step away from the original. It had occurred to me that under ideal conditions, readers of my history would be able to hear the songs while reading. This would remedy the incompleteness caused by the reader's encounter with the mere lyric content of the songs. But the rewriting occasioned by the copyright stance of Oxford and the music publishers took the book an additional step away from concreteness. Even fragments of the lyrics could not be presented. I had written a history that was at two removes from its subject. There were no musical sounds and no lyrics, yet I was attempting to document my history and draw responsible, convincing inferences about them. The effect on my manuscript was devastating.

It would be interesting here to publish a "before" and "after" section of my manuscript in order to demonstrate the effect that unwriting *The Story of Rock* had on its vividness and credibility. (Though even now there would be a problem about permissions, I suspect. It's not clear that one can even discuss the problem without encountering the permissions barrier.) But in my anger and frustration over the effects of the alterations on my book, I eventually disposed of the correspondence and the original manuscript during a move from one location to another. I never suspected that anyone would take an interest in the difficulties that I had faced in having the book published. I had hoped that the lonely Beach Boys quotation would stand out like a sore thumb and evoke a cynical smile from readers who knew something about problems with music rights. A few of the people who read the book did ask why I had so strangely omitted lyric quotations from my work. This response came particularly from those familiar with scholarly conventions of quotation generally, who therefore brought scholarly expectations to my book, especially since it had been published by a leading scholarly press. People with business backgrounds were inclined to think that the publisher could somehow have circumvented the obstacles. On the contrary, the publisher had left it up to me and the $1,500 advance provided—a sum hardly equal to buying the right to discuss the popular music of our time.

I am not learned in the law of copyright nor in the nuances of "fair use" that are associated with it. I do not know how music publishers managed to convince book publishers that they must abridge the freedom of speech which they accept in publishing other kinds of material. I am aware of the problems of piracy in the music industry and have no sympathy with those who exploit the creations of performing artists in such a way that their livelihoods are threatened. But it seems to me that scholars should have the right to discuss the music of their time. What could help the performing artist more than discussions that acknowledge the cultural importance of what they convey to us through their lyrics? Why should they want to prevent a permanent record of their accomplishments in the histories of their time by charging fees that place their cultural performances beyond the capability of most scholars and publishers? In a field that has often prided itself on its revolutionary sentiments, it appears that yet another revolution is in order.

A RESPONSE TO MR. CARL BELZ
By Leonard Feist

Before commenting on Mr. Belz's account of his frustration, it will be useful to make some general observations about music—popular songs particularly—and fair use. Of all types of copyrighted works, none are as vulnerable to economic injury as songs. In a typical popular song, brief by its very nature, there is much repetition both in words and music so that a short excerpt may, in effect, be a very substantial part of the whole. There have been many protracted and complex lawsuits over the similarity of the melody of one song with another. Judicial determinations often based on a very few notes in a particular sequence have meant the difference of tens of thousands of dollars to one or the other of the contestants.

Moreover, although the lyric may be only half of a song, it is nevertheless a complete entity on its own and, for better or worse, stands on its own metric feet as a poem. There is a market for lyrics. The contents of several monthly magazines are made up entirely of lyrics of songs both current and standard for which the magazine publishers pay music publishers consequential sums of money. Exclusive agreements frequently are concluded which bar the music publisher from granting anyone else the right to reprint the lyric.

The author of another book published by Oxford University Press seemed to have better success in securing permissions from music publishers. *American Popular Song: The Great Innovators 1900–1950* by Alec Wilder, published in 1972, is jam-packed with quotations from various copyrighted songs, literally hundreds of them. In the case of one composer, there are no examples since he chose not to grant permission to use any musical excerpts, but there are almost ten pages in all of copyright acknowledgments.

It is difficult to make either a fair use interpretation or a business practice comment on Mr. Belz's frustrating experiences with music publishers. There is just not enough information. He says that he included "several dozen" songs in his original text. Elsewhere he refers to requests for "quotations from lyrics." How extensive a "quotation?" How many complete lyrics? He apparently wrote to "fifteen or twenty" publishers for permissions for "several dozen songs" including ten quotations from the Beatles. Did Mr. Belz seem to be approaching what might have been viewed by some publishers as an anthology? It is unfortunate that Mr. Belz disposed of his correspondence with the publishers. I might have been able to shed some light on the situation if I had known what he had requested and how he had asked for it. (Requests for permission to include lyrics in scholarly works is not commonplace in popular music publishers' experience.)

I do not intend to avoid meeting the issue of fair use of excerpts of lyrics (or music) of popular songs. Mr. Belz's situation as he presents it, however, just doesn't seem to me to be an example on which comment can be made. It seems to me that the four criteria of Section 107 of the Copyright Act, plus the music education guidelines which were developed by publishers and educators, provide a reasonable basis for a determination of fair use by a reasonable person. Lord knows, it took long enough to arrive at the language. Perhaps it will require judicial interpretation to provide the answers to some marginal questions, but I hope not. I hope that the rule of reason will prevail.

I do regret (and apologize to Mr. Belz for) the failure of half of the publishers to whom he wrote to answer his inquiries. Although there is no excuse for such cavalier treatment of polite requests, there are several explanations. The rock era and the instantaneous success of the rock artist or group has created new publishers who may find themselves fully occupied with meeting business demands. Fewer and fewer music publishers today print their own music. Often, they contract with specialists in the print field to handle all aspects of this facet of their business. A letter relative to any print right would be forwarded to the sub-publisher who, in turn, might be an innocent in dealing with the problems of permissions. For these failures of publishers, I can only express my regrets and hope that we, at NMPA, may encourage prompt responses even though the answer may be "no."

One last word—I read Mr. Belz's book shortly after its publication and found it an exemplary work. I'm glad that it has gone through two hardcover editions, been reprinted in paperback and translated several times. *The Story of Rock* is a real contribution to the literature on the subject. I wonder what it might have been with the lyrics included?

Belz-Feist: Unwriting *The Story of Rock*

The comments of Leonard Feist are instructive in several ways. They indicate some of the precise economic and artistic reasons why composers and publishers are reluctant to allow even small units from song lyrics to pass into publication without prior review. He also suggests some of the bureaucratic conditions of music publishing houses that result in their failure to correspond.

The reference to Alec Wilder's *The American Song,* although supporting the claim that persistence and skill with publishers make well-documented publication feasible, may also suggest that heavy investments are necessary to carry out music scholarship. Ten pages of copyright acknowledgments would be a very expensive undertaking if the fees cited by Belz are truly representative of the contemporary pop music field.

Furthermore, the legislative fair use music education guidelines to which Mr. Feist refers, and which NMPA assisted in working out, do not provide clear criteria for publishing. The "Guidelines for Educational Uses of Music" (see HR *Report* No. 94-1476, pp. 70–72) restrict themselves to nonpublishing situations—copying for classrooms, archival holdings, emergency replacements, etc. And these guidelines are accompanied by this disclaimer from the Committee on the Judiciary:

> ... the following statement of guidelines is not intended to limit the types of copying permitted under the standards of fair use under judicial decision and which are stated in Section 107 of the Copyright Revision Bill. There may be instances in which copying that does not fall within the guidelines below may nonetheless be permitted under the critieria of fair use. (70–71)

The new legislation therefore invites scholars and publishers to use their judgment about what is reasonable and fair. Some publishers adhere to the safest strategy of seeking permissions in all cases and encouraging their authors to pay whatever fees are requested; others attempt to pursue "reasonable" policies in different ways.

Rolling Stone magazine, for example, which probably quotes as much music as any U.S. publisher, has created the following arbitrary rules in the absence of any clear guidance from statutes. According to Associate Editor Sarah Lazin,

> For many years we cited every lyric [i.e., quoting a lyric and accompanying it with an acknowledgment of the author, copyright date, and publishing company] and when we checked with other magazines and found that they didn't cite anything, we asked our copyright lawyers to explain the law to us. . . . The law is very vague, and they couldn't decide whether we should cite and get permission from the publishers (which runs into a lot of money), or whether we could cite and not get permission, or not cite at all. So we made up some rules and have followed them for years: a lyric of four lines or over but under 1/5th of the song must be cited, but permission need not be asked, defining under 1/5th of a song as fair use. . . . Over 1/5th of the song must be cited and permission must be obtained. . . .

> For books. . . we have to follow book rules and cite all lyrics and obtain permission for every citation. . . That is a huge problem for us, and a very expensive one as well. (Letter, Sara Lazin, Associate Editor, *Rolling Stone*, April 6, 1978.)

Rolling Stone sees such requirements as restrictive, but has considerable sympathy with "popular artists, who, without these laws, would have no income or credit from their material."

Rolling Stone's rules for its journalistic publication seem "reasonable," and its invention of fractional percentages of lyrics has the virtue of applying definite limits on a consistent basis. The "book rules" referred to do not appear to have any basis in law, but rather represent self-imposed restrictions. The policies at *Rolling Stone* illustrate how much latitude there is within the law for creating individual policies and carrying them out successfully.

The courts, mentioned by neither Carl Belz nor Leonard Feist, have on occasion rendered decisions about copyright infringements of song lyrics appearing in publications. *Nimmer on Copyright* mentions a group of such cases as illustrating the "functional test" that has often been applied in attempting to determine "the effect of the use upon the potential market for or value of the copyrighted work." (17 USC 107 [4]). In a number of cases where quoted material performs a different function than in its original context, the fair use defense has been held legitimate.

> . . . The unauthorized reproduction of the chorus lyrics of songs were held noninfringing fair use where such reproductions appeared in magazine articles. . . . In each such instance the plaintiff and defendant in a sense employed the same medium. However, the functions differed in that plaintiff's music sheet was intended to be used for singing or musical presentations, while defendant's article was a literary presentation which incidentally included the disputed lyrics. Persons interested in obtaining plaintiff's music would not find that need fulfilled through the purchase of defendant's magazine article. (Nimmer on Copyright, 13.05 (B), 55-56; cases cited are Karll v. Curtis Publishing Co., 39 F.Supp. 836 (E.D. Wisc. 1941); Broadway Music Co. v. F-R Publishing Co., 31 F.Supp. 817 (S.D.N.Y. 1940); Shapiro Bernstein & Co. v. P.F. Collier, 26 U.S.P.Q. 40 (S.D.N.Y. 1934))

These cases would support the conclusion that in book publication a critical function of scholarly quotation and a reasonable caution about supplanting the producer's market are, along with other fair use considerations, sufficient guiding principles for publishers to come to fair use decisions that avoid frustrating, book-delaying correspondence and economically prohibitive fees.

Donald Duck v. Chilean Socialism

One product of the socialist revolution in Chile (1970–73) was a work of popular, polemic scholarship called *Para Leer al Pato Donald* (*How to Read Donald Duck*). Written by Marxist scholars Ariel Dorfman and Armand Mattelart, the book in its various translations became an international bestseller, with sales through 1978 totaling more than 250,000. Because of anticipated and actual opposition from Walt Disney Productions, however, a U.S. edition was not published and a mere 1,500 copies became available to the United States audience because of import restrictions.

Detailed documentation of Disney's arguments in this matter has not been possible, since it is maintaining its legal readiness to prevent any future United States edition that contains Disney comics imagery. Its vice-president and counsel, Franklin Waldheim, has implied that the reproduction here of statements from their letters of brief to the United States Treasury Department in their attempt to prevent importation would be disadvantageous pre-trial publicity and thus result in the obstruction of justice. (See the letter in the Appendix.) For related reasons, the editors and the publisher have not deemed it prudent to reproduce the contested Disney images from *How to Read Donald Duck*.

Walt Disney Productions argued that this cover conveyed the piratical intent of the authors and publisher. They found it to be designed so as to deceive unsuspecting parents into the purchase of material representing itself as Disney's own. Cover from Ariel Dorfman and Armand Mattelart, *How to Read Donald Duck: Imperialist Ideology in the Disney Comic* (David Kunzle, translator) 1975; reproduced courtesy of the publisher, International General, New York.

4

DONALD DUCK v. CHILEAN SOCIALISM: A FAIR USE EXCHANGE

JOHN SHELTON LAWRENCE

The new media of mass communications have occasionally stimulated visions of an international community that exchanges its cultural creations and enriches its consciousness through the resultant diversity. Marshall McLuhan's phrase, "the global electronic village," expresses this optimism, as did Thomas Hutchinson's prophecy of 1938 regarding the future of television:

> Television means the world in your home and in the homes of all the people of the world. It is the greatest means of communication ever developed by the human mind. It should do more to develop friendly neighbors, and to bring understanding and peace on earth than any other single material force in the world today.[1]

To such minds, the notion of art as universal language has come of age with the technologies for the world-wide distribution of imagery.

The belief that popular, commercial art and entertainment will advance the cause of humankind found an eloquent proponent in Walt Disney, whose moralism and sense of cultural mission are widely known. More than a decade after his death, the corporation he formed seeks to give embodiment to his visions of commercial entertainments that would have a salutary effect on all the peoples of the world. For example, in announcing the Experimental Prototype Community of Tomorrow (EPCOT) to be constructed in Florida, the Disney corporation's president Card Walker wrote:

> There never has been a greater need for the communication of information about the diverse peoples of our planet, the new systems evolving to meet the need of those people, and the alternatives we face. . . .

45

> EPCOT Center and its two major themes, Future World and the World Showcase, will be devoted to . . . the advancement of international understanding and the solution of the problems of people everywhere.
>
> Our dedication. . . . will extend as far as the Disney ability to communicate can reach, including films, television, educational materials and even the licensing of concepts and products.[2]

Disney's *Annual Report for 1977* provided this view of EPCOT's potential:

> It will be a "communicator to the world," . . . "a permanent international people to people exchange," advancing the cause of world understanding. . . . a much needed symbol of hope and optimism . . .[3]

The tensions between enlightenment and enjoyment, American national and foreign interest, corporate profit and service to mankind are to be dissolved in this last of the great theme parks conceived by Walt Disney before his death.

Turning from the appealing rhetoric of "sharing," "communication," "understanding," and "peace" to examine actual patterns of exchange in the world's popular media, one discovers important inequalities among nations. In film and television, where Disney Productions has had great success, United States dominance is immediately evident. Although there is significant global *distribution* of media products, there is relatively little *exchange*. Some major countries, for example, import as much as 69 percent of their foreign films from the United States.[4] About television, Elihu Katz and George Wedell report in their survey of international programming:

> On Monday, July 15, 1975, at 8:30 p.m. the viewers of Bangkok could choose among three American series: "Manhunt," "The FBI," and "Get Christie Love!" On a Saturday night in Tehran the viewer had a choice of "A Family Affair" and "Days of Our Lives" on one channel and "The Bold Ones" and "Kojak" on the other. The examples are handpicked, of course, for the choice sometimes includes—as in Thailand on Sundays—wrestling (local), a Disney film, or "Hawaii Five-O."[5]

Some countries import as much as 100 percent of their programming, resulting in choices like those just mentioned; the United States imports only 1 percent of its commercial television offerings and a mere 2 percent of its public television.[6]

In the field of children's comics there are similar patterns of dominance by United States exports, led, of course, by Disney, whose publications are translated into eighteen different languages, including Arabic, Flemish, Serbo-Croatian, and Thai.[7] Millions of the Disney comics are distributed monthly, not to mention the additional millions sold by Marvel and DC Comics, but United States entrepreneurs import almost nothing from foreign countries for distribution to their own people.[8] Communication in "the global village," then, goes one way: the United States transmits cultural messages but receives very few from those to whom its communications are directed.[9]

DONALD DUCK AND THE CHILEAN REVOLUTION

The relations of dominance and passivity in world cultural exchange have not escaped the attention of observers in host countries for United States media products. One of the more forceful attempts to analyze the influence and values of imported United States culture and of the Disney universe in particular occurred in Chile during its short-lived socialist government under Salvadore Allende (1970–73). Ariel Dorfman and Armand Mattelart wrote *Para Leer al Pato Donald* (translated into English as *How to Read Donald Duck: Imperialist Ideology in the Disney Comic*)[10] which was widely read in Chile, Latin America, and eventually in a number of other countries—the United States excluded. Details of its English translation and attempted importation are an unrecounted episode in the evolving tradition of copyright and fair use. It is a story that turns on the presumed unique status of imagery as understood by image-producing corporations and the correlative timidity of publishers about viewing such images within the fair use tradition.

At the time of the socialist revolution in Chile, the communications industries there exhibited a typical Third World configuration. More than 50 percent of its television programming was imported from foreign countries, with a predominance of United States offerings like "Bonanza," "Mission Impossible," "FBI," "Disneyland," etc.[11] Half-hour episodes that would cost from $3,000 to $5,000 in Japan or West Germany could be obtained for sums like $65–$70. Feature length United States films priced at $24,000 to $60,000 in Japan or Germany were available for $350 to $400. As Jeremy Tunstall has explained,

> The standard American practice in all media fields is initially to undercut the opposition through price competition; this follows from the enormous numbers of publications and broadcast outlets in the USA. Since an extra "copy" of news agency service, or the use of a feature film or a television series, has no obvious or "rational" price, there is more than the usual scope for price cutting and variation.[12]

Clearly such pricing policies will depress native production in market economies, since the cost of a program or film copy can be held below the costs even for lighting a studio or providing film stock. The virtually free distribution of programs and films at "country prices" is thus a good initial investment in an economy that may rise to greater affluence without ever developing its own media production facilities. Furthermore, United States programs are undeniably popular with foreign audiences and help foreign television networks to fill up programming hours once they have made a commitment to use television as a form of national entertainment.

The Chilean comics market also imported American products like *Superman*, *The Lone Ranger*, and others, as well as the Disney comics.[13]

Responding to these circumstances in December 1969, the Popular Unity party formulated a program for mass communications that received the approval of allied political groups.

> The means of communication (the radio, the press, publishing, television and the cinema) are fundamental aids to the formation of a new culture and of a new man. They should therefore be imbued with an educative spirit and freed from their commercial character. Measures should be taken to make the media available to the social organizations and to cast off the brooding presence of the monopolies.[14]

When the Popular Unity party came to power in 1970, it did make an effort to reshape a culture for the Chilean population, though it left commercial television largely intact. The state took over the largest publishing house in Chile, Zig-Zag, and used it to launch Empresa Editorial Quimantú, an operation that eventually published several million inexpensive books for wide distribution.[15]

It was through Quimantú (meaning literally "Sunshine of Knowledge") that a counteroffensive against the Disney comics was launched. Rather than forbidding further publication of Disney materials, Quimantú created *Cabro Chico (The Little Kid)* as an alternative, progressive-revolutionary comic. Two associates at Quimantú, Ariel Dorfman of the Juvenile and Educational Publications Division and Armand Mattelart, head of Investigation and Evaluation of the Mass Media Section, collaborated on *The Little Kid* and also wrote *How to Read Donald Duck* (1971), a popular and radical exposé of the values and worldview of Walt Disney material.

How to Read Donald Duck deals with several topics ranging from the peculiar sexual and familial values of Disney's "funny animals" to the political and social values that lie close to the surface in the episodes of Donald, his nephews, and the surpassingly rich but stingy Scrooge McDuck. It analyzes attitudes toward work, ownership, leisure, and the other perpetual themes of conflict in Duckburg. Many of their observations are paralleled by those found in the works of James Agee, Richard Schickel, and other critics of Disney.

But the central weight in the Dorfman-Mattelart critique falls upon the political and economic values of Disney as they relate to peoples of the less developed countries who have fallen into the U.S. orbit of influence—often symbolized by Disney fantasies about the Ducks as global travelers.

Roughly half the Disney comics sampled in their study showed the heroes from Duckburg confronting the peoples of other continents and ethnic groups. Plots in the stories and the imagery used to convey them—images that Quimantú reproduced without authorization from Disney—reveal a population of childlike noble savages on the one hand and political revolutionary thugs on the other. The former are easily tricked out of their wealth by the greedy ducks since they do not understand the value of their assets, and they are perpetually in need of redemption from problems that they cannot solve with their own resources. The political revolutionary thugs terrorize the natives of imaginary countries like Unsteadystan, though they are easily defeated once exposed by the super-intelligent ducks.[16] The Disney comics, which to some extent permit the regional production of Disney material, at times engage freely in antirevolutionary political propaganda. An episode appearing after the seizure of power by the junta featured the Allende government in the form of buzzards named Marx and Hegel, who attack helpless kittens as Jiminy Cricket watches. They are eventually chased away by a farmer with a shot-gun. "Ha! Firearms are the only thing those bloody birds are afraid of." Marx and Hegel (in their Disney-buzzard form) are of course "immune to the voice of conscience."[17]

In generalizing about the implications of Disney materials for a country like Chile, Dorfman and Mattelart suggest

> The threat derives not so much from their embodiment of the "American way of life." as that of the "American dream of life," It is the manner in which the U.S. dreams and redeems itself, and then imposes that dream upon others for its own salvation. . . . It forces us Latin Americans to see ourselves as they see us. . . . The Disney cosmos is no mere refuge in the area of occasional entertainment; it is our everyday stuff of repression.[18]

The socialist critique of Donald Duck found a fairly wide audience in Chile, resulting in twelve separate printings before the military coup that destroyed the Popular Unity government in 1973. Like many other artifacts of the socialist period, the book was burned; the authors were compelled to seek refuge in other countries. A New York *Times* article reported that "after the coup the president of the neighborhood council ripped down the socialist calendars and slogans that hung on the wall of his two-room wooden shack. In their place he put up some posters of Mickey and Donald."[19] In the wake of socialist criticism, the Disney characters had become antirevolutionary symbols.

The book was, however, destined to survive its burning and banning in Chile, and its exiled authors survived the mass executions carried out by the military junta. A Latin American edition had been published in Argentina in 1972. Feltrinelli in Italy published its translation *Come Leggere Paperino* in the same year. By 1975 *Para Ler o Pato Donald* had appeared in Portugal, followed in rapid succession by the French edition, *Donald l'imposteur* (1976); the Swedish, *Konsten All Lasa Kalle Anka* (1977); the German, *Walt Disney's Dritte Welt* (1977); the Danish, *Anders And i den tredje verden* (1978); and the Dutch, *Hoe Lees ik Donald Duck* (1978). Other editions are forthcoming in Greek, Finnish, Japanese, Hungarian, and possibly Serbo-Croatian. English language edition sales are now in the region of 10,000, with total world sales around 250,000.[20]

In their modest way, these figures rival the global reach of Disney's distribution.

One might have expected that the book would become widely available in the U.S., but here intervened the consideration of copyright. The art historian David Kunzle, who has written a major social history of the comic strip and who has also studied the art of revolutionary Chile, prepared a translation and introduction for *How to Read Donald Duck* while attempting negotiations with American publishers. Random House, which had an option through Feltrinelli, considered publication, as did Beacon Press, which had fearlessly published the Gravel edition of the *Pentagon Papers*. Both were eventually deterred by their fear of litigation from Disney, according to Kunzle.[21] Disney comic book frames provided visual documentation for the book's argument about prominent themes and stereotypes. Disney's reputation suggested that it would never give permission for such a use and that it would cause expensive litigation if these frames were published without permission. Eventually, International General of New York, which specializes in Marxist publications, agreed to publish the book and had it printed in England; 3,950 copies of *How to Read Donald Duck* left England in May 1975 and arrived at the New York docks in June. At that time, Donald Duck in his corporate form began to fight back, confronting the thieving revolutionary thugs of an "Unsteadystan" that no longer existed.

THE DETENTION AND RELEASE OF HOW TO READ DONALD DUCK

The Imports Compliance Branch of the Customs department, a subdivision of the Treasury Department, has the authority to review imported material for its "piratical" character. When *How to Read Donald Duck* arrived, Imports Compliance made a preliminary judgment that the book might infringe upon Disney copyrights. The Chief of Imports Compliance, Eleanor M. Suske, informed International General in a letter of July 10, 1975, that the book was being seized and held in custody pending a final determination. Walt Disney Productions was similarly informed in a letter of August 12. Both parties were invited to submit briefs, as the Treasury Department has authority to consider evidence and arguments in such cases.

International General sought legal assistance from the Center for Constitutional Rights (CCR), which argued for the release of the book both on fair use and First Amendment grounds. The letters were vigorous and detailed.[22]

In its response to the notification, Walt Disney Productions was represented by its Eastern counsel, Franklin Waldheim, who declared that the books were piratical infringements of Disney's character copyrights.[23] He anticipated the fair use defense by suggesting that the use of the illustrations was in no way necessary to document what the authors were attempting to prove, since the mere description of the plots and quotation of literary text would have sufficed—a use which Disney did not choose to contest. In interpreting the purposes behind the book's use of the images, he saw the attempt to embellish a book at the expense of Disney. He also suggested that the use of a Disney-like image of Scrooge McDuck on the cover (reproduced at the beginning of this chapter) was an effort to deceive unsuspecting parents into believing that they were buying one of the Disney comics—thus depriving Disney of income that rightfully belonged to it.[24]

A central contention in the Waldheim letters is that imagery, unlike the words in the comic text, is not susceptible to fair use; verbal equivalents are in all cases sufficient—except where the nature of the art work itself is discussed. (Phenomenological differences between verbal and visual symbolism are discussed at length by both Bernard and Sigmund Timberg in Chapters 20 and 23.) It was this point that the attorneys for International General and the authors confronted in their briefs and rebuttals.

The Center for Constitutional Rights is a nonprofit legal assistance group in New York City that provides counsel in issues related to the Constitution and Bill of Rights. Lawyers for the Center, Peter Weiss, Rhonda Copelon, and William H. Schaap, defended *How to Read Donald Duck* against the accusation of piracy by an appeal to both the fair use concept and the First Amendment. In their letter of August 8, 1975, to the Imports Compliance Branch of Customs, they argued that in relation to recognized fair use questions,[25] Donald Duck could pass traditional tests. They cited Judge Lasker in *Marvin Worth Products v. Superior Films Corp.* (S.D.N.Y. 1970, 319 Fed. Supp. 1269; 168 USPQ 693, 697):

> The cases and commentaries attempting to define the quicksilver concept of "fair use," although varying and overlapping in their definitions, appear to agree that there are at least four tests appropriate to determine whether the doctrine applies: (1) Was there a substantial taking qualitatively or quantitatively? (2) If there was such a taking, did the taking materially reduce the demand for the original copyrighted property? (3) . . . Does the distribution of the material serve the public interest in the free dissemination of information, and (4) Does the preparation of the material require the use of prior materials dealing with the same subject matter?

Taking Judge Lasker's decision as the point of departure, the center's lawyers answered his questions in the following way:

> 1. No.—There is no substantial taking. On the one hand, the cartoons reproduced represent but a very small portion of the entire book. On the other,

each representation consists, as a rule, of but one or two frames taken from an entire comic strip or book.

2. Definitely not.—The taking, such as it is, in no way reduces the demand for the original copyrighted property, since no one would buy "How to Read Donald Duck" as a substitute for the original copyrighted property.

3. Most certainly.—The public interest in the free dissemination of information—in this case the views of the author-scholars concerning the values and attitudes evinced in Donald Duck comics—can only be served by the publication of their book, complete with representative samples of the comics which are the subject of their criticism and analysis.

4. Absolutely.—As discussed at greater length in the enclosure [provided by authors and publisher], reproduction of some of the cartoons is a categorical prerequisite to the publication of the book in a meaningful, readable way.

Having formulated the fair use defense, the CCR memorandum turned to the question of the First Amendment and argued as follows:

> ... we would contend that preferred position of the First Amendment in the spectrum of constitutionally guaranteed rights must be recognized in the field of copyrights as well. The book at issue, while a serious work of scholarship, is also a frankly political statement which is, or should be, of interest to a large number of readers. In view of this, the greatest reticence should characterize its evaluation by an agency of the government, lest property rights be given preference over rights of free speech and political expression. In other words, only the grossest and most unambiguous case of piracy—such as clearly is not present here—could possibly justify an assault on free speech in the guise of copyright protection. On the other hand, given a delicately balanced situation from a pure copyright point of view, First Amendment considerations should always tip the balance in favor of publication (or, in this case, importation).

The CCR lawyers concluded their First Amendment argument with a citation from Judge Wyatt's decision in the *Time v. Bernard Geis* case, where he appealed to the public interest in being permitted to share important information about the assassination of President Kennedy.

An author-editor letter, written immediately upon receipt of the Customs Compliance notification and included with the CCR statement, addresses itself primarily to the question of whether the contested images are necessary to their critical analysis. The text of that letter reads as follows:

6 Reasons Why No Cartoon Matter, No Book

1. The book is a criticism of the Disney *cartoons*, not Disney literary values. Cartoons are a unique mass medium which are an *inseparable* marriage of literary and visual matter. If it is possible for the book to capture the essence of Disney with written language only, we would ask: Why didn't Disney just write a novel? Obviously, he didn't.

2. It is not just the language used, but even more important, the relation between Disney language and graphic matter which is in question. This is particularly the case in the incredible use of racial, ethnic, professional, political slurs and stereotypes which are the very essence of Disney graphic matter. For example, the bearded captain (p. 58) which is obviously an unwritten slur

against Fidel Castro. See all cartoons for Disney's family of clichés, particularly of foreign peoples (the Vietnamese, p. 57; Africans, p. 50; Arabs, p. 51, etc.).

Also, the depiction of "villains" throughout as big, black, ugly and stupid; all so cliché-ridden they are literally undescribable without using the cartoon itself.

Similarly, the sexuality and coyness in the visual matter—in opposition to asexuality and prudery in the language.

In brief, the written text is the thesis, and the cartoon reproductions are the evidence and proof.

Just as the essence of Disney is both literary and graphic, the essence of the criticism of Disney is both literary and graphic.

3. Being given the foreign authorship and origin of the book; the US government's and US mass media's well publicized opposition to the Chilean Popular Unity government; the equally well orchestrated promotion of the Disney image of "purity, innocence," etc., etc., the environment in the US has been so poisoned by these well publicized campaigns, that to criticize Disney without the use of graphic proof would substantially reduce its impact and credibility in the USA.

Furthermore, many of the cartoons were never published in the USA, and thus a written text without cartoon reproductions would further decrease the credibility of the analysis, because the USA audience is not aware of this aspect of Disney, particularly Disney's very political character, which is the very essence of the book's thesis.

4. The changes of language in the translation from the original Spanish are significant in the case of those few original English-language cartoons—often poorly translated and altered in function for Latin American political conditions. An aspect not known to the USA public.

5. Disney comics were a phenomenon of the 40's and 50's in the USA, and for the most part are no longer available and have become "collector's items" (READ: "speculator's"), and thus the average reader would have no public means to find the original comics to check the veracity of just a literary description without the use of the visual matter. The reader would have to rely on his/her memory, which being given No. 3 above, would further decrease the credibility of the book.

6. Last, but certainly not least. The book is EDUCATIONAL. It was written primarily for young students, in Chile, among others, and intended as a simple, popular and readable book—like the Disney comics themselves. If each frame had to be described with language only, its complete popular and mass essence would be changed: instead of a short and popular book which now exists, it would become a long and unpopular tome of 1,000 pages, accessible and readable only by a limited group of (boring?) introverted scholar-types.

Again to repeat, if the essence of Disney can be captured solely by language, why did *they* take the trouble to make graphic matter?

Answer: In reality the verbal and visual matter are inseparable (also insufferable).[26]

As letters from the conflicting parties were received at the Customs Compliance office, they were duplicated and transmitted for response to both Disney Productions and to CCR. The parties reiterated their positions in a variety of ways and engaged in a more detailed debate regarding the necessity to reproduce Disney images. Franklin Waldheim, Disney's attorney, found in Point 6 of the author-editor memorandum, a confirmation of the piratical intent upon which Disney was resting much of its case.[27] It was held to be a concession to the accusation that the taking was designed to enhance the entertainment value of the book. But this taking in its larger context served the ultimate purpose of dissuading anyone from ever buying Disney commodities in the future. The Disney argument thus contained at least three distinct strands:

1. The contention that the unauthorized reproduction was merely illustrative

2. The claim that International General and the authors had pirated for the purpose of deceiving prospective comics buyers into believing that they were buying the genuine Disney product

3. The argument that the ultimate purpose of such taking and deception was to deprive Disney of its rightful markets

Responding to these contentions about the alleged cloaking of its uses behind the mantle of fair use—as opposed to honestly flying the black flag of piracy—the CCR responded to the Customs Department as follows:

> As for Disney's statement that inserting copies of the comic book frames is not necessary since the book is not a criticism of artistic style, we submit that the Disney comics primarily convey their message through pictures, not just dialogue or situation. For example, on p. 58 of *How to Read Donald Duck*, the authors discuss the situation of a comic in which Donald becomes involved with revolutionaries. The reproduction of selected frames is necessary in order to demonstrate both Disney's negative portrayal of the revolutionary leader through his pictured actions and to show the strong resemblance he bears to Fidel Castro. These subtle statements cannot be described in mere words, but must be shown in order to discuss their impact intelligently. As in *Time v. Geis*, 293 F. Supp. 130 (S.D.N.Y. 1968) the excerpts from the copyrighted work are necessary to make the authors' theory comprehensible.[28]

Thus it is clear that both of the disputing parties held the visual matter of Disney to have a unique status. The authors contended that imagery conveys information that becomes available for discussion only when it is reproduced. The Disney corporation argued, on the other hand, that except in the context of art criticism, copyrighted visual contents are wholly susceptible to evocation through verbal equivalents; images, unlike words, thus have a legal status that prevents their reproduction for the mere purpose of message analysis.

It was probably the failure to produce specific law or precedent on this point that pushed the Customs Department toward a decision favoring the importation of *How to Read Donald Duck*. On June 9, 1976, Eleanor M. Suske rendered an opinion "that the books do not constitute piratical copies of any Walt Disney copyright recorded with Customs, within the meaning of Section 106 of the copyright law."[29] Disney challenged the decision by seeking further representation from the firm of Donavan, Leisure, Newton and Irvine of New York. Upon their restatement of the Disney contentions of piratical infringement in a letter of October 6, 1976,[30] the Treasury Department (the parent administrative agency for Customs) articulated the reasons for its decision more fully through a letter from Leonard Lehman, Assistant Commissioner for Regulations and Rulings. "No specific copyright recorded with Customs has been cited as the basis for the exclusive action sought by Walt Disney Productions."[31] There had, in fact, been doubt about whether the Latin American comic book images had ever been copyrighted in the countries where they had been published—a point made by CCR and never addressed by Disney in its representations. But more important, from the standpoint of the fair use controversy, was the Treasury Department's acceptance of both the fair use and First Amendment arguments.

> The spotty use of one, two, or three cartoon "frames" throughout the work in question, does not appear to be a substantial appropriation of a material part of any one copyrighted work so as to come within the infringement test of *Arnstein v. Porter,* 154 F.2d 464 (2d Cir. 1946), *cert. denied,* 330 U.S. 851. Furthermore, the total of 68 frames does not constitute a substantial portion of the 112-page book. Finally, we do not believe the questioned item, priced at $3.25, and consisting overwhelmingly of ponderous text, could be confused for a Disney.... Most of the issues are related to the sociopolitical "message" of the work in either a specific or general context. We believe the following quotation is very apt for this case:
>
>> The spirit of the First Amendment applies to the copyright laws, at least to the extent that the courts should not tolerate any attempted interference with the public's right to be informed regarding matters of general interest when anyone seeks to use the copyright statute which was designed to protect interest of a quite different nature. (*Rosemont Enterprise, Inc. v. Random House, Inc.* 366 F2d 303, 35 C.O. Bull. 1965–66, p. 683)

This final ruling, of course, represented substantial concurrence with the arguments advanced by CCR. Walt Disney Productions did not choose to protest the matter any further at that time, though it was clear from their final memorandum issued by Donavan, *et al.* that they did not regard the Treasury Department as even having the jurisdiction to render a decision of fair use.

But in spite of sympathy for the arguments of CCR and International General, there was a serious snag for them in the final determination of the Customs Department. In her letter of June 9, 1976, Ms. Suske indicated that the entire shipment of 3,950 copies could not be accepted for importation because of the manufacturing clause of the copyright regulations. Although 1,500 copies could be admitted,

> The balance of 2,450 booklets in this shipment remain prohibited importation under Title 17, United States Code, Section 16, and are subject to seizure and forfeiture, however you may petition for remission of forfeiture and request approval to export this merchandise under Customs supervision.[32]

Somewhat ironically, the manufacturing and importation clause of the copyright law is a vestige of a period in history when American book publishers, newspapers, and magazines, freely pirated the works of foreign authors—to the severe disadvantage of both English and American authors. The final price exacted by the pirate industries in the struggle over international copyright that persisted from 1836 to 1891 was a provision in the copyright law that would prevent more than minimal importation of books manufactured in foreign lands.[33] Thus, the claims of an earlier generation of pirates, combined with the authors' inability to find a wholly American publisher, prevented the widespread circulation of their critique in the land that created and sustained the Disney perception of the world.

CONCLUSIONS

The story of *How to Read Donald Duck* is in important respects unique in the history of visual scholarship and publication. To my knowledge, it is the only case in which a substantial number of images belonging to a major media corporation have been exactly reproduced for purpose of political argumentation—such use being subsequently vindicated by a public decision-making agency. True, a considerable amount of reproduction has occurred surreptitiously, without the asking of permission or resulting challenge by copyright holders. The Donald Duck case squarely confronted the philosophical question regarding the image's status as a prerequisite to informed and precise analysis and proved to be persuasive, even though Dorfman and Mattelart's Marxist point of view about Disney's politics would hardly be considered plausible by the average United States citizen.

It would be a mistake, however, to exaggerate the significance of the Donald Duck affair as legal precedent. Granting that the Treasury Department had jurisdiction to make a determination of fair use—a point that Disney has contested through its counsel[34]—the case can carry little weight for the American legal system. As an affirmation of the rights of critical inquiry, it has a necessarily *ad hoc* rather than generalized implication for future fair use decisions.

A greater value of the Donald Duck case lies in its illumination of the residual powers and uses of copyright—as opposed to its normal justification emphasizing incentive and income for creators. Here we can see censorship in the form of prior restraint with its usual attendant evils. The absence of a domestic edition of *How to Read Donald Duck* and its minimal importation—a mere 1,500 renders it virtually a collector's item—deprives the American audience of a commentary upon the Disney imagery and stories and thereby prevents them from passing their own judgment upon its message. Furthermore, this restraint is exercised in an arbitrary way; the book has been published in nine other major languages, appearing in countries where Disney maintains branch offices.[35] America alone is chosen as the territory from which the book is to be excluded through administrative or legal action.

The visions of world community promoted by the Disney Corporation could come closer to realization if we could hear more of the world's people as they assess our cultural impact. To the extent that copyright law restricts such a hearing, its functions and privileges need reassessment.[36]

NOTES

[1]Quoted in Horace Newcomb, *TV: The Most Popular Art* (N.Y.: Doubleday, 1974), p. 2.

[2]*Annual Report 1977, Walt Disney Productions*, p. 1.

[3]*Ibid.*, p. 8.

[4]Jeremy Tunstall, *The media are American* (N.Y.: Columbia, 1977), table 3, pp. 282–83. India is cited as having the 69 percent figure.

[5]Elihu Katz and George Wedell, *Broadcasting in the Third World: Promise and Performance* (Cambridge, Mass.: Harvard University Press, 1977), p. 161. Cf. also table 5.4, pp. 158–60.

[6]Tunstall, table 1, pp. 278–79.

[7]David Kunzle, *How to Read Donald Duck: Imperialist Ideology in the Disney Comics* (N.Y.: International General Editions, 1975), p. 14.

[8]For one study of American comics and their dominance of a foreign market see Dagmar von Doetinchem and Klaus Hartman, *Gewalt in Superhelden Comics* (Berlin: Basis Verlag, 1974), esp. p. 149*ff*.

[9]Herbert Schiller has published several studies, including *Mass Communication and American Empire* (Boston: Beacon Press, 1971); *Communication and Cultural Domination* (White Plains, N.Y.: International Arts and Sciences Press, 1976), which contains "Afterword, Chile: Communications Policies of Reform and Counterrevolution," pp. 98–109.

[10]See note 7. Ariel Dorfman is currently Professor of Spanish at the University of Amsterdam; Armand Mattelart is a professor and researcher in the Audiovisual Department at the University of Paris.

[11]Cf. Tunstall, table 1, pp. 278–79. Chile is listed at 55 percent of imported programming.

[12]*Ibid.*, p. 43. Cf. table 17, pp. 301–303.

[13]Kunzle's Introduction, p. 12.

[14]Salvador Allende, *Chile's Road to Socialism*, Joan E. Garces (Ed.), (Harmondsworth, England: Penguin, 1973), p. 48.

[15]Mike Gonzalez, "Ideology and Culture under Popular Unity," in Philip O'Brien (Ed.), *Allende's Chile* (N.Y.: Praeger, 1976), p. 117.

[16]A good summary review of themes in the book is provided by J.A. Hoberman, "The Donald Duck Report," *Village Voice*, July 26, 1976.

[17]See the reproduction in Kunzle's Introduction, p. 13.

[18]Dorfman and Mattelart, pp. 95, 98.

[19]Quoted by Hoberman.

[20]Information from the title page of *How to Read Donald Duck* and through correspondence with Seth Siegelaub of International General, Dec. 10, 1978.

[21]Details provided through conversation.

[22]A correspondence file, from which information and quotations are taken, was provided by Peter Weiss and Ellen Seeherman of the CCR.

[23]Waldheim to Suske, Sept. 10, 1975.

[24]Waldheim to Regional Commissioner of Customs, Imports Compliance Branch, Sept. 25, 1975.

[25]CCR, Weiss, Copelon, and Schaap to Suske, Aug. 8, 1975.

[26]Letter "6 Reasons Why No Cartoon Matter, No Book" (slightly edited here for publication) is dated Aug. 12, 1975. It was written by the authors and the editor, Seth Siegelaub.

[27]Waldheim to Darrel D. Kast, Acting Director, Entry Procedures and Penalties Division, U.S. Customs Service, Washington, D.C.

[28]CCR, Seeherman, and Weiss to Darrell Kast, Jan. 12, 1976.

[29]Suske to Weiss, June 9, 1976.

[30]Donavan, Leisure, Newton, Irvine to Leonard Lehman, Assistant Commissioner of Customs, Regulations and Rulings, Washington, D.C., Oct. 6, 1976.

[31]Lehman to Donavan, Leisure . . ., July 7, 1977.

[32]Suske to Weiss, June 9, 1976.

[33]Cf. Aubert J. Clark, *The Movement for Copyright in the Nineteenth Century*, (Washington, D.C.: Catholic University Press, 1960), especially chap. 2.

[34]Donavan, Leisure . . . to Lehman, Oct. 6, 1976, raises this point.

[35]Disney has foreign subsidiaries with Principal Marketing Executives in Australia, Belgium, Canada, Denmark, England, France, Germany, Italy, Japan, Spain, and Sweden. *Annual Report 1977*, p. 40.

[36]The Copyright Act of 1976 provides that the manufacturing and import restrictions will be phased out by 1982 (see Section 601). In 1981, however, the Register is to report to Congress on the probable effects of discontinuing the restrictions, at which time the issue may be reexamined.

APPENDIX: Correspondence between John Lawrence and Franklin Waldheim

(a) A letter of request to reproduce statements from the Disney letters of brief to the Treasury Department was sent to Franklin Waldheim, vice-president and Eastern counsel for Walt Disney Productions (Nov. 28, 1978). After an introduction to the project and its publisher, the text of the letter reads as follows:

> One of the case studies in the book deals with the administrative action taken against the *How to Read Donald Duck* booklet which was detained temporarily at your request in 1975. I have corresponded with the Center for Constitutional Rights, which represented International General and they made available to me all of the letters in their possession, including letters that you had written to the U.S. Customs Service in connection with the matter. Dates of your letters are September 10 & 25, and December 29, 1975. An additional letter representing Disney was written October 6, 1976 by Donavan, Leisure, Newton, and Irvine.
>
> In the interest of representing as forcefully as possible the protectionist point of view and representing as accurately as possible the stance taken by Disney in this matter, I would like to obtain your permission to quote freely from the letters referred to. I have obtained this permission from the Center for Constitutional Rights and the authors of the contested book. I do hope that you can grant this request.
>
> In any case, I appreciate the attention that you give to this matter and look forward to hearing from you.
>
> Sincerely,
>
> John Lawrence (signed)
> Professor of Philosophy

(b) A letter of response was written by Franklin Waldheim on January 10, 1979. Its entire text is reproduced here.

Dear Professor Lawrence:

I have your letter of November 28. I am troubled by the thought of having my company's brief (embodied in the letters you refer to) quoted by someone who does not represent my company. Our point may be missed or buried in quotations of cases which have upheld the right of critics to copy portions of a copyrighted work.

These judicial holdings have been prompted by the fact that a critic cannot make his opinions clear without quoting some selections from the work which illustrate his view. We do not quarrel with this principle. The book "How To Read Donald Duck" discusses about eighty different comic strips; and the authors make their points by telling the reader what the situation in the comic strip is and by quoting the dialogue where relevant. Their views are expressed in each instance.

These quotations from our comic strips would in themselves be copyright infringements—but we do not quarrel with them because they represent a fair use. But the comments of the authors have nothing to do with the artwork. It adds nothing more to what the authors have already said in the text. By the admission of the authors, the artwork was added for the purpose of making the book look more inviting to prospective readers.

We do not want to argue our position to the readers of your book through selections from the letters we have written. We will present our case, when and if necessary, to the proper tribunal in our own way.

We would like to be cooperative. If this matter were finally closed, we would not be too concerned about what any writer may have to say about it. But there is always the possibility that this book might be published in the same form in this country and if so, the same issues would be raised in our courts. So long as that possibility still exists, we must regard this as a pending matter in which we will be heard at the proper time.

Sincerely yours,

Franklin Waldheim (signed)

Other People's Images: Advertising and Fair Use

> Originally we had intended to make this advertising assertion analysis a fairly comprehensive study of advertising. However, we were denied permission to reprint many of the company ads we selected.
>
> Donald A. Hiatt, *True, False, or In Between:*
> *An Elective Course in Logical Thinking*[1]

Advertisement is a ubiquitous, ritual form of communication possessing central economic and social importance. It exerts influence on language, cultural stereotypes, the style of political campaigns, and a host of other phenomena. As advertising has become more creative and expensive, advertisers have adopted the practice of copyrighting their texts and images. Donald A. Hiatt's experience is typical in the field of advertising scholarship. Two related stories are provided in the materials that follow. William Stott, author of *Documentary Expression and Thirties America* (Oxford, 1973), describes his prolonged attempt to secure permissions to reprint two Lucky Strike advertisements. His story is followed by our account of another scholar's unsuccessful attempt to reproduce an advertisement.

William Stott reproduced these advertising images in Documentary Expression and Thirties America after prolonged correspondence with the corporations.

61

5

OTHER PEOPLE'S IMAGES:
A CASE HISTORY
WILLIAM STOTT

In the spring of 1972, with no more than usual agony, I finished my dissertation. Three anonymous readers approved it, and I had a doctorate. Then—oh, dream of those dim nights when I bled out sentences—a publisher wanted to publish it. "With illustrations?" I asked. The dissertation discussed particular photographs, drawings, and advertisements of the 1930s, but had no pictures in it. "Well, we'd like illustrations," said the editor. "If you can get the rights without too much trouble." "Oh, sure," I said, knowing no better.

Fortunately I did know that I didn't know what I needed to. I phoned the law school at the university where I teach and said I wanted to speak with the professor who taught copyright law. "You mean Professor Treece?" said the secretary. "Yes, of course," I said.

James M. Treece, at that time Charles I. Francis Professor of Law at the University of Texas at Austin, specializes in copyright law—the field of law which, he says, is most like theology. Treece has strong opinions about fair use of copyrighted materials for scholarly purposes, and he generously agreed to give me counsel.

Looking over my proposed illustrations, Treece noticed that some were photos and drawings made for agencies of the U.S. government. "These are public property," he said. "They are uncopyrighted and anyone can publish them."

As for the other illustrations, he said that to protect myself and my publisher I had to make an earnest effort to get the permission of the copyright owner of each photo, drawing, and advertisement. What, I asked, constituted an earnest effort? "Well, you write them a letter. If they don't reply, you write them another. You keep copies of the letters."

He said that some of the photographers would no doubt want to be paid for giving me the right to print their work. If they wanted more than seemed reasonable, I could point out that mine was a scholarly book, one that was hardly to be a bestseller. He said I might have to leave some pictures out because the rights cost too much.

"But what if someone won't give me permission even if I'm willing to pay?" I asked.

"Then you've got a dispute," Treece said. Though the fair use provisions in copyright law protect writers who want to quote small amounts of published copyrighted prose, it has never been clear how this doctrine applies to the graphic arts. "After all," Treece said, "you can't 'quote' a small portion of a picture and have it mean anything."

Treece's own opinion is that in certain cases the fair use doctrine may justify a scholar's quoting an entire work. An art historian discussing a painting at length, for example, may be allowed to publish a reproduction of the painting without the artist's permission. "This, however, is *my* view," Treece emphasized. "It is not the law—not yet, anyway." But he said that if a copyright owner refused me permission I might then want to suggest to my publisher that we consider publishing the illustration regardless, on the assumption that it was fair scholarly use.

I thanked Treece, promised to report back, and set about following his advice to the letter—and in many letters. I wrote the individuals who had taken the photographs I wanted to publish. Where I couldn't find the photographer's address, I wrote the book publisher or the magazine that had printed the photograph. In the case of advertisements I wrote the director of public relations of the company advertising.

I began each letter approximately thus:

> In fall 1973 Oxford University Press (New York) will publish a scholarly analysis I have written of the documentary literature of the 1930s. This study, tentatively titled *Documentary Expression and Thirties America,* will have approximately 90,000 words, will cost about $12.00, and will appear in a cloth edition of 6,000 copies. I plan to have an illustration section in the book with about 60 pictures in it, and this is why I'm writing you.

I went on to explain that they had made, published, or sponsored a picture or ad I wanted to reprint in my book. I cited the place I had seen the image and said briefly why I wanted to use it. I said that I would of course credit them for it and thank them in the book's acknowledgments. In closing I asked if I might publish their image.

Some letters were misdirected. One magazine didn't own a certain photo and didn't know the photographer's whereabouts (through the

New York Times' obituary index I learned that the photographer had died thirty years earlier and that, presumably, his photo's copyright wasn't renewed). One publisher didn't have a current address for the author of a book published in 1942 (an address later turned up, I forget how, and the former photographer was pleased to have one of her pictures back in print).

Many photographers wanted payment for rights to their work. The most expensive rights I purchased were those controlled by *Time-Life*. *Time-Life* assured me that because mine was a scholarly book the rate I paid was one-half that charged "commercial" books.

The rights that proved hardest to get were those for two advertisements. The first was a 1940 General Electric radio ad I had noticed in *Life* magazine. I wrote GE's director of public relations and received a genial reply from Ford C. Slater in GE's corporate advertising division. Slater said, in part: "We see no reason why our 1940 GE radio advertisement could not be used in the manner in which you describe. We would, however, appreciate an opportunity to see the ad reproduced and the associated caption or text materials prior to publication next fall. Pending only that review, which we presume would be pro forma, non-exclusive permission could be granted."

I replied:

> I plan to reprint the ad, picture and full text, in the illustration section of my book. It would have only a credit caption, "Advertisement for GE Radio, 1940." In the text of the book I argue that in the 1930s the new medium of radio "sold itself precisely as a way of making unimagined distant people real and objects of human concern." I speak about the listening audience's generous response to the crisis of the 1937 floods and then continue:
>
>> A GE advertisement of the period shows a mother dabbing her eyes with a handkerchief while her daughter comforts her. Near them stands the radio, a genial brown idol. The head-text reads: "'Don't Cry Mother . . It's *Only* a Program!'" The ad continues:
>>
>> Of course daughter is wrong. It's not just a program—it's real and the people in it live! Mother's tears and smiles are the natural reaction of one good neighbor to another neighbor's everyday problems.
>>
>> She shares the heartbreak of a girl who is hundreds of miles away—yes, farther than distance itself, for she lives in the land of make-believe. But it isn't make-believe to this lady because, thanks to the golden tone of her General Electric Radio, every program is close, intimate and personal.
>>
>> And persuasive, like anything we know, or feel we know, firsthand. Radio demonstrated its enormous power to arouse belief the night the Martians landed in Orson Welles' "War of the Worlds." The nationwide panic the show created suggests how much Americans then accepted the rhetoric of radio as a rhetoric of reality.
>
> This is the full use I intend to make of the ad. I trust there is nothing offensive to your Company in it and hope that you will grant me your permission to reproduce the ad.

To which, Slater responded: "Thank you for expanding upon the context in which you wish to use our GE radio ad from 1940. You have our permission to use it in the way you've described."

GE gave me permission to use the ad because they saw, quite rightly, nothing unfavorable in my use of it. The second ad proved more difficult. It was a 1938 ad, also in *Life,* for Lucky Strike cigarettes. I wrote asking permission from the American Tobacco Company, a division of American Brands. P.H. Cohen, Director of Advertising, replied: "This will acknowledge receipt of your letter of September 14, 1972 with regard to your proposed use of a LUCKY STRIKE Cigarettes advertisement which appeared on the back cover of the Life Magazine dated June 27, 1938. I regret to advise you that we must decline to consent to the proposed republication of this or any similar advertising."

If I had not had access to legal advice, I would have let the matter drop here and published the book without the Lucky Strike ad. The point I used the ad to make—that there was a bias toward "firsthand" and proletarian experience in the 1930s—was made by other artifacts I cited, though not with such economy. But I was angry. I felt then—and I feel now—that it is unjust that advertisers can force their ads upon the public in print and broadcast and then forbid the public to play the ads back, elucidating their various meanings. Furthermore, intrigued by Cohen's mention of "similar advertising," I had looked further and found a 1939 Lucky Strike ad in the same "Witnessed Statement" series that even more brilliantly served my purposes. I was willing to pursue whatever tactic Treece suggested that might enable me to publish this ad.

Treece and I had a second consultation. There were, he said, several paths open to me. One which he did *not* recommend was to try to beat the American Tobacco Company's copyright on a technicality. It was unlikely that the ad was published without a copyright notice on it. If this were the case, one could argue that the ad wasn't copyrighted. However, the American Tobacco Company could counter that the ad was protected by the copyright of that issue of the magazine, a position Treece thought very weak but not baseless. I decided not to rely on technicalities. (Curiosity got the better of me, and I later checked the ad. It had the copyright notice; the underhanded approach wasn't open to me.)

Treece next said that I could and should inquire whether the ad's copyright had been renewed. Since the original ad appeared in 1939, the American Tobacco Company would have had to renew copyright in about 1967 under the law then in effect or the ad would enter the public domain. Treece recommended that I write the Copyright Office in the Library of Congress, which for a small fee (then $5.00) would search the copyright renewal for me.

He said he thought it unlikely that the ad's copyright had been renewed. But in case it had been and to make our claim for fair scholarly use, he said that if I allowed him to he would write the American Tobacco Company on my behalf, stating our belief that, according to the doctrine of fair use, I had the right to reprint the ad for scholarly purposes. I, of course, said yes; yes, by all means.

Treece wrote his letter on his law firm's letterhead:

> Dear Mr. Cohen:
>
> Our client, Professor William M. Stott, advised us that you refused his request for a gratuitous, non-exclusive license to reproduce one of the advertisements from the Lucky Strike "Witnessed Statement Series" in a scholarly work to be marketed in England and the United States.
>
> Professor Stott has now focused upon another advertisement in the series titled "Eye Witness at 2,000 Tobacco Auctions," which appeared on the back cover of the *Life* Magazine for September 18, 1939.
>
> He wishes to use a reproduction of that advertisement in his book to advance the scholarly observation that advertisers relied heavily on the testimonial advertisement in the Twenties and Thirties.
>
> I have advised Professor Stott that he can undoubtedly make the use he contemplates of the mentioned Lucky Strike advertisement—under the fair use doctrine if the copyright in the advertisement was renewed, or under the public domain doctrine if the copyright was not renewed.
>
> I also advised him that I saw no reason not to inform you of this advice and no reason not to accede to any reasonable request you may make concerning the manner in which the advertisement is described or attributed to a source in his book.
>
> Professor Stott's book will go to press in December, so there is sufficient time for us to implement any suggestion you may make about identifying the original copyright proprietor of the advertisement or identifying the magazine in which the advertisement appeared.

For the sake of the story, I would now like to be able to say that Treece's bold letter got us involved in an elaborate correspondence with the American Tobacco Company which eventuated in a court trial that triumphantly vindicated a scholar's right to publish copyrighted images. Happily for my peace of mind, though, this didn't happen. The American Tobacco Company never answered Treece's letter. And after a six-week wait, Eugene R. Lehr of the Reference Search Section of the Copyright Office answered mine:

> This refers to your letter of January 18, 1973. The following search report is made.
>
> Search in the indexes and catalogs of the Copyright Office covering the period 1938 through 1970 under the title EYEWITNESS AT 2,000 TOBACCO AUCTIONS disclosed only the following separate registration for a work identified under this specific title.
>
> EYEWITNESS AT 2,000 TOBACCO AUCTIONS (Earl Forbes), by W. Griffin. (Witnessed statement series) (Lucky Strike Cigarettes) (In "True De-

tective Mysteries," October, 1939, back cover). Registered in the name of American Tobacco Co. under A5 101519, following publication September 6, 1939.

Search in the Renewal Indexes under the above names and title failed to disclose any renewal registration relating to this entry.

So the Lucky Strike ad I wanted to reprint wasn't the American Tobacco Company's property any more. The company had no right to stop me from using it. My book came out with the ad in it, and to this day only three or four readers, James Treece paramount among them, have known that behind the trumped-up excitement of the ad's sanitized tobacco auction (note the man at back right, with his Dennis Day hairdo and his reporter's hat impossibly far back on his head) there had been some real excitement.

What conclusions do I have? Darned few. In general I would recommend that, in matters of fair use, scholars obtain legal counsel and not rely on the timid advice their publishers are likely to give. More specifically, I consider it unfair, as I've said, that advertisers can billboard the world with their images and then restrain scholars from explicating them. The illustrations in my book made me write perhaps a hundred letters and spend hundreds of dollars, but I was lucky. I got to use everything I wanted.

What if my period of study had been more recent? What if the American Tobacco Company still owned an ad I needed to make my point? What if I wanted to use a company's ad to show something detrimental to its interest—show, for instance, how cigarette advertisers tried to comfort the public about the hazards of smoking in the 1940s and early 1950s ("More Doctors Smoke Camels Than Any Other Cigarette," "Chesterfield—Gentler in Your 'T' Zone," "We're Tobacco Men, Not Medicine Men")?

Treece believes that a strong case can be made that *fair use* includes the right to reprint the whole of a graphic work for scholarly purposes. I hope his view prevails. Under the new copyright law it appears that a copyrighted advertisement may be unpublishable, except by its owner or with its owner's consent, for as long as seventy-five years. Who can wait that long to know what we are really being sold in the ads, our national daydream?

Stott: Advertising

The happy ending of William Stott's story turns ultimately on the failure of the American Tobacco Company to renew its copyright registration. He raises the question, "What if my period of study had been more recent? What if the American Tobacco Company still owned an ad I needed to make my point?" An answer to these questions is provided by the experience of J. Michael Sproule, a university professor and author of the book *Argument and Persuasion* (McGraw-Hill).[2]

Sproule's book discusses subliminal devices in a chapter on the ethics of argument and persuasion. He wanted to use an "Early Times" ad appearing in *Newsweek*, February 16, 1976. Following some of the suggestions in Wilson Brian Key's book, *Subliminal Seduction*,[3] Sproule believed that he had found a confirming instance of subliminal and unethical appeals on the part of Early Times. In addition to using "overt, sexually interesting symbols" (the female models), he also found

> . . . covert appeals to the reader's sexual interests: For example, The Early Times bottle, a phallic symbol, pointing to the "privates" of the model, above it; and an apparent effort to suggest the word "sex" (last letter of the top caption, "s"; "E" suggested by the ice in the glass; and "x" appearing twice in the words below the glass).[4]

Directed by his publisher to obtain copyright clearance as a condition of using the Early Times ad, Sproule began his correspondence with the General Offices of the distillery.

> Dear Staffmembers:
>
> I am preparing a textbook tentatively entitled *Argument and Persuasion* to be published by McGraw Hill Book Company in 1980 and intended for use by undergraduate college students.
>
> I would like to have your permission to reproduce in my book and in its future editions, the material indicated below.
>
> > Advertisement for Early Times Kentucky Straight Bourbon Whiskey captioned, "Early Times. To know us is to love us," which appeared in *Newsweek*, February 16, 1976. pp. 46–47.
>
> It is understood, of course, that full credit will be given to your organization, either in a footnote or as a reference within the text, or both.[5]

In response to his letter, Sproule received the following letter from Mr. Robert Panther, Sr. vice-president at B-F Spirits, Ltd.

> Your recent letter to the Early Times Distillery Company requesting permission to reproduce one of our Early Times ads has been referred to me for consideration as National Brands Director for Early Times.
>
> I have a dual purpose in writing to you Mr. Sproule. Generally speaking, we are happy enough to permit use of our advertising and/or some of our

marketing experiences by educators, but there are two points which should be brought to your attention before we grant permission.

(1) The ad theme of "Early Times. To Know Us Is To Love Us." has been de-emphasized in our advertising and will be de-emphasized in the future. This is merely a result of consideration of creative strategy on the brand.

(2) Some time ago we granted permission of use of our product to appear in a movie scene without full understanding of how it would be presented; unfortunately, the presentation of the brand was extremely unflattering to the product, and embarrassing to us as a company, and for this reason we would be interested in knowing the manner in which our advertising may be discussed.

Please be assured as Brands Director, I am always interested in the marketing and advertising aspects of our industry, not just of our product, and I am most sincere in the hope that your reply to this memo will invite our approval of your request. Thank you very much for your attention and for your interest.[6]

In response to the letter from Vice-President Panther, Sproule stated his subliminal sexual message theory and added that "the actual wording of the caption ["To Know Us Is To Love Us"], which your organization is de-emphasizing—is not of preeminent importance. Secondly, my work is scholarly in nature and probably would not be comparable to the movie scene you mentioned."[7]

After thus straightforwardly indicating his aim in discussing the ad, Sproule received a prompt and unequivocal denial of permission.

Since we nor our advertising agencies deal in the area of subliminal advertising in creative preparation of our ads or in selection and final execution of the ads actually produced we prefer not to have our advertising analyzed in such manner for publication. Therefore, we are not willing to grant permission for use of our ad in your study.[8]

For Sproule, there was little hope of adequately discussing an ad without being able to test his judgment and that of the readers against the perceptual cues on which he based his interpretation. His disappointment was heightened because he *had* obtained permission to publish a Black Velvet advertisement. One can't discuss a *pattern* in advertising on the basis of a single example. He was also a bit galled to discover through correspondence with Wilson Brian Key that *no* permissions had ever been sought for the dozens of advertisements that appear in Key's published studies: "there is no copyright problem with reproducing ads, as long as you do not retouch them or use them to sell something: free comment and criticism."[9] However, in the end, Sproule and his publisher decided to abide by the B-F Spirits–Early Times refusal of permission to reprint the advertisement.

At least in the current stage of publishing practice, William Stott's conclusion seems apt as a comment on the Sproule–Early Times episode: "I would recommend that in matters of fair use scholars obtain legal counsel and not rely on the timid advice their publishers are likely to give."

NOTES

[1]Donald A. Hiatt, *True, False, Or In Between: An Elective Course in Logical Thinking* (Lexington, Mass.: Ginn, 1975), p. 21.

[2]Forthcoming, 1980.

[3]Wilson Brian Key, *Subliminal Seduction: Ad Media's Manipulation of a Not So Innocent America* (New York: Signet, 1973).

[4]J. Michael Sproule to the editors of this book, Dec. 26, 1978.

[5]Sproule to General Offices, Early Times Distillery, July 28, 1978.

[6]Robert E. Panther, senior vice-president, B-F Spirits Ltd., Aug. 7, 1978, to Sproule.

[7]Sproule to Panther, Aug. 22, 1978.

[8]Panther to Sproule, Sept. 7, 1978.

[9]Key to Sproule, Sept. 4, 1978. Key has also published *Media Sexploitation* (Englewood Cliffs, N.J.: Prentice-Hall, 1976).

Film Study and Copyright Law

Writing as film theorist, film historian, and archive collection builder, Gerald Mast explores the relationships between copyright law and the growing field of film studies. He deals in detail with the question of fair use and permissions in film image publication as well as the complex problems associated with film rental and ownership. His overall judgment on the Copyright Act of 1976 is that it achieved little in clarifying the activities required by film scholarship and publication.

6

FILM STUDY AND THE COPYRIGHT LAW
GERALD MAST

One clear academic trend of the last decade is the increasing and increasingly serious study of motion pictures by scholars and their university students. The growing number of film students, teachers, and courses (which can be documented by consulting the American Film Institute's *Guide to College Courses in Film and Television*) has produced one of the few expanding disciplines in the generally shrinking field of humanistic studies. This growing interest has been accompanied by an increasing number of serious books devoted to film study—textbooks, purely scholarly studies, and high-level critical studies designed for both the specialist and the general reader. Given the need to draft a new copyright law, one that took notice of such technological facts of twentieth-century life as motion pictures and television, film scholars and instructors might have expected a law that would reflect their concerns and remedy their problems. Unfortunately, the Copyright Act of 1976 fails as completely as the law of 1909 to address those problems.

The two specific issues which the new law fails to address explicitly—and which are the two most important problems facing film research and teaching today—are (1) the legal restrictions on using individual production stills or frame blow-ups from whole films in publications; (2) the legal restrictions against owning prints of copyrighted films for classroom teaching or scholarly research. This article will examine each of these legal problems in detail. But behind these specific issues lie two general attitudes that plague the serious film scholar and have undoubtedly produced the new law's muteness on the preceding two key issues.

The first is the general prejudice against looking at films (and therefore film study) as worthy of serious attention. This prejudice can be traced to the beginning of the century and the earliest movies themselves, which were considered casual, banal, and superficial amusement for the unlettered and unthinking segment of the populace. That movies were even protected by the 1909 copyright law was a 1912 afterthought, for no one believed that there was anything about them worth protecting—except their commercial value. Before 1912, only still photographs were protected by the 1909 copyright act; the only way to protect a motion picture from the era's blatant piracy was to send the Library of Congress a complete paper reel of still photographs, corresponding to the individual frames of the motion picture. The landmark Supreme Court decision in *Mutual Film Corp. v. Industrial Commission of Ohio* (1915) summed up the general early attitude by stating that movies were plain and simple entertainment, like circuses and vaudeville shows, designed solely to make money; therefore, unlike books and newspapers, films were not entitled to the freedom of speech guarantees of the the First Amendment. (As if the publishers of books and newspapers did not intend to make money!)

These attitudes may seem to have been altered by the passage of time, the making of so many good movies, and the obvious artistic excellence and importance of many of those who have made them. The Supreme Court's decision in the *"Miracle* Case" of 1952 (*Burstyn v. Wilson*) reversed the 1915 opinion, granting movies their freedom of speech. The bemused, cynical diatribes of the twenties and thirties against the artificialities of Hollywood and the stupidities of the "pants pressers" who ran it by the Menckens, Hechts, Parkers, Nathans, and Fitzgeralds have faded into the cultural history of an earlier era. The cultural elite greets a new film by Antonioni, Bergman, Kurosawa, or Altman with the same enthusiasm as the cultural elite of an earlier generation greeted a new novel by Fitzgerald or play by O'Neill. And, after all, film is now taught in the university.

But these facts are deceptive. A major university may need a faculty of forty to assure coverage of all the periods, genres, and figures of English and American literature, but it may employ only one or two faculty members to cover the entire history, theory, and criticism of cinema in all nations of the globe. Although university deans are frequently pleased with the large enrollments in film-study classes, they just as frequently restrict budgets for film rentals to absolute minimums and refuse to purchase any films at all (even though buying saves money over a period of years) because of the initial cost and the implied commitment of such an investment. The most concrete proof of the *de facto* academic prejudice against film study is the university's library, which probably does not own a single film. Although a new generation of librarians has become "media conscious"—more sensitive to the needs of media study and more qualified to serve them—than their exclusively book-bound predecessors, shrinking library budgets in an era of academic austerity have made significant academic investments in a new educational resource almost impossible.

This academic insensitivity to film study undoubtedly contributed to the continued silence of the new copyright act on the subject of owning copyrighted films. There was considerable academic influence on Congress in shaping the 1976 law; an entire section of the law (108) was devoted specifically to library exemptions from provisions of the law; another entire section (107) was devoted to "fair use" exemptions, especially for educational purposes. But Sections 107 and 108 reveal that, despite the new law's intention to acknowledge twentieth-century technological advances, the 1976 law is, like the 1909 law, a "book law"; the primary technological advance it seeks to regulate is the photocopying of copyrighted books. The thrust of the academic influence on the new law was to preserve the right to photocopy printed material for classroom teaching and for legitimate scholarly and archival purposes. Three special groups were formed to articulate specific guidelines for the educational use of copyrighted material, the committees composed of members of both the academic community and the relevant publication or media industry for each field. Two of the three groups "were successful in agreeing upon guidelines stating the minimum standards of 'educational' fair use" of (1) printed material and (2) music.[1] The third group was, unfortunately, not successful at articulating specific guidelines—on the educational fair use of audiovisual material.

The failure of this group reveals the second general attitude with which the serious film scholar must contend—not only the prejudices, insensitivity, and ignorance of colleagues about his needs but the commercial structure of the film marketplace. Although many problems of the audiovisual group stemmed from the film and television industries' fear of the new home videotape recorders (the most extreme early position of the media industry was that the use and manufacture of such machines should be banned altogether), the educational use of films is also influenced and determined by commercial considerations. Unlike a published book, which produces revenue by the sales of individual copies, a film produces revenue by a distributor's renting it to an exhibitor, who then collects money from individual patrons and sends a portion of it back to the distributor. Whereas the optimum commercial situation for a book publisher is to sell as many copies as possible, the optimum commercial situation for a film distributor is to keep as few copies of a print in existence as possible. Other than the two copies of a film which the distributor or producer must send to the Library of Congress to copyright it, all other extant prints of a film should be those several dozen in commercial distribution. The film industry under-standably sees any attempt to tamper with this commercial convention as detrimental to its interests and income. Yet film study on a university level must tamper with it if the study is to be worth serious attention and worthy of serious people.

This conflict and paradox underlies much of the specific discussion that follows.

PRODUCTION STILLS AND FRAME BLOW-UPS

Ten years ago the primary copyright problem facing the film scholar was obtaining permission to use still photographs from motion pictures in his publications. The first edition of my *Short History of the Movies* (published in 1971, but completed by 1969) contained the following note on the acknowledgments page:

> The author wishes to apologize for the obvious scarcity of stills from Ameri-can motion pictures made between 1929 and the present. That scarcity must be blamed on the American film companies who either demanded exorbitant permission fees or withheld their permissions altogether.[2]

The second edition of the book (published in 1976) contains many of the same photographs that I had been unable to use in the original edition. Over the last decade each of my books has encountered less trouble in securing permissions to use photographs and less exorbitant demands for fees to use them. There are three reasons for this gradual improve-ment: First, the film industry has become more sensitive to the existence of serious film books that require stills for legitimate illustrative pur-poses. Second, both the film and the publishing industries have become conscious of the highly questionable legal status of these photographs. Third, the concept of fair use has been increasingly applied to these photographs, although there is no explicit language (including that of the new act) to necessitate this inference.

Film books require photographic stills for the same reason that critical books on poetry require quotations of verse and critical books on drama quotations of lines of dialogue. The photograph serves either to illustrate the verbal discussion (particularly if the reader is unfamiliar with the specific scene, shot, or figure, or if his memory cannot recall its details) or to support the claim that a particular "reading" of a scene, shot, or film is valid. There have been film books (perhaps the great majority) which merely use photographs decoratively—to make a more attractive publication. And there have been film "books" that have been nothing more than collections of hundreds of photographs. There have also been film books which deliberately refuse to use any photographs at all since the frozen, still image does not correspond to anything that the viewer actually experiences in a film.³ But for other kinds of film books, the photographs are as important as the text; indeed, the photographs are a part of "the text."⁴ This fact is far more widely recognized today than it was ten years ago.

A still photograph that represents a shot from a film can be one of two kinds of things: (1) a production still, (2) a frame enlargement. The ontological difference between these two kinds of photographs has caused both confusion and consternation in the past. A *production still* is a photograph, taken by a still photographer with an ordinary still camera, on the set of a motion picture. Sometimes the photograph has been carefully posed; sometimes it has caught the actors while rehearsing a scene that exists in the finished film (it is never snapped during a take, since the "click" would disturb the microphone and the actors' concentration). Although one purpose of the production still was simply to be a record, a journal of the film's shooting, its primary purpose has always been to publicize a film—either in display advertisements in front of the theater or in stories or advertisements published in magazines and newspapers.⁵ Production stills, then, have been made expressly to be published, to be seen by as many people as possible, in order to "sell" the picture. According to the old copyright act, such production stills were not automatically copyrighted as part of the film and required separate copyrights as photographic stills. The new copyright act similarly excludes the production still from automatic copyright but gives the film's copyright owner a five-year period in which to copyright the stills. Most studios have never bothered to copyright these stills because they were happy to see them pass into the public domain, to be used by as many people in as many publications as possible. There is, then, some irony in a publisher's paying a healthy permission fee on a public domain photograph to advertise a company's movie. One might suppose that the movie company should pay a fee to the publisher and not vice versa. There is no question that publishers have paid thousands (perhaps hundreds of thousands) of dollars to film companies for precisely this purpose on public domain material.

A frame enlargement (or blow-up) of a film is a still photograph of an actual frame of the final motion picture. If the whole film is copyrighted, then this single frame, being part of the whole, would also be protected. But a single frame is an extremely small fraction of the work (a two-hour film would contain 172,800 frames). Although one can make such enlargements chemically in a processing laboratory, the least expensive and most functional way to make a frame enlargement is to use some kind of apparatus to take a still photograph of the movie frame.⁶ The advantage of the frame blow-up over the production still is that the resulting photograph is actually a part of the film itself. If the photograph is to illustrate something about a film or to serve as a piece of data for a "reading" of the film, it is obviously best to use something actually in the film. Even when a production still appears to resemble a shot in a finished film, the result is a resemblance rather than an identity, for the photograph does not duplicate the camera angle of the shot, and a rehearsal of a scene is not the take itself. The disadvantage of the frame blow-up is that the resulting photograph is grainier and blurrier than the visual perfection of the production still, which has been produced specifically to be as visually perfect in publication as possible. My own tendency has been toward the exclusive use of frame blow-ups since they are the most legitimate evidence for arguments about a film, but the sacrifice of photographic clarity (especially when the frame enlargements are printed in books, which further diminishes their sharpness) is indeed a sacrifice.

One might expect that the use of a frame blow-up or two from a film would be a legitimate application of the "fair use" exemption (since the frame is only 1/172,800 of the whole film), but there is no explicit confirmation of this principle in the new copyright act. But whether the photograph be a production still or a frame enlargement, there seems no reason whatever for any author or publisher to request permission to use it and to pay any kind of fee for doing so. The attitude of those film companies that have requested (and still request) fees has little to do with these principles and everything to do with finance. They reason that because they own the film they are entitled to "a piece of the action" on any money that might be made as a result of the film's existence.

Many of their procedural and financial demands have been quite extraordinary and deserve recounting. One major film company demanded a permission fee of $200 per photograph in 1969. To use, say, ten stills from this studio's films might well amount to the entire royalty an author could expect from the book. Another studio demanded that permission to publish a photograph be obtained from every person depicted in it. Since one of the stills was from a *Golddiggers* musical (featuring the faces of 100 anonymous blondes alongside their dancing pianos) and another was of a stagecoach in the wilderness (with no visible faces in it at all), I did not know how to comply with the studio's demand. The copyright owner of Charlie Chaplin's films refused to allow permission to publish any photographs from the copyrighted feature films. The listed copyright owner of the Soviet silent classics requested $25 per still. Since I wanted to demonstrate entire montage sequences from five classic Eisenstein and Pudovkin films, I needed to use over fifty stills. He eventually settled for a fee of $25 per film (which he increased to $50 per film for the second edition), plus citing the film library of his mother as the source of the still (although I had made the frame blow-ups myself). But since all those Soviet films are in the public domain, it seems strange to pay anything or cite any sources for use of stills from them. Another man considers himself the copyright owner of Laurel and Hardy (and everything related to them); not only does he request high fees for using photographs of the comedians (although he never had anything to do with the making of any of their films, nor was he ever connected with any company that made them), but he also demands a fee should anyone want to, say, draw a cartoon of the two comedians on a package of cornflakes. Although I can understand how Walt Disney can own Mickey Mouse, I cannot see how two formerly living (and highly public) persons can be owned in the same way.

According to Section 107 of the new copyright law:

> The fair use of a copyrighted work, including such use by reproduction in copies or phonorecords or by any other means . . ., for purposes such as criticism, comment, news reporting, teaching (including multiple copies for classroom use), scholarship, or research, is not an infringement of copyright. In determining whether the use made of a work in any particular case is a fair use the factors to be considered shall include—
>
> (1) the purpose and character of the use, including whether such use is of a commercial nature or is for non-profit educational purposes;
>
> (2) the nature of the copyrighted work;
>
> (3) the amount and substantiality of the portion used in relation to the copyrighted work as a whole; and
>
> (4) the effect of the use upon the potential market for or value of the copyrighted work.[7]

A photographic still or frame blow-up obviously satisfies the third and fourth strictures; one can argue that the publication of a film still in a book achieves precisely the purpose for which the production still was made—it increases the market value of the film by giving the potential audience member the desire to see it. The first factor is the tricky one for photographic stills, for almost all books are published with the commercial intention (or, at least, hope) of making *some* profit. Many film books, however, have an almost exclusively "educational" value. Further, the "commercial nature" of a film book in no way conflicts or competes with the "commercial nature" of a motion picture production but, in fact, complements it.

In articulating these four explicit factors, the new act has merely transcribed the implications of previous legal decisions on the issue of fair use under the old law.[8] Except for this explicit listing, the new law is as fuzzy as the old one on the applicability of fair use to film stills. Significantly, there has never been a legal test of the copyright status of film stills, although at least one prolific and well-known author-editor of books on film has always made it his policy to publish stills without seeking permissions.

Seeking permissions to publish stills will continue as a general practice for film books (as I think it will), because publishers would rather pay a little insurance than a lot of damages. Commercial publishing houses have been unwilling to risk the danger of a lawsuit (although a university press with which I am currently working on a book will publish photographs without seeking permissions; but perhaps a university press feels more secure about its "non-profit educational purposes"). The usual recent practice of the commercial presses with which I have worked is to attempt to obtain permission to publish all photographs from copyrighted films at a reasonable fee. If the requested fee seems unreasonable, the publisher bargains for a cheaper one. If the listed owner of a copyright fails to answer a letter (as frequently happens with foreign films), or if the owner refuses to grant permission to publish, the publisher then goes ahead and publishes the still. At least the correspondence between publisher and copyright owner can establish that a legitimate effort was made to obtain permission to publish.

OWNERSHIP OF PRINTS

Imagine that the following procedures determined the organization and pedagogy of a college course in the modern novel. Each week, thirty copies of the assigned novel would arrive from the publisher. The instructor would pass copies out to students in the class, who would then read the novel for the next two hours, during which time the instructor would also freshen his memory of its details. Then a discussion, lasting one to two hours, would follow, after which the books would be collected, packed up in the box, and shipped back to the publisher. The process would be repeated each week for the entire quarter or semester.

Imagine that a student, stimulated by one of the novels, decided to write a paper on the novelist's concerns and major works. After perusing the newspaper and entertainment guides to cultural events within a 100-mile radius, the student discovers that he can get his hands on two of the author's other novels during the next month of the semester. The university library fortunately collects a certain number of secondary sources on the novelist and his works—critical books, journal articles, and newspaper critiques; it unfortunately provides no access to any of the primary works by the author himself.

Imagine that the instructor of the course also takes an interest in the author and decides to write a major study, requiring the detailed explication of all the author's works. After letter writing and catalogue reading, the scholar discovers that he can get access to the material he needs by logging 15,000 miles of travel between archival collections in New York City, Los Angeles, Washington, D.C.; Rochester, New York; Madison, Wisconsin; London, Paris, and Moscow.

These fanciful impossibilities, intolerable for the literary teacher and scholar, are actualities for every film instructor in every course. Films for most film courses are usually rented from a 16mm distributor, perhaps at a special classroom rate,[9] which requires observing the following restrictions: no admission can be charged; only thirty-five or fewer students can be enrolled in the class; there can be only one showing. To comply with the distributor's rights and to observe these restrictions usually requires very long classes (for a film takes about two hours to screen and time must remain for discussion, during which sections of the film might be shown again for detailed analysis). The other option is to hold special screening sessions for film courses (perhaps during the evening), followed by class periods of a regular length during the day (but if the instructor shows sections of the film in a class on a different day from the original screening, he fails to comply with the "one showing" regulation).

Film instructors usually solve the most serious of these problems by trying to "get around" them (a euphemism for violating the letter of the agreement with the copyright owner). Because a film usually arrives on campus about one week before its scheduled screening date, many instructors feel they can show the film, in whole or in part, as many times during that week as necessary. Because administrators often require film students to pay something to subsidize the cost of film rentals, many film courses collect a "laboratory fee" (parallel to science courses), which may or may not be considered an "admission charge." And because some film courses are very large (perhaps 1,000 students or more in a large university's course in "Introduction to Film"), the instructor might observe the limit of thirty-five students per class by limiting each discussion section of the course to thirty-five students or less.

The impossibility of observing the literal requirements of a film's copyright owner if one is to teach it (according to any acceptable definition of the term, *teach*), guarantees deceit, the stretching of terminology, and even, perhaps, outright illegality. Although some issues about a film can be discussed as a result of a single viewing—its general "theme," styles of dress and decor, its political or social implications—none of its internal complexities can be discussed because these cannot be discovered and deciphered by even the most perceptive and practiced viewers in a single viewing, except in a very fragmentary way. (If there is any doubt about this difficulty, consider the blindnesses of the journalistic film critics—even the very best ones—who make all kinds of mistakes about a film's details because their *métier* allows them to see it only once.)

Film is the *densest* of all the arts—that is, to understand and feel the effects of a film we must integrate an immense number of signs and stimuli both simultaneously and consecutively. There is simply no way to understand how the artist has made the work—even a very simple film—without the detailed dissection and interrelation of such details as its narrative structure, dialogue, music, sound effects, lighting, camera angle, decor, color scheme, camera movement, physical motion, compositional patterns, use of depth and flatness, and so on and on and on. Because those details come at us both all at once and ceaselessly during a film screening, it is simply impossible to understand the care, craft, and conception that have dictated the choice of each without detailed analysis.[10] This analysis necessarily requires multiple viewings of a film and multiple class sessions devoted to a careful examination of its parts and their relation to the whole. In addition, the student should have the opportunity to study a film more deeply on his own, over the course of a semester, if it engages him, and should have the opportunity to study related films by the same filmmaker, or of the same period, or of the same genre if the subject stimulates him. This is what the term, *study*, means on the university level.

The obvious pedagogical solution to this problem would be for the university, willing to commit itself to the serious and proper study of film, to invest in its own collection of films, which would be considered one of its intellectual resources, like the books and records in its library. Although few universities have yet been willing to make this kind of expensive commitment, several have made at least beginnings in this direction.[11] Such collections should be large enough to provide not only a basic core of films to be taught in various courses but a large group of supplementary titles to provide both scholars and students an adequate background in the various major figures, periods, and genres of film. In addition to screening its prints in film courses, the university would also maintain a film-study facility where students could check films out to study them on special analytic viewing machines, analogous to the tape recordings of a language laboratory or the record-listening room of the library.[12] But the university that makes this kind of commitment soon discovers that it cannot legally buy all the films it needs to build such a collection; only films in the public domain can become part of a university's film collection.

Many important films are in the public domain and readily available for purchase from several competing companies at attractive prices:[13] almost every classic of the silent period (Griffith's entire work, Eisenstein's, Pudovkin's, the German Expressionists, the French surrealists, all of Mack Sennett, much of Chaplin, some of Keaton, and so forth); a large number of foreign classics of the 1930s (for example, Hitchcock's British films, Renoir's French films, the British and American documentary classics). A public domain collection, however, will have two serious gaps: all of the American sound films of the last fifty years and some of the "New Wave" foreign classics of the last thirty years (amazingly enough, many of the "New Wave" foreign films have never been copyrighted). There are some significant exceptions—American sound films that, for whatever reason, were never copyrighted: Frank Capra's *Meet John Doe* and *It's a Wonderful Life*, the MGM musical, *Till the Clouds Roll By*, Mel Brooks' *The Producers*. But except for these accidents, such a collection will be clearly deficient in the most recent half of film history—particularly lacking films in color and the wide screen, the dominant film formats of the last twenty-five years. Despite the gaps in such a collection, the pedagogical advantages of using prints that are always on hand, available for study on more than one day, are so great that I have become increasingly committed to teaching only those films which the university owns.

One major difference between the old and new copyright acts on the subject of owning prints is to provide precisely for the kind of desirable pedagogical possibility that I have described. The 1909 act implied that no one could own a print of a copyrighted film except the owner of the copyright. This implication produced several FBI raids on private film collections—the most famous being the seizure of actor Roddy MacDowell's personal film collection—as a violation of copyright law. Some very serious constitutional problems follow from such an implication (how can it be illegal to own something which one uses privately, without any commercial gain, in screenings at home for one's friends?). The new copyright act, therefore, shifts the legal issue from ownership of a print to the manufacture and selling of the print. Whereas the owner of an illegally made or sold print was legally responsible under the 1909 act, the film laboratory that makes the illegal print and the person who sells it are liable under the 1976 act.[14] But one of the specific exemptions from this copyright protection are "non-profit educational institutions," which have been granted the use of copyrighted films in the way that serious film study requires.

The key section of the new act is 110, "Limitations on exclusive rights: Exemption of certain performances and displays." Section 110 "allows non-profit educational institutions and their faculty to exhibit motion pictures or to display portions of them in face to face teaching activities. The exhibition or display must occur in a classroom or similar place of instruction."[15] This section, then, specifically adapts the principles for the fair use of printed material (Section 107) to the use of films and videotaped material. But before moving on to the second requirement of Section 110, which, ironically, nullifies these very principles which the act tries to establish, let me explain and explore the language of the foregoing exemption.

The terms, "face to face teaching activity," and "classroom or similar place of instruction," are designed to separate the university teaching of film from the activities of campus film societies, which show films to members of the university community for a profit. Both the film industry and the framers of the copyright act understandably wanted to protect the campus film-society market, estimated at producing as much as $100,000,000 revenue per year, from the educational use exemptions of the copyright act. To take one example, the oldest campus film society, the Documentary Film Group at the University of Chicago, founded in 1928, rents some 200 films each year, generating over $25,000 in rental fees, for an audience exceeding 100,000 admissions. This group is only one of several on one of many campuses in the United States. These groups and their film suppliers deserve protection for both commercial and educational reasons. Not only do these groups produce significant revenues for the film industry, but they serve the cultural function of introducing millions of new audience members each year to the traditions and richness of film art, both past and present.

The language of this exemption, however, leaves another question quite muddy. If the student wishes to write a paper on, say, the Western, and if the campus owns prints of several Westerns and provides a film-study center for viewing them, would it be a legitimate exemption from copyright restrictions for the student to view a number of these films by himself in order to write the paper? On the one hand, this is not a "face to face teaching activity"; on the other, it surely fulfills an educational purpose and takes place in a "classroom or similar place of instruction." The spirit of the new copyright act would probably be interpreted to apply to such a situation.

But an additional restriction in Section 110 violates the spirit of these educational exemptions and, in effect, makes them impossible to apply to copyrighted films. "The person responsible for the exhibition or display must not have had reason to believe that the copy of the motion picture being exhibited was not 'lawfully made.'"[16] An educational institution is exempt from observing copyright restrictions in teaching activities only if it owns lawfully made prints. Although this restriction sounds sensible, it really introduces a vicious, Catch-22 circle—for heretofore it has been impossible for a university to purchase a lawfully made print from the copyright owner of a copyrighted film. "The members of at least the theatrical motion picture industry have had a long standing practice of never selling copies of their motion pictures. . . ."[17] If a university in the past succeeded in acquiring a print of a copyrighted film, it might well have been an unlawfully "made" one. The print could either have been a pirated copy, sold by a private film collector with access to the print and a film laboratory (hence the new law's concentration on the laboratory that prints the films), or a videotape copy of a film, produced by some form of private videotaping machine (hence the industry's fear of these machines). And even if the print were lawfully made originally (made for, and sold to, a television station, say), would it still be a "lawfully made" print if the station sold it to a collector, who then sold it to a university?

Film piracy is a deplorable act, costing the film industry millions of dollars in revenues each year. The most notorious recent piracy cases have concerned pirated copies of new films, the industry's richest source of revenue. In one recent case, film pirates provided prints of new feature films for the home-box-office systems of hotels and in-flight motion picture systems of airlines before the legitimate copyright owner had even been able to release the film to the general public. Film piracy of new films is especially rife abroad, where exhibitors are less familiar with the legitimate local representatives of copyright owners. It is in the interest of both film educators and the film industry for the industry to make its legitimate profits from a film. Without a healthy film industry there would be no new films to study.

In comparison to the high-finance thievery of such infringements of copyright, the film industry's losses as a result of private film collectors, who make prints of copyrighted film classics available for university purchase, are very small indeed. So small, in fact, that the film industry may deliberately have decided to permit such minor piracy to continue for nonprofit educational institutions in order to preserve the general rule against film duplication and print ownership without exception. Even so, the film industry has targeted the private film collector as one of its major foes and selected several private collectors for individual and exemplary prosecution. But the private film collector has been the university's only source for prints available by no other means.[18]

So Section 110 of the new law allows the educational exemption from copyright restriction only so long as the print is not "believed to be illegally made." How could the not-beliefs of university scholars and administrators be tested in court? The double negative in the phrase is strangely evasive. And who exactly is *"responsible* for the exhibition"? And what if a print be "lawfully made" but not lawfully sold? Any university committed to collecting films would prefer to buy a copyrighted film from its copyright owner, rather than from a private collector who obtained his print who knows how or where—if the copyright owner would be so flexible as to sell or lease the university a print at a reasonable price.

There has been some movement in this direction in recent years, perhaps as a result of Section 110 of the new act, although this movement has not yet produced a satisfactory solution. The first development is that the copyright owners of films have increasingly permitted Super-8 copies of whole copyrighted films or excerpts of copyrighted films to be made and sold to private collectors and universities. Such whole films as John Ford's *Stagecoach* and all the protected Charlie Chaplin features can be bought in Super-8 and one can buy a 25-minute compilation of excerpts from *Psycho* and dozens of other major films. There are probably two reasons for making these films available in 8mm. First, Super-8 is a noncommercial film gauge; there is little chance that Super-8 sales can compete with 16mm rentals, 16mm being the standard gauge for college film society screenings and those of other, nontheatrical exhibitions. Second, Super-8, though a vast improvement over standard 8mm,[19] is limited by the size and clarity of its image to use in rather small rooms.

This fact, which protects the commercial market for 16mm, also makes Super-8 unsatisfactory for university use (as well as for private collectors, who usually are extremely scrupulous about obtaining the highest visual quality). If the university must project films in a large classroom or auditorium (many universities have only one screening facility), Super-8 would not produce an adequate image. Even in a small classroom, the Super-8 image is less brilliant, less sharp, less detailed (by its very size) than a 16mm image, which is already a reduction from an original 35mm negative. If one is teaching how the details of the image—its lighting, composition, color, balance, decor—control our responses to it and understanding of it, the Super-8 image is inadequate to demonstrate such detail. Further, because Super-8 film is only half as wide as 16mm film, it is only half as strong, tending to break more easily, which would impair its usefulness as a research resource to be frequently checked out and studied by individual scholars and students. University film study therefore requires 16mm prints.

A second development is the increasing tendency for distributors of certain 16mm prints to consider selling or leasing a print (for five years, seven years, or "life of the print") to universities for film study purposes. But there are two problems. First, the 16mm distributor often does not have the legal right to sell or lease most prints on a long-term basis, according to the contract he has signed with the film's original producer or distributor in 35mm. Such 16mm distributors have the exclusive right of nontheatrical, short-term rentals, and no other distribution rights. Some 16mm distributors, however, have negotiated recent contracts to give them long-term leasing rights or have discovered loopholes in older contracts that give them such rights. The second problem is that, unfortunately, the rates they have established for such long-term leasing of selected prints (they cannot legally "sell" a print to anyone) are exorbitant—approximately $1,200 per film. When one considers that the average cost of renting a film for a single classroom showing is, say, $75, this long-term lease price is almost eighteen times the rental price (the cost of making a feature-length, black-and-white print is about $200). The 16mm distributors argue that a film leased in this manner can be used many times in many different kinds of courses to justify the cost; they further argue that they must earn enough money on the long-term lease to justify the loss of one-time rentals. But if the university wants to build a large film collection (rather than simply own two dozen or so films that would be used repeatedly), and if the purpose of buying a film is not necessarily to show it to classes but also to make it part of an archive for possible study, the $1,200 price makes such use totally impractical.

Perhaps the principle of "Fair Price," as stated in Section 108 of the new act can be applied to film purchases as well. In the discussion of library exemptions from copyright restrictions, subsections 108 (c) and 108 (e) of the copyright act permit reproduction of an "entire work . . . or . . . a substantial part of it" if an unused copy "cannot be obtained at a fair price."[20] What, however, would be a "fair price" for a print of a film not previously obtainable lawfully at any price?[21] One possible standard that could be applied is some multiple of the rental price (i.e., five times, ten times, fifteen times the price of a single rental). But precisely what multiple would be a "fair" one? Another standard (and, I think, a more satisfactory one) would use the current selling prices of public domain films as some indication of a fair price. A black-and-white, public-domain, feature film, such as *Hiroshima Mon Amour,* can be bought for approximately $300. A color, public-domain feature, such as *Till the Clouds Roll By,* can be purchased for approximately $500. Further, companies that specialize in the sale of short, public-domain films charge approximately $35–$50 for a one-reel film and $60–$80 for a two-reel film, or about ten cents per foot.[22] Since ten reels (or 4,000 feet) is the approximate length of most feature films, the present market indicates that a price of $350–$450 per black-and-white feature film and $500–$600 per color feature film are adequate to strike the print, advertise it for sale, ship it to the customer, cover salaries for a small staff, and produce a sufficient profit. If copyrighted 16mm prints of feature films were available for purchase or long-term lease by educational, "not-for-profit" institutions at these prices, copyright owners might discover a rich source of revenue that previously never existed, and those institutions that wished to commit their resources and budgets to film study would be able to do so at a fair price.[23]

The new copyright act contains inherent contradictions that affect and afflict the serious academic study of film texts. Although the new act was designed to protect the commercial rights of copyright owners while, at the same time, guaranteeing the rights of educational institutions, the foregoing discussion indicates that the new act is patently unsuccessful at balancing those needs and claims. The film industry and the professional educator have antithetical interests in film prints—the one to make as much money on them as possible, the other to study them as closely and fully as possible. Although it was the intent of the new act to balance these claims, the internal contradictions of Section 110 (between the classroom exemption and the "lawfully made" print) and the failure of Section 107 to articulate specific principles of fair use have left film study more or less where it was before the drafting of the new act.

There are several possibilities for the future. Perhaps the film industry and film educators can come to some agreements (either *de jure* or *de facto*) about obtaining legally made prints at a fair price. Or perhaps the conflict between not using unlawfully made prints and the university's right to access of information will be tested in court. Given the costs of such legal action and the dangers of either side's losing such a case, the most probable course of future action will be no course of action, as has been true in the past.[24] University scholars will need to make the uncomfortable choice between obtaining a questionably legal print or not studying a film properly at all, and the film industry will need to make the uncomfortable choice between prosecuting an educational, not-for-profit institution for the legitimate study of a film it could not legally obtain or closing its eyes to the possible existence of such copyright violations completely. The new copyright act ought to have made both sides less uncomfortable, eradicating the sources of such legal, moral, and intellectual dilemmas.

NOTES

[1]Quotation from Stephen Freid, "Fair Use and the New Act," XXII *New York Law School Review*, 510 (1977).

[2]Gerald Mast, *A Short History of the Movies* (Indianapolis and New York: Bobbs-Merrill, 1971), p. 5.

[3]Leo Braudy's *The World in a Frame* (Garden City, N.Y.: Anchor Press/Doubleday, 1976) refuses to include a single photographic still because of the way such photographs falsify the experience of film (see pp. x, xi). It is a matter of some debate as to whether written prose (because it is sequential) or photographs (because they are spatial and visual) can more accurately convey the experience of watching a film. This debate would indicate that either method is partial since a film communicates both sequentially and simultaneously.

[4]An extreme example of the integration of stills and text is Charles Affron's *Star Acting* (N.Y.: Dutton, 1977), which weaves the verbal text and frame blow-ups from films together into verbal-visual sentences and paragraphs. There was simply no other way for the author to convey details of facial expression and transitions of emotional reactions on the faces of the stars.

[5]For this reason one could frequently find stills in front of the theater that depicted scenes one never saw in the film, scenes that undoubtedly ended on the cutting-room floor. Another kind of still camera frequently used on movie sets over the last two decades has been the Polaroid Land camera, which helps the script girl remember precisely how actors were made up and dressed, what props they carried, what directions they faced, and so forth, so that different shots would match, without bothersome mistakes in continuity.

[6]The essential parts of such a mechanism include a rear light source (to shine through the film), a lens capable of extreme close-up photography, and a reflex viewing system to center and focus the lens perfectly on the movie frame. Although many scholars

have improvised their own systems, the easiest one to use is the Honeywell Repronar 800, originally manufactured to make copies of photographic slides but adaptable to movie frames as well. One can also photograph a projected motion picture directly from the screen (see Herbert Keppler, *The Honeywell Pentax Way*, Garden City, N.Y.: Amphoto Books, 1973, pp. 287–88), but the visual results are far less satisfactory.

[7]As quoted in Freid, p. 498.

[8]*Ibid.*, 498–99.

[9]The average film rental for classroom use is about $75, perhaps 60 percent of the regular rental rate for the film. A whole film course (fifteen weeks, one film each week) would cost about $1,200 per semester in rentals. For a course that uses classic silent films, most of them in the public domain, film rentals are significantly lower (perhaps $750 for fifteen films). The cost of a course that uses recent and popular American films, especially those in color and Cinemascope, can be twice or three times the average amount, for many film distributors will not rent the film for classroom use at a rate lower than its regular rental (such films cost as much as $300 for a single showing).

[10]This kind of detailed analysis also demands the use of special analytic projectors which can stop the film on individual frames, run it backward, run it forward very slowly, and so forth. Several competing companies manufacture these analytic projectors (average cost between $2,000 and $2,500). Originally employed by athletic teams to evaluate the play of their personnel and analyze the play of their opponents, the machines also do very well at aesthetic analysis.

[11]Among the universities that I personally know to have begun collecting prints of films are Harvard University, the University of Massachusetts, New York University, the City University of New York, the University of Chicago, the University of Illinois, the University of Wisconsin, Northwestern University, and the University of California (both Berkeley and Los Angeles). A variant of the individual university collection is the regional film archive and study center, an extremely useful idea that the American Film institute is attempting to organize, modeled on the University Film Study Center in Boston. The Boston archive serves a dozen of the area colleges and universities with a collection of about 200 prints, splitting the costs of purchase and maintenance among them. They also maintain a study center facility where students from any of the supporting campuses can come to study a film more closely. The advantage of sharing costs, however, produces the disadvantage of sharing prints. Occasionally a print is not available precisely when the instructor needs it. And the danger of shipping prints is that they can be lost; the danger in their frequent use is that even if not abused by inadequate projectors and projectionists, their use shortens the life of the print.

[12]Analytic film viewing machines, which allow a viewer to stop the film, move it forward or backward quickly or slowly, are manufactured by several companies. They are extremely gentle to the film, preserving its life far better than any projector. These machines begin at a price of $4,000 (variant versions of them can be purchased for up to three times this amount), but adequate used machines can be bought for perhaps half this sum.

[13]One of the signs of the times is the proliferation of these companies offering prints of public-domain films for purchase. At least a dozen new companies have sprung into life within the last five years.

[14]See Peter F. Nolan, "A Brighter Day for the Magic Lantern: Thoughts on the Impact of the New Copyright Act on Motion Pictures," *Loyola of Los Angeles Law Review* (December 1977).

[15]*Ibid.*, p. 26.

[16]*Ibid.*

[17]*Ibid.*, p. 35.

[18]In their own defense, private collectors maintain that without their concern for the preservation and integrity of prints—a care not matched by the industry itself—complete prints of any number of important films would simply not be extant today. Peter F. Nolan, a spokesman for the industry, is incapable of referring to film collectors without sneeringly putting the term in quotation marks ("collectors").

[19]Super-8 film is the same width as standard 8mm, but the individual frames have been made twice as large by eliminating one of the two sets of sprocket holes at the sides of the film and reducing the width of the separation lines between frames.

[20]Leon E. Seltzer, "Exemptions and Fair Use in Copyright: The 'Exclusive Rights' Tensions in the New Copyright Act," *Bulletin, Copyright Society of the U.S.A.* 215 (1977): 306.

[21]The problem with determining the fair price of out-of-print books is at least as complicated and difficult as that of film prints. See Seltzer, pp. 307–310.

[22]The term *reel* here does not refer to a projector reel of 16mm film (which might contain as much as 2,000 feet of film) but to the original 35mm reels of a film. Although 35mm cameras and projectors can now accommodate reels of 2,000 feet of film, the original machines could accommodate only 1,000 feet. A ten-reel film, then, would be one requiring a maximum of ten 1,000-foot reels of 35mm film, a maximum length of 10,000 feet. When reduced to 16mm, this film would have a maximum length of 4,000 feet and would fill either two or three projection reels, depending on their size. A one-reel film, then, has a maximum length in 16mm of 400 feet and a two-reel film a maximum 16mm length of 800 feet. The D.W. Griffith Biograph films are one-reelers; the Chaplin Mutual comedies are two-reelers.

[23]Private collectors predict, however, that if major distributors enter the sale or long-term lease business, the prices of prints will soar.

[24]The dangers of the film industry's losing such a suit are especially great, for the result would be public affirmation that either universities were entitled to own pirated prints or entitled to lease or buy any film they wanted from the copyright owner. Because of these dangers, and because instigation of the suit would necessarily come from the industry, it is not likely that there will ever be a test case.

Television Research and Fair Use

In the chapter that follows, Douglas Kellner expresses the television scholar's frustrations in attempting to locate, study, and reproduce for publication images from programs. Relatively few scholarly studies include television images; their absence is partially accounted for by the major network and producer policies Kellner describes and by the correlative reluctance of some publishers to risk fair use publication.

As was evident in the Stott and Sproule episodes described in Chapter 5, copyright practice can exhibit elements of what First Amendment law labels *prior restraint*—the prevention of publication or broadcast before actual or potential damages have been ascertained. Among instances of restraint directed against television commentary, two that have acquired a public character are worth mentioning here. The first involves Professor Robert Alley's book, *TV: Ethics for Hire?* (Abingdon, 1977). In writing on "Kojak," Alley sought to challenge Benjamin Stein's characterization of Kojak as "a very decent, law-abiding guy" and of the show's message as "moral, kind behavior always wins" and "that justice is done." Stein's article had appeared in *TV Guide*, where a related editorial (appearing after Alley's book) extolled the way in which "Kojak" carried America's standards to the rest of the world. "When Kojak is shown reading his (sic) rights to the apprehended suspect—*by demand of the law of his land*—the message of human dignity and respect for the individual is not lost on the citizens of other lands" (*TV Guide* 25:25, A-6; italics in original). Alley does not find such descriptions convincing and wanted to quote twenty lines of dialogue from an episode to place the program in a different light. Among them were these relevant words spoken by Kojak himself, in justification of his own violation of the law.

> Sure I stretched the law, so what? Maybe it ought to be stretched in the reverse once in a while. You know, instead of freeing any punk who comes along with a misspelled word on an affidavit, you ought to come into my court house one night.

When Alley's book had reached the galley stage, Abingdon requested that permission be obtained from Universal Studios. When Alley inquired by telephone, he was asked whether his treatment would be "favorable or unfavorable." Alley's answer was not satisfactory to the permissions employee at Universal and he was thus requested to send his manuscript for review. Permission was eventually denied and the galleys were reset to include these words:

> A casual viewer of *Kojak* may have difficulty relating such words as "moral," "kind," and "justice" to the plots of this series. An example from a *Kojak* script would be beneficial. Unfortunately, Universal Studios, which owns the legal rights to the show, refused to grant permission to reprint twenty lines of dialogue from a *Kojak* episode probably viewed by over 20 million persons. While we are inclined to believe that such a brief excerpt from a program broadcast over public channels can be considered fair use when employed for purposes of critical analysis, we will honor the wishes of Universal and seek to do justice to the dialogue through a paraphrase (p.110).

It is clear in this case that a scholar was deprived of evidence that would have proved more credible than a mere paraphrase. [Account provided by Professor Alley, University of Richmond, Virginia.]

A different type of effort at restraint upon publication—this time unsuccessful—arose in connection with Horace Newcomb's widely read study of narrative formulas, *TV: The Most Popular Art* (Doubleday, 1974). The cover of the book caricatures Archie Bunker (played by Carroll O'Connor) of the "All in the Family" series. After seeing an advance copy of the cover, CBS wrote to Doubleday, requesting it not to use the cover since such treatment would detract from the commercial value of the Bunker character. Doubleday was not persuaded to abandon the visual parody and the original cover has now been through several printings without resulting litigation. [Details provided by Professor Newcomb, University of Texas at Austin and Doubleday editorial staff.] The case is one of many illustrating the crucial and discretionary role of the publisher in responding to efforts at prior restraint.

There are, then, a large number of potential areas of conflict between scholars and television copyright holders, including image reproduction for publication, off-air taping for classroom use, permission to quote the words from a program, and the less frequently encountered problem of visual parody (see the related discussion in Chapter 23). Taken together, the experiences of Alley, Newcomb, and Kellner typify problems faced by many scholars attempting to document their perspectives on television.

7

TELEVISION RESEARCH AND FAIR USE

DOUGLAS KELLNER

Television is widely recognized as America's most powerful cultural force. The statistics of television interaction are overwhelming: over 97 percent of American homes have a TV; the average set is on more than six hours a day; by the time most children enter grade school they will have spent more time watching television than they will devote to their entire school career. Television nurtures Americans from the cradle to the grave and is the one major agent of socialization that will continue to influence its viewers during their entire lifetime.[1] The varied and complex effects of television on human behavior are a subject of national concern. Less attention has been directed to how television programming is constructed and what images and messages it communicates.[2] The reasons for the relative neglect of television as a cultural artifact have to do with the newness of the medium, its ubiquitousness, and the seemingly random nature of its programs. New mass media of communication seem to resist scholarly study during their first stage of development. Only as they mature are they studied as cultural forces and later as art forms. Perhaps McLuhan is right that a once dominant medium comes to be viewed with a combination of nostalgia and critical distance only after another new medium has displaced it.[3] It seems that the passage of time, research by social scientists, and journalistic controversy finally force the scholarly community to see that what was taken as mere leisure-time entertainment is really a powerful social-cultural force as well as an interesting aesthetic artifact.

There are now some encouraging indications that the academic community is beginning to assume its responsibilities to take television and popular culture seriously. Significant and pioneering books on television culture are appearing;[4] scholarly journals are increasingly publishing articles on television;[5] and university courses are being given that deal seriously with American television. A consensus is forming that television is a worthy subject for serious research, and as a result, research centers with videotape collections of television programs are rapidly expanding. As an example of the expanding resources, my own study of TV cop shows was aided by daily reruns of major crime dramas which were transmitted by cable into my home from Dallas, San Antonio, and Waco, providing material for analysis alongside the regularly scheduled glut of cop shows. To make possible a more careful analysis, I bought a Sony Betamax videorecorder and built up a small library of tapes. After repeated viewing of programs and the development of a system of analysis, I found that each television genre has its own formulas, codes, rituals, mythologies, and ideologies; that each series within a genre also has its unique images, values, and messages; and that each program is generally a distinct text. For instance, it is often assumed that all crime dramas are the same, and although there are overarching genre codes and formulas, my research has discerned five distinct types:

1. Authoritarian Law and Order Crime Dramas
   (e.g., "Dragnet," "The Untouchables," "The FBI");
2. Liberal Morality Plays
   (e.g., "Mod Squad," "The Streets of San Francisco," "Police Story");
3. Mythic-Moral Redeemers and Supercops
   (e.g., "Kojak," "Baretta," "Hawaii-Five-O");
4. Corporate Cops
   (e.g., "Ironside," "The Rookies," "S.W.A.T.");
5. Individualist Cops
   (e.g., "Columbo," "Serpico," "Starsky and Hutch").

Within each category, there are interesting differences. "Dragnet," for instance, emphasizes the force of Jack Webb's authoritarian personality. "The Untouchables" focuses on the power of Elliot Ness's incorruptible team of federal agents. "The FBI" increasingly suppressed the personalities of the agents and pictured the technical apparatus of the agency as the effective force of law and order. "Kojak" features the mythical power of Theo (read "God") Kojak in a corrupt urban environment. "Mod Squad" promotes the commitment and dedication of "mod" youth; "Starsky and Hutch" champions the macho individualism and personal relationship of its two heroes. "S.W.A.T." utilizes mechanistic-militaristic teamwork and a technical apparatus to crush its foes. And "Baretta" breaks many crime drama codes by showing its hero as part of an urban ghetto subculture, one who shares the lives and mythically redeems the suffering of the little people.[6] Situation comedies, soap operas, melodramas, game shows, and other TV genres also communicate quite different values, ideologies, and messages.[7]

As a result of these preliminary investigations, I resolved to write a book on the crime drama and began visiting and corresponding with several of the new TV archives in the country. I wanted to discover where the tapes of past TV programs were stored and to ascertain their availability for public scrutiny and scholarly research. The following report focuses on the resources of television material I found and the obstacles I encountered along the way.

The newly formed Committee for Television Archives lists fifteen centers in the United States and I shall discuss the most important ones with which I am familiar.[8]

THE LIBRARY OF CONGRESS NATIONAL ARCHIVES

The Television, Motion Picture and Sound Recording Branch of the National Archives and Records Service at the Library of Congress in Washington has a large collection of tapes of television programs. TV films are catalogued along with motion pictures, and the scholar is allowed, by appointment, to use a Steinbeek machine to study the films. This machine allows freezes, replays, and speedups, but the picture is quite small. The National Archives' collection of television programs was assembled in a curiously haphazard fashion. Some TV producers began sending films of their programs, scripts, plot summaries, and other material for copyright purposes in the early days of television, but other producers did not, since there was no legal requirement to do so. Thus the collection of cop shows that I examined was sketchy and random. From the programs of the 1950s there were several films of "Dragnet," a couple of "Naked City" and "M-Squad," but none from such programs as "Highway Patrol," "Racket Squad," or "Mr. District Attorney." In the 1960s, things began to improve and there were many films of shows like "The FBI" and "Hawaii-Five-O," but none of "Mod Squad," "N.Y.P.D.," or "Felony Squad."

Only a few scholars have made use of the Library of Congress Archives to do research on television genres or series. One study of the TV Western, *The Horse, The Gun, and the Piece of Property* by Ralph and Donna Brauer, made extensive use of the archives,[9] but I know of no other comparable study done there. While using the Library of Congress material, I found the staff helpful, the viewing conditions tolerable, and although the collection was sketchy in the area of my interest, it nonetheless contained material not readily accessible elsewhere. Neither cameras nor tape recorders are allowed in the archives, thus preventing the recording of media images or dialogue for more detailed analysis, classroom use, or publication.

The new copyright law signed in October 1976 mandates the creation within the Library of Congress of an archive that will preserve "television and radio programs which are the heritage of the people of the United States," programs that are of "present or potential public or cultural interest, historical significance, cognitive value, or otherwise worthy of preservation."[10] The new law directs the library to provide access "to historians and scholars without encouraging or causing copyright infringement." Under copyright deposit rules, the library already contains over ten thousand television films and it now plans to increase storage facilities. Under the direction of broadcast historian Erik Barnouw, plans are being drawn up for a new archive. Barnouw hopes that it will be opened some time in 1980 and states:

> The new archive will acquire material in several ways, including traditional methods: (1) deposits under the copyright law—which under new provisions should bring a larger flow of material than in the past; (2) exchanges and gifts; (3) transfers from other collections of the Library. To these is added something new and valuable: (4) the right to tape certain kinds of material off the air "for archival purposes."

It seems clear that this combination can create an enormously diverse and representative archive. Barnouw continues:

> It must be emphasized that the Library of Congress collection will not be for rental or classroom use. The programs will be there for study by scholars on an individual basis. Yet they represent a historic step in providing documentation concerning media that have become so powerful in our society and our individual lives.[11]

Considering its current material and the prospects for an expanded archive, the Library of Congress has the greatest promise of providing a master collection for television research material and should be cultivated to its full potential. Unfortunately, it will not lend its materials to universities or to individuals, nor will it allow any kind of picture taking on the premises. The Library of Congress policy seems to have stiffened since the spring of 1978, when poor quality audiocassettes were allowed for note keeping. At least one factor—admitted off the record by a Library of Congress employee—is that major producers have exerted considerable pressure against allowing any copyrighted materials to leave the building.

It is very desirable here to consider facilities for a loan library and tape reproduction center. As Vanderbilt University now does with TV news programs, such a service could produce tapes at cost for universities or individuals engaged in scholarly research. The National Archives should also provide such a service. In fact, the fair use provisions of the copyright law would seem to require them to assist legitimate scholarly research. Noncompliance with the fair use intent of the law would provide a rather poor example for other archives.

UNIVERSITY RESEARCH ARCHIVES

UCLA, Vanderbilt University, the University of Georgia, the University of Winconsin, and George Washington University have begun to establish TV archives.[12] Vanderbilt, for instance, has tapes of the three network news programs from August 5, 1968, to the present; its fascinating history is told elsewhere in this book.[13] Here I shall simply discuss its resources and facilities. News videotapes are available for viewing at a minimal charge on premises; the Vanderbilt archives will send tapes of specific news broadcasts and will even compile tapes of specific subject matter for loan at a reasonable cost. Vanderbilt also publishes *Television News Index and Abstracts*, which is distributed to almost 500 libraries. The staff is extremely friendly and helpful, and its services have provided material for many scholarly studies. Their huge news-tape collection of the entire Nixon era—including the full Watergate and Impeachment Hearings—provide important material for study of the Nixon presidency.[14] The Vanderbilt Archive loan contract, however, at present refuses permission to duplicate for more extensive later study or for classroom use—another sign of the undue conservatism and fear of lawsuit that is prevalent in many media resource archives across the country.

UCLA probably has the largest collection of TV films and videotapes outside the National Archives. In 1965, the Academy of Television Arts and Sciences Foundation and the regents of the University of California established a television library on the UCLA campus. Its goal is "to acquire and preserve the full spectrum of television programing."[15] The collection is intended for use by students and researchers. It has amassed about 15,000 programs received from production studios, foundations, or individuals within the industry; it has received nothing directly from the networks. Material can be used only on the premises and nothing can be copied or removed from the archive. Its holdings include the complete John F. Kennedy campaign material, the "Jack Benny Show," the "Loretta Young Show," the "Ann Sothern Show," the complete "Hallmark Hall of Fame," and the "Alcoa" series. The material is on an assortment of formats: 16mm, 35mm film, one-half and three-quarter-inch videocassettes, and two-inch tapes. The equipment for viewing includes two 16mm flatbed movieolas, the necessary playback formats for the tapes, and two 35mm Steinbeeks. The UCLA collection has recently received between 20,000 and 25,000 programs that are not yet catalogued. It is working on methods to permit parts of the collection "to be made available for learning institutions throughout the country as well as overseas."[16]

Many more university archives are needed to facilitate the scholarly study of television. The price of videocassettes and the forthcoming videodiscs will make the costs of acquisition for libraries comparable to those for books. Since television is so important a part of our culture, it is surely as important to have available programs like "Roots" as it is to possess the bestsellers that libraries routinely stock. The impact of popular television programs in our time probably exceeds that of our books. If universities are to assume their responsibilities as learning centers, providing skills for understanding and critically judging the realities of contemporary society, then the requisite materials must be available in video libraries and research centers.

PRIVATE FOUNDATION ARCHIVES

There are several private foundation archives of which the most important is the Museum of Broadcasting in New York. Background work for the museum began in 1967 when the William Paley Foundation commissioned studies by William Bluem of Syracuse University "to determine how many broadcast materials of the past had been saved, what they were, and where they were."[17] Studies reported that "despite some losses, a great deal of meaningful material still existed: at the networks, in universities, and in private collections."[18] In November 1976 Paley announced the opening of the Museum of Broadcasting and stated: "The precious body of broadcasting history that is still in existence—discs, kinescope film, and audio and videotape—must be preserved. Otherwise, it will simply, by neglect, disintegrate or disappear."[19] The museum negotiated agreements with CBS, NBC, ABC, PBS, and National Public Radio for material. The museum staff selected for their archives what they deemed the most important material and resolved to preserve an entire typical television day recorded every eight months in different parts of the country. Their first five-year plan is to collect over 20,000 broadcasts, representing the whole spectrum of radio and television broadcasting by period, genre, series, and program. Video preservation copies are made on three-quarter-inch tapes; copies for use in the museum are made on one-half-inch cassettes. The public is allowed to watch cassettes on Sony Betamax videorecorders. One can become a yearly member and reserve time on the machines. The public may use the facilities when available for a $1.50 fee.

The Museum of Broadcasting is a fine institution, but of limited use for scholars. Lately, it has been swamped with visitors, and it makes no official provisions for scholarly research. A scholar can become a member and reserve a certain amount of time, and the staff is most cooperative in providing time priorities for serious research, but there is a space limitation of only eight videocassette machines in the face of tremendous public demand. Often there are long lines outside the museum waiting entry. There is also a limited amount of material available. For instance, while researching the cop show genre, I found that the museum had pilot programs of only a few series, although it continues to add to the collection. Generally, the museum is concerned with collecting the best of television and often is content with one episode of a popular series. Such selectivity is admirable, but it is not of great use to scholars doing more specialized work. The museum's personnel protest that they have neither the money nor the facilities to process and show a greater variety of material. In fact, the networks have contributed such an immense amount of material that it will take years to process it all. Despite such limitations, several interesting research projects have begun at the museum. The collection is particularly valuable for studying the history of broadcasting.

Other private foundation or institutional collections of video material are found at the Academy of Television Arts and Sciences in California, the American Film Institute in Washington, the Museum of Modern Art in New York, the Donnell branch of the New York Public Library, and George Eastman House in Rochester.[20] Since this material consists largely of video art or documentaries it is not of essential interest to students of mainstream television culture, although it may well be useful to scholars who specialize in those areas.

PRIVATE COLLECTIONS

New videocassette recorders and cable-satellite TV make it possible to build a personal videocassette library for study, research, and teaching material. I bought a Sony Betamax recorder (they were sold for less than $800 in 1978) and obtained a $500 grant from the University of Texas to make a collection of tapes on crime dramas for my book and to use in Philosophy of Communication courses. Other television scholars, such as Horace Newcomb and Paul Hirsch, have received grants to buy videorecorders and cassettes. TV buffs are now taping reruns of their favorite shows, and one can amass a large personal collection of cassettes for research and teaching at a reasonable expense. Cable and satellite TV makes possible access from 12 to 40 channels on current systems, which could provide a scholar with sufficient material for research of a television series or genre. Someone studying the mythologies of "Star Trek," the thematic developments of "All in the Family" in relation to changing social conditions, or the images of war or sexuality on "M.A.S.H." could rather quickly tape enough material from daily reruns to establish a basis for serious analysis.

Projections of future home-video entertainment centers forecast the possibility of connecting one's home television to a central computer that could play for home use virtually any film or TV program in existence. Such a system could instantly provide the material necessary for cultural analysis of any given TV program or series as well as of television history as a whole. It is also conceivable that entire series like "Star Trek" might be recorded on videocassettes and sold for home use; hundreds of films have already been recorded for cassette sale at $39–$79 a film. Videodiscs will cut these costs dramatically. That we may be living in a future video environment with four-foot to seven-foot TV screens, videorecorders, and cassette collections as everyday household equipment only underscores the urgency of developing adequate analyses of images, providing the audience with skills to analyze and critically to interpret the messages communicated—preconditions for avoiding television manipulation.

But we are not yet in a video Utopia. Meantime, it is important to know where one can find access to preserved TV material. One might think that the networks would hold the most extensive and important collections of television material. Is this indeed the case, and what is Network[21] policy concerning research? Do they accept the principle of fair use of their materials for research, teaching, and publication?

NETWORK ARCHIVES

While visiting New York in the summer of 1978, I tried to interview Network personnel about their policies on the accessibility of materials for scholarly research and their interpretations of fair use as concerns the use of broadcast images in the classroom. I encountered either refusal to answer, ignorance about policies, or flatly contradictory answers from members of the same corporations. Therefore, I sent letters to the three networks seeking written, official clarification. (See my letter in Appendix B.) None answered my first letter of request, but I persisted with additional letters, including copies of letters from the editors of this volume requesting some sort of documentation. I finally heard from NBC (see its letter in Appendix C) and from CBS, which requested that its letter not be printed. ABC never responded.

The three networks seem to have different policies on access to their own news and research archives by the general public or by scholars. ABC has a "media concepts" department that makes available transcripts and pictures of ABC-produced shows for books, articles, and other uses. One employee told me that they had no facilities for viewing materials and no archives on their premises, although they did have a news archive, the Sherman-Grinberg Library, that the public could use. CBS also has a news archives library with material available for public viewing at about $15 per hour; it will also make copies of some material on a cost basis. Further, after dropping its Vanderbilt University suit and

acquiescing in the right of an archive to tape news broadcasts and prepare indexes, CBS started publishing its own yearly indexes and transcripts of news programs in 1975.[22] CBS in 1974 and NBC in 1976 began
to make tapes of news broadcasts available to the Library of Congress
and six presidential libraries. Both NBC and CBS allow taping of their
news programs for a yearly fee related to the size of the institution or
school system. But none of the networks allows off-air copying of any
other type of programming. The Network letters to me express a limited
willingness to provide materials to the public on a commercial basis.
Neither of the letters received contains a reference to the concept of fair
use. Clearly we shall have to contend with Network insistence on its
monopoly over television imagery for the foreseeable future.[23] How
strange this is as regards the public interest can be understood by imag-
ining that newspapers like *The New York Times*, or books and articles,
were available only for a single reading—and then withdrawn by management and never seen again.

FAIR USE IN TEACHING AND SCHOLARLY
PUBLICATION

I have discussed the need for adequate archival resources and
Network's recalcitrant attitudes. The negative and ambiguous policies
are least tolerable in the areas of teaching and publication. Because of
the cultural-social importance of American television, TV education
courses should be instituted at every grade school, high school, and
university in the U.S. Since we live in an increasingly media-mediated
environment, people must be taught to analyze, understand, and
criticize the images of their symbolic environment. It is the duty of
scholars to provide methodologies and theories to facilitate this process
and to teach courses that survey and criticize our symbolic landscape.

With respect to my own teaching in the philosophy of
communication—where it is essential to use film, television, popular
music, and radio, as well as print—I have inquired among lawyers about
the legality of my instructional practice. With respect to my use of Sony
Betamax cassettes, lawyers confidently told me that fair use would permit me to tape programs for research and to display portions of them in
class. They warned, however, that I could not keep tapes in any of the
university libraries. University administrators, in their turn, told me that
I had to erase such tapes after three uses or one semester. Such pieces of
advice are improvisational and reveal a characteristic confusion among
university officials, technicians, and others with administrative responsibilities. The law itself is not clear and does not really direct or restrict in

clear ways. Fears in the university lead to a conservative policy that prevents scholars from teaching and conducting research to the fullest of their capabilities—and that works to the detriment of social interest. This is an arena where teachers and scholars should press for their legal rights despite Network and university attempts to give *de facto* restrictions a *de jure* appearance.[24]

There is no sound reason why a democracy should not subject its most important cultural productions to critical scrutiny, and any restrictions on such educationally important pedagogy should be resisted. Putting television programs on large screens in the classroom provides alienation effects that allow one to gain critical distance in the analysis of a work. The same effect is achieved by freeze frames. Critical analysis calls attention to TV as cultural artifact and as complex aesthetic structure, and provides a critical awareness of how television is constructed and how it communicates. Such study enables the student to gain new understanding of television culture and to resist media manipulation. This gain in critical-media consciousness, what I call *media competency,* provides an increase in individual autonomy and makes possible more effective social participation. Why should we allow restrictive Network monopoly of images to interfere with this educational process? Clearly it should not, and as educators we should unite in struggling for more explicit guarantees of fair use of media materials in the classroom.

Scholarly uses of media images in publishing have been an even thornier and more vexing enterprise. Several authors in this anthology describe how their requests to publish images in studies of cultural history or popular culture were denied or inhibited by prohibitive charges for publication of copyrighted images or by mere failure to respond. Effective study of television genres, series, or programs demands publication and analysis of images, and quotations of dialogue, which Network now prohibits or ruthlessly controls and censors. Although the current law is not perfectly clear on this issue, publishers tend to be afraid of Network lawsuits and often prohibit publication of media images for which permission is denied or not explicitly granted. This is extremely unfortunate since it restricts critical analysis and exposition. As I watched tapes of TV cop shows at the Library of Congress on the Steinbeek machine which allowed freezes of images, I experienced the powerful effect of Jack Webb's authoritarian bearing, Dan August's macho individualism, and Kojak's mythic godlike qualities that would illustrate some of my theses. With a good camera, one could take pictures of such images for publication, but cameras are not allowed. Evidently the broadcast industry is able to pressure research archives into protecting its commercial interests at the cost of disregarding the requirements of scholarship.

CONCLUSION

The prevailing university attitude is hostile to television studies,[25] a stance that mirrors the corporate indifference so frequently encountered. Many popular culture scholars have encountered it while applying for university research grants, trying to institute popular culture courses, or qualifying for tenure. Yet, some institutions are establishing popular culture study centers, and the yearly conferences of the Popular Culture Association show a growing interest in this field for study. To make further advances, we must emphasize the importance of television, the need for media literacy in our population, and the social responsibility of scholars to teach critical skills as a part of this basic literacy. The increasing importance of mass media and the new forms of media communication will accelerate the need for media education. Universities must encourage the necessary research by opening curricular and financial space for it. Those scholars who share the convictions expressed here must deepen their commitment and engage in the struggles necessary to produce significant changes in the academy.

NOTES

[1]For data on the ubiquity of television in our society and theses on its social function, see Douglas Kellner, "Television Socialization," *Mass Media/Adult Education* No. 46 (Fall/Winter 1977/78).

[2]I have been engaged for the past several years in a study group that is researching these issues; it is now preparing for publication a collection of *Critical Studies of Television and American Capitalism.*

[3]Marshall McLuhan, *Understanding Media* (New York: Signet, 1964); he develops this thesis in detail in an article, "Laws of the Media," *et cetera* 34, No. 2 (June 1977).

[4]The best recent book on American popular culture is Robert Jewett and John Shelton Lawrence, *The American Monomyth* (Garden City, N.Y.: Anchor Press/Doubleday, 1977). See also Horace Newcomb, *TV: The Most Popular Art* (Garden City, N.Y.: Doubleday, 1974); Horace Newcomb (ed.), *Television: The Critical View* (New York: Oxford, 1976); and the Aspen Institute anthologies, *Television as a Social Force* (New York: Praeger, 1975) and *Television as a Cultural Force* (New York: Praeger, 1976).

[5]See the *Journal of Popular Culture* and *American Film*, which have published many interesting articles on TV. The *Journal of Popular Film* is expanding to include television criticism and will now be called the *Journal of Popular Film and Television.*

[6]These categories are developed in my forthcoming study of the crime drama genre, *Television Cops and Violence.*

[7]See my articles "Ideologies in Advanced Capitalism," *Socialist Review,* 42 (November-December 1978); "Television, Ideology, and Emancipating Popular Culture," *Social Review* (forthcoming); and my "Television Images, Codes, and Messages," *Praxis* (forthcoming).

[8]See the appended list of television archives for their addresses and contact personnel.

[9]Ralph and Donna Brauer, *The Horse, The Gun, and The Piece of Property* (Bowling Green, Ohio.: Popular Press, 1975).

[10]The new American Television and Radio Archive was discussed by Erik Barnouw in a speech at the American Studies Association convention in Boston, October 29, 1977.

We are grateful to Professor Barnouw for sending Bernard Timberg a copy of the summary of the speech which I am quoting here.

[11]Barnouw.

[12]See the appended list of TV archives for addresses and contact personnel.

[13]See Chapter 8.

[14]There is also a news archive in the making at George Washington University's Regional Center for the Study of Television News. This center will collect and make available the Vanderbilt Archive material and will establish its own archive.

[15]Robert Rosen, letter to *American Film*, December-January 1978, p. 4.

[16]Robert F. Lewine, letter to *American Film*, December-January 1978, p. 4.

[17]Cited in "Preserving Broadcast History," *American Libraries*, October 1977, p. 515.

[18]*Ibid.* The report downplays the immense amount of broadcast material lost and the ensuing tragic gap in broadcast history due to Network greed and stupidity.

[19]*Ibid.* Although we should be thankful to Paley for helping fund this venture, we should be aware that the museum was set up as much as a public relations gimmick to promote American commercial broadcasting as to aid serious study of broadcast material.

[20]See Appendix A for a comprehensive listing of archives.

[21]I use the term *Network* to describe the system of commercial broadcasting in America, and the term *network* to describe a particular broadcast corporation like CBS. For an elaboration, see my forthcoming article "Network and American Television."

[22]On the CBS News Archive, see Jody McMahon, "Keeping History Alive: Videotape Archives," *Videography* 3, No. 1 (January 1978): 16 *ff.*

[23]The Brauer study, pp. 239-40, contains a rueful reflection: "Probably the only answer to the research problem is the networks themselves. The local stations and networks seem unbelievably paranoid about people investigating them and researching them."

[24]For a sensible interpretation of fair use in the classroom, see Donald Wylie, "An Unconventional Look at Copyrights," *Audiovisual Instruction* 23, No. 7 (1978): 14 *ff.*

[25]A study of the United States television audience showed that a surprisingly large number of well-educated people, university professors among them, were heavy television watchers. Do they uncritically share its value system? For viewer data, see Robert T. Bower, *Television and the Public* (N.Y.: Holt, Rinehart & Winston, 1973).

Appendix A: Film and Television Archives

United States Archives

1. Academy of Motion Picture Arts
and Sciences
The Margaret Herrick Library
8949 Wilshire Boulevard
Beverly Hills, CA 90211

2. Academy of Television Arts
and Sciences
6363 Sunset Boulevard
Hollywood, CA 90024

3. (a) American Film Institute Center for
Advanced Film Studies
Charles K. Feldman Library
501 Doheny Road
Beverly Hills, CA 90210
(b) The American Film Institute
John F. Kennedy Center
Washington, D.C. 20566

4. Anthology Film Archives
80 Wooster Street
N.Y., NY 10012

5. ATAS-UCLA Television Library
Department of Theater Arts
UCLA
Los Angeles, CA 90024

6. Brigham Young University
Harold B. Lee Library
Provo, UT 84602

7. Broadcast Pioneers Library
1771 N. Street, N.W.
Washington, D.C. 20036

8. CBS News Archives
524 West 57 Street
N.Y., NY 10019

9. Corporation for Public Broadcasting
1111 16 Street, N.W.
Washington, D.C. 20036

10. Walt Disney Archives
500 South Buena Vista
Burbank, CA 91521

11. East Coast Motion Picture Unit
Television Film Archives
U.S. Marine Corps Base
Quantico, VA 22134

12. George Washington University
Library: Regional Center for the
Study of Television News
2130 H Street, N.W.
Washington, D.C. 20037

13. International Museum of Photography
at George Eastman House
Department of Film
900 East Avenue
Rochester, NY 14607

14. J. Walter Thompson
Creative Library—8th Floor
420 Lexington Avenue
N.Y., NY 10017

15. Library of Congress
Motion Picture, Broadcasting
and Recorded Sound Division
Washington, D.C. 20540

16. Museum of Broadcasting
1 East 53 Street
N.Y., NY 10022

17. Museum of Modern Art
Department of Film
11 West 53 Street
N.Y., NY 10019

18. National Anthropological Film Center
Smithsonian Institution
Washington, D.C. 20560

19. National Archives & Records Service
Audiovisual Archives Division
GSA
Washington, D.C. 20408

20. National Library of Medicine
8600 Rockville Pike
Bethesda, MD 20014

21. Naval Photographic Center
Washington, D.C. 20374

22. NBC News Film Library
30 Rockefeller Plaza, Room 896
N.Y., NY 10020

23. The New York Public Library
at Lincoln Center
The Library and Museum of the Performing Arts
Theater Collection
111 Amsterdam Avenue
N.Y., NY 10023

24. Pacific Film Archive
University Art Museum
Berkeley, CA 94720

25. Public Television Library, PBS
475 L'Enfant Plaza West, S.W.
Washington, D.C. 20024

26. State Historical Society of Wisconsin
    Mass Communications History Center
    8l6 State Street
    Madison, WI 53706

27. University of California, Los Angeles
    Film and Television Archive
    University Research Library
    405 Hilgard
    Los Angeles, CA 90024

28. University of Georgia
    School of Journalism and Mass Com-
    munication
    Peabody Awards Program
    Athens, GA 30602

29. University of Southern California—
    Warner Brothers Collection
    427 North Cañon Drive
    Beverly Hills CA 90210

30. University of Southern California
    Department of Special Collections
    Doheny Library
    University Park
    Los Angeles, CA 90007

31. Vanderbilt University
    Vanderbilt Television News Archive
    Joint University Libraries
    Nashville, TN 37203

32. Wisconsin Center for Film and Theater
    Research
    516 State Street
    Madison, WI 53706

Foreign Archives or Information Sources

National Film Archive
395 Wellington Street
Ottawa K1A ON3
Canada

Fédération Internationale des Archives du
Film (F.I.A.F.)
Secrétariat
Galerie Ravenstein 74
1000 Bruxelles, Belgique

Fédération Internationale des Archives de
Television (F.I.A.T.)
Secrétaire Générale
I.N.A. 1
Place de Mercuriales
93170 Bagnolet
France

Appendix B: Questions from Letter of Request for Policy Information to ABC, CBS, NBC from Douglas Kellner, October. 23, 1978

(1) What archives do you have available for public or scholarly use to study TV broadcast materials? i.e., What archives of your news, entertainment, and special events programs do you have and what, if any, public or scholarly access do you allow? Would you, for instance, open your news archives to a scholar studying images of Africa in American television news and documentaries? Would you allow a TV scholar writing a book on variety specials, for instance, to view programs that your Network has produced?

(2)What is your policy on fair use of images for scholarly research and publication? Would you give permission to use stills of TV shows you broadcast in a book analyzing popular culture? Would you give permission to a professor at a university to tape and analyze programs you broadcast for publication of an article or book on TV? Would you give a professor permission to tape a program you broadcast and show it to a university or high school class? How would you construe "fair use" of TV images for educational purposes? What limitations would you put on "fair use?"

(3) Finally, would you give me permission to publish the answer to my letter in the article I am writing?

Appendix C: Letter of Response from NBC to Douglas Kellner, December 7, 1978

In response to your letter to NBC of October 23, the following are some of the considerations that govern NBC's handling of requests about archival research and other outside use of our program materials. We can't give you a statement of hard-and-fast "policy" because we treat each case on its own merits.

NBC is a commercial broadcasting company. It is essentially designed to provide the viewing and listening public with a program service, funded by sale of air time to advertisers. It is *not* a public archive or library, and NBC generally does not have the staff or facilities for providing regular research services to scholars and the general public. While NBC retains audio and video tapes, film, transcripts and other broadcasting records, these are primarily intended for use by NBC employees in the conduct of NBC business.

On the matter of archives, NBC does support the principle of archival preservation of broadcast material by an appropriate institution, with provision for access by the public and by scholars. We have demonstrated this by making a major donation of historic radio and television records, including film and videotape, to the Museum of Broadcasting in New York City, which opened in 1976. We intend our collection in the Museum to serve as a single, central repository whereby research institutions, scholars, students and the public will be able to have access to memorable NBC news and entertainment broadcasts of the past. These donations—with some others made to the Library of Congress which has a cooperative arrangement with the Museum—are the only archival gift NBC contemplates at this time.

NBC News has an archival service through which news film and tapes may be purchased for file and reference use only. Costs of printing, dubbing, research and other related services are borne by the purchaser.

Most importantly, NBC is unable to permit any outside use of its program materials unless it has first been satisfied that copyright and other contractual rights have been protected.

NBC does not own many of the programs it broadcasts. Instead, it is licensed by independent program suppliers merely to broadcast the program locally or on a network basis. In most instances, therefore, permission for taping or otherwise reproducing the images or sounds we broadcast has to be obtained directly from the program suppliers themselves.

As for the few programs NBC does own, a combination of copyright considerations and various union and other clearance problems prevent us from letting these shows be taped off the air. This restriction applies to most news and documentary programs as well as to entertainment.

NBC does have a limited licensing arrangement in the news area for taping by schools and libraries. It provides a one-year license, for a fee of fifty dollars, to tape off the air *only* the following programs: "NBC Nightly News,"

"Meet the Press," NBC News elections coverage and NBC coverage of Presidential press conferences.

NBC tries in another way to accommodate the interest of education institutions in documentaries and other programs of educational value. Wherever possible, we make these programs available, after broadcast, for educational distribution in the form of videotape cassettes and 16 mm. film prints. There is a fee for the service. Information on this, with a catalogue of titles available, can be obtained by writing to our educational distributor, Films, Inc., 1144 Wilmette Avenue, Wilmette, Illinois 60091.

We appreciate your interest and hope this information is useful to you. I have no objection to your publishing this letter.

Sincerely,

Robert O'Neil (signed)
Administrator, Corporate Affairs Department

CBS replied but requested that the letter not be published. ABC did not reply. Neither CBS nor NBC mentions question (2) Appendix B, regarding fair use.

III

THE IMPACT OF COPYRIGHT LAW ON EDUCATIONAL RESOURCE INSTITUTIONS

CBS v. Vanderbilt University:
Taping the Evening News

> In a free and open society, no subject matter of a claim to copyright is vested with more public interest than television network news broadcasts; to preclude their reasonable use by members of the public for research and study contravenes the Free Speech and Free Press Clause of the First Amendment.
>
> Defendant's Rebuttal in *CBS v. Vanderbilt*

To our knowledge, *CBS v. Vanderbilt,* here described by Cosette Kies of the George Peabody Library School, is the only litigation between a major media corporation and a university. In 1973, CBS objected to Vanderbilt's Television News Archive as a violation of its copyrights. Today, the archive continues its operation after an out-of-court settlement in 1976 and the passage of the Baker Amendment that granted statutory protection for Vanderbilt.

In the context of this volume, an especially interesting feature of Vanderbilt's defense was its denial that CBS could copyright its news programs; a corollary of this was its refusal to employ the fair use defense. In addition to its denial of the copyrightability of television news, Vanderbilt relied on a First Amendment defense.

As indicated by the current policy statements included by Kies, Vanderbilt has retreated from its outright denial of television news copyrightability. It now urges users to "be advised that some of the materials in the collection contain a notice of copyright" and that they should "be guided by provisions of the [copyright] statute in using materials. . . ." Vanderbilt is also extremely cautious about uses of its archival material and requires the presence of an archive employee at any location where a public "performance" of its tapes (as opposed to a class or study session) is made. Copying the tapes is also forbidden.

8

THE CBS-VANDERBILT LITIGATION: TAPING THE EVENING NEWS

Cosette Kies

On December 21, 1973, a complaint was filed by the Columbia Broadcasting System against Vanderbilt University. Nearly three years later to the day, December 20, 1976, the lawsuit was dropped. The subject of the suit was CBS's claim that Vanderbilt University was violating the network's copyright and making unauthorized and illegal use of network property by renting at less than cost the tapes, or segments of them, to individuals requesting them.

The defendant in the case, Vanderbilt University, originated and presently maintains the Vanderbilt Television News Archive, which is administered by the Joint University Libraries of Vanderbilt University, George Peabody College for Teachers, and Scarritt College in Nashville, Tennessee. This service consists of videotaping, preserving, abstracting, and indexing the evening newscasts of three major commercial television broadcasting networks: ABC, CBS, and NBC. The Television News Archive has also taped special news events, such as President Nixon's trip to China, national political conventions, and the Watergate hearings. Taping is presently restricted to the evening news broadcasts and other special newscasts. The programs are recorded and included in the archive's abstracts and indexes exactly as aired, in Nashville, complete with commercials. Since 1971, each frame is recorded with an overprint of the network's initials, the date of the broadcast, and the time of day (Central Standard Time) at ten second intervals.[1]

The Television News Archive was the idea of a Vanderbilt alumnus, Paul C. Simpson, who discovered on a visit to the broadcasting networks in New York in 1968 that no permanent records were being kept of national television news. Simpson was informed by network officials that the cost of preserving such tapes would be prohibitive. As a result of Simpson's concern, the Television News Archive was founded at Vanderbilt, funded primarily from private sources.[2] In 1968, the Archive started taping. A paid staff was added in 1971. Additional sophistications since that time include the abstracts and indexes and the network/date/time overprinting on the tapes.[3]

Seen by the founders primarily as a library service for scholars, students, and historians, the archive has been used by students (individually and in classes), authors, scholars, and public officials.[4] The New York State Commission investigating the Attica uprising used the archive tapes, as has the Council on Children, Media, and Merchandising. Archive personnel categorize most individual users as being from the fields of communications, history, and political science. The House of Representatives used it during the hearings on charges of news staging by the networks.[5] The index and abstracts were abused, according to Fred Friendly, by The Institute for American Strategy in its Lefever report on national defense coverage by television.[6] The National News Council has used the abstracts on broadcasts that pertained to their study of presidential complaints about the news media.[7]

The complaint in *CBS v. Vanderbilt* was based on twenty-three points delineating CBS's claims about the extent of its control of copyright.[8] CBS President Arthur R. Taylor stated in a letter to Alexander Heard, Chancellor of Vanderbilt University:

> If Vanderbilt is allowed the misuse of our property, there is the danger that other, perhaps less reputable individuals and organizations would use our materials for their own ends. The harm to the CBS journalistic product and reputation could be incalculable.

The Vanderbilt reply to this argument, as stated in the two motions to dismiss the CBS suit, included:

> Claims of copyright . . . cannot stand because of the free-speech and free-press clauses of the First Amendment of the United States Constitution. . . . The speech present on the "CBS News with Walter Cronkite" is not merely the speech of CBS or of Walter Cronkite, it is the speech of Presidents, senators, congressmen, governors, and other citizens, speech which exercises a vital influence on the lives of all Americans, and which is, indeed, "the essence of self-government."

Vanderbilt's second motion stated that the U.S. Copyright Office "exceeded its statutory authority in registering a claim for copyright of a television news broadcast as an unpublished motion picture."[9]

In another letter to a mass-circulation periodical investigating the case, President Taylor wrote:

> CBS has stated repeatedly that its only interest in this dispute is protection of its copyrighted materials from misuse by others. . . . CBS cannot permit the

> unauthorized duplication, editing or trafficking in CBS broadcasts any more
> than authors, scholars, newspapers, or book publishers would allow such
> violation of their copyrights.[10]

This argument reiterates the ninth point of the CBS complaint against Vanderbilt:

> Each such program is therefore entitled to the full protection afforded by the
> statutes of the United States for the protection of the copyrighted works, and
> the Plaintiff, as the owner of such works and such copyrights, is entitled to all
> the remedies provided by law for any infringement thereof.[11]

Barbara A. Ringer, Register of Copyrights, observed in 1974:

> Judging from the briefs I have seen there appears to be a deliberate effort to
> provoke a confrontation over the extent to which copyright should be al-
> lowed to control the fixation and later dissemination of matters of current
> interest and historical value. Vanderbilt seems much less interested in de-
> fending the case on the basis of fair use than on the ground that copyright
> registration over materials such as national news broadcasts should be sharply
> limited or eliminated altogether.[12]

This comment seemed appropriate, since Vanderbilt's defense indeed pointed out that news broadcasts could not be copyrighted. It also argued that copyright conferred primarily "the right to control the use of the copyrighted work for economic gain."[13] The main thrust of Vanderbilt's defense, therefore, did not rely on the fair use concept, since it was argued that "this doctrine is not applicable unless a work is protected by a valid copyright."[14]

The case has been dropped without prejudice by CBS and the new Copyright Law which went into effect on January 1, 1978, specifically authorizes the taping of audiovisual news programs.[15] That would seem at first glance to relegate the aborted CBS-Vanderbilt case to the classification of an interesting historical footnote. Certain occurrences while the case was active, however, and other unresolved issues involving fair use and copyright make this case currently important in its own right, as well as providing a framework for the exploration of copyright issues which may be tested in the future by means of other lawsuits and settlements.

BACKGROUND

One area repeatedly discussed during copyright revision was that involving technological advances not covered by the Copyright Law of 1909 or its amendments. Works covered by that law were published, printed items—including books, periodicals, newspapers, lectures, sermons, addresses, dramatic and musical compositions, maps, works of art and reproductions of works of art, scientific and technical drawings, photographs, prints and labels, including those used for articles of merchandise, motion picture photoplays, motion pictures other than photoplays, public performances, and recording rights for nondramatic literary works.

In simple terms, *copyright* is the right of authors and artists to benefit from the sale of the product of their intellectual labor. This right was established in Article 1, Section 8 of the U.S. Constitution: "The Congress shall have power . . . to promote the progress of science and useful arts, by securing for limited times to authors and inventors the exclusive rights to their respective writing and discoveries." The House committee that recommended the 1909 act said, however, that copyright was "not primarily for the benefit of the author, but primarily for the benefit of the public."[16] Supreme Court decisions dealing with the 1909 act made plain the precedence of free access over reward to the owner:

> Courts passing upon particular claims of infringement must occasionally subordinate the copyright holder's interest in a maximum financial return to the great public interest in the development of art, science, and industry.[17]

The new copyright law, passed in 1976 and enacted in 1978, has been modernized to make specific references to newer forms of communication, but legal interpretation will still be necessary, particularly in dealing with Section 106, exclusive rights in copyrighted works, and Sections 107 and 108, limitations on exclusive rights: fair use; and limitations on exclusive rights: reproduction by libraries and archives.[18]

OWNERSHIP

The legal aspect of the actual ownership of broadcasts, the news specifically, is an area that requires further clarification. News itself is not copyrightable. In other words, the information, or news itself, is not protected by copyright, but the actual newspaper article, television broadcast, or periodical article is protected. Some court decisions that have dealt with this problem include the *Fortnightly Corporation v. United Artists Television*, the *Teleprompter Corporation v. CBS*, and the *Williams and Wilkins* case.

The ownership issue in the CBS-Vanderbilt suit was complicated by the CBS claim that the network had offered Vanderbilt, prior to 1968, a royalty-free, nonexclusive license to make videotapes of the evening news and permit use of these tapes at the university. Vanderbilt claimed that it received no such formal offer.

Taping

A possible outgrowth of the CBS-Vanderbilt case was the practice of television networks providing schools with a license for a fee in exchange for the right to videocopy.[19] At present there is no clear-cut set of guidelines for legal copying in school use, as evidenced by the BOCES case and preliminary injunction (see Chapter 13). In the absence of guidelines, individual distributors and producers have established their own licensing requirements. In the spring of 1978, a survey of nearly thirty program distributors revealed no common patterns. CBS News, for example, charges an annual license of $25.00 and up, depending on size of the school system, with the right to hold for thirty days. NBC, on the other hand, requires negotiation for an annual license to record and hold hard news programs.[20]

Storage

The primary motivation for founding the Television News Archive was that the three major commercial television networks were not retaining copies of their news broadcasts. This may have been due, in part, to television news being originally, in the words of Erik Barnouw, ". . . an umpromising child . . . the schizophrenic offspring of the theater newsreel and the radio newscast, and was confused as to its role and future course."[21] However, since its inception in the early 1950s, television, within a twenty-year period of growth, became the source of news for an estimated 64 percent of Americans.[22] During that twenty-year period, the growth and intrigues of CBS News have been discussed and written about by former staff and CBS observers.[23]

Since early 1974 both CBS and NBC have been recording and storing copies of their evening news broadcasts. CBS entered into an agreement with the National Archives in Washington, D.C., to distribute videocassettes of CBS News broadcasts to libraries according to the American Library Association's Interlibrary Loan Code, as did NBC at a later date. Also, CBS's chairman, William Paley, was instrumental in setting up the Museum of Broadcasting in New York, which stores radio and television programs.[24] Neither of these archives, however, has complete runs of evening news of all three networks from 1968, as does the Vanderbilt Television News Archive.

In addition to these archives and the Television News Archive at Vanderbilt, the new copyright law provided in Section 113 for the establishment of the American Television and Radio Archive at the Library of Congress. Although presently in planning stages, this government-authorized archive has the potential to systematize and provide leadership to the broadcasting archives founded earlier.

Access to stored materials in the various archives is generally provided by traditional indexing methods. The Vanderbilt Television News Archive has an index and abstract. The indexing is based on descriptive abstracts of the news items, designed to enable retrieval from the tapes. These indexes and abstracts have been published monthly since January 1972, and a project to index and abstract the 1968-71 tapes will soon be completed. Approximately 500 copies of the *Television News Index and Abstracts* are distributed worldwide.[25] Since 1974 CBS has provided an index to its news tapes retained since that date.

The indexes and abstracts of the Vanderbilt Television News Archive permit the user to request compilations of videotapes which are compilations of news items on certain subjects. CBS objects to such compiling of tapes by subject matter upon request and to the lending of these compilations along with total or partial broadcasts. Vanderbilt does charge a minimal user fee which does not, it contends, even pay for the user costs involved. Vanderbilt officials also argue that putting together compilations of subject tapes and lending tapes outside the archive itself is a traditional library service. Since books can be sent to scholars by means of interlibrary loan, it should be possible to send information in tape form for the same purpose.[26] No changes in the administration, policies, and charges for the archive materials have been made by Vanderbilt officials since CBS originally brought suit in 1973,[27] although rising production costs necessitated charging a subscription fee for the abstracts and index early in 1979.[28]

USE

Even though the new Copyright Law protects the Vanderbilt Television Archive, the materials used in the archive adhere to the stipulations of the new law. The descriptive brochure for the archive contains the following statement regarding copyrights:

> The General Revision of Copyright Law (Public Law 94-553), in provisions effective January 1, 1978, includes specific references to copyrights in audiovisual works and to the archiving of television news broadcasts by archives such as the Vanderbilt Television News Archive. Users of the Archive should be advised that some of the materials in the collection contain a notice of copyright and be guided by the provisions of the statute in using materials from the Archive.

Every applicant for use of the tapes signs the following:

LOAN AGREEMENT

> It is hereby agreed and confirmed by signature below that the loan of materials from the TELEVISION NEWS ARCHIVE of Vanderbilt University is subject to the following conditions:

1. That no copy of this material, on audio tape, video tape, or motion picture film will be made.

2. That this material will not be rebroadcast over television or radio.

3. That this material will not be publicly exhibited except in the presence of a representative of the Vanderbilt Television News Archive, whose expenses for this purpose are to be paid by the exhibitor.

    NOTE: "Publicly exhibited" means being displayed in a place to which the general public has unimpeded access or to groups not otherwise regularly assembled for the purpose of study.

4. That use of this material is subject to the stated service charges, including costs of any tape damaged in use.

DATE_____ SIGNATURE _____

In provisions effective January 1, 1978, the General Revision of Copyright Law (Public Law 94-553) includes specific references to copyrights in audiovisual works. Users of material from the Vanderbilt Television News Archive should be aware that some telecasts in the collection carry a notice of copyright and be guided by the statute in their use of material from the Archive.

User statistics from 1977 for the Television News Archive tend to show in-depth, specific use of the tapes for scholarly purposes. Over the course of the year 654 services were requested, including reference questions. In a hundred and one instances tapes were loaned to individuals and institutions in forty-two states and six foreign countries. Current projects involving archive tapes include studies on busing and the energy crisis. Duke University has embarked on an extensive analysis of political elections as shown on television. George Washington University Library in Washington, D.C. has established a department of audiovisual materials which involves the use and study of videotapes from the archive.[29]

The use of the archive's tapes appears to fall within the guidelines of the proviso in Subsection 108 of the new copyright law.[30] Although there is no definite statement pertaining to the tapes, it could be argued that a news item for the evening news is similar to that of an article in a periodical. From the "limited" use of the tapes it would seem reasonable to argue that the use of the archive would not be in violation of the spirit of the new copyright law.

CONCLUSION

When CBS filed its suit against Vanderbilt in 1973, it was a clouded case from the beginning. Certainly the old Copyright Law of 1909 was inadequate to base a court decision on. There was apparent reluctance on the part of the court in Nashville to place the case on the docket, possibly for this reason. The new copyright law, although it acknowledges the existence of electronic media and archival aspects of copyright, still awaits clarification.

Another aspect which cannot even be speculated about is the motivation behind the original filing of the suit and its subsequent withdrawal. The legal implications are such that this case, and others like it, are not "settled," nor can they be until there is further clarification. Certainly, the value of the Vanderbilt Television News Archive is beyond question. The historical achievement alone of providing precise material to scholars not yet born is obvious.[31] The issue is not really the value of the project but its legality. Fair use and the First Amendment as opposed to copyright in its guise of exclusive control is the issue. The balancing of interests will be a prolonged and delicate task.

NOTES

[1]An earlier account of this lawsuit was published by the author, "Copyright versus Free Access: CBS and Vanderbilt University Square Off." *Wilson Library Bulletin* 50 (November 1975): 242-46.

[2]It seems ironic that it was a businessman, Paul Simpson, who recognized the potential scholarly worth of the national news broadcasts rather than the university officials and faculty. Skip Wollenberg, "Archives of TV News Unique," *Austin American-Statesman*, Sept. 17, 1978, p. 13.

[3]Kathy Sawyer, "The Battle for Walter Cronkite," *The Tennessean Magazine*, July 7, 1974, p. 16.

[4]Interview with James Pilkington, Director, Television News Archive, Joint University Libraries, Vanderbilt University, Nashville, Tennessee, April 23, 1978.

[5]Sawyer, p. 16.

[6]Fred W. Friendly, *The Good Guys, the Bad Guys and the First Amendment: Free Speech vs. Fairness in Broadcasting* (New York: Random House, 1975), pp. 180-81. The report claimed to have examined actual tapes and transcripts to analyze news coverage, but actually there was reliance on the abstracts. This circumstance was not mentioned in the report's account of its methodology. Ernest Lefever, *TV and National Defense: An Analysis of CBS News, 1972-1973* (Boston, Va.: The Institute for American Strategy Press, 1974), p. 25.

[7]"CBS Asks Vanderbilt to Halt Outside Use of Tapes," *Broadcasting*, Jan. 7, 1974, pp. 32-33.

[8]Columbia Broadcasting System, Inc. v. Vanderbilt University, complaint filed in the United States District Court for the Middle District of Tennessee, Nashville Division (Dec. 20, 1973).

[9]"CBS, Vanderbilt Battle over Taping News," *The Chronicle of Higher Education*, Sept. 30, 1974, p. 11.

[10]John Weisman, "The Network vs. the University," *TV Guide*, June 29, 1974, p. 3.

[11]CBS complaint, p.3; see footnote 8 above.

[12]Barbara A. Ringer, "The Demonology of Copyright," R.R. Bowker Memorial Lecture, New Series, Oct. 24, 1974, p. 9.

[13]CBS v. Vanderbilt, No. 7736, Defendant's Rebuttal, p. 18.

[14]*Ibid.*, p. 36.

[15]The clear position in the new copyright law was due, in part, to the Baker Amendment. Senator Howard Baker stated, "Inasmuch as this activity is strongly impressed with the public interest, it seems to me that my amendment asks little of the three major networks who have been given licenses which are conditioned solely on their obligation to serve the public interest, convenience, and necessity." U.S. Congress, Senate,

Senator Baker introducing the Amendment of the General Revision of the Copyright Law—Amendment, S. 2487. Amendment 1803, 93d Cong., 2d Sess., Aug. 15, 1974 *Congressional Record,* vol. 120.

[16]H.R. *Report* No. 2222, 60th Cong., 2d Sess., p. 7.

[17]Berlin v. E. C. Publications, Inc., 329 F.2d 541 (2d Cir. 1964).

[18]Michael H. Cardozo, "To Copy or Not to Copy for Teaching and Scholarship: What Shall I Tell My Client?" *The Journal of College and University Law* 4 (Winter 1976-1977): 62.

[19]F. William Troost, "Off-the-Air Videotaping: An Issue of Growing Importance," *Audiovisual Instruction 81* (June-July 1976): 63.

[20]"Videotaping of Copyrighted Films Enjoined Despite Educational Use," *BNA News and Comment* 370 (March 16, 1978): A-2.

[21]Erik Barnouw, *A History of Broadcasting in the United States from 1933.* 3 vols. (New York: Oxford, 1970), 3: 40.

[22]Weisman, "The Network," p. 4.

[23]Examples are Fred W. Friendly, *Due to Circumstances Beyond Our Control. . .* (New York: Random House, 1967) and Gary Paul Gates, *Air Time: The Inside Story of CBS News* (New York: Harper and Row, 1978).

[24]Jody McMahon, "Keeping History Alive," *Videography* Jan. 1978, pp. 16-18.

[25]Pilkington interview.

[26]Interview with Frank Grisham, Director, Joint University Libraries, Vanderbilt University, Nashville, Tennessee, Mar. 28, 1975.

[27]Pilkington interview.

[28]"VU Sets $60 Fee for TV News Index," *Nashville Banner,* Oct. 31, 1978, p. 27.

[29]Pilkington interview.

[30]Pilkington interview.

[31]Melinda Golub, "Not by Books Alone: Library Copying of Nonprint, Copyrighted Material," *Law Library Journal,* May, 1977, p. 165.

Seeking Copyright Clearances for an Audiovisual Center

The copyright owners of audiovisual material have consistently pressed for restrictive interpretations of fair use. This official stance generally urges potential users of their material to secure advance permission. The Copyright Office takes a neutral stance on unresolved fair use issues but tells the public, "The safest course to follow is to get permission before using copyrighted material" ("*Fair Use" of Copyrighted Works*, Circular 20, June 1976). Government-funded institutions often align themselves with the policy of caution; a typical directive to users of AV center services will contain a statement, such as—"Evening educational programs (Public Broadcast Network or commercial broadcast) will be duplicated only if the request is accompanied by a written release of copyright from the producer" (*Copyright Law Information for Educators, 1978*, Area Education Agency 12/Iowa/Media Center; pamphlet combines Copyright Office interpretations and local policy adaptation).

But what happens when one goes by the book? Jeanne Masson Douglas was director of a media center when she wrote this essay, which first appeared in *Audiovisual Instruction* (December 1974; reproduced here by their permission.) Although her experiences date back several years, they remain typical for the permission seeker. In the fair use conferences that have brought together producers and users, there has been a frank acknowledgment that producers have not really been organized to cope with requests for permissions and that some sort of centralized clearing house operation may be necessary to remedy the complaints registered by Douglas and others. (See especially, *Conference on Video Recording for Educational Uses*, July 19-22, 1977, Airlie, Va.)

9

SEEKING COPYRIGHT CLEARANCES FOR AN AUDIOVISUAL CENTER

JEANNE MASSON DOUGLAS

One of the major responsibilities of the instructional developer is that of making instructional materials available in an appropriate medium. Materials are often not useful in their existing forms; they may have to be altered to fit specific course objectives, to accommodate a preferred instructional mode, such as independent study or inter-active instruction, or simply to provide multiple copies. Whatever the reasons for wanting to modify commercial instructional media, the copyright issue is unavoidable, and obtaining copyright clearances often becomes the responsibility of the instructional developer.

Having been involved for the last five years in instructional development activities, either in a management role or as a consultant, I have accumulated considerable data related to acquiring copyright clearances. During this time, I have communicated with several publishers, producers, chairmen of national associations and organizations, and even with presidents of private corporations in attempts to obtain permissions to reproduce their materials. The results have been interesting, and at times, surprising.

In my early attempts as a copyright agent, I made use of a form letter. I soon learned that this technique was getting only delayed responses or no response at all. An original letter for each transaction was found to be much more successful. Every letter had two things in common, however: the specification that the media we produced would be used only within our own institution, and that the materials would be used by our students only. (Sometimes phone calls have been necessary to prompt a response, but since I never make a duplication permission agreement except in writing, a written document is ultimately needed.) To demonstrate good faith in complying with the fair use principle, I always explain the purpose and effect of the use of the reproduced material, the quantity needed, and the nature of the reproduction.

My respondents have been of an amazing variety. At times, I have been fortunate to deal with someone known as the Rights and Permissions Officer or the Contract and Copyright Officer, or even the Product Development Director. On other occasions, I have been directed to the Public Relations Officer or the Editor-in-Chief. Often, it has been necessary to negotiate with the Vice-President, Executive Vice-President, or the President of a firm. On one occasion, the producer concerned would not communicate except through his lawyer.

Another variation which keeps things interesting is what I have decided to call *passing the buck*. For example, a New Jersey distributor referred me to a California producer who referred me to a New York photographer. And a Middle Western publisher referred me to the copyright holder, who happened to be based in Japan. (Actually, this latter transaction took less time, in number of mail days, than many more localized arrangements.)

As varied as the respondents are the responses themselves. These have ranged from the law firm's "no . . . and furthermore . . ." to the following: "I am happy to grant you permission. . . . I will also be pleased to supply lists of other materials that you may wish to consider for your programs . . ." and "I appreciate your courtesy in requesting permission. Thank you for asking. I hope we have helped in designing and developing improvements in your curriculum." One producer scolded, via telephone, "Why did you ask? Why didn't you just go down behind the barn and do it?" In extreme contrast to this attitude, however, is that of the publisher who sends along a printed copy of the company's policy statement related to copyright. One New York film producer responded to my letter with a telephone call, explaining that he was willing to grant permission verbally but would not "put it in writing because of possible complications." Again in contrast, a New Jersey publisher responded with a Permission to Reprint form which I had to complete in triplicate. An Illinois media producer responded, "Enclosed is our duplication policy statement to accommodate those making legitimate requests and to inform those duplicating illegally that a policy does exist. Dealers are asked to make positive identification of known illegal duplicators."

A review of some specific examples of clearance policies is helpful. For clarity, I categorize by media type.

PRINT MATERIALS

Print→print

A New York publisher granted permission to make 500 copies of a short story for a $12 fee and use of a credit line on each copy.

A New Jersey publisher granted permission to reproduce a series of tests.

A Colorado publisher would not grant permission to duplicate an article because reprints were available at 50¢ each.

Print→nonprint

An Ohio publisher granted permission to copy pages from a dictionary and a thesaurus as slides.

A New York publisher granted permission to convert all the illustrations of a book to slides and the text to tape.

An Illinois manufacturer granted permission to copy as slides all the illustrations in a textbook.

A New Jersey manufacturer granted permission to copy all the illustrations of three of its books.

A California manufacturer provided permission, or sources of permission, by chapter and page of every illustration in its book, a listing consisting of five pages of single-spaced typing.

A national organization granted permission to convert all the illustrations in its book to slides.

NONPRINT MATERIALS—AUDIO

Disc→Cassette

A New York producer's vice-president would not grant permission. In response to a later inquiry, the company's vice-president for copyright granted permission.

A California producer permitted six copies each of ten recordings.

A New York producer would not grant permission for reasons of "deprivation of royalty."

An Illinois producer allowed two copies only for independent study use.

A Colorado producer allowed one copy only, and that only to protect the original.

Reel→Cassette

A New York producer granted permission for a first copy, and charged 40 percent of the initial cost for each additional copy.

A Massachusetts producer of language tapes granted permission to convert an entire course from reel to cassette.

Cassette→Cassette

A New York science materials producer and a New York language materials producer allowed the making of one copy to protect the master tape.

An Illinois producer refused permission to duplicate, but agreed to replace damaged tapes for $1.00.

A university's audiovisual production facility allowed one copy of each cassette purchased.

NONPRINT MATERIALS—VISUAL

Filmstrip→slides

A New York producer granted permission to cut filmstrip and mount the frames as slides, but would not grant permission to duplicate photographically.

A New York producer would not grant permission to duplicate, but offered to produce slides from the filmstrips for $20 per set above the cost of the filmstrips.

A California producer replied that permission could not be granted because the material (regretfully) was in the public domain.

A California college audiovisual production facility would not grant permission.

A Massachusetts producer granted permission to make two slides only from each frame in a filmstrip.

Slides→slides

Illinois, New York, New Jersey, and California producers would not grant permission. One producer did offer to provide multiple copies of sets at reduced cost.

A New York producer agreed to grant permission at 40 percent of the list price of the sets.

NONPRINT MATERIALS—PROGRAMS

Filmstrip/Record→slide/cassette

A New York producer replied, "Since it is not for commercial use, do what is best for your purpose."

Slide/Cassette→slide/cassette

A California producer said "yes," no conditions.

NONPRINT MATERIALS—TELEVISION

CBS Affiliate Station

Program Director replied, "Go ahead (videotaping off-the-tube, prime-time), since it is for one-time use and erase the tape after that use."

PBS Affiliate Station

Program Director replied "Yes, We can't give you permission, but neither can we deny you the right to do. (!) O.K., for onetime use."

In many cases, I have found that permission depends on the type of media being converted. A New York producer, for example, would not allow the duplication of slides, but agreed to converting disc recordings and text to cassette recordings. In other cases, permission would be granted if you were willing to pay the price. In one case, the fee was equal to the cost of the material itself; in another, fees were set at $100 per tape, $100 per filmstrip, and $50 per booklet. Sometimes, on the other hand, agreements seemed to be more reasonable, such as granting permission to convert transparencies to slides and text to cassette for an entire program, the only condition being that you adopt their text and cite publication information in your reproduction.

It is not easy to draw simple conclusions from these many experiences. Every situation has its unique set of circumstances, and constraints, and will differ as the educational institutions and the commercial suppliers differ. Every transaction must be worked out formally and diplomatically. It often becomes the responsibility of the instructional developer to assure that this is done. Faculty who do not fully understand the complexities of the problem should be provided with in-service programs or other means of becoming aware; the instructional developer will need all the sympathy he can get from his colleagues. Meantime, more publishers and producers are making their media available in a variety of formats. This fact, and new copyright legislation, should result in a less complicated and more satisfying task for the instructional developer charged with acquiring copyright clearances.

The Duplication of Audiovisual Materials in Libraries

Jerome K. Miller is author and editor of several books on the educational implications of copyright law. In his essay, he describes the likely impact of the
Copyright Act of 1976 upon libraries with audiovisual holdings. He sees a frustrating situation for the librarian confronted with patron requests for duplication. Because the law either forbids duplication of audiovisual materials or fails
to give clear authorization for types of duplication not explicitly forbidden,
Miller does not believe that librarians will soon be able to resolve conflicting
demands placed upon the law and library patrons.

10

THE DUPLICATION OF AUDIOVISUAL MATERIALS IN LIBRARIES

Jerome K. Miller

Most articles on the new copyright law appearing in library literature pertain to the photocopying of printed materials and the transfer of photocopies in response to interlibrary loan requests. This is certainly a legitimate concern but it overlooks another important area of library service. Most libraries include audiovisual materials in their collections and these materials are subject to demands for copying. Although the new copyright law gives libraries fairly clear guidelines for the duplication of printed material, it is much less clear in the guidance it gives for the duplication of audiovisual materials. The relevant provisions of the law are found in Sections 108 and 107.

A library's right to make photocopies for patrons is provided in Section 108. It also gives libraries certain rights to duplicate audiovisual materials. This right is quite limited by the provisions of Section 108, subsection (h):

> The rights of reproduction and distribution under this section do not apply to a musical work, a pictorial, graphic or sculptural work, or a motion picture or other audiovisual work other than an audiovisual work dealing with news, except that no such limitation shall apply with respect to rights granted by subsections (b) and (c), or with respect to pictorial or graphic works published as illustrations, diagrams, or similar adjuncts to works of which copies are reproduced or distributed in accordance with subsections (d) and (e).[1]

A quick reading of this subsection would suggest that all or almost all audiovisual materials are protected from copying. A closer reading reveals several exceptions. The right to duplicate "audiovisual works dealing with news" stems from the *CBS v. Vanderbilt University* suit. (This point is treated at length in Chapter 8.)

Two additional rights are granted in subsections (b) and (c) of Section 108. Subsection (b) permits a library or archive to duplicate *unpublished* works (including audiovisual materials) in facsimile form for the purpose of preservation and security or to deposit a copy of the work in another library or archive for research purposes. A copy made under this provision cannot be given or sold to library patrons. The copy must remain the property of the library or archive, although it can be loaned to patrons under the usual procedures.

Subsection (c) gives libraries and archives the right to reproduce *published* works (including audiovisual materials) for the purpose of replacing damaged, deteriorating, lost, or stolen copies, if "an unused replacement cannot be obtained at a fair price."[2] If the copy is missing or if it is so badly damaged that it cannot be copied, then the library or archive may reproduce a copy found in another library or archive. This subsection opens the way for duplicating out-of-print sound recordings, prints, posters, pictures, etc. As in subsection (b), a copy made under this provision cannot be given or sold to a patron. The copy must remain the property of the library or archive, although it can be loaned to a patron under the usual loan procedures.

Subsection (h) also provides for the duplication of diagrams, charts, and pictures accompaning textual matter in books and periodicals. When a patron asks a library or archive to photocopy a journal article or part of a book, the library or archive may also duplicate the illustrations accompanying the textual matter. This also applies to photocopies made in response to interlibrary loan requests.

The thorniest problem centers on the injunction in subsection (h) against the copying of audiovisual materials: "The rights of reproduction and distribution under this section do not apply to a musical work, a pictorial, graphic or sculptural work, or a motion picture or other audiovisual work. . . ." This seems to rule out the duplication of almost all audiovisual materials outside the four exceptions just identified. The House committee report accompanying the copyright law provides an interesting comment on this prohibition:

> Although subsection (h) generally removes musical, graphic, and audiovisual works from the specific exceptions of section 108, it is important to recognize that the doctrine of fair use under section 107 remains fully applicable to the photocopying or other reproduction of such works. In the case of music, for example, it would be fair use for a scholar doing musicological research to have a library supply a copy of a portion of a score or to reproduce portions of a phonorecord of a work. Nothing in section 108 impairs the applicability of the fair use doctrine to a wide variety of situations involving photocopying or other reproduction by a library of copyrighted material in its collections, where the user requests the reproduction for legitimate scholarly or research pruposes.

This indicates that Section 108 does not exclude libraries and archives from using the provisions of Section 107, on fair use.[4] The fair use section provides greater latitude for the duplication of audiovisual materials. Section 107, for all its importance, is very brief:

> Notwithstanding the provisions of section 106 [which outline the rights of the copyright owner], the fair use of a copyrighted work, including such use by reproduction in copies or phonorecords or by any other means specified by that section, for purposes such as criticism, comment, news reporting, teaching (including multiple copies for classroom use), scholarship, or research, is not an infringement of copyright. in determining whether the use made of a work in any particular case is a fair use the factors to be considered shall include—
>
> (1) the purpose and character of the use, including whether such use is of a commercial nature or is for nonprofit educational purposes;
> (2) the nature of the copyrighted work;
> (3) the amount and substantiality of the portion used in relation to the copyrighted work as a whole; and
> (4) the effect of the use upon the potential market for or value of the copyrighted work.[5]

The four criteria were drawn from the common law and they are not always easy to apply. The congressional reports which accompanied the law provide some help in applying them to the duplication of audiovisual materials.

THE PURPOSE AND CHARACTER OF THE USE

The first criterion speaks to the purpose and character of the use, including whether the application is of a commercial or a nonprofit nature. Tax-supported libraries are obviously nonprofit institutions, but what of other types of libraries? Section 108 indicates that libraries of business firms can enjoy the benefits of that section as long as (1) the library itself is operated as a nonprofit unit within the firm, (2) the library's collection is open to qualified researchers from outside the firm. This would seem to provide some guidance in the application of this section to the libraries of commercial dance academies, photography schools, art schools, art galleries, advertising agencies, etc.

In applying the first criterion, it is also important to consider the purpose of making the copies. If they are made for teaching, research, criticism, or news reporting, then greater latitude applies. If the copies are to be made for direct financial gain, then the fair use doctrine must be narrowly construed. Finally, we must ask whether the copies are to be given away, or to be sold. If the copies are given away, or if a small cost-recovery fee is charged, then one enjoys greater latitude; if the copies are sold for a profit (as is the practice in a small number of libraries) then the copying must be carefully limited to remain within the bounds of fair use. The few libraries that attempt to profit from their duplicating services—they cover other operating expenses with the surplus income—would probably be wise to reconsider this policy.

The criterion of the purpose and character of the use also addresses itself to the question of the number of copies being made from a work. The committee reports provide specific guidance on this point. A library may make enough copies of an item to enable a teacher to distribute the copies to a class. (This assumes, of course, that all the other criteria have been met.) The copies must be limited to the class for which they were made and only enough copies for that class may be made. Only a single copy may be made for the other applications, such as research, news reporting, criticism, etc. This does not prevent a library from duplicating the same visual or aural materials a number of times to meet a number of requests. It requires only that the copies be made one at a time, as the demand arises. Copies cannot be stockpiled to meet anticipated needs.

Some of the most generous provisions in Section 107 pertain to copying by students. The Senate report provides rather clear guidelines on this point:

> For example, copying of extracts by pupils as exercises in shorthand or typing classes or for foreign language study, or recordings of performances by music students for purposes of analysis and criticism, would normally be regarded as a fair use unless the copies or phonorecords were retained or duplicated.
>
> Likewise, a single reproduction of excerpts from a copyrighted work by a student calligrapher . . . in a learning situation would be a fair use of the copyrighted work.[6]

The fair use section of the copyright law has clear applications to the use of duplicating equipment owned by the library. It is not limited to the traditional copying on coin-operated photocopying machines or microfilm reader-printers. It also applies to tape recorders, cameras, and video equipment provided by libraries for student use. But this generous provision has two obvious limitations: the copies must be made for the direct purpose of learning, and they should be erased or destroyed when they have served their purpose. They must not be included in a library collection. The requirement that the copies be erased or destroyed should not be interpreted so rigidly as to prevent students from saving a few sample items for an employment portfolio.

The congressional reports provide one final warning about the purpose and character of the use. It is acceptable for a teacher, critic, reporter, scholar, etc., to have a library copy part of an in-print, copyrighted work for use in the patron's scholarship. If, however, these copies are accumulated over a period of time with other parts of the same work, or with copies from other works so as to constitute a collection or an anthology, the copies made as a fair use can constitute an infringement. As long as the library employees are unaware that a patron is developing such an infringing collection or anthology, it does not create a problem for the library. If, however, a library employee know-ingly assists in the development of such a collection or anthology of visual or aural materials, then the library and its employee(s) share in the liability for the infringing activity. This injunction against collections and anthologies clearly prevents a library from building collections of slides, tape recordings, etc., copied from items that are available on the market. It does not prevent libraries from employing Section 108 (c) to duplicate out-of-print materials for the purpose of replacing damaged, deteriorat-ing, lost, or stolen items in its collection. In short, the prohibition of collections and anthologies of materials made under the terms of fair use does not prevent a library from copying a small part of a work for a patron. It only prevents libraries from (1) knowingly helping a patron build a collection or anthology, (2) maintaining such a collection in a library.

THE NATURE OF THE COPYRIGHTED WORK

The amount of copying that may be done under the terms of fair use is determined, in part, by the type of work being copied. The committee reports speak to the duplication of different types of works for classroom use. This statement of legislative intent from the Senate Report may provide some guidance to copying for other purposes, as well.

> For example, in determining whether a teacher could make one or more copies without permission, a news article from the daily press would be judged differently from a full orchestral score of a musical composition. In general terms it could be expected that the doctrine of fair use would be applied strictly to the classroom reproduction of entire works, such as musical compositions, dramas, and audiovisual works including motion pictures, which by their nature are intended for performance or public exhibition.[7]

The injunction in Section 108 (h) against the duplication of musi-cal, pictorial, graphic, and sculptural works surfaces again. In this in-stance, it is not a total prohibition on copying these performance and display materials. It is only an indication that very limited copying may be made from these materials under the terms of fair use. It is not always easy to know how much copying may be made from these materials. Some guidance is found in the "Guidelines for Educational Uses of Music" which appeared in the Conference Committee report. It is de-signed to offer guidance to fair use copying of sheet music by or for teachers. Some parallels may be drawn from it for the copying of other performance and display materials.

> The purpose of the following guidelines is to state the minimum and not the maximum standards of educational fair use under Section 107. . . .

Moreover, the following statement of guidelines is not intended to limit the types of copying permitted under the standards of fair use under judicial decision and which are stated in Section 107. . . . There may be instances in which coping which does not fall within the guidelines stated below may nonetheless be permitted under the criteria of fair use.

A. *Permissible Uses*

    1. Emergency copying to replace purchased copies which for any reason are not available for an imminent performance provided purchased replacement copies shall be substituted in due course.

    2. (a) For academic purposes other than performance, multiple copies of excerpts of works may be made, provided that the excerpts do not comprise a part of the whole which would constitute a performable unit such as a section, movement, aria, but in no case more than 10% of the whole work. The number of copies shall not exceed one copy per pupil.

    (b) For academic purposes other than performance, a single copy of an entire performable unit (section, movement, aria, etc.) that is, (1) confirmed by the copyright proprietor to be out of print or (2) unavailable except in a larger work, may be made by or for a teacher solely for the purpose of his own scholarly research or in preparation to teach a class.

    3. Printed copies which have been purchased may be edited or simplified provided that the fundamental character of the work is not distorted or the lyrics, if any, altered or lyrics added if none exist.

    4. A single copy of recordings of performances by students may be made for evaluation or rehearsal purposes and may be retained by the educational institution or individual teacher.

    5. A single copy of a sound recording (such as a tape, disc or cassette) of copyrighted music may be made from sound recordings owned by an educational institution or an individual teacher for the purpose of constructing aural exercises or examinations and may be retained by the educational institution or individual teacher. (This pertains only to the copyright of the music itself and not to any copyright which may exist in the sound recording.)

B. *Prohibitions*

    1. Copying to create or replace or substitute for anthologies, compilations or collective works.

    2. Copying of or from works intended to be "consumable" in the course of study or of teaching such as workbooks, exercises, standardized tests and answer sheets and like material.

    3. Copying for the purpose of performance, except as in A (1) above.

    4. Copying for the purpose of substituting for the purchase of music, except as in A (1) and A (2) above.

    5. Copying without inclusion of the copyright notice which appears on the printed copy.[8]

It is very important to remember that these are minimum guidelines and that copying in excess of these terms may also be a fair use. These guidelines provide some guidance to scholars or to music critics who may wish to copy a part of a work to assist them in their creative efforts. It provides almost no help for composers who might be tempted to include a passage from a copyrighted work in their own compositions.

It is unfortunate that the congressional reports did not include clearer information about the application of this section to musical recordings or illustrative materials. Clearer guidelines will probably have to await legislative or legal action.

THE AMOUNT AND SUBSTANTIALITY OF THE PORTION USED IN RELATION TO THE COPYRIGHTED WORK AS A WHOLE

Generally speaking, a library may reproduce a small part of an audiovisual work for its patrons. The comments on this point in the Senate report are oriented to the copying of printed materials by teachers and they offer almost no guidance to the copying of nonprint materials. In essence, this criterion states that one may make a single copy (or multiple copies for classroom distribution) of a small part of a copyrighted work. On that basis, one may assume that it is acceptable for a library to copy a few frames from a film or filmstrip or a few illustrations from a book of illustrations, or a small passage from a musical work for a patron who requests it, provided that the other three criteria are met.

THE EFFECT OF THE USE UPON THE POTENTIAL MARKET FOR, OR VALUE OF, THE WORK

This criterion is probably the easiest to understand and apply. If a single instance of copying deprives the copyright owner of a legitimate sale, the copying is an infringement of the copyright. Furthermore, if the repeated copying from a work has the cumulative effect of depriving the copyright owner of a sale, that is also an infringement. In applying this point it is particularly important to consider the problem of availability. This is a difficult problem for those working with the visual media. Art historians and art teachers make an extensive use of slide copies of works of art. These slides usually reproduce the art work in its entirety, although occasionally a close-up shot of a part of a work is used to emphasize a point. Some of these slides are readily available from commercial slide libraries and from art galleries. Many others, however, are not available from any known source. To limit art teachers and art historians to the small pool of available slide reproductions of art works would create a substantial hardship. The problem is usually resolved by making slides of the pictures found in art books. It is not uncommon to find an art department or art history department asking a library to make slides of all, or almost all, the pictures in a given book. This action is not motivated by unwillingness to purchase the slides from normal trade sources; the service is requested because the items needed cannot be bought. The Senate report provides some assistance in resolving this problem.

> *Availability of the work:* A key, though not necessarily determinative, factor in fair use is whether or not the work is available to the potential user. If the work is "out of print" and unavailable for purchase through normal channels,

the user may have more justification for reproducing it than in the ordinary case, but the existence of organizations licensed to provide photocopies of out-of-print works at reasonable cost is a factor to be considered.[9]

In short, if the copies are available from the original copyright owner or from an authorized distributor, the library has little justification to make more than an occasional copy of a small part of the work. If, on the other hand, copies are not available, then the library has some justification for making the copies for a patron. The lack of good sources for this type of information creates a real problem when librarians or library patrons try to find the sources of illustrative materials.

SPECIAL PROBLEMS IN THE USE OF LOCALLY PRODUCED INDEPENDENT STUDY AUDIOVISUAL PROGRAMS IN LIBRARIES

Up to this point, we have considered the library's role as a duplicating service for audiovisual materials. Many libraries, especially those in schools and colleges, offer a variety of independent study audiovisual programs which are produced within the institution. These programs are designed to meet a specific need for a specific course. They are frequently employed to introduce students to factual information (vocabulary, principles, concepts, etc.) which are basic to a course. In some institutions, entire courses or the entire curriculum is taught through these programs. In these institutions, the instructors meet students individually or in small groups for coaching, supervising laboratory sessions, and administering examinations. In a few libraries, audiovisual independent study units embody critiques of films shown in film study classes. The programs consist of stills of selected scenes along with a recording of the instructor's comments or critique. The presence of these audiovisual independent study units does not of itself create a problem with the copyright law. The problem usually occurs when the creators of these programs borrow heavily from copyrighted works to create the study units. This borrowing usually takes three forms: (1) copying pictures, charts, and diagrams from books, periodicals, and audiovisual programs; (2) copying the organization or pattern of presentation from another work; (3) using copyrighted music as background music. The problem may be compounded when the programs are produced in multiple copies to facilitate simultaneous use by a number of students.

If teachers can make multiple copies of a small part of a work for classroom distribution, one might assume that they also have the right to have multiple copies of a small part of a work made to be incorporated in an audiovisual instructional program. This comforting assurance is undercut by several other points. First, the teacher's right to make multiple copies for a class is limited. The copies are to be used only one time by the students in one class. The cost of audiovisual instructional programs mandates that they be used by many students in several successive terms. A second and more important consideration centers on the first fair use criterion (the purpose and character of the use) which prohibits the creation of collections or anthologies of materials copied from copyrighted works. These two points seem to preclude the legitimate use of very much copied material in these programs. This problem has two solutions: creativity and permission. If the designers of these programs are to remain within the law, they must either create their own materials instead of copying them, or they must obtain permission to duplicate the materials they cannot or do not want to create. Obtaining permission to duplicate musical recordings is almost impossible.

It is best either to omit music from the programs or to use cleared music. *Cleared music* is created under special licenses which enable the distributor to allow others to copy it upon the payment of a fee. Cleared music libraries may be identified in *The Audiovisual Market Place* and in other reference sources; obtaining permission to duplicate visual materials is not quite as difficult, the greatest problem is identifying the name and the address of the copyright owners. Most book publishers, with the possible exception of textbook publishers, are quite cooperative about granting permission to duplicate graphs, charts, illustrations, and textual materials from their publications. In obtaining permission, it is advisable to use a standard application form provided by a trade association and to supply all the information it requires. If the items being copied or being produced are in the television format, it is important to explain that the material will not be broadcast or electronically transmitted. If the copyright properietors are not so informed, they may charge broadcast permission rates, rates which could quickly consume an entire library budget.

Although the use of copyrighted materials in audiovisual instructional programs creates serious problems, one should assume that a certain amount may be copied under the terms of fair use. Fair use has three important applications: First, one may include a segment of copyrighted material in the program, if it is a small and insignificant part of the original work and if it is a small and insignificant part of the locally produced program. Second, in dealing with scientific and technical topics, there may be only one correct way to perform a given task. If a locally produced program is teaching students to perform that task (e.g., a chemistry experiment or a welding technique), it is acceptable to incorporate the correct procedures described in the standard scientific or technical manuals, without fear of copyright infringement. This applies only to duplicating the organizational structure of the description in the standard reference manual. It does not necessarily permit word-for-word copying or the duplication of the accompanying illustrations or bibliographies.[10] The third category pertains to criticism. Literary and artistic criticism is a legitimate form of creativity that is possible only when the critic can incorporate portions of the work in the critique to illustrate the points he or she wishes to make. This usually involves quotations from literary works. This can also be applied to musical and artistic criticism; and it can be applied to critiques employing the audiovisual format instead of the more familar written format. A tape-recorded critique of a particular piece of music may include a few brief passages of the music as examples of the critic's points. A critique of a film produced in a visual (e.g., sound-slide) format may include a few stills from the film to show examples of the acting or cinemagraphic techniques employed in the film. In each of these, the basic content of the work must be created by the critic. The excerpts can constitute only a small part of the work.[11]

CONCLUSION

Librarians who observe the detailed guidelines in the new copyright law for the duplication of textual materials may feel that the new law has left them with inadequate guidance for copying audiovisual materials. This feeling of helplessness is compounded by the need to consult two sections of the copyright law to find the answers. Sections 107 and 108 are both based on the broad concepts of fair use, but they employ radically different approaches. Section 108 provides lengthy but prescriptive guidelines for duplicating textual materials, illustrations accompanying textual materials, television news programs, and out-of-print and unpublished materials. The remaining applications are covered by Section 107, which is based on an interlocking set of brief but vague criteria; their brevity and vagueness should warm the hearts of those who make their living through litigation. They will be a source of some irritation to librarians who must interpret them to patrons who want the library to duplicate audiovisual materials. Quick solutions do not appear to be in the offing. Library supervisors who find themselves in the unenviable position of having to apply the law in this situation must do their homework so they will have a better idea of their rights, and so they can explain them to their employees and patrons. In time, decisions of the courts will offer some guidance. It seems unlikely that voluntary or legislative guidelines will be provided soon. The tension between users and proprietors has been so exacerbated in recent years that it is improbable that the two groups will be able to arrive at mutually acceptable guidelines for the duplication of most visual and aural materials. Having recently passed a controversial copyright bill, it seems unlikely that Congress will want to engage itself in this difficult matter again soon. It is a situation in which Congress can only alienate its conflicting constituencies.

NOTES

[1]*Copyright Revision Act of 1976* (Washington, D.C.: Government Printing Office, 1976), Section 108 (h).

[2]*Ibid.*, (c).

[3]U.S. House. *Copyright Law Revision*, 94th Cong., 2d Sess., H.R. *Report* 94–1476 (Washington, D.C.: Government Pringint Office, 1976), Section 108.

[4]*Copyright Revision Act*, Section 108 (f) (4).

[5]*Ibid.*, Section 107.

[6]U.S. Senate. *Copyright Law Revision*, 94th Cong., 2d Sess., 94-473 (Washington, D.C.: Government Printing Office, 1976), Section 107. (Hereafter cited as Senate Report.)

[7]*Ibid.*

[8]*General Revision of the Copyright Law, Title 17 of the United States Code:* Conference Report House of Representatives, 94th Cong., 2d. Sess. H.R. *Report* 94–1733. (Washington, D.C.: Government Printing Office, 1976) Section 107.

[9]Senate Report, Section 107.

[10]Melville B. Nimmer, *Nimmer on Copyright: A Treatise on the Law of Literary, Musical and Artistic Property, and the Protection of Ideas* (N.Y.: Matthew Bender, 1963-78), p. 644.

[11]See Note 6, Senate Report on its intent for Section 107. The phrase, "quotation of excerpts in a review or criticism for purposes of illustration or comment . . ." is here interpreted to permit copying small visual excerpts of a film or other visual material for the purpose of criticism or comment. The practice of quoting a small part of a work in a review or critique was established by the courts as a form of fair use long before the new copyright law was written. The new law upholds this longstanding practice. Although it does not mention its application to critiques of the visual media produced in visual format, it clearly does not prohibit or discourage this new practice.

Library and Learning Resources:
How Will Copyright Apply?

The previous essay by Jerome K. Miller concentrates on commonly available library resources and technologies of reproduction. This essay by Billie Grace Herring discusses several of the technologically more advanced resources, access systems, and means of information reproduction that may well become more common—in spite of their undefined legal status with respect to copyright. Among technologies discussed here are remote access terminals, cable communications, microform, cathode ray tube terminals, and helical scan video. These are likely to raise fair use questions, as will the general issue of "the fair use of a data base." In connection with the latter, the National Commission on New Technological Uses (CONTU) has now issued its report (published after Herring's essay had been completed) recommending that "computer programs, to the extent that they embody an author's original creation, are proper subject matter of copyright" and " that the Act of 1976 should be amended to apply to all computer uses of copyrighted data bases and other copyrighted works fixed in computer sensible media. . ." *(Final Report of the National Commission on New Uses of Copyrighted Works,* July 31, 1978; p. 2). CONTU's work over a three-year period was exceptionally thorough, and its recommendations are likely to become embodied in legislation amending the existing copyright law. Herring's essay suggests many of the complications inherent in applying copyright law to future library-housed information systems.

11

LIBRARY AND LEARNING RESOURCES: HOW WILL COPYRIGHT APPLY?

BILLIE GRACE HERRING

In the conference committee reports and in the new copyright law itself, careful attention was given to library photocopying of materials and to classroom use of copyrighted materials. Since "photocopying" seems to imply the *reproduction of hard-copy print materials* and since "classroom" appears to imply *face-to-face teaching*, the legality of new media extensions of these practices becomes dubious. How do new communications technologies affect the rights of user and copyright holder?

How does copyright protection relate to materials which are stored in machine-readable but not in eye-legible form? To what extent do the guidelines for use of materials in classrooms apply

—when the classroom is remote and scattered in many geographic locations?
—when instruction is being carried via cable system?
—when instruction is given via carefully designed materials for self-paced individualized instruction?

Is there a dividing line between instructional use and performance of creative works in the classroom or in extensions of classroom activities? Aspects of these questions are addressed below.

ACCESS TO INFORMATION IN LIBRARIES AND LEARNING RESOURCE CENTERS

Section 108 of the new copyright law seems to imply that material in libraries and learning resource centers exists in tangible form, that it is supplied to the patron as a physical entity either on site or through interlibrary loan, and that the patron will either use the material in the library or will charge it out for use at home. The implication is that the patron will have *physical access* to materials. Today, not all information is stored in eye-legible, manually manipulable form.

Furthermore, the law appears to distinguish between entertainment and instruction, but ambiguity remains concerning the broader educational use which may be generated by the individual for personal inquiry or by *ad hoc* groups of persons whose intention is learning, but not in a structured, institutional setting. For example, a neighborhood group of parents meets informally and decides to explore the community library to obtain materials on parent-child communication. Or an informal self-help club decides to enclose the patio at a member's home and approaches the public library to find visual materials on electricity and wiring which they will study together at their supper meeting. Or a study group examining issues in health care for the community seeks copies of interview tapes and health care proposals to use in its programming. Such uses cannot be labeled *entertainment*; they are instructional, but not in the usual "classroom" or institutional sense.

As new communications technologies continue to evolve and as current technologies become more readily available, individual learning and information-seeking may be accomplished without physically going to the library or information center. Patrons may request information from their homes or offices and have it delivered by various combinations of communications technologies. We can expect devices for utilizing these technologies to become as widely available as today's pocket calculators and touch-tone telephones. As microminiaturization of such equipment continues, personal computers with sizeable memories will be found in more and more homes. Two-way cable communications systems also show signs of developing more widely. Thus, the library of the near future must deal not only with information in many formats, but with variable means of transmitting the information to the potential user. At times, the information will be sought to further research or scholarship; at other times, it will be for personal enrichment or amusement.

The means by which libraries will store information, access data about what is available in the holdings of a given library (or a cooperating group of libraries), access the materials themselves, and lend materials to users will take a much wider variety of forms than they have in the past. As remote access becomes routine, how will the copyright law meet the challenges presented by such access?

Storage of Materials

Libraries today store most of their materials as hard-copy print. Some material is stored as audio recordings, as audiovisual recordings, as microforms, and in some libraries, as machine-readable files (data not intended to be eye-legible but to be read by computers, optical character recognition, or punched card or tape devices). Print materials, recordings, microforms, and the output from machine-readable files in hard copy or computer output microforms may be considered to be in tangible form, although some of the materials may be accessed only with special equipment. Other information, such as that which appears on a cathode ray tube (CRT) display screen without hard-copy output, is temporary in its visible manifestation and thus appears to be more intangible.

Microforms. As both space and conservation considerations become more critical, the use of microforms[1] in place of hard-copy print materials is becoming more commonplace. Some journals are being published only in microform. Because they anticipate limited sales for a work, a few publishers have begun to publish books only in microform, usually microfiche. Some publishers may produce microform copies only "on demand" when a copy is ordered. Using microforms as the output medium for machine-stored graphic and print data is another current alternative that may be expected to expand rapidly. "Ultrafiche" and other miniaturizations allow increasing density of storage.

With the advent of color microform technologies, it becomes feasible to store "still" visual materials, such as pictures, slides, diagrams, charts, maps, and graphs, on microforms. Business and industry have long used microform aperture cards to store engineering drawings and other graphic materials. Now that color is available, microforms are reasonable storage choices for museums, art libraries, architecture collections, anthropology collections, map collections, health science libraries, and other collections which have three requirements in common: (1) that information be stored visually; (2) that it not require motion for comprehension; (3) that it does require color to convey its meaning. Computer output graphics (drawings, graphs, lettering, etc., generated by a computer on a CRT) can be transferred to microforms for storage. Given the problems that many libraries face in finding sufficient storage space for existing documents and visual materials, and given the possibility that personal microfiche readers will soon be as commonplace as personal pocket calculators, it appears that many libraries could benefit from conversion of many documents and visual materials to the microform format; under copyright provisions, however, such conversions would appear to be violations.

An excellent example of the efficiency of color visual information stored on microfiche may be found in the collections serving art history students who must study reproductions of paintings. Rather than use black and white photographs (as is commonly done now) or be confined to a library carrel for slide viewing, the student could buy a set of microfiche of the slides cheaply and thus have ready access to all slides shown in class or assigned for study. The student then could study the paintings wherever a microfiche reader was available, and many students would probably buy a portable reader, which costs little more than a textbook. What seems to be an ideal solution to a nagging educational problem may be negated, however, by the apparent illegality of copying such slides onto microfiche, since it results in an "anthology."

Jerome Miller's contribution to this book has addressed the complex problems faced by curators of art slide collections which have been developed from photographs of pictures in art books. A further transposition of the slide collection to microfiche greatly complicates the problem of permissions. In neither of the situations cited does the law appear to allow full exploitation of existing technologies to help the student learn more efficiently without the college, teacher, or library investing inordinate quantities of time and resources in tracing the original copyright holders.

Audio formats. Libraries have stored information or aesthetic experience in audio forms since before 1915.[2] Since patrons often have playback devices in their homes, audio materials are circulated in the same manner as print materials. Existing technologies provide opportunities, however, for modification of audio materials. We see such modification in the use of the more dense cassette tape recordings used by the Library of Congress Division for the Blind and Physically Handicapped, in the use of rate-controlled speech playback devices either to compress or expand the time required for listening, and in the modification of audio tracks accompanying visual materials by adding inaudible advance pulses to synchronize the visual and audio portions of a program. Developments in laser technology may soon make possible storage and transmission of sound by light waves rather than by electronics, bringing more rapid and lower-cost transmission together with greatly compressed storage.

Audiovisual formats. Films, sound filmstrips, and sound slide programs are widely used in libraries today, but distribution of such formats is usually to a limited clientele of teachers, representatives of clubs or organizations, or library staff who use the materials in library programming. But video technology has vastly expanded the possibilities for capturing and distributing materials in audio and visual modes. Helical scan videotape equipment that allows original production, off-air recording, as well as playback of prerecorded materials, has put the video format within the reach of almost all libraries. The consumer-oriented one-half inch video recorder/player has made recording and playback possible at many locations and in a variety of situations.

Although considerable progress on off-air taping for schools was made by the joint statement of policy for school rerecording of public instructional programs,[3] it is still unclear whether institutions such as public libraries are covered by the agreement. Most programs that may be rerecorded for later playback in schools are instructionally oriented. Yet library patrons often see program series, such as *Roots, Civilization,* or *The Long Search,* and expect that, since their public library has videorecordings, these programs will be available for viewing at the library or for circulation to be played back on home video systems. Patrons often request tapes to "catch up" on a missed broadcast. Since such programs were not cleared for off-air recording and since permissions or licenses to record off-air are either prohibitively expensive or will not be granted at all, libraries must wait until the series becomes available through a commercial distributor. Often the purchase price is prohibitive. Meanwhile, during the time immediately following open broadcast of such programs, many moments of optimum educational use occur when it would be useful to review a portion of the program. At present, there seems to be no way of having such portions available short of illegal off-air taping.

It must be recognized that many video producers are willing to negotiate licenses for duplication of tapes, including changing the format to another size of videorecording. As the consumer market demands more prerecorded tapes for purchase, libraries may expect increasing demands from patrons for videorecordings, either in tape, disc, or some yet undeveloped format.

Machine-readable files. At present, the technology for creating and searching large machine-readable files is readily available. Except for proprietary libraries that are responsible for storing company records in machine-readable form, few libraries (except national institutions, such as the Library of Congress and the National Library of Medicine) are creating their own original data bases. Fewer yet are creating full-text data bases. Word-processing technologies, however, simplify text storage, editing, and display and may be considered one prototype for full-text data bases, especially in the publishing industry.

Most data bases currently in use are composed of (1) bibliographic/catalog data which can be used for numerous outputs, (2) citations to documents which the patron must then locate in hard copy or in microform. Although bibliographic citations cannot be copyrighted, the data bases usually contain additional information that has been generated by the creator of the data base.[4] Furthermore, the user of the data base may select for output only part of the stored data and may format the output according to specific needs. Does copyright apply to either the additional information generated by the creator of the data base or the particular format of the output?

Often bibliographic/catalog data bases are created on shared or cooperative bases, with numerous libraries supplying input. If the information in the data base can be copyrighted, then the determination of copyright ownership may become extremely complex.

Most data bases of citations to works on a given subject or combination of subjects have been created on a proprietary basis because of the cost and complexity of providing in-depth subject indexing. Both search and communications fees are involved in using such bases. Since subject descriptors have been created by the proprietor who makes the base available to libraries, to individual users, or to individual users through information brokers (who perform searches for a fee), such bases are usually copyrighted. Since access is controlled by passwords and search keys, only authorized patrons can use the data bases.

The output of citations or of bibliographic/cataloging information from a data base may appear in several forms depending on the needs of the user: hard-copy printout, screen displays with no hard copy, or computer output microforms. Since most of the output is in alphanumeric characters, videorecording has not been used extensively as an output or a storage medium. But video discs provide exciting possibilities for other forms of storage and output because of their density of storage and easy indexibility.

Given the complexity of these systems and their methods of transmitting information, what will determine fair use of a data base? When may information-seekers "tap in" to the system on fair use grounds?

Access to Information about Library Holdings

The card catalog and printed periodical indexes have been the traditional means of locating information about the holdings of a given library or group of libraries. The Library of Congress, which sets the pace for many aspects of library practice, has announced that it is "closing" its card catalog as of January 1, 1981; subsequently, it will produce its catalog only in machine-readable form. Since the Library of Congress was the source for printed catalog cards in use throughout the world, almost all academic, large public, and other research libraries are making plans to change to some form of catalog other than the card catalog. Some are electing to use computer output microform. Others are planning on-line catalogs with interim book catalogs printed out from the machine-readable data base of the library's holdings. In all instances, creation of a machine-readable file of bibliographic information forms the basis for these catalog formats. The machine-readable file must be unique to a given library because it must contain locational information, data about unique aspects of copies held by that particular library (such as autographs), and other local information. Since a machine-readable file can be duplicated more easily than a traditional card catalog, will libraries find it necessary to copyright the file which constitutes the base for its catalog?

Often substituting for the printed periodical indexes are the citation data bases discussed in the previous section. Furthermore, with improving automatic indexing techniques, libraries and information centers may find themselves creating more and more specialized indexes for both local uses and for sale to other users. Libraries may publish such indexes or catalogs themselves or may contract with a commercial firm for publication and distribution.[5] The nationally available printed indexes and the data bases that parallel them are copyrighted; should an individual library also require such protection for its locally generated special indexes?

Patron Access to the Information-Carrying Materials

Given existing technologies and those which are feasible but not readily available, patrons have two choices regarding access to the materials stored in a library. They may go to the library to charge out the physical items, or they may obtain remote access through home television receivers, keyboard and/or cathode ray tube terminals, telephone, dataphone, facsimile receivers, or videophones. Such remote access raises all manner of copyright questions. But so too does the problem of accessing directly many kinds of visual and audiovisual materials.

Direct access. The patron who elects to go to the site where the physical materials are stored or asks that materials or copies of parts thereof be made available through interlibrary loan faces a much less complex problem than does the patron who wishes to have remote access to the materials. Although obtaining portions of visual and/or audiovisual works via interlibrary loan may be impossible, the law is relatively clear about the availability of photocopied materials or reproduced phonorecords through interlibrary loan.

Even the patron who goes to the library to "check out" materials, however, may be faced with some problems. If material is in machine-readable form and the patron has no CRT or print terminal available at the site where materials will be used, it may be necessary to print out the machine-readable materials into hard copy or onto microform before lending them to the patron. The patron who needs visual materials, such as maps, graphs, art reproductions, or slides, may find that the library has a "building use only" policy for such materials because of the need to protect and conserve the originals. If the originals are copyrighted, the library is prohibited from making copies. If a copy can be reproduced by the patron for his own use by using a typical photocopying machine, there appears to be little difficulty. Slides, however, require a different copying process. Is a library justified in providing a slide-copying device so that the individual patron may make a copy of a slide for his own study? How would making a copy of a slide differ from making a copy of a graphic stored on microfiche by using a microfiche reader/printer? How would it differ from copying a map on a photocopying machine? If the patron wishes to use an old and rare phonograph record for study, but the record cannot be taken out of the library, should the library provide a record-to-tape copying system (just as it provides photocopy machines or microform reader/printers) so that the patron may make his own copy for study and research?

If the researcher locates a videotape of a news broadcast which has been made legally by the library but is needed in a format compatible with the patron's home video system, may the library provide a duplication device which will convert from one format of videorecording to another?

Essentially, if photocopying of printed materials by the individual user for personal use is permissible, is similar copying of audio, visual, and audiovisual works permissible, provided that the library has posted the appropriate copyright notices on the copying machines?

Remote access. Almost all futurists suggest that rather than moving people to information stores or to classes or meetings, energy shortages and economic factors will force adoption of remote access technologies, such as telelectures and teleconferences, to allow people to study or work together from remote sites. Futurists see uses of other message-carrying technologies, such as broadcast TV, cable communications, dataphones, picturephones or videophones, CRTs, and facsimile devices as information circuits between people. All these remote access technologies appear to raise copyright questions.

The permissible use of copyrighted works in telelectures appears to be especially ambiguous. The law makes some allowances for transmission of copyrighted materials for in-service education of teachers and government employees (Sec. 110.2 iii), but use for other continuing

education or administrative purposes may be questioned. Is the telelec-
ture, whether or not accompanied by telewriting or some other visual
display, to be considered a transmission, a performance, or classroom
instruction?

Telecourses offered by community colleges are a further use of
telecommunications to take instruction to people where they are rather
than to bring people to the instruction on campuses. The copyright law
makes provision for delivery to handicapped persons (Sec. 110.C ii), but
is ambiguous about general dissemination of education through telecommunications technologies; thus, producers of telecourses now spend
enormous amounts of time requesting permissions to quote from audio
and visual, as well as print works, in telecourses.

The individual library patron who wishes to use available communications technologies to "see" materials in a library immediately encounters the question of transmission of copyrighted materials. In some
communities, the cable television system has assigned one or more public
access channels to a library in the community and sometimes one of
these channels is used for video reference. The patron who needs to see
a map, chart, picture, or other visual material that can be "read" on a
television screen telephones the video reference desk of the library and
makes a request; the staff locates the information and tells the patron to
turn his television set to cable channel 'X'. The desired material is then
placed under a camera and the image is transmitted on the cable channel
to which the inquirer has turned. Video reference may also be available
through closed-circuit television systems on a campus, with teachers requesting transmission to classrooms, or on some campuses, with students
requesting transmission to their dormitories.

If cable channels are available to a library, remote preview of audiovisual works, such as films, slide-tape programs, or videorecordings,
is simple to accomplish technologically but would appear to involve illegal transmission. If such previewing were being done in one school
building or for in-service training of teachers or government employees,
its legality could be argued. If, however, the program chairperson of the
local study club requested remote preview of a film from the library,
would this constitute a performance of the work and thus an illegal
transmission? If a film which has been ordered for preview by an inter-
mediate school district or regional media center were transmitted to
twenty different campuses via CCTV so that teachers and librarians
could preview the film, would this also be considered a performance?
Under the premise of moving information to people rather than people
to information, wider use of remote transmission technology seems desirable.

Patrons who need hard copy of a video transmission may prefer to
request that a facsimile be sent rather than a video display. If the infor-

mation is time-critical to the user, he may find that investment in a facsimile transceiver is justified, although he will then be limited to using the materials in libraries which have facsimile transmission devices. Material composed of only alphanumeric characters may be read by optical character recognition devices and transmitted via dataphone or other electronic mail devices. Is transmitting a document via facsimile devices any less acceptable than photocopying a document and transmitting it through the postal system?

If the patron has a terminal available, he may perform remote and/or interactive searches of the library's catalog or of the data bases of citations mentioned earlier. Once citations to appropriate articles have been located, low-cost disposable copies of the documents may be printed out for the user on microform and the microforms mailed to the user, or the user may pick them up at the library. Hard-copy reproductions might also be provided. Because information on microforms requires a special reader to light and to enlarge the images, are they to be considered audiovisual media?

If the user elects to have audiovisual materials transmitted for use via cable, minor modifications may be possible without altering the original. For example, a second sound track in another language or with simplified vocabulary may be carried along with the video and audio signals on the original videorecorded work. Special effects equipment may allow for captioning materials or for presenting them in sign language for the deaf patron. Even when cable communication is not available, spoken audio materials may be compressed or expanded in playback time to meet the needs of special users. To what extent are such modifications permissible without violating copyright?

Technologically, we may anticipate that in the future messages will be sent and received with increasing ease and speed, and with decreasing costs. Whether the library of the near future will be able to capitalize on these communications technologies will be determined, in part, by copyright regulations. How can the technologically up-to-date library balance its primary purpose—the dissemination of ideas and the free and efficient flow of information—with the proprietary rights of the creators of the works? We appear to be at a stage in which many questions have been raised with no clear answers. A great deal rides on the answers.

INSTRUCTIONAL DESIGN IN LEARNING RESOURCES PROGRAMS

The storage, retrieval, and display of information is usually considered to be the primary purpose of libraries and learning resource centers. In schools and colleges, however, the institution often makes the learning resources center staff responsible for working with departments in instructional design. Thus, the learning resources center staff must address use of copyrighted materials in the design of instructional systems that will transmit educational content, allow students to learn at their own pace, and permit them to study at locations remote from the classroom or library.

Such systems may be designed commercially, but more commonly, the systems are designed by departments or divisions within the educational institution itself. Such designs are seldom the work of a single teacher.

Consider these examples: a college English department decides to design the initial freshman composition course so that students move through it in a self-paced, self-instructional pattern. In basic math, a high school math department designs from existing textbooks and workbooks a self-instructional tutorial system to assist students who are having difficulty; the system is so successful that it is adopted by the entire school district. A community college develops a telecourse on government and political science using film clips and excerpts from many news broadcasts. A college-level program in education wishes to teach students to evaluate instructional materials and prepares a series of audio-tutorial laboratory sessions incorporating excerpts from tapes, filmstrips, and videorecordings which each student previews and evaluates individually.

In each of the foregoing examples, the programs of instruction have clearly been developed on the instruction of "higher authority" [H.R. *Report* 94-1476 IIIB (b)]. They are not dictated by a printed curriculum guide, but neither are they the result of a single teacher's face-to-face classroom teaching. Are uses of copyrighted material in such situations fair uses?

When major independent study programs are developed, especially those which are a full course length, it is common practice in curriculum design to develop several variations of the course first, to test these variations on different groups of students for one or more semesters, and then to complete the independent study course plan on the basis of the results of the field test and tryout with the various groups of students. The intent of designers normally is to use the tested and revised program over a period of years. The law is clear that permission must be sought if copyrighted print material is to be duplicated for student use for more than one successive semester, but little consideration seems to be given to the time needed for field testing and learner verification. During the field-test stage, a course may be highly volatile, changing from one day to the next according to the responses which are being received from students. Once a course design is selected, however, copyright permissions are usually sought, although further verification and refinement may be done at a later stage. It appears that materials used by only one class in one semester during the early stages of field testing would be considered fair use. If the "class" tested is made up of 1,200 students in freshman biology, is that still to be considered one class? Testing a course for longer than one semester or with several sections of a course taught by different teachers also would appear to violate the "spontaneity" principle of the House Committee guidelines.

Curriculum developers may rightly feel that their freedom to experiment with many different materials is being curtailed. Will designers of instructional systems be restricted to originally produced audio, visual, and audiovisual materials if they anticipate that course development and field testing will take more than one semester and will apply to more than one section of a course?

What about instructional systems developed before the current copyright law? Learning resource centers contain many derivative works created before 1978. Are retroactive permissions required? Are learning resource centers violating copyright law by housing and circulating materials for which permissions have not been obtained? To complicate the permissions problem, further, one often cannot determine the origin of materials for systems that have been in use for a number of years. Is the system developed before 1978 to be discarded?

In Chapter 10, Jerome Miller addresses problems that arise from the use of copyrighted materials in locally produced independent study programs in libraries and suggests several solutions that appear to be within the scope of the law. In the process of developing such programs, another question arises, however, concerning the occasional need to borrow audiovisual materials from another library. Borrowing print material generally is not a problem (the creator of the independent study program still has the responsibility of seeking copyright permission in this case), but borrowing an audiovisual work is almost impossible, even when prior permission has been obtained. In general, it appears that libraries take into account the low volume sales of audiovisual works, especially of film and videorecordings, and do not duplicate them, arguing such duplication violates point four of the primary fair use guidelines—the potential effect of the use upon the potential market for or value of the copyrighted work.

All these questions point to the larger question of how user access can be balanced with compensation to the creators of audiovisual works. Librarians, teachers, and educational administrators have not even begun to receive answers to these questions.

PERFORMANCES THAT LEAVE THE CLASSROOM

Staff members in learning resources center programs carry the additional responsibility of helping teachers plan for effective utilization of library materials to achieve instructional goals. At times, such utilization involves student development of creative works derived from copyrighted works. The learning resources staff may work directly with students or with teachers on such assignments.

Within the last five years, teachers and learning resources specialists have shared with the writer the following examples which dramatize the problem:

One was a puppet show produced in a classroom situation by children whose dominant language was Spanish. It originally began as an English language-arts activity designed to require students to read a particular copyrighted children's book, to use oral English in presenting a classroom skit based on the book, and to use written English in adapting the story to the dramatic puppet show format. When the puppet show, which had consumed many days of class time in its production, was finished and presented to the class, it was so successful that the students were asked to present it to classes taught by other teachers, to a primary grades assembly of the school, and later to the local parent-teacher group. The school decided to videotape the performance for exhibition to classes in subsequent years.

Although the law is not entirely clear regarding dramatization of an entire copyrighted work within one classroom by one teacher's class, it could be assumed that this "face-to-face" use was indeed fair and met the criteria for spontaneity, if not for brevity. When the program was later "performed" for other classes, for a school assembly, for the PTA, and was subsequently videotaped, it would appear to have gone beyond the guidelines for classroom use; yet, since all these performances took place within a two-week time span and evolved from a spontaneous suggestion by a group of students, there was not sufficient time to get written permission from the holder of the copyright of the book. And if permission had been requested and not given, what would have happened to the value of the learning experience for the students? A "teachable moment" would have been missed.

In another instance, a fictional work read by students in several grades of an elementary school was adapted into a musical play by a teacher and group of students. The music and lyrics were written and composed by the teacher and students, but the plot and characters were drawn from the book. The creation went into rehearsal and permission was sought from the book's copyright holder. Permission was denied, but by this time a performance had been announced and the production was ready. Frantic telephone calls back and forth finally resulted in permission to give *one* performance, but had a dampening effect on all who were involved in the learning project.

In a different school, a junior high school orchestra teacher, in attempting to demonstrate string instruments to students who would be enrolled in the school, arranged for a demonstration performance of many varieties of musical works at a school assembly to show the range and versatility of string instruments. Among the selections he wished to have performed were two popular songs currently being played by local radio stations, but for which there was no orchestration for strings. In creating such orchestration of the two songs, the teacher was acting within the scope of instructional activities but not within a classroom since the work was played at a school assembly.

Finally, a teacher of visual and film literacy in a high school in which students not only view works created by others but also produce audiovisual works of their own, required that students learn techniques by producing a "see a song" slide program which illustrated the mood and/or words to a song selected by the student. The teacher directed students to make slides from a number of sources, including magazines, books, and real-life situations. The assignment was the teacher's own idea and did not stem from directives in a curriculum guide. The slide-tape programs were then presented for the class and also entered in the annual media fair of the state film society. The winning entries were later presented to the school assembly. Does the entry in the media fair constitute performance? Does the teacher's direction to choose a song and one's own slide sources (including copyrighted sources) constitute "higher authority"?

In short, considering the four cases just listed, where is the line between classroom and performance?

All parties involved in fashioning the new copyright law recognized that it is, at best, a compromise. On the one hand educators are concerned with fair use, the free flow of ideas, and the teachable moment. On the other hand, proprietary interests are concerned with fair remuneration of copyright holders for their works. Perhaps one helpful step in the direction of balancing these diverse interests will be further definition of the adjective *fair* when it is used to modify *remuneration* and when it is used to modify *use* when the use employs newer communications technologies.

NOTES

[1]*Microforms* is a generic term for such specific formats as microfiche, roll microfilm, cassette or cartridge microfilm, microcards and other opaque images.

[2]"Music Rolls for Circulation," *Library Journal* 40 (August 1915): 619, describes how

the Kansas City Public Library circulated player piano rolls in 1913-14. "Victrola Records for Library Use," *Wisconsin Library Bulletin* 11, No. 3 (March 1915): 73.

[3]*Joint Statement of Policy: School Rerecording of Public and Instructional Television Programs.* Public Broadcasting Service; Great Plains National Instructional Television Library; Public Television Library, Agency for Instructional Television. 1975.

[4]Information in addition to bibliographic data may include subject descriptors, annotations or abstracts, classification numbers, holdings data, or locational symbols.

[5]G. K. Hall Company is an example of a commercial publisher that produces and distributes printed book catalogs of selected libraries or special collections.

SELECTED REFERENCES

Annual Reviews and Handbooks

Advances in Librarianship, Melvin J. Voigt, Ed. Vol. 1. New York: Academic Press, 1970-.

Annual Review of Information Science. Vol. 1. New York: Knowledge Industry Publishing, Inc., for American Society for Information Science, 1966-.

The Bowker Annual of Library and Book Trade Information. Vol. 1. New York: R. R. Bowker, 1955/56-.

Educational Media Yearbook. Vol. 1. New York: R. R. Bowker, 1973-.

Selected Periodicals

Advanced Technology Libraries. White Plains, N.Y.: Knowledge Industry Publishing, Inc., 1972-.

Cable Libraries. Ridgefield, Conn. C.S. Tepfer Publishing Co., 1973-.

Datamation. Barrington, Ill.: Technical Publishing Co., 1955-.

Educational and Industrial Television. Ridgefield, Conn. C.S. Tepfer, 1972-.

Information Hotline. New York: Science Associates International, 1976-.

Journal of Library Automation. Chicago: ALA, 1969-.

Online Review. New York: Learned Information, 1977-.

IV

THE IMPACT OF COPYRIGHT LAW ON CREATORS, PRODUCERS, AND DISTRIBUTORS

The Administration of Copyrighted Imagery at Walt Disney Productions

The *How to Read Donald Duck* episode discussed in Chapter 4 had exceptional features related to foreign publication, import restrictions, unsubstantiated claims about copyright registration, and the issue of the Treasury Department's authority to render fair use decisions.

The essay that follows describes the routine, domestic policies and procedures at Walt Disney Productions. These have a general significance for the understanding of copyright because the corporation has such an enormous number of copyrighted items in its inventory and because it has developed a very firm, efficient machinery for the administration of permissions requests. In addition, Disney enforces its policies with legal vigor that is probably unequaled by any other media corporation. It litigates often and successfully in matters of copyright infringement. Significant recent prosecutions (all decided in Disney's favor) include *Walt Disney Productions v. Air Pirates,* 345 F. Supp. 108 (N.D. Cal. 1972); 581 F.2d 751 (9th Cir. 1978); *Walt Disney Productions v. Mature Pictures Corp.,* 389 F.Supp. 1397 (S.D.N.Y. 1975)—both cases involve pornographic parodies of Disney characters. *Walt Disney Productions v. Alaska Television Network,* 310 F.Supp. 1073 (W.D. Wash. 1969) involved off-air taping for delayed cable television transmission. Disney is also a coplaintiff in the major suit against Sony Corporation of America mentioned in the following essay and discussed in more detail by Eugene Aleinikoff in Chapter 14.

12

THE ADMINISTRATION OF COPYRIGHTED IMAGERY: WALT DISNEY PRODUCTIONS

JOHN SHELTON LAWRENCE

An anecdote told by composer-performer Larry Groce ("Junk-Food Junkie") illustrates copyright practice at Walt Disney Productions. Groce had contracted with Sears to write, record, and publicize a record called "Winnie-the-Pooh for President." Sears manufactures a Pooh line of clothing under an exclusive license from Disney Productions, which had purchased rights for Pooh from its original owners. At a promotional "campaign" rally in Chicago, Groce obtained a Pooh sweater, of which a mere two dozen had been created. Some weeks later, Groce had occasion to visit the Disney Studios at Burbank in connection with a Little Golden Book project. He wore his rare Pooh sweater to the meeting. After the session with Disney personnel, Groce was followed by a Disney vice-president who asked him where he got the sweater. "At Sears," Groce answered. The disbelieving executive seized the collar of the sweater, forcing the astonished musician into a nearly kneeling position. Once the label had been twisted out for close inspection, Groce was released by the executive, who explained that he was just verifying the origin of the sweater.[1]

This unmannerly incident, not so important in itself, symbolizes well the role and philosophy of Walt Disney Productions as a meticulous and aggressive copyright administrator. Disney carefully registers copyrights for every item that it acquires or creates—including even its corporate *Annual Reports*. And more than any other major media corporation, Disney brings administrative and court actions against copyright infringers. In so doing, Disney sometimes deviates from corporate as well as personal etiquette. For example, Philip M. Hawley is a member of the Board of Directors of Walt Disney Productions and of its audit committee. He is also president of the Carter-Hawley-Hale Stores, Inc., a retail chain named as codefendant in the recent suit of Disney and Universal City Studios against the Sony Corporation for its manufacture and marketing of the Betamax home videorecording system.[2] A corporation with less zeal would have exempted Hawley's firm from the expense of extended litigation, particularly since so many other retail chains are equally liable.

Speculation about the unmannerly and vigorous legal behavior of the corporation sometimes reverts to the personality of Walt Disney himself, who was reported to have been covetous of fame and obsessively preoccupied with the personal control of his creations. Even friendly biographies of Disney contain a sprinkling of anecdotes that evidence this. In one of them, Walt Disney reprimands a young employee, Ken Anderson, who seems to want too much public recognition for his contribution to Disney's products:

> I'm impressed with what you're doing, Ken . . . You're new here and I want you to understand one thing: there's just one thing we're selling here, and that's the name "Walt Disney." If you can buy that and be happy to work for it, you're my man. But if you've got any ideas of selling the name "Ken Anderson," it's best for you to leave right now.[3]

It is doubtless true that Walt Disney's ego shaped to some extent an aggressive corporate policy in protecting items to which the Disney name and copyright had been attached. But objective, economic factors are more decisive in the company's history and suffice to explain the continuity of policy a decade after the death of the founder.

Walt Disney learned early in his career as a film maker the importance of retaining control over his copyrighted creations. In a stinging experience of the late twenties, Disney lost control of Oswald the Rabbit, a successful cartoon creation. Disney had made an agreement with Charles Mintz and Universal Pictures to supply the Oswald films, for which they held the copyrights, even though Disney was creating and producing the material. Universal apparently decided that it could increase its profit margin with the Oswald films either by compelling Disney to produce them on a less-than-cost basis or by dispensing with Disney himself. When Disney refused to provide the films at a loss, Mintz hired away the members of Disney's studio who had been working on Oswald. Disney not only lost his staff but was also unable to continue Oswald cartoons because he lacked the copyright for the character. Particularly galling was the circumstance that Oswald was becoming popular enough to appear on merchandise: a chocolate-coated marshmallow bar, a badge, an Oswald Stencil Set all bore the likeness of Disney's creation.[4]

Disney resolved at that time to retain a higher degree of control over his creations and to become wholly independent. He probably insured thereby his long-term success as a film maker, for it was the administration of copyrights for licensed merchandise that brought large and dependable revenues to an enterprise that often took enormous and expensive artistic gambles.

After losing Oswald, Disney went on to create Mickey Mouse. And by 1930, he received his first merchandising offer for Mickey: in exchange for a mere $300, badly needed at the studio, he allowed Mickey Mouse's image to be used on school tablets. By 1934, the Mickey merchandise had snowballed and required Disney to employ fifteen persons at a product-licensing office in New York. In the words of Richard Schickel:

> Some eighty concerns, including such blue chips as General Foods, National Dairy, and International Silver, were moving some seven million dollars' worth of stuff carrying what amounted to the Disney imprimatur. For this privilege they paid royalties in the range of 2½ to 5 percent—occasionally as much as ten percent—and Disney was grossing $300,000 on the operation and clearing half that amount, which made up almost one third of his net profit.[5]

Since Disney was losing substantial amounts on some of his major films in the thirties and forties, the impact of these revenues was decisive. *Fantasia,* for example, cost $2,275,889 to produce but returned only $676,380 from its initial release. *Pinocchio* was produced at a cost of $2,596,751 and earned only $1,584,498, a loss of $1,012,253.[6]

After several decades of successful licensing for its copyrighted imagery and characters, the Disney Corporation could begin to conceive of a film as a kind of "loss leader" that would repay its investment through so-called exploitation—the licensing, manufacturing, and marketing of items derived from the themes, images, characters, or music of a film. The corporation's experience with its TV series, *Davy Crockett, Indian Fighter,* is the best example of this process. Disney had made the series at a cost of $700,000 but received a mere $300,000 from the network. However, an extended merchandising campaign had been planned that eventually made up this deficit. "The Ballad of Davy Crockett," the copyrighted theme song for the program made the *Hit Parade* as the number one tune during a period of thirteen weeks and eventually sold ten million copies, as well as stimulating demand for sheet music from a company that Disney had formed—the Walt Disney Music Company.[7]

An avalanche of posters, rifles, toys, costumes, and coloring books fed the American appetite for Crockettiana. More than ten million Davy Crockett coonskin hats were sold. It was in this arena of Davy Crockett licensed merchandise that Disney's reputation as a fearsome copyright enforcer proved advantageous. Many of the items marketed, such as coonskin hats, were not really patentable or copyrightable, since they had long been firmly established in the public domain. Davy Crockett himself was part of the national legacy and his name could hardly be copyrighted. But Disney had copyrights on the program material, licenses for merchandise bearing *his* name along with that of Crockett's, and an imposing reputation for copyright enforcement.

The Bob Thomas biography of Disney reports that the corporation was surprised at the scale of the Crockett boom and found itself without a full line of products to exploit it. In order to buy time for themselves to saturate and capture the market, the Disney Corporation sought to deceive retailers into believing that they would be infringing Disney copyrights if they sold "unauthorized" Davy Crockett products.

> ... Vincent Jefferds ... sent telegrams to major department stores warning that they would be liable for damages if they sold unauthorized merchandise. It was a bluff, but it gave Disney time to enfranchise manufacturers for products bearing the title, "Walt Disney's Davy Crockett" and a picture of Fess Parker.[8]

The financial implications of these efforts were substantial. Merchandising income at Disney almost doubled from the "pre-Crockett" to the "post-Crocket" era. For 1953, total income stood at $2,314,360; by 1955, it had risen to $4,416,057. (The Mickey Mouse Club income caused another surge to $5,513,762 in 1956.)[9]

The Crockett merchandising bonanza, in its turn, helped to build a large audience for a theater film version of the TV series. When *Davy Crockett, King of the Wild Frontier* (the popular refrain from the best-selling tune chosen as the title for the film) was released, it earned $2,500,000. Since the content of the film had already been seen free of charge on television, its theatrical success was at least partially a tribute to the shrewd licensing and merchandising that had made Davy Crockett the dominant center of American fantasy experience for a period of several months.

In light of the corporate history of success in licensing and merchandising its copyrighted materials, it is clear why the Disney organization continues to maintain an aggressive stance. Analyzing its gross revenues and operating income for 1977, one sees that motion pictures and television contributed $118,058,000 and $50,394,000 respectively.[10] Its Consumer Products division, on the other hand, contributed $97,191,000 in gross revenues and $35,826,000 in operating income. Thus the secondary uses of copyrighted material are almost as important economically as the primary film or television vehicles through which they are launched. Indeed, when one considers that the theme parks— Disneyworld in Florida and Disneyland in California—are organized substantially around Disney themes and characters and contribute revenues of $414,576,000 and income of $93,431,000, it is clear why the corporate control of copyrights is so strenuous. These revenues truly dwarf those derived from film material alone.

With the continuing dependence upon revenues from the reproduction of copyrighted imagery and music, it is not surprising that the Disney corporation would have a large and efficient organization for the administration of permissions. At other places in this book, some authors complain about difficulties experienced in getting media corporations to acknowledge their correspondence. Long delays and exorbitant fees are customary. The Disney organization cannot be faulted for such reasons, since it is surely unequaled among major media corporations in its promptness and decisiveness. This does not mean that the corporation is always sympathetic with what appear to be legitimate scholarly requests for permission to reproduce. It denies many requests, but at least does so quickly. Nor does Disney acquiesce in the concept of fair use as applied to its copyrighted visual imagery, tunes, or lyrics. It wishes to keep every secondary use of its material under its own careful control, lest a major source of profit slip into the public domain. No object reproduced under license from the Character Merchandising Division is too small or insignificant to bear the Disney copyright notice, whether it be a drinking glass, a child's toothbrush, a magazine advertisement for the Mickeyphone, or an image of a Disney-related book jacket in a remainder catalogue.[11]

For the administration of its copyrights, Walt Disney Productions has created two major divisions: the Consumer Products Group and the Legal Department. The Consumer Products Group develops record albums, books, games, educational materials, home movies, and a variety of other Disney theme-related items. In addition to developing its own marketable items, Disney licenses other companies to manufacture items that bear Disney images. In a large-scale product campaign, such as was orchestrated for the release of *Pete's Dragon* in 1977, Disney developed character merchandise arrangements with more than thirty licensees and collaborated with an additional six companies that were basing promotions on material from the film. Records, books, posters, sweepstakes, popcorn, key chains, necklaces, and a variety of other items emblazoned with Pete's image were marketed.[12]

The Legal Department at Disney, working closely with the Consumer Products Group, formulates contracts for the use of copyrighted material and oversees administrative or legal actions when infringements occur. In addition to pursuing court litigation, it can appeal on occasion to an administrative agency, such as the U.S. Customs Bureau (as it did in the *How to Read Donald Duck* case) or to the Patents and

Trademarks Office. Two corporate officers, Peter F. Nolan of Disney's Office of Counsel, and Franklin Waldheim, vice-president and Eastern counsel, share responsibility for managing such actions. The volume of Disney's litigation against infringement is so great that some fifty outside legal firms are employed on a world-wide basis.[13] As of 1978, for example, Disney was conducting some 500 lawsuits and administrative procedures, fifty to seventy-five of which are lawsuits. Domestically, some eighteen to twenty new cases are filed annually.

The most typical causes of action for Disney are film piracy and character merchandise infringement. Unauthorized duplication and selling of films and tapes occurs on a world-wide basis, with numerous cases in England, Europe, and South Africa, as well as in the U. S. This is the basis, of course, for Disney's current action against the Sony Corporation.[14] Character merchandising infringement occurs often with the illegal use of Disney characters on watches, T-shirts, stuffed toys, and other consumer items. A less frequent cause of litigation, because most publishers respect Disney's readiness to litigate, is the illegal publication of Disney materials in books. This occurred in the *Air Pirates Comics* case, where Disney characters were presented in pornographic fashion.[15]

Apart from the occasional ripples caused by an important litigation, the bulk of the Disney copyright administration consists of coping with a large number of requests for permission to reproduce imagery. The corporation receives about 25 requests per week to use or to reproduce Disney copyrighted material, amounting to some 1,300 requests per year. The largest percentage of the requests, about 60 percent, comes from primary or secondary schools that wish to make some instructional or entertainment use of Disney material. Another large group, 32 percent, comes from PTA's, churches, and individuals. Scholarly and publication-related requests account for a mere 5 percent. Only 3 percent of the requests—the only ones that promise any immediate return for the corporation—are related to commercial ventures.

A request to Disney for the right to reproduce is handled in the following way: when it arrives, the Legal Department is first assigned the task of making a determination of rights. Images with actors, for example, require a review of the contracts to determine whether the actors retained a "right of privacy" limiting the corporation to promotion and publicity. Similarly, images contained in stories purchased from outside authors require a review of their contracts.

If the Legal Department determines that Disney has the rights to the material requested, the question of whether the use can be granted is determined by the Disney management. According to Peter F. Nolan of the Legal Department, decisions are guided primarily by a public interest and a business criterion.

Disney sees its relationships to schools and scholarly publication as an aspect of its public interest in education. According to Nolan, Disney grants those uses that appear to serve the public. It approves 85 percent of the requested school uses for carnivals, assemblies, classroom adaptations, etc., on a royalty-free basis. Where use for publication is granted, a scholar pays a standard, minimal fee of $50 and receives a high-quality photographic reproduction prepared by the Disney Archives. Because of the photographic and administrative costs, Disney sees its handling of requests for rights to reproduce as a fairly expensive form of public service. On a purely short-term, economic basis, form letters of denial might prove to be the most convenient way of responding to the noncommercial proposals that come to the corporation.

In addition to its "public service" criterion, Disney also applies business criteria to requests, even where scholarly publication is the proposed use. Because there are so many Disney images circulating, the corporation is concerned about the "dilution of market" that may occur if every publication request is granted. Disney sees publication of images, even in a book context, as a "competing use" that may dilute the market for the corporation's images generally. Therefore, the public interest criterion may be overruled by commercial considerations.

Not acknowledged officially is a third criterion that is often masked as a purely commercial, contractual one. Disney would probably like to avoid any unfavorable associations that may arise from uncontrolled secondary uses. For example, Richard Schickel reports that the producers of Edward Albee's *Who's Afraid of Virginia Woolf?* were denied permission to use the "Who's Afraid of the Big Bad Wolf?" tune from *Three Little Pigs*. The words in the play were sung instead to "Here We Go 'Round the Mulberry Bush," which does not enjoy copyright protection. Schickel's conjecture that Disney did not wish to tarnish its reputation through association with the unwholesome household of George and Martha is plausible.[16] And Richard Schickel himself, who has written the only major critical study of Disney's work to date, *The Disney Version,* was denied permission to reproduce a single image in his book. Schickel had entertained some very cordial relations with the Disney Studio personnel until Walt Disney's death in 1966. Thereafter, as the drift of his analysis began to be apparent, he "was given to understand that the studio did not approve of this study . . ."[17] Schickel received the impression that the studio wished only favorable biographies to appear and was unwilling to collaborate with anyone taking a critical stance.

Another, more peculiar refusal has been related by Maurice Sendak, the children's book author and illustrator. He reports that Mickey Mouse was one of the recurring figures in his own childhood fantasies. In his book *In the Night Kitchen,* he wished to pay tribute to the hero of his youth by fusing the Mickey of his book with the Disney Mouse—not in a prolonged treatment but in a single scene where the composite character became a decoration on a stove. But even this innocent transmutation came to the attention of the Disney permissions staff, doubtless through voluntary consultation by Sendak's publisher. Sendak was forbidden this use. He "put it down to the general decay of civilization" that "the Disney studio irritatingly refused to let me paint his revered image on a cooking stove that figured in my plot . . ."[18] Disney was perhaps concerned about the safety of children around stoves or interested in preserving the dignity of Mickey for state occasions when he meets visiting foreign dignitaries, such as the Emperor Hirohito.

On other occasions, Disney has denied permission without knowledge of a book's content—though there are cases in which they have asked for review of a manuscript as a condition for reaching a decision. Leslie Fiedler, for example, requested to reproduce an image from *Snow White and the Seven Dwarfs* to accompany his text of *Freaks* (Simon and Schuster). Fiedler's text—which Disney did not ask to see—simply observed that Disney had catered to a widespread human interest in the grotesque with his extremely popular dwarfs. Perhaps the Disney corporation did not wish the dwarfs to be associated with carnivals, circus side shows, and other "unwholesome" forms of American life that were avoided in the creation of Disneyland. Or perhaps the Disney corporation was still smarting from Simon and Schuster's publication of Shickel's *Disney Version* ten years earlier. It is hard to say what the decisive considerations were in denying a major cultural commentator like Fiedler the opportunity to document visually his claim concerning the public prevalence of curiosity about human aberrations. The reason that Disney gave in its correspondence was a variant of the "dilution of market" concept.

> As you may know, our characters are protected by copyright, and the nature of the United States Copyright is such that unless we exercise a high degree of control over every use thereof, we endanger that valuable property. In addition, this company licenses numerous others to reproduce our copyrighted characters in connection with many different publications and our commitments to them must be respected. . . . We hope that you will understand our position and will appreciate that our refusal is based in large part on legal considerations.[19]

But other publications reproducing Disney's images, some with rather unfavorable judgments, had appeared recently with the permission of the corporation.[20] Why should Leslie Fiedler be singled out and forbidden to incorporate images in his commentary? When questioned about all the elements entering into a decision—the letter concedes that the "refusal is based *in large part* on legal considerations" (italics added)—the Disney corporation will emphasize that it need not give reasons, since it is a privilege attaching to copyright that the holder may deny a request without providing an account of his precise reasons.

As in the somewhat extraordinary case of Donald Duck and the Chilean critique, it is appropriate to distinguish more routine dealings from their censorship implications. Clearly, the copyright mechanism at Disney can be used to deprive a critique of the visual evidence it may demand or a cultural history of the concrete documentation necessary for a substantial recreation of the past. The cooperation of the corporation and its archives is at times exemplary and public-minded—and should be commended accordingly.[21] But the mechanism it commands, in conjunction with its fearsome resources for prosecution, give it a discretion and selectivity unworthy of the presidential Medal of Freedom bestowed on Walt Disney. Copyright is, in effect, a means through which Disney's full entry into cultural history and commentary is administratively foreshortened. No institution—corporate, ecclesiastical, or political—merits that exemption, least of all in a land that professes a heritage of democratic discussion.

NOTES

[1]Letter from Larry Groce, Aug. 1, 1978.

[2]Phillip M. Hawley listed as board member in the *Annual Report 1977*. Carter-Hawley-Hale Stores is named as a defendant in the complaint against the Sony Corporation.

[3]This anecdote is in Bob Thomas, *Walt Disney: An American Original* (NewYork.: Simon and Schuster, 1976), p. 192.

[4]*Ibid.*, p. 85.

[5]Richard Schickel, *The Disney Version: The Life, Times and Art of Walt Disney* (New York: Avon Books, 1969), pp. 135-36.

[6]Cost and revenue information provided by Disney Archivist, David R. Smith, letter of July 31, 1978.

[7]Thomas, p. 258.

[8]*Ibid.*, pp. 257-58.

[9]Merchandising income data provided by Disney Archivist, David R. Smith, letter of July 31, 1978. As an "exploiter" of secondary revenues, Disney showed the way for later films like *Jaws, Star Wars*, and *Superman* (1978) which earned enormous sums from merchandising and character licenses. Similar long-term exploitations have occurred with the *Peanuts* characters.

[10]Revenue and operating income figures are taken from *Annual Report 1977, passim.*

[11]Bell Telephone is conducting a nationwide advertising campaign for decorative telephones. Each ad containing a picture of the Mickeyphone carries a Disney copyright notice. (It appears in *Texas Monthly*, August 1978, p. 47, and in national magazines.) Publisher's Central Bureau carries Christopher Finch's *The Art of Walt Disney: From Mickey to the Magic Kingdoms*. The picture of the book jacket (with Mickey's image) carries the copyright notice. Copyright notices are placed on letterheads and mailing labels that bear Mickey's image.

[12]Details on the *Pete's Dragon* campaign appear in the *Annual Report 1977*, p. 28.

[13]Details about the structure and process of copyright administration were graciously provided in an interview with Peter F. Nolan, Office of counsel, at Walt Disney Studios, Burbank, May 12, 1978.

[14]One should note that Disney's stance in the Sony case is seen as bad business practice by some critics in the investment community. Theodore W. Anderson at Argus Research Corp. suggests that Disney should have exploited the video bonanza by marketing tapes of its films, as other motion picture companies are. See "Can Disney Still Grow On Its Founder's Dreams?" *Business Week*, July 31, 1978, pp. 60-61.

[15]Disney won its litigation against Air Pirates. See Walt Disney Productions v. The Air Pirates, 345 F. Supp. 108 (N.D. Cal. 1972) and the appeal Walt Disney Productions v. The Air Pirates, 581 F.2d 751 (9th Cir. 1978).

[16]Schickel, p. 136.

[17]*Ibid.*, p. 311. Schickel reports in a letter, March 4, 1978, that he did not really regret the lack of pictures for his volume, since he felt that his study would be taken more seriously without them.

[18]See Sendak's account in "Growing up with Mickey," *TV Guide* 26 (Nov. 11, 1978): 75.

[19]Details of Fiedler's experience provided by conversation and letter of April 5, 1978. The statement of Disney's grounds for refusal is contained in a letter to Fiedler of March 8, 1977.

[20]See for example, Robert Jewett and John Shelton Lawrence, "Disney's Land: Saints and Sanitary Animals," in *The American Monomyth* (New York.: Doubleday, 1977), which reproduces several images by permission.

[21]See David R. Smith, "A Mouse is Born," *College and Research Libraries*, November 1978, for an account of the Disney archives, where it is described as "a great benefit to scholars who hope to tell the history of America and American businesses during the past half century" (p. 492). It is also described as a legal tool for Disney's use where others "infringe, knowingly or unknowingly, on its rights in its copyrighted characters" (p. 493).

The Unauthorized Reproduction
of Educational Audiovisual Materials (1)

In the important suit of Universal City Studios and Walt Disney Productions against the Sony Betamax, allegations of economic harm carry a surface plausibility, even though the pretrial memoranda of the plaintiffs did not suggest any exact way of measuring this harm. In contrast, discussions of the off-air reproduction of educational programs and the illegal copying of films and videocassettes have been more specific in identifying degrees and amounts of economic damage. In his brief statement, "Golden Egg Production: The Goose Cries 'Foul,' " R.B. Churchill, president of his own independent film-producing company, suggests the impact that bootleg reproduction has on his operations. His statement was written for a popular rather than scholarly audience and has achieved wide circulation, including reproduction in the *Hearings* volumes of the House Judiciary Committee. Complementary and more specialized statements of evidence regarding the educational film producer can be found in the testimony of Edward Meell, representing the Educational Media Producers Council before the House Judiciary Committee. [See 1975 *Hearings before the Subcommittee on Courts, Civil Liberties and the Administration of Justice of the House Committee*, Serial No. 36, Pt. 1, pp. 316-32. Another important related statement is James E. Lemay, "The Producer's View," in "Off-Air Taping, Piracy, and the New Copyright Law—A Symposium," *Educational and Industrial Television 10* (July 1978): 32-36.]

13

THE UNAUTHORIZED REPRODUCTION OF EDUCATIONAL AUDIOVISUAL MATERIALS—

GOLDEN EGG PRODUCTION: THE GOOSE CRIES "FOUL"

ROBERT CHURCHILL

I am a goose with tears in my eyes. People laugh at me in the street. Children stick out their tongues. A big grown-up goose. Crying!

It's about these eggs that I lay. Our eggs . . . well, maybe *golden* is too strong a word, but with out-of-pocket production costs averaging about $20,000 a film, nobody is eating them for breakfast.

What's all this crying nonsense? It's about videotape duplication. It's about a very real concern of producer-distributors that they will be forced out of business if educators duplicate 16mm films without authorization.

This article isn't going to belabor the illegality of videotape duplication under the copyright law or even the ethics of a little benign larceny (after all, it's for the benefit of the children, isn't it?). Rather let's examine the economics of egg production and why there soon may be no more eggs.

I will have to speak, of course, from the experience of our own small company, but I believe that it is reasonably representative. Let us assume that we produce a film for $20,000 and sell prints for $200. About 65 percent of that $200, give or take a few percents, pays for print costs, distribution (including preview prints), and overhead. The 35 percent pays off the production costs. In our example, production cost would be recouped with the sale of 285 prints.

Sounds like a great little enterprise, you say. Only 285 prints before we begin to make a profit. Ah, but it will take us two and a half to three years before we have sold 285 prints. You thought that this was big business, that we sold thousands of prints? No, film companies will sell perhaps 500 to 800 prints during the life of an average film. That's all.

Further, most of that 35 percent "profit" after the first 285 prints is what we use to produce new films.

The educator's position is that 16mm prints are so expensive that they can afford only a fraction of their needs. Why then couldn't videotape duplication solve the problem of providing all those extra copies that schools so desperately need?

If a fee is paid to the producer for the right to make copies, it's quite possible that the producer can still make a living and the schools can at last have as many copies of a film as they need. Personally, I profoundly hope that this will happen. Today films are too rare, too hard for the teacher to get. Availability will cause a great increase in use, understanding of the medium, and consequent further demand. Eventually I suspect that the producer will benefit as more funds are channeled into a teaching medium that has finally come alive.

Let's leave the heady vision of tomorrow's cornucopia long enough to notice that the last paragraph begins with an if. If on the other hand, the producer's films are duplicated without compensation, soon there will be no films. The goose is dead.

It works this way. A producer counts on a number of purchasers who buy not just one print, but from two to ten or more. Also, after a few years many users will replace a print that has worn out. If he loses these sales, the producer is in trouble.

An even greater potential hazard comes from the tape-happy media director who doesn't buy even the first print. A person from our company saw this happen in the office of an unself-conscious media director in northern California last spring. The director, who had on his desk a number of audio tapes sent in for a demonstration project from various producers, was calling across a partition to an assistant, conferring on the number of tapes of each title they thought they should run off on their high-speed duplicator. These were not 16mm films, but they might have been.

An ingenious way to save the taxpayers' money, by George! Next year perhaps they can set up a plant and print all their own textbooks by facsimile.

Even if this last imaginative kind of larceny doesn't become the rage in film duplication, the goose will succumb if there is loss of duplicate print orders and replacement sales. Conservatively these will account for 25 percent of a company's sales. And there isn't a film producer in the country, whether it's EBE or little old us, who wouldn't be out of business before you could say "videotape duplication" if its gross income dropped by 25 percent.

No duplication without compensation! Don't kill poor old granny goose! That's the word. Pass it on.

The Unauthorized Reproduction
of Educational Audiovisual Materials (2)

Proving the actual extent of bootleg copying may be as difficult as proving the economic harm caused by home off-air taping. But it has never been publicly argued that unauthorized film print duplication of educational films was fair use. Like piracy, it has been a surreptitious practice. Off-air taping of educational films by educational institutions, on the other hand—sometimes of the same films that were bootlegged in an earlier period—was rather widely assumed to be legitimate. Taping was done on a large scale and its results advertised for potential users. These are at least the surface facts in the BOCES case, where three educational film producers, Encyclopaedia Britannica Educational Corporation, Learning Corporation of America, and Time-Life Films brought suit against the Board of Cooperative Educational Services of Erie County, New York, and its administrators, C.N. Crooks and others. Their complaint was filed on October 19, 1977. A preliminary injunction favoring the plaintiffs was granted on February 27, 1978. No date for a full trial of the issues has been set as of this compilation. The value of the preliminary injunction reproduced here in part lies in its disclosure of the reasons that may weigh heavily with courts in future assessments of the claims of nonprofit institutions to engage in fair use off-air taping.

PRELIMINARY INJUNCTION AGAINST BOARD OF COOPERATIVE EDUCATIONAL SERVICES (BOCES)

JUDGE JOHN T. CURTIN

Encyclopaedia Britannica Educational Corporation, et al.
v. C.N. Crooks, et al.
No. 77-560 (W.D.N.Y. Feb. 27, 1978—
District Judge John T. Curtin Delivered the Decision)

The plaintiffs are three corporations engaged in the business of producing, acquiring, and licensing educational motion picture films. On October 19, 1977, the plaintiffs filed this copyright infringement suit against the Board of Cooperative Educational Services of Erie County (BOCES), a nonprofit corporation organized under the Education Law to provide educational services to the public schools in Erie County. The complaint alleges that BOCES has videotaped a number of their copyrighted films without their permission and distributed the copies to the school districts for delayed viewing by the students. The plaintiffs demand that the defendants be enjoined from videotaping copyrighted films and they seek both actual and statutory damages for past infringement. They also request an award of costs and fees, and the surrender or destruction of all infringing copies of the films.

At the time of filing the complaint, the plaintiffs moved for a temporary restraining order to prevent the destruction of the existing videotapes and records pertaining to the tapes in BOCES' possession pending a final decision in the case, and also to obtain accelerated discovery privileges. This motion was granted by the court, upon the plaintiffs' agreement to post a $10,000 bond to indemnify the defendants against possible loss. Both parties proceeded to engage in preliminary discovery.

The case is now before the court on the plaintiffs' motion for a preliminary injunction. The plaintiffs seek to temporarily enjoin the defendants from videotaping plaintiffs' copyrighted motion pictures from television broadcasts, recopying the videotapes, distributing these tapes to the school districts, displaying the copies in classrooms, and transmitting the videotaped films to the schools over closed-circuit television cables. A hearing on the motion was held on December 27, 1977, at which the attorneys agreed not to call witnesses in connection with the motion but to rely on filed affidavits, exhibits, memoranda of law, depositions, and oral argument.

All three of the plaintiffs are engaged in the business of producing, acquiring, and licensing educational audiovisual materials. Although the percentage varies among the three, all derive substantial income from the sale and licensing of copyrighted educational motion pictures, both to television networks and to educational institutions. Each of the plaintiffs owns copyrights to some of the films on which this infringement suit is based.

Since 1969, plaintiff Learning Corporation of America [LCA] has been entering into licensing agreements with BOCES for the purchase of 16-millimeter prints of educational films. In 1975, its revenues from BOCES reached a peak of $12,676.25, but declined to $1,703.75 by 1977. Some of the films on which LCA's infringement claim is based have been the subject of licensing agreements. Neither of the other two plaintiffs has at any time entered into licensing agreements with BOCES.

BOCES was created under §1958 of the New York Education Law for the purpose of providing educational services and specialized instruction on a cooperative basis to the school districts within its geographic district. The Erie County BOCES services twenty-one school districts, including over one hundred separate schools. The focus of this lawsuit is one of BOCES' services, its practice of videotaping educational programs from television broadcasts and distributing the tapes to the schools for delayed viewing in the classrooms.

BOCES admits that it has been videotaping television programs of educational value since 1966. Since 1968, it has been openly distributing catalogs to the teachers within the twenty-one school districts which describe the available programs and provide ordering instructions. Each of the educational films involved in this lawsuit has been listed in one of BOCES' catalogs as available to the schools.

When a program of educational value is broadcast on television, BOCES makes a master videotape of the entire film. The vast majority of films it tapes are broadcast by the local public broadcasting channel WNED-17, but some also are broadcast by commercial stations. The catalog describes the programs and provides that if a teacher wants to order a copy, the school district must supply BOCES with sufficient blank videotape and allow two weeks for processing.

When a school files a written request for a videotape, BOCES copies the master onto the blank tape and delivers the copy to the requesting school. BOCES holds the master in its videotape library for varying periods of time before erasure. The copies are viewed by the students in the classroom, and in most instances then are returned to BOCES for erasure and reuse in videotaping other programs. However, BOCES does not require the schools to return the tapes. A few of the school districts keep the copies for their own videotape libraries. BOCES also does not monitor the use of the tapes by the schools, but presumes they are used solely for educational purposes. Copies are distributed only to the schools within its twenty-one school districts and then only upon written request. Copies are supplied to the schools at cost, and no admission is charged to the students.

With the exception of the 1974-75 school year, BOCES has records of the number of copies made of each particular television program. These records show that the volume of copying is substantial. During the 1976-77 school year, for instance, BOCES duplicated approximately ten thousand videotapes. BOCES has not kept records of the number of times a copy has been displayed in the classroom or the ultimate disposition of the tapes.

According to the defendants' affidavits, this program is a significant component of the instructional support services provided by BOCES, and is relied upon by the teachers in planning their school curricula. Since many of the programs are televised when classes are not in session or at times that do not coincide with coverage of the subject in a particular course of study, it is claimed that the students cannot view these programs unless videotapes are available. In order to provide this service, BOCES has invested a considerable amount of money in videotape equipment, which has an estimated replacement cost of one-half million dollars. BOCES has between five and eight full-time employees working to provide the service. The defendants claim that if the program is discontinued, public education would be greatly disrupted.

All three of the plaintiffs have been aware that educational institutions were videotaping their copyrighted television programs for some time. Time-Life has had knowledge of this practice since at least 1972, and LCA and Encyclopaedia Britannica have known since 1973. The Association of Media Producers, a trade organization to which all three of the plaintiffs belong, has been negotiating with the National School

Board Association and other representatives of educational institutions in an attempt to define what constitutes fair use in the area of videotaping educational programs. These negotiations are still in progress, and no compromise has yet been reached.

BOCES' practices came to LCA's attention approximately in December 1976, when it received a copy of the BOCES videotape catalog. The catalog was thereafter supplied to the other two plaintiffs, and this action was commenced.

The plaintiffs' theory of infringement is straightforward. As the copyright owners of the films in question, they claim that they have the exclusive rights under federal copyright law to copy and perform the films. These exclusive rights were infringed by BOCES each time it videotaped one of the films off the air without permission and again each time it distributed a copy of a tape to a requesting school for performance in the classroom. They argue that in copyright infringement actions, irreparable harm is presumed once a prima facie case of infringement is established, and that therefore they are entitled to preliminary injunctive relief.

BOCES admits that it has videotaped the plaintiffs' copyrighted films without paying license fees or obtaining permission, but opposes the motion on three grounds. First, it raises the fair use doctrine as a defense and argues that noncommercial videotaping of television programs off the air for purposes of delayed viewing in the classroom is not a copyright infringement. Second, BOCES argues that the plaintiffs are barred by the doctrines of laches and estoppel from obtaining preliminary relief. Finally, it contends that any presumption of irreparable harm is rebutted by the existence of a clear measure of damages provided by the plaintiffs' licensing agreements, coupled with BOCES' records of the number of copies it has produced. In the post-argument papers, BOCES makes the additional claim that most of the television programs videotaped by BOCES were purchased by the local educational channel, WNED-TV, with state funds, and that these appropriations were made to WNED for the purpose of providing instructional broadcasts for the public schools at no cost to the schools. BOCES argues that the plaintiffs are seeking to force the state to pay twice for the use of their films and that the appropriations would not have been made if the instructional programs could not be utilized by the schools through videotaping. Although BOCES voluntarily stopped distributing tapes to the schools when the suit was commenced, it claims that this has caused a substantial hardship to the educational institutions served and wishes to reinstate its program.

As a general rule, a motion for preliminary relief should be granted only upon a clear showing of either probable success on the merits and possible irreparable injury or sufficiently serious questions going to the merits to make them a fair ground for litigation and a balance of hardships tipping in the plaintiff's favor.

I.

Turning first to the question of irreparable injury, the plaintiffs claim that BOCES' videotaping is depriving them of licensing fees and is irreparably impairing their market for educational films. They point out that BOCES could readily avoid any disruption in its educational services pending a final decision in this case by entering into licensing agreements with the plaintiffs for the copying and performance of their copyrighted films. They contend that these licenses would provide a ready measure of damages, payable out of the $10,000 bond should BOCES ultimately prevail.

BOCES contends that the presumption of irreparable harm in copyright infringement cases can be rebutted by showing that monetary damages would provide full compensation for any infringement. They claim that the plaintiffs' licensing agreements, taken in conjunction with BOCES' records of the number of videotapes being made, provide a clear measure of damages, and that therefore preliminary relief is inappropriate.

I find that the plaintiffs' showing of irreparable harm is sufficiently detailed to meet the standard enunciated in *Wainwright*. The plaintiffs allege that BOCES' practices threaten to destroy or substantially impair their market for educational films. This claim, if true, encompasses injury beyond lost licensing fees, which cannot readily be reduced to monetary terms. Moreover, BOCES does not keep records of the number of times each film is displayed in the schools, and it does not guarantee return of the videotapes. Absent such records and guarantees, the licensing agreements would not provide a clear measure of damages caused by distributing copies of the films to the schools.

II.

The question of probable success on the merits poses a more troublesome issue. Educational institutions have been videotaping television broadcasts for strictly educational purposes for some time. The legality of such copying has never been determined, either by the courts[1] or by the legislature. The problem of accommodating the competing interests of both educators and film producers raises major policy questions which the legislature is better equipped to resolve. However, Congress has not as yet provided a legislative solution to the problem, but has left the issue to the courts.[2]

I assume for purposes of this motion that the plaintiffs are the copyright owners of the films providing the basis for this lawsuit,[3] and that BOCES has videotaped and distributed copies of these films without the plaintiffs' permission, either by license agreements or otherwise.[4] This squarely raises the issue of infringement.

Section 1 of the Copyright Act of 1909 declares that a copyright owner shall have the exclusive rights to copy the copyrighted work and to exhibit or perform it publicly. Infringement of these rights entitles the copyright owner to injunctive and monetary relief.[5] Substantially the same general provisions were reenacted by Congress in the Copyright Revision Act of 1976,[6] which applies to any alleged infringements occurring on or after January 1, 1978. Act of October 19, 1976, *Pub. L. No. 94-553*, Transitional and Supplementary Provisions, §102, 90 Stat. 2598.

Viewed solely in reference to the copyright law, BOCES' videotaping activities would seem to constitute a blatant violation of the plaintiffs' exclusive rights to copy and perform their films. However, the statutory language is qualified by the judicial doctrine of "fair use." Although the doctrine is a defense to claims of copyright infringement, *Nimmer on Copyright* §145, its application nevertheless must be considered in determining the existence of a prima facie case for purposes of preliminary relief. *Wainwright, supra* at 94.

[Omitted from the text here are (1) a passage defining the statutory and judicial definitions of fair use, and (2) an analysis of defendants' appeal to the *Williams and Wilkins* precedent, in which the validity of the analogy is rejected. See Harriet L. Oler, Chapter 21, Section II, 3 "Off-air videotaping for nonprofit educational institutions" for a summary of the reasoning on the latter point.]

The scope of BOCES' activities is difficult to reconcile with its claim of fair use. This case does not involve an isolated instance of a teacher copying copyrighted material for classroom use but concerns a highly organized and systematic program for reproducing videotapes on a massive scale. BOCES had acquired videotape equipment worth one-half million dollars, uses five to eight full-time personnel to carry out its program, and makes as many as ten thousand tapes per year. For the last twelve years, these tapes have been distributed throughout Erie County to over one hundred separate schools.

Considering all of these factors, I find that the plaintiffs have established a prima facie case entitling them to preliminary relief. As BOCES points out, the applicability of the defense of fair use raises numerous questions of fact which cannot be resolved without a full trial on the merits. At this stage in the proceedings, I find that the substantiality of the copying and the possible impact on the market for education films tip the balance in favor of the plaintiffs, outweighing BOCES' noncommercial, educational purpose in copying the films.

In its post-argument papers, BOCES raises the additional claim that most of the television programs which it videotaped were purchased by WNED-TV with state funds, and that these appropriations were made to WNED for the purpose of providing instructional broadcasts for the public schools at no cost to the schools. BOCES argues that the plaintiffs are seeking to force the state to pay twice for the use of their films and that the appropriations would not have been made if the instructional programs could not be utilized by the schools through videotaping. At this time, the record does not contain sufficient information pertaining to this claim to defeat the plaintiffs' application for preliminary relief. This possible defense should be developed at trial.

[Omitted from the text here is the court's analysis of defendant's *laches* defense—the claim that plaintiffs had delayed too long in bringing their action.]

III.

The plaintiffs have established their entitlement to preliminary relief. Accordingly, I direct that BOCES be enjoined from videotaping the plaintiffs' educational films or programs off the public airwaves. If this order unduly disrupts educational plans, BOCES can obtain licenses from the plaintiffs for use of the films. As to films which have already been videotaped and are incorporated into the curricula of the BOCES' school districts, however, I find that the public interest would be served if BOCES is allowed to continue distributing such tapes to the schools. The interests of the plaintiffs will be adequately protected if BOCES, in cooperation with the school districts, implements a plan to monitor the use of the tapes in the schools and to require their return and erasure within a specified time period.

The parties are directed to meet with the court on March 3, 1978 at 9:00 A.M. to frame an order complying with the decision.

So ordered.

NOTES

[1]Walt Disney Productions v. Alaska Television Network, 310 F. Supp. 1073 (W.D. Wash. 1969), is not in point. The defendant in that case was engaged in commercial videotaping for profit and no question of fair use was raised.

[2]The Copyright Revision Act of 1976, Act of Oct. 19, 1976, *Pub.L.No.* 94-553, 90 Stat. 2541, codified in 17 U.S.C. §101-810, makes extensive changes in the copyright law, many of which were designed to address issues raised by rapidly changing technology. . . .

However, the Act does not address the question of whether off-the-air videotaping of copyrighted motion pictures for classroom use is an infringement. The legislative history clearly demonstrates Congress' intent to leave the problem to the courts pending further negotiations between the film industry and educators aimed at developing guidelines to protect the interests of both groups. . . .

[3]When the complaint was filed, the case concerned nineteen copyrighted films owned by the plaintiffs. Since that time, preliminary discovery has uncovered additional films owned by the plaintiffs and copied by the defendant. At this stage, BOCES is not contesting the plaintiffs' ownership of the copyrights. As additional films are added to the complaint, however, BOCES is entitled to investigate plaintiffs' ownership of particular films and object where appropriate.

[4]As to LCA, some question of permission may exist. Some of the films providing the basis of this lawsuit were at one time the subject of licensing agreements between LCA and BOCES. In addition, as pointed out in the defendants' Brief in Opposition to Motion for Preliminary Injunction at 36-37, LCA agreed to allow videotaping off the air by schools which subscribed to educational television for seven-day periods after the program was broadcast, and some question arises as to whether BOCES' practices fall within this express permission. These issues should be resolved at trial.

[5]Derived from Act of Mar. 4, 1909, ch.320, §§l, 25, 64, 35 Stat. 1075, 1081, 1088, and previously codified in 17 U.S.C. §§1(a), 1(d), 101.

[6]Now codified in 17 U.S.C. §§106, 502-03.

Fair Use and Broadcasting

Eugene N. Aleinikoff has served for a number of years as broadcast counsel to the Corporation for Public Broadcasting. His essay gives a balanced picture of the considerations and the interest pressures that will shape future applications of the fair use principle in the broadcast field.

Part I deals with fair use as applied on a case-by-case basis to the creation of broadcast programming. He suggests a margin of uncertainty here that will continue to require careful review of uses and user interests. (Many decisions of this kind may be eliminated by the compulsory license and Copyright Royalty Tribunal features of the Copyright Act of 1976. See Section 118 and Sections 801-810. *The Federal Register,* Vol. 43, No. 111, June 8, 1978, contains the CRT's determination of rates for public broadcast uses of particular types of material.)

Part II reviews the off-air taping controversies and suggests that generally the scope of fair use may be diminished through restrictions on use-period and transferability, and through the creation of compulsory licensing and stricter policing arrangements. These evolutions in practice are being prompted by a greater willingness of producer interests to assert their copyright prerogatives and to litigate in securing them.

14

FAIR USE AND BROADCASTING

Eugene N. Aleinikoff

FAIR USE OF COPYRIGHTED MATERIALS IN BROADCAST PROGRAMS

Whether one views electronic broadcasting as essentially different in kind or merely in degree from earlier print media, the sharp contrast in audience circulation and impact, and the revolutionary technological developments of the past few years, cannot but raise serious questions about the applicability of traditional standards of fair use to broadcasting. The obvious differences within the broadcasting world itself between television and radio, between commercial and public broadcasting, between entertainment and informational programming, and even between news reporting and documentary features—all make for additional complexity.

To add to the difficulty, judicial guidance on the extent of the fair use privilege in broadcasting has so far been sparse. Commercial television, heavily loaded with weekly film series, live sports coverage, feature motion pictures, and the rest of usual American television fare, is not the type of arena where fair use of previously copyrighted works often comes into play. Public television is apparently too new, underwatched, and poorly financed to have stirred copyright owners to take program producers to court to test fair use defenses.

There have, however, been sporadic broadcasting cases in the general realm of fair use. Perhaps the oddest permitted Jimmy Durante's poetry reading on NBC Radio in the 1930s.[1] Although that ruling was premised on a statutory omission in the author's rights—which led to legislative amendment of what was then Section 1(c) of the Copyright Law specifically to include nondramatic literary works within radio-reading prohibition—the spirit of fair use could be discerned. In the 1950s came the twin cases involving Jack Benny in "Autolite" and Sid Caesar in "From Here to Obscurity" which highlighted the extent of noninfringing parody in copyright law.[2] And in the 1970s, a television biography of Ezra Pound was found not to infringe upon an earlier biographical book on assorted grounds of noncopyrightability of public domain material, noncopying of the book, and fair use of historical facts in the television program.[3]

As the Supreme Court has indicated recently in the context of "indecency,"[4] broadcasting is so very different from print in immediacy and accessibility, directness and persuasiveness as perhaps to justify more restrictive legal standards. Thus, it can presumably be argued that free broadcasting exposure cannot help but adversely affect the financial return from copyrighted works included in television and radio programs. That premise is, of course, not without question—namely, the large amount of "payola" that disc jockeys are reputedly offered for radio promotion of popular records. It can also be contended that television, with its tremendous budgets and immense financial resources, should compensate creative authors and their publishers for all but the most insignificant uses of their works. As far as most commercial television is concerned, there seems to be some justification for that philosophy: "fair use" has always been narrowly applied to commercial material and theatrical entertainment. But television documentaries must be viewed as a different category, with the same First Amendment considerations as in the Howard Hughes biography and Kennedy assassination film cases,[5] whether on commercial or public television. And certainly news broadcasts and educational television must be accorded all the "public interest" considerations implicit in the copyright clause of the Constitution.

There are further differences from the print media. Television programs are shot and recorded, edited and assembled in ever new and more complicated ways which adapt and use subject material far beyond original anticipation. A photograph can be shown for a split second or on a split screen; a few lines of poetry may be used for continuity or coloration on either radio or television. Both may have major program importance and wide audience viewing, however brief the broadcast exposure or limited the program allusion.

On the other hand, a complete theme from a symphony performed by a large orchestra may be used in an undoubtedly informational or instructional manner, well within usual fair use criteria. And in many cases, use of extensive portions of copyrighted works will provably fail to so result in competition with, reduction of value of, or other adverse effect on the included works as to preclude fair use treatment.[6]

Fair use must thus be applied to broadcasting, as in other areas, primarily on a case-by-case basis in the light of the factors set forth in Section 107. Yet perhaps some general guidelines can be perceived. Both the Senate and House reports on Section 107 specifically endorsed the Copyright Register's 1961 report which included, among other examples, "incidental or fortuitous reproduction, in a newsreel or broadcast, of a work located in the scene of an event being reported."[7] And the House and Senate reports repeated previous indications of possible fair use application in the realm of educational broadcasting, albeit somewhat circumscribed by emphasis on the size of audience, payment to performers and producers, etc., as countervailing factors.[8]

There seem to be three clear types of fair use in television and radio: first, incidental appearances in news and documentary broadcasts, which are not artificially contrived but are part of the actual reportage—e.g., a background painting on the wall, music played by a band in a public parade, an identifiable poster shown in a street scene, a radio soap-opera heard in a television documentary sequence;[9] second, brief examples used for exemplary, analytic, or critical purposes in educational or instructional programs—e.g., a passage from a book, an excerpt from a ballet, a clip from a movie, or short portions of a television program;[10] third, minimal broadcast inclusions for noncompeting purposes—for example, hand puppets seen in the course of a musical performance on a children's television show;[11] 15 seconds of a political campaign song record included in the opponent's radio commercial.[12]

On the other hand, it seems equally undeniable that copyrighted works cannot be used merely for program decoration or augmentation under the aegis of fair use. A producer is not, and should not be, free to score a dramatic film from assorted passages of copyrighted music. A visual collage of copyrighted photographs should not be freely available for a documentary film irrespective of lack of content connection. Feature film clips cannot be used simply to spice instructional programming without direct educational justification.

There is, of course, a wide middle ground where no exact guidelines presently exist. Frequently, for some reason, this area of doubt has come up in the instance of television commercials recorded off-air for inclusion in public broadcasting programs. Since they are so short, it is difficult to believe that one or more copyrighted radio or television commercials cannot be demonstrated in an educational program on the techniques of advertising writing or production. But is that use equally justified as historical commentary, or for humorous purposes in a variety-type program? Does it make any difference whether the program use is pejorative, rather than complimentary, in terms of the economic injury inflicted or educational benefit derived? And should the commercial's having been made for widest possible dissemination and viewing be a compelling factor in permitting its use for dissimilar television purposes?

Other examples of uncertainty abound: a phonograph record played or poem read as part of the action of a television drama; a radio segment utilized in a broadcast retrospective; a motion picture sequence included in a biography of its director. They attest to the restless ingenuity of television and radio producers and to the unparalleled need for new creativity to interest easily bored home audiences. And they never cease to provide broadcast lawyers with new problems that can be answered only by considered judgment in the light of the length and manner of program use as well as the nature and type of program in which used.

FAIR USE AND THE OFF-AIR TAPING OF BROADCAST MATERIALS

Even more uncertainty is encountered in considering the legal status of reproducing copyrighted television and radio programs without permission for school or home use.

Off-air school recording came up too late in the revision process for legislative action, but the House report discussed the probable application of fair use under Section 107 as follows:

> The problem of off-the-air taping for non-profit classroom use of copyrighted audiovisual works incorporated in radio and television broadcasts has proved to be difficult to resolve. The Committee believes that the fair use doctrine has some limited application in this area, but it appears that development of detailed guidelines would require a more thorough explanation than has so far been possible of the needs and the problems of a number of different materials affected, and of the various legal problems presented. Nothing in Section 107 or elsewhere in the bill is intended to change or pre-judge the law on this point. On the other hand, the Committee is sensitive to the importance of the problem, and urges the representatives of the various interests, if possible under the leadership of the Register of Copyrights, to continue their discussions actively and in a constructive spirit. If it would be helpful to a solution, the Committee is receptive to undertaking further consideration of the problem in a future Congress.[13]

The House report comment on off-air videorecording thus looks toward educational guidelines akin to the classroom print and music guidelines negotiated between the educators and authors/composers/publishers which are included verbatim in the House report. In the absence of such guidelines, or indeed of further congressional action, off-air recording for school use, a practice widely prevalent in American school systems, must be viewed under general Section 107 standards.

And since what is at issue is the use of complete recordings of entire radio and television programs for nonprofit educational purposes, Factors (1) and (3) in Section 107 are fixed from the start. Thus Section 107 consideration must concentrate on Factors (2) and (4): "the nature of the copyrighted work" and the "effect of the use on the potential market for or value of the copyrighted work." But there is little reason to believe that Factor (2) "the nature of the copyrighted work" is of much significance here. Given the desirability of a specific television program for teaching, there seems to be no real differentiation to be made between a documentary like "Sixty Minutes," or "docudrama" like "Roots," or drama like "Masterpiece Theatre."

That leaves as crucial Factor (4)—i.e., the economic effect on the marketing of, or income from, the radio or television program which is reproduced. This adverse effect can be measured as in other cases by decreased profits—but peculiar to broadcasting, can also be judged in terms of increased costs to the program owner. The latter is the result of the residual pattern of talent compensation in television production; actors and announcers, writers and directors all receive additional fees for extended program exposure—typically television reruns, foreign broadcasts, and audiovisual exhibition. The talent unions, having won those battles, can be presumed to insist upon supplemental fees for off-air school recording, whether authorized by the television producer or automatically permitted under the copyright law. These additional off-air recording fees can be borne by the television producer only out of special license fees charged to school users, or increased charges to the broadcasting organizations. In view of recent CATV experience, it appears highly unlikely that commercial television would concur in increasing broadcast fees to permit wider school use where the student audience is not the type of buying audience generally sought by television advertisers. And special off-air license fees to schools could be directly competitive with standard audiovisual distribution fees, and hence presumably would not result in increased income to cover additional costs.

Thus the economic emphasis returns to decreased profits. There is, no doubt, potential market value for television programs in educational post-broadcast use. Historically, this school distribution has been accomplished through so-called nontheatrical distribution agencies selling or renting directly to schools along the same lines as educational films and apart from broadcast channels. It is difficult to persuade television producers, let alone major motion picture distributors, that off-air recordings of their stock in trade are not going to supplant usual educational audiovisual distribution—especially now that 16mm film prints are being replaced by videocassettes using virtually the same exhibition equipment as off-air recordings.

On the other hand, educators find it hard to understand how classroom use the next morning of a previous evening's television program can be viewed as inconsistent in any way with the hoped-for exposure of the original broadcast. If CATV commercial relay did not require additional license or payment under the former copyright law (before the compulsory license now in Section 111), they ask, why should educational delay be considered an infringement simply by nature of off-air recording for that purpose?

The argument goes further in terms of precedent. The Supreme Court, among others, has expressly emphasized the need to interpret the copyright law in light of the public benefit achieved rather than the private monopoly promoted.[14] The Federal Communications Act is premised on the public ownership of the air waves, and their utilization in the public "convenience, interest and necessity."[15] Certain educational copying prerogatives have already been established by agreed-upon guidelines for literary and musical materials for teaching purposes. And indeed, the Senate Report specifically recognized the application of fair use principles to off-air school recordings under limited conditions.[16]

The educational television community has also made the point that off-air recording and classroom playback, so long as accompanied by appropriate time and place restrictions, can perform a promotional rather than substitutional function. Instructional resource materials, once used, can easily come to be regarded as mainstays for the classroom teacher—in which case, audiovisual copies must be specially purchased or rented from the program distributor. It may be difficult for film and television production organizations to accept the nature of off-air recording as abetting or creating, rather than diminishing or destroying, their market, but that economic position has been urged—and in the absence of real data to the contrary, could be convincing in the courts and Congress.

Even assuming potential financial loss of the post-broadcast educational market, however, there are public interest arguments for protected fair use. Comparatively few television and radio programs are easily available for separate delivery in a nonbroadcast format—and then presumably considerably after the "teachable moment" that has been so often cited. The importance of this lack of ready availability has not only influenced the classroom literary and music guidelines. It is reflected as well in the library photocopying provisions for out-of-print books under Section 108(c) and (e), and in the recording privileges for "audio-visual news programs" in Section 108(f). To round out the circle, there is specific statutory authorization in Section 110(1) to display motion picture films and television programs among other works "in the course of face-to-face teaching activities of a non-profit educational institution, in a classroom or similar place devoted to instruction," so long as by lawfully made copies.

The copyright owners' answer is simple and forthright: copying a full television or radio program is a clear violation of the most basic copyright right of all, the right to copy under Section 106(1)—and "fair use" can never justify copying an entire program for widespread viewing. As a matter of economics, the audiovisual producers point to the current vision of popular videodisc sales at very low prices, and the consequent increase in the home and institutional market for all types of programs—which off-air copying availability could conceivably curtail. And most practically, there is the claim that no matter how limited the free permission for off-air recording, little policing is practically possible and the probability of educational piracy beyond those limits is too great to risk under the guise of restricted fair use.

This feared lack of educational moderation is presumably the cause of the current suit in New York by several film producers against the Erie County BOCES educational audiovisual agency, *Encyclopaedia Brittanica v. Crooks.* Erie County BOCES, like many other agencies across the country, had followed a practice of recording television broadcasts of local commercial and educational television stations. BOCES then circulated catalogs of its television recordings to the school systems in its area and, upon request, furnished duplicate recordings to interested teachers or administrators, apparently without any time or place restriction on the use of these recordings.

The federal judge hearing the case issued a preliminary injunction temporarily prohibiting BOCES' off-the-air recording activities (while permitting previously videotaped films to continue to be distributed to schools which already included them in their curricula so long as strictly maintained and subsequently erased) pending final judicial determination of its claim of fair use. His opinion, in effect, indicates probable denial of a fair use privilege on the rationale that, given the probable availability of film licensing from the plaintiffs:

> the substantiality of the copying and the possible impact on the market for educational films tip the balance in favor of the plaintiffs, outweighing BOCES' non-commercial, educational purpose in copying the films.

But there is a serious question whether the balance might not be tipped the other way if off-air recording activities are limited to a single school and the resultant recordings used for classroom purposes in that school only during the same week before destruction or erasure. That practice has already been permitted by such major educational television agencies as the Agency for Instructional Television, the Great Plains Instructional Television Library, and the Public Television Library—all three of which have subscribed to a joint statement of policy excluding only programs for which underlying rights restrictions do not permit off-air videotaping. Seven-day school rerecording is also referred to in

Section 118(d) as appropriate exposure of public radio and television programs for which copyrighted musical and pictorial works are subject to compulsory license.

Whatever its ultimate outcome, the BOCES suit indicates strongly that the prerevision era of nonaction by film producers and television companies is rapidly drawing to a close, and that the off-air recording guidelines sought by the House Copyright Subcommittee are urgently needed. Many film and television distributors have indicated their willingness to establish a practical and reasonable clearance process that would make fair use redundant. Consequently, only by espousing fair use privileges that can be judicially defended under the Section 107 criteria will the educational community find it possible to withstand producer-distributor pressure to paint fair use altogether out of the picture.

That the commercial stakes are high is further evidenced in the current lawsuit by major Hollywood film companies, including Universal Studios and Walt Disney Productions against Sony Corporation, its distributors and customers, to prevent Betamax home recording of feature films shown on television.[18] The Universal City Studios v. Sony Corporation of America case involves, if anything, an even more fundamental copyright issue than the BOCES litigation.

Before the advent of home off-air videorecording equipment at marketable retail prices, it had generally been assumed that a single copy of a copyrighted work for an individual's own personal use would not constitute actionable infringement. The usual analogy of a handwritten copy of a library book was easily extendable in the library copying provisions of Section 108 to permit photocopies and phonorecords for "private study, scholarship or research" under certain conditions. As another example, the Senate report, in commenting on the revision bill, noted that "the making of a single copy or phonorecord by an individual as a free service for a blind person could properly be considered a fair use under Section 107."[19] Even more directly, the House report accompanying the 1972 Copyright Act Amendment initiating copyright protection for sound recordings, clearly indicated the view that off-air tape recordings of phonograph records would not infringe upon the newly created right, as follows:

> Specifically, it is not the intention of the Committee to restrain the home recording, from broadcasts or from tapes or records, of recorded performances, where the home recording is for private use and with no purpose of reproducing or otherwise capitalizing commercially upon it.[20]

This philosophical view of the exclusion of private use from the copyright owners' exclusive rights is, of course, consistent with the limitation of the Section 106 "performing" and "display" rights to cover only performances and displays "publicly," with the added definition in Section 101:

> To perform or display a work publicly means (1) to perform or display it at a place open to the public or at any place where a substantial number of persons outside of a normal circle of a family and its acquaintances is gathered; or (2) to transmit or otherwise communicate a performance or display of the work to a place specified by clause (1). . . .

Similar is the provision in Section 109(b) authorizing owners of lawful copies to display them publicly "to viewers present at the place where the copy is located." Finally, the United States Supreme Court had, at least indirectly, lent emphasis to the protected nature of private in-home activities in a 1969 "obscenity" decision,[21] as well as in its disinclination in the cable television cases to hold CATV operators liable under the copyright law for separate performances when reaching at-home viewers by broadcast relays.[22]

Indeed, it was perhaps their defeats in the protracted CATV litigation that caused the major motion picture companies to attempt more immediate legal action on home videotape recording. Also undoubtedly of importance was the anticipated advent of cheap videodiscs for home consumption, arousing the film companies to serious fears of unfair competition from widespread homerecording equipment that could well undercut the demand for videodisc availability of previously produced feature films and television series.

As a consequence, whatever the earlier assumptions among the copyright fraternity, Universal and Walt Disney brought suit in the California federal court in 1976 against Sony, along with assorted Betamax dealers, retailers, and buyers. As outlined by the film companies, their basic contentions are

> (a) that whenever a Betamax owner records their copyrighted motion pictures off of television, such conduct infringes the copyrights of the plaintiffs, and (b) the naked sale of a Betamax recorder-player (a machine which is admittedly designed for the main purpose of recording television shows off the air) makes all those in the chain of sale liable for infringements which are thereafter committed with Betamax.

Apart from this rather novel application of the doctrine of contributory infringement, there is throughout the Betamax suit the flavor of the plaintiffs' serious concern about Sony's refusal to indicate potential copyright infringement by home television recording in its advertisements, and its encouraging, as their brief puts it, "building libraries of copyrighted television material, omitting commercials from the recordings they make, and trading tape-recorded television shows with other Betamax owners."

Like the BOCES case, the Betamax suit was begun under the

preexisting copyright law, alleging infringements of the general right to "copy" any work under old Section 1(a) and the specific right to make a "transcription or record" of a dramatic work, along with the accompanying right to "exhibit" or "perform" such dramatic work therefrom, under old Section 1(d). There seems little question but that Section 106 of the new act provides equal if not greater protection in its broad definition of the first exclusive right as to "reproduce the copyrighted work in copies or phono-records" read in conjunction with Section 101 definition of "copies" as:

> Material objects . . . in which a work is fixed by any method now known or later developed, and from which the work can be perceived, reproduced, or otherwise communicated, either directly or with the aid of a machine or device. The term "copies" includes these material objects . . . in which the work is first fixed.

A literal reading of the statute would therefore appear initially to be in the plaintiffs' favor.

The Sony defenses can be summarized along three general lines: first, that private off-air videotape recording is not within the proscriptions of Sections 1(a) and (d); second, that public policy requires an exclusion for off-air home recording either to be read into Sections 1(a) and (d) or considered to be derived from implied consent by the copyright owner; third, that the doctrine of fair use should be applicable. The emphasis is clearly on private use, rather than educational purpose, with a sprinkling of First Amendment considerations.

None of these defenses is, of course, predicated on clear statutory language or unarguable legislative intent. The 1909 statute could never have envisioned electronic television recording and playback, and the prerevision language was sufficiently general to permit almost any interpretation.

Nor are the copyright revision proceedings of much assistance in this effort. True, all the participants laid great stress on "public performance" and the difficulty, if not impossibility, of preventing private recording. But that does not alter the direct and unequivocable exclusive right to "copy" under Section 106(1). And whereas home audiotapes of radio programs were apparently expressly intended to be permitted in the sound recordings copyright amendment in 1972, the economic consequences of home videotaping may well be far different from that of home audiotapes—just as the economic importance of videodiscs is probably far greater than long-play record albums.

The public policy argument inherent in the Supreme Court's emphasis on the constitutional "public interest" objectives of the copyright law in recent "performance" cases seems more difficult to bring to bear in the Betamax case. At least one federal court has already distinguished the concurrent live relay permitted in cable television decisions from off-air recording for subsequent CATV origination, and explicitly held CATV recording to be a gross copyright violation.[23] Nor has the Supreme Court ever cited the "public ownership" of the airwaves as justification for making free with copyrighted programs and indeed, in the cable television cases, specifically refused to subscribe to an "implied consent" theory that might have been hinted at in an earlier hotel-system radio-reception case.[24]

The fair use considerations in the Betamax case are not markedly different from the BOCES litigation—involved are full recorded copies of complete audiovisual works of all types. Here, however, the prime question is the balance of possible damaging consequences for motion picture companies against undoubted benefit to equally large commercial concerns servicing the personal interests of individual viewers. It is possible that fair use guidelines could be constructed to reach an accommodation through express restrictions on use-period and transferability—along similar lines as has been proposed for the guidelines for school off-air recording in the House report. In their absence, however, the California court will be faced with the same kind of hard decision as in the celebrated *Williams and Wilkins* decision on reprography,[25] and with equally unpredictable results.

In any event, the Betamax case is a prime example of the increasing necessity of copyright law to create new mechanisms for handling old rights. Modern technology has made it virtually impossible to prevent easy copying of any copyrighted work. What is necessary, therefore, is exploration of ways in which the use of copies can be enforceably controlled and copyright owners can be properly compensated. The Betamax case may not presently be aimed in that direction, but its outcome in the courts either way may well lead to legislative action that will force the same kind of solution that has already been accorded similar conflicting interests in cable television—namely, a form of combined minimal exemption and compulsory license, coupled with policing requirements, that will insure both availability and payment.

NOTES

[1]Kreymburg v. Durante, 22 U.S.P.Q. 248 (S.D.N.Y. 1934).

[2]Loew's Inc. v. Columbia Broadcasting System Inc., 131 F. Supp. 165 (S. D. Calif. 1955), 239 F.2d 532 (9th Cir. 1956), 356 U.S. 43 (1958) and Columbia Pictures Corp. v. National Broadcasting Co., 137 F.Supp. 348 (S.D. Calif. 1955).

[3]Norman v. Columbia Broadcasting System Inc., 333 F.Supp. 788 (S.D.N.Y. 1971).

[4]FCC v. Pacifica Foundation, 98 Sup. Ct. 3026 (1978).

[5]Rosemont Enterprises, Inc. v. Random House, Inc., 366 F.2d 303 (2d Cir. 1966) and Time Inc. v. Bernard Geis Associates, 293 F.Supp. 130 (S.D.N.Y. 1968).

[6]See Meeropol v. Nizer, 560 F.2d 1061 (2d Cir. 1977).

[7]Senate *Report* No. 94-473, 94th Cong., 1st Sess., p. 62; House *Report* No. 94-1476.

[8]Senate *Report* No. 94-473, 94th Cong., 1st Sess., p. 65, House *Report* No. 94-1476, 94th Cong., 2d Sess., p. 72.

[9]E.g., Italian Book Corporation v. American Broadcasting Company, 4 Med.L.Rptr. 1762 (S.D.N.Y. 1978).

[10]Cf. House *Report* No. 94-1476, 94th Cong., 2d Sess., p. 72.

[11]Mura v. Columbia Broadcasting System Inc., 245 F.Supp. 787 (S.D.N.Y. 1965).

[12]Keep Thomson Governor Committee v. Citizens for Gallen Committee, No. 78-331 (D.C. New Hampshire 1978).

[13]House *Report* No. 94-1476, 94th Cong., 2d Sess., p. 71.

[14]Twentieth Century Music Corp. v. Aiken, 422 U.S. 151 (1975).

[15]47 U.S.C.A. Sec. 303, 307, 309.

[16]Senate *Report* No. 94-473, 94th Cong., 1st Sess., p. 66.

[17]Encyclopaedia Brittanica Educational Corp. v. Crooks *et al.,* 447 F.Supp. 243 (W.D.N.Y. 1978).

[18]Universal City Studios Inc. v. Sony Corp. of America No. CV 76-3520F (D.C.W.D. Calif.)

[19]Senate *Report* No. 94-473, 94th Cong., 1st Sess., p. 66.

[20]House *Report* No. 92-487, 92d Cong., 1st Sess., p. 7.

[21]Stanley v. Georgia, 394 U.S. 557 (1969).

[22]Fortnightly Corp. v. United Artists Television Inc. 382 U.S. 390 (1968) and Teleprompter Corp. v. CBS Inc., 415 U.S. 394 (1974).

[23]Walt Disney Productions v. Alaska Television Network Inc., 310 F.Supp. 1073 (W.D. Wash. 1969).

[24]See Buck v. Jewell-La Salle Realty Co., 283 U.S. 191 (1931).

[25]Williams and Wilkins Co. v. United States, 287 F.2d 1345 (1973), 420 U.S. 376 (1975).

V

COPYRIGHT AND FAIR USE TRADITIONS IN INTERNATIONAL PERSPECTIVE

International

Everyone has the right to the protection of the moral and material interests resulting from any scientific, literary, or artistic production of which he is the author (Article 27, §2, *Universal Declaration of Human Rights,* December 10, 1948 United Nations General Assembly).

Through its Declaration, the United Nations asserted, in effect, that copyright is a basic human right—"a common standard of achievement for all peoples and all nations," as its Preamble suggested. Unlike so many other rights enumerated there, e.g., "the right to work, to free choice of employment, to just and favorable conditions of work" (Article 23), the rights of copyright have been substantially achieved by the industrialized nations.

But internationally, as well as in the United States, both technological evolution and ideals of free discussion have led to copyright debates. Recording and replication technologies can diminish the protection of material interests in scientific, literary, or artistic productions. And the speech interest-copyright conflict is implicit in the Declaration itself, becoming evident when we juxtapose against Article 27 another asserting the claims of free expression.

Everyone has the right to freedom of opinion and expression; this right includes freedom to hold opinions without interference and to seek, receive, and impart information and ideas through any media and regardless of frontiers. (Article 19)

Does copyright impose restraints against the freedom "to seek, receive and impart information and ideas through any media"? Because the major media-producing nations are sympathetic with *both* speech rights *and* copyright protection, they too are debating the implicit conflict.

The formulations in this debate vary as does the degree of intensity. The contributors to this section allow us to see the copyright discussions from the vantage point of their own national experience and the particular range of materials with which they possess special familiarity.

All the countries represented here have some kind of statutory recognition of the fair use principle, though in none does it seem to be defined with any more explicitness than in Section 107 of the 1976 Copyright Act of the United States. In its application, the principle has the status of a "rule of reason" whose determinations are governed by a consideration of particular circumstances.

The new media generally, and visual media especially, have proved to be troublesome areas for fair use. For example, the reports on Great Britain, Canada, and France indicate intensive recent discussions involving government-appointed commissions, position papers, or the formation of private associations for the stricter regulation of authors' rights.

Some rough generalizations may be ventured on the basis of these reports.

195

— There has been very little application of fair use principles to the new media. Compulsory licensing, for example, in the area of off-air taping by educational institutions, is either already a requirement or seems likely to be adopted among all the nations represented. For an extensive survey of compulsory licensing arrangements and international practice on off-air taping, see Franca Klaver, "The Legal Problems of Video-cassettes and Audiovisual Discs," WIPO/Unesco/IGC/XR.1 (1971)/13, October 24, 1975; also in *Bulletin of the Copyright Society of the USA* 23 (Fall 1976):152-85.

— Whereas the laws reported on are not markedly less restrictive than those of the United States, the foreign experience seems less prone to practices that might be labeled *prior restraint* and also less prone to litigation. The reports on Great Britain and Japan emphasize rather amiable relations between scholars and copyright holders. (Japan has a mediating mechanism to circumvent the court system entirely in copyright disputes, but it has not been necessary to use it in cases related to research.)

These foreign contributions provide some perspective on current United States issues and hint at a potential wealth of distinctions and alternative practices that might be relevant to dealing with current disputes about the aims and proper limits of copyright protection.

Some of the scholars, in writing for this volume, were guided partially by a questionnaire prepared by the editors. This questionnaire is printed as an Appendix to the following section.

Great Britain

Harry S. Bloom is Senior Lecturer in Law at the University of Kent, Canterbury. His report summarizes the deliberations of the Whitford Committee, a major study group appointed by the British government in 1973, reviews the philosophy of copyright, and sketches some areas of current practice in permissions procedures and off-air taping. Britain has a "fair dealing" concept, but its scope is more restricted than that of the United States statute in that visual materials are specifically excluded. In practice, however, there seems to be greater availability of new media artifacts through mutually satisfactory negotiations between copyright holders and scholars.

15

THE COPYRIGHT POSITION IN BRITAIN

HARRY S. BLOOM

PART I: THE WHITFORD COMMITTEE

The British government set up in 1973 a departmental committee chaired by Mr. Justice Whitford and known as the Whitford Committee, to "consider and report on whether any and if so what changes were desirable in the existing law of copyright in Britain."

The committee produced a bulky report in March 1977 after nearly three years of intensive evidence taken from several hundred persons and organizations. These covered a wide span of subjects: book publishing, broadcasting, photocopying, television and radio, gramophone records, education, newspapers, audio and visual recording, rediffusion, typefaces, libraries, as well as the international aspects of the far-flung spread of copyright interests of what could now with proper justification be called the *copyright empire.*

Among the subjects on which the Whitford Committee wanted special guidance from practitioners and experts in the industry was the subject of computers and especially computer programs and software generally. The response was encouraging—leading computer business organizations, prominent academics, the Post Office (Telecommunications), The British Computer Society, and a large number of organizations and persons involved in the computing industry presented written and oral evidence, giving their views and offering suggestions.

The Whitford Committee in its general review managed to produce a uniform study from such a great variety of submissions. That in itself is an achievement. But first, the committee felt it necessary to point out that "unless the principles on which protection is to be given are clearly understood, the drafting of a comprehensible new Copyright Act will be impossible." Thus, it said, it was necessary to start by considering copyright protection and design protection separately, for they had developed separately.

The following is the committee's definition of (i) copyright and (ii) industrial design.

Copyright

Copyright is one form of what is comprehensively described in today's jargon as *intellectual property*. Copyright protection finds its justification in fair play. A person works and produces something. The product of his skill and labor ought to belong to him (or possibly his employer). A baker, everyone will agree, is entitled to be protected against thieves who seek to steal a loaf of bread baked by him. The baker, however, is plainly not entitled to a monopoly in baking. Further, anyone who buys a loaf from him is entitled to do what he likes with it. He can eat it, he can sell it to somebody else, if he can find a buyer, or use it as a decoration. Competition is healthy. If rival bakers bake bread, each does his work and makes his profit without helping himself to the product of the skill and labor of his rival.

A writer writes an article about the making of bread. He puts words on paper. He is not entitled to a monopoly in the writing of articles about the baking of bread, but the law has long recognized that he has an interest not merely in the manuscript, the words on paper which he produces, but in the skill and labor involved in his choice of words and the exact way in which he expresses his ideas by the words he chooses. If the author sells copies of his article, then again a purchaser of a copy can make such personal use of that copy as he pleases. He can read it or sell it secondhand, if he can find anyone who will buy it. If a reader of the original article is stimulated into writing another article about bread, the original author has no reason to complain. But it has long been recognized that only the original author ought to have the right to reproduce the original article and sell the copies thus reproduced. If other people were free to do this they would be making a profit out of the skill and labor of the original author. For this reason the law has long given to authors, for a specified term, certain exclusive rights in relation to so-called literary works. Such rights were recognized at common law at least as early as the fifteenth century.

The first Copyright Act was enacted in 1710 and dealt only with books. This act may be likened to a modest Queen Anne house to which there have since been Georgian, Victorian, Edwardian, and finally twentieth-century additions, each adding embellishments in the style of the times. To follow the history in detail would take far too long. Briefly, it was soon realized that the Act of Anne did not go far enough to protect the interests of authors of books. Further, it came to be realized that the creators of other kinds of works were equally deserving of protection. The basic philosophy being that the fruits of a man's creative labor should be protected, so far as profitable exploitation was concerned, it was realized that in the field, for example, of books, giving the author sole right to print and distribute was not enough. What of translations or dramatic versions; what of public performances of the work; and of course, more recently broadcast or television performances? From time to time the rights of authors have been extended, and under the existing act a long list of so-called restricted acts exists.

The way in which the law relating to copyright has grown, by steady increase in the types of works protected and the area of protection given, accompanied by relatively small but by no means unimportant erosions in the form of an increasing number of exceptions, has inevitably resulted in an act of some complexity. The Act of 1956 is a remarkable feat of draftsmanship, but even if it is a draftsman's dream, it has proved a nightmare to those who must try to understand it—whether as laymen for their own purposes or as lawyers seeking to guide their clients. For this reason, no doubt, one of the most constant themes in the submissions received by the committee has been the request that something be done to simplify the law. A principal objective in any future legislation must be that copyright law should be "placed on a plain and uniform basis" to adopt the words of the 1952 (Gregory) Committee echoing the words of the 1909 Committee. The committee stated that it was as well aware of the difficulties and dangers of oversimplification as it was that, over sixty-five years later, the goal aimed at in 1909 has not been reached. In the introduction to its report (paragraph 9) the Gregory Committee said:

> It will not be out of place to say at the start that copyright is a right given to or derived from works and is not a right in novelty of ideas. It is based on the right of an author, artist or composer to prevent another person copying an original work, whether it be a book, tune or picture, which he himself has created. There is nothing in the notion of copyright to prevent a second person from producing an identical result (and himself enjoying a copyright in that work) provided it is arrived at by an independent process. Although such an action does not constitute an infringement of Copyright Act 1911, we think it is desirable that a point of such fundamental importance should be clearly stated.

This recommendation was not adopted. The committee thought it should be in any future act, coupled with a clear statement that there is no copyright in ideas as such, only in the form in which they are expressed. It recognized, too, that copyright protection not infrequently involves a conflict between public and private interests and that there is a need in certain cases for the exclusive right of the author to be limited. On the whole, the committee agreed with the generally held view that the balance between the rights of the copyright owner on the one hand and the exceptions in favor of copyright users on the other is approximately right, and that no abrupt change in the balance is called for. It also took the view that if in any particular case the author's exclusive right is to be removed, as by way of blanket licensing, this should not interfere with his right to be adequately compensated for the use involved.

Industrial Designs

If the law is to be placed on a "plain and uniform basis," one very important question which must be considered is the relationship between the protection given to industrial designs and the protection given to other works classified as *artistic*. A good many people plainly do not understand that many of the words used in the copyright act have to be given a meaning, arising from definition and interpretation, rather different from that which would probably be given to them by most individuals. Few people for example, would think of a mathematical table as being a *literary* work, but it is one for the purposes of the Copyright Act. So too are street directories, football pool coupons, and lists of Stock Exchange prices. These are only a few examples of written matter in fact protected under the Copyright Act as *literary* works. For the purposes of the act they are as much literary works as any novel or poem. Everyone would agree that they are, of course, *works*, but it is a little absurd to continue to classify them as *literary* works, and *this sort of misdescription leads to misconceptions as to the scope and extent of copyright protection, having regard to the way in which the law has developed in this country, and indeed in most others.* What has been thought worth protecting is a man's skill and/or labor. If a man's skill and/or labor is to be protected, as a practical matter it can be protected only if it has been reduced to some permanent form, such as writing or drawing, by which it can be identified. Some works may involve much skill but little labor; with others, the reverse is the case.

Another frequent source of misunderstanding in the field in which the committee was dealing arises out of the different ways in which people use the word *monoply*. To the lawyer the distinction between copyright protection and monopoly protection is clear enough. *Copyright* gives protection only against copying. *Monopoly* protection arises only if a person enjoys a right in some product of his skill and/or labor which will enable him to stop anybody else making or using the same or a similar product—even if it is made wholly independently and without any copying. In this report, when monopoly protection is mentioned, it refers to this latter kind of protection.

If a mathematician works out a set of tables and writes them down he acquires copyright in the set of tables as written down by him on a piece of paper. Nobody else can, without his authority, take that piece of paper and, copying from it, print off the tables and sell them. Anyone, however, is entitled to make copies of an identical set of tables if he can find them in some noncopyright source. Equally, anybody is entitled to work out an identical set of them. This second set of independently devised tables will be a copyright work because it is an "original" work in the sense that it owes its existence to the skill and /or labor of the person making the calculation.

In the field of artistic works it has long been recognized that in certain cases protection is in no sense dependent on artistic quality, and the 1956 Act specifically so provides. Drawings of all descriptions, diagrams, maps, charts, and plans are all protected "irrespective of artistic quality." Moreover, the making in three-dimensional form of an article depicted by a drawing in two dimensions is an infringement if the article is made, directly or indirectly, from the copyright drawing. It should perhaps be added that this is subject to a qualification introduced in the 1956 Act which is dealt with in the report. "Industrial designs," a description used to cover designs for articles manufactured in quantity on a commercial basis, have always been the subject of separate protection— with, at various times, specific and complex provisions to avoid overlap between such separate protection and any protection which might otherwise be available under the general law of copyright. One main difference between the protection given to artistic works under the Copyright Act and protection given to industrial designs under the Registered Designs Act lies in the circumstance that, for an industrial design, the protection given is not copyright protection, but a true monopoly. Quite how this happened is by no means clear. Designs as such were never protected by the common law, which was concerned only with the protection of literary copyright. Copyright statutes in the eighteenth and nineteenth centuries dealt with copyright in literary works, engravings, musical and dramatic works, and fine arts generally.

Modern Developments

Like the Gregory Committee, the Whitford Committee stated that it had been faced with a number of problems raised by technical developments in various fields. The developments which had taken place since the passing of the Act of 1956 had arisen in three main fields: (1) the improvements in the techniques by which documents can be reproduced; (2) the development of techniques for recording sound and sequences of visual images on magnetic tapes; (3) computer technology. The committee pointed out:

> There are undoubtedly difficulties in fitting some of these developments into the framework of the 1956 Act. Further, the ease with which copyright works can now be reproduced creates problems in the field of enforcement of copyright owner's rights. These various problems are separately dealt with in succeeding chapters of the report, but the general question remains as to how any new Act can best be framed adequately and intelligibly to deal with them.

In brief the Whitford Committee recommended that the Copyright Act of 1956 be revised in order that the law may be placed on a plain and uniform basis, but this would in some cases be practically impossible because of deeply embedded habits and conventions and of the need to line up with international conventions.

Thus the Whitford Committee felt itself faced with a problem of vast complexities since it is difficult, in English law, to discard old established precedents and principles.

In anxiety to solve all the problems, several of them contradictory, the committee took many short cuts and omitted important issues which are habitually studied in copyright legislation. In many respects, the Whitford Committee ducked crucial arguments and at the same time came to conclusions that, in the writer's opinion, were based on fallacious reasoning. Furthermore, critics thought one of the committee's most glaring deficiencies was the lack of attention to providing for the protection of innovations in new technologies, such as computing and, to a certain extent, photocopying—questions to which admittedly, no one, it seems, has yet found the perfect answer.

PART II: THE NEED FOR NEW LEGISLATION FOR COPYRIGHT IN COMMUNICATIONS

For some two hundred years copyright legislation has constantly needed updating, primarily because of the introduction of new technologies of communication. New copyright acts tend to be adopted about three times in a century, prompted, at least in modern times, by the need to provide legislation for new technologies. Our last copyright act, as mentioned earlier, was in 1956 (following the previous Copyright Act of 1911).

In the United Kingdom, particularly in the field of education, the British government policy—and perhaps that of academics and the teaching profession generally—has been somewhat reluctant to adhere strictly to copyright principles because of desire to make both sides happy and balance the rights of users and producers. For instance, the British Council of Education Technology reports that schools, colleges of further education, and universities are able to videotape material made specially for transmission to them freely, without charge (though the Independent Channels ask for a nominal   25 per annum license fee to do just the same thing). This, of course, is an agreement based entirely on trust. Other programs may not be videotaped from any channel at any time and the Council of Education Technology says it is extremely unlikely that any permission would be given to any party to do so. There is no precedent on this.

Since computers were not in sight or in mind when our own 1956 Copyright Act was passed, it was natural to expect that the Whitford Committee would pay special attention to computers and the myriad problems they create. The advice given to the committee by the computer fraternity was voluminous and much of it was contradictory. Briefly, the Whitford Committee said that computer programs (and software) are none other than—hold it!—*literary works*! (Those who do not grasp this incredible statement should see later explanation.) There was something miraculous in the way the Whitford Committee found this magical short cut. According to this view, the whole question of the transition to different computer languages culminating in the particular computer-readable language would be equivalent to the translation of a book into a foreign language.

This shows that the Whitford Committee regarded a computer program as protectable at copyright in the same way as a novel, a poem, or a play. Were this so, it would be a revolutionary new way through the jungle of legislation dealing with technological innovation. It is as though the committee, being asked to draft a law dealing with intercontinental airline traffic, should have rediscovered the old Canals and Inland Waterways Act and spotted that there was a lot of similarity between aircraft and barges—after all, they both deal with freight and passenger traffic: the wizardry in this analogy would be equivalent to a small amendment in the original act reading something like "In this legislation barges shall include aircraft, notwithstanding that aircraft do not ride on the surface of the water and are not towed by horses!"

What is the purpose of copyright and the philosophy behind it? The question, which was posed by the Whitford Committee, was only half answered because the committee chose not to answer many of the crucial questions troubling the computer world internationally today.

Here it suffices to say briefly that having begun as a censorship institution to protect the interests of the Crown, copyright eventually emerged as an institution with a *dual public purpose*:

1. Encouragement to writers and publishers to disseminate knowledge among the general public.
2. Compensation to authors and publishers for their work and expenditure in preparing the necessary works.

These purposes are also very evident in the Unites States understanding of copyright law.

These purposes have been analyzed minutely in the courts, from which it would appear that, as with the Queen Anne Act, the predominant public interest is the spread of knowledge, education, and intellectual activity. In other words, a monopoly for a limited time for the exploitation of the work is granted to the author and publisher so that they can gain a headstart on rivals by securing for their exclusive profit the commercial exploitation of the works. The prime function, however, is not to curtail or limit the spread of literacy.

PART III: ACADEMIC AND SCHOLASTIC ACTIVITIES

This is most obvious, of course, in the field of education where there are many anomalies.

It is by no means certain, for instance, who owns the copyright in books or theses written by scholars or academic staff members for use in connection with scholastic activities. But the matter somewhat falls to the ground owing to the paucity of attempts to apply the copyright laws to scholastic material. For instance, according to Section 4 (4) of the Copyright Act, a teacher producing material as an aid to his teaching is clearly acting within the course of his employment and therefore that work must belong to the educational institution unless they enter a written contract to the contrary.

Surprisingly, most people on this side of the ocean have been blissfully unaware of the consequences of this interpretation. There is no record of a university's trying to stop a lecturer from publishing his lecture notes, diagrams, statistics, or other educational aids or having claimed the royalties on books written by its staff. Publishers cheerfully pay royalties to writing dons. Only the Open University—a case all on its own—has steered clear of possible pitfalls in this direction by providing clearly in its charter that the copyright of material produced by its staff for Open University courses will automatically belong to the Open University.

In fact, if one were to look in the United Kingdom for conflicts in the field of education, say, between producers (copyright holders) and users (scholars, teachers, publishers) one would find the position hopelessly involved because of Section 4. Thus there is a minimum of litigation. There are, of course, countless cases of infringements of the Copyright Act in education, but most people complacently accept that it costs too much to sue.

Reluctance to sue is further encouraged by the widespread employment of the custom of "fair use" which enables one writer to use a certain amount of the work of another without asking permission. Where one draws the line on number of words which may be lifted has always remained indefinite legally. The Publishers Association of Great Britain has, however, drawn up a code of practice which sets a limitation of copying from another's literary work of 400 words of prose and 40 lines of poetry.

Usually authors simply write for permission to the publisher, and the rules of payment are arbitrary. They may explain why they want to use the material but there is no enforcement to review the text of the manuscript. Very rarely would a writer withhold his permission on the grounds that the material is derogatory. One educational publisher we asked said that in twenty years she had known only of two cases of a refusal. The *droit moral*, despite numerous attempts to introduce it in the United Kingdom, has never been part of the law of copyright in this country.

Thus there appears to be a contradiction in our principle of copyright. How can you develop knowledge, education, etc., among the public at the same time as you appear to tie up the commercial exploitation of the work by bestowing a statutory monopoly? How could scientists work in developing scientific research if they could not build on the work of other scientists who could have a monopoly in the knowledge involved in the research? How could a literary work on history, for example, be written if the knowledge of the historical era being investigated was "frozen" by a monopoly in favor of another writer on that period of history? This dilemma was neatly solved in both the United Kingdom and the United States by providing that there cannot be a monopoly or any other form of restriction over *ideas* as such. The free use of ideas is sacrosanct. The term *ideas* can be expressed in numbers of ways, e.g., as systems of knowledge, theories, prescriptions, the logical structure, knowhow, or usage. Another way of saying this is that nobody can own a fact or facts. Einstein has no rights, economic or otherwise, to the theory of relativity. Obviously, a scientist or a writer could not be expected to start at square one or from the beginning of time whenever he embarked on an experiment or a work of literature. An American judge has expressed the matter by saying that a pigmy standing on the shoulder of a giant can see further than other giants and that the whole of intellectual progress is dependent on this idea that knowledge advances by building on previous knowledge.

What then does copyright secure? It secures the legal protection of the expression of the idea. Thus, a very simple solution to the dilemma was reached by limiting copyright to the form in which the idea was couched but not the idea itself. Copyright goes further in requiring a fixation, i.e., the expression of the idea, in some material form, e.g., in a printed book or a gramophone record, films, magazines, etc. In the

United Kingdom, as mentioned before, attitudes have been somewhat magnanimous. This has been aided and abetted by Government policy which tends to help make both sides happy by (1) giving wide copyright protection and (2) making it easy for fair use and infringement to carry on happily.

PART IV: FAIR USE

Some would consider that one of the most useful parts of the Whitford Committee report is that of "fair dealing," since the 1956 Act skirts the issue. The law here reflects how Professor Nimmer describes it in his "Defense of Fair Use"—that the scope and limits of this judge-made rule of reason are most obscure, so that the issue of fair use has been called "the most troublesome in the whole law of copyright."

The 1956 Act provides in Section 6 that fair dealing with literary, dramatic, and musical works for the purpose of

> (i) research or private study;
> (ii) criticism or review (provided there is an acknowledgment); or
> (iii) reporting on current events in newspapers, magazines and periodicals (an acknowledgment must be given), by broadcasting or in a cinematograph film;

shall not constitute an infringement of copyright.

Fair dealing, which is not defined in the act, is judge-made, probably one of the reasons why it causes numerous complications—especially in the courts (see *Hubbard v. Vosper*). In this case, the court allowed a complainant to quote almost the entire contents of certain documents on the grounds that their publication would be for the public interest.

In Section 6 (10), however, *sufficient acknowledgment* is defined as "an acknowledgment identifying the work in question by its title or other description, and, unless the work is anonymous or the author has previously agreed or required that no acknowledgment of his name should be made, also identifying the author."

In the old days, when copying from protected works was generally kept within reasonable bounds by the limitations of copying by hand, fair dealing did not offer special difficulties. There is no doubt that the advent of mechanical processes of copying, and in particular the photocopying machine, has made this issue one of the most controversial and complicated of the whole practice of copyright.

As far as the status of film publicity photographs, frame blow-ups, screen photographs of TV images, and similar photographs is concerned, the Copyright Act of 1956 says that all copyright in this area shall continue to subsist until the end of the period of 50 years from the end of the calendar year in which the author died, and shall then expire, provided that:

(a) in the case of an engraving, if before the death of the author the engraving had not been published, the copyright shall continue to subsist until the end of the period of fifty years from the end of the calendar year in which it is first published.

(b) the copyright in a photograph shall continue to subsist until the end of the period of fifty years from the end of the calendar year in which the photograph is published, and shall then expire.

The acts restricted by the copyright in an artistic work are

(a) reproducing the work in any material form;
(b) publishing the work;
(c) including the work in a television broadcast;
(d) causing a television program which includes the work to be transmitted to subscribers to a diffusion service.

In practice, however, the whole area is very undefined and one finds that publishers, film historians, photographic editors, and studios act according to their own circumstances or make their own rules and prices.

The Society of Authors and the Publishers Association justifiably pointed out in *Photocopying and the Law*:

> Proper regard for copyright is essential to the continued publication of works of all kinds (technical, scientific and educational, no less than biography, travel and fiction) for, if free copying so reduces sales of the original commodity that publication becomes uneconomic, in the last resort important publishing in many fields must wither away. Without some reasonable control the source material upon which those who wish to make photocopies depends will cease to exist.

This applies equally to images. The practice of fair dealing, although not applying specifically to photographs, nevertheless has made it difficult for anyone to lay down strict guidelines.

In Section 9 (4) of the act it is provided that the copyright in a work of architecture is not infringed by the making of a painting, drawing, engraving, or photograph of the work, or by the inclusion of the work in a cinematograph film or in a television broadcast.

Under Section 9 (5) it is not an infringement of the copyright in an artistic work to include it in a cinematograph film or in a television broadcast if its inclusion therein is only by way of background, or is otherwise only incidental to the principal matters represented in the film or broadcast.

One of the biggest problems in this area is proof of the ownership of photographs. One hears of studios or agencies closing down and often the contents of their photographic libraries are made free to anyone who is interested.

Most people feel that as long as they provide an acknowledgment they will be protected from any breach of the law. Fees for use of photographs vary considerably from agency to agency or library to library, but are usually very modest, such as $1.25 per still, plus an acknowledgment.

Sometimes the free publicity from the acknowledgment is enough. If the photographs are much sought after and the owner is interested in making money rather than the publicity, obviously the stakes will rise. For instance, a publisher wanting photographs of Brigitte Bardot from *Paris Match* had to pay $15 a photograph for United Kingdom rights; $20 for world rights. The same publisher using stills from a well-known film for a book was required only to put in an acknowledgment.

If scholars or academics or anyone requiring photographs find the price too high, usually persuasive arguing will bring the price down. There is very little litigation in the courts in this area. Although one publisher described the practices that go on as being "built up like a house of cards," the *laissez-faire* attitude has meant that there are few problems that cannot be solved over the telephone.

The area of photographic and moving film imagery well illustrates the complexities of fair dealing practice. Taking such complications into consideration, the Whitford Committee admitted that it was in "something of a dilemma over the whole problem." It is tempting, they reported, to suggest that the specific cases set out in Sections 6 and 9 be replaced by a general formula, applicable to all works and subject matter, whether existing now or yet to be invented. Such a formula might follow the words of Article 9 (2) of the Berne Convention, namely, that a dealing is fair if it does not conflict with normal exploitation and does not unreasonably prejudice the legitimate interests of the author. This, admittedly, would have the merit of uniformity and flexibility for the future.

They go on to examine how difficult this umbrella approach would be since there are usually good reasons for differing exceptions in relation to different classes of works and subject matter.

The Committee has, however, at last come up with a positive suggestion in its Chapter 14.

> We recommend a general exception in respect of "fair dealing" which does not conflict with normal exploitation of the work of subject matter and does not unreasonably prejudice the legitimate interests of copyright owners. We think this would be sufficient to cover the interests of the press, publishers, broadcasters, reviewers and commentators. Such an exception should also cover "fair dealing" for the purposes of "research or private study" and there should be no need to refer to this field expressly. If the reference is, however, retained, it should be in the form "private research or private study."

Let us hope that should this be incorporated in a future British copyright act, it will help bring about a whole new outlook on copyright.

Canada

A.A. Keyes is Special Advisor to the Secretary of State Department, Government of Canada. He consults often on copyright matters and has written a position paper for the government in an effort to clarify the debate between copyright holders and the academic community regarding the meaning and application of Canada's fair dealing statute. Keyes favors a retention of negotiated access (as opposed to an extension of fair dealing or compulsory licensing) as the most socially beneficial practice.

16

COPYRIGHT AND FAIR DEALING IN CANADA

A. A. KEYES

It is with some trepidation that one ventures into the complexities and pitfalls of one of the most controversial aspects of copyright law: the "fair dealing" exception. In discussing any question of exceptions one should not lose sight of the reality that it is necessary to provide rights in order to make exceptions. Thus arises the perennial creator-user equation: the role, scope, and importance of copyright may change, but the basic social conflict remains between encouraging, nurturing, and rewarding intellectual creativity on the one hand and, on the other, providing access to particular copyright material.

Copyright, as an economic phenomenon, is an accepted and integral part of the general business climate, and the extent to which it structures markets, and indeed, particular industries, is fully recognized. As a social phenomenon, however, there is continuing dispute as to the objectives to be achieved by copyright law.

Much has been written, and more said, about the alleged origins, theories, and purpose of copyright law, and when copyright laws are to be revised, speculation is aroused. Although, undoubtedly, theories of copyright have played a major role in the legislative and judicial developments of copyright law in various countries, theory should not blind us to social necessities or cultural imperatives. Of prime importance are the social and public policy objectives to be expressed in a copyright law.

In the Anglo-American legal tradition, the origins of copyright law are usually traced from the Statute of Anne[1] and its purpose viewed in terms of privileges based on monopolies handed out by the Crown, in the pursuit of censorship as a means of religious oppression, or alternatively, as seeking control of the technical means of reproduction. It is also said the origin of copyright is associated with the European invention of printing. Though convenient, this appears not to be entirely accurate.

The origins of copyright can be traced back to ancient Rome, where the term *plagiarism* is said to have originated. If printing was a condition precedent for copyright, it would have had to exist since A.D. 770, printing being a technological fact in the Far East. Moreover, some centuries before Caxton and European printing, copyright cases had been decided. For example in A.D. 561, an Irish copyright case arose from the hand copying of a prayer book without permission. The action was for delivery up of the infringing copy and the decision of King Diarmid was "to every cow her calf, to every book its copy."[2] The action was, perhaps, the only known instance where a defendant, found to be a copyright infringer, was subsequently canonized (as St. Columba)!

"North Americans" themselves recognized the inherent rights of creators before the Statute of Anne and provided a somewhat drastic remedy; the practice where each Indian had his own song, which no other Indian dared sing without receiving in return a blow from a tomahawk.[3] Thus, in North America, seventy-five years before the Statute of Anne, the concept of owning, of having a right in, the result of intellectual work was recognized.

Much further back in time, there is an even more authoritative source for the assertion of rights of authors. Jehovah is reported as saying, when angry with the prophets of falsehood: "therefore, here I am against the prophets . . . the ones who are stealing away my words."[4] From this awesome beginning many theories have been developed which attempt to explain the nature of copyright and its place in a legal system.[5]

In civil law jurisdictions, theories of copyright have been developed which place great emphasis on the moral or personal rights of authors, in addition to their economic rights. Creativity is seen as an expression of an author's personality. Thus, the French phrase *droits d'auteur* embraces the personal and economic rights of authors, meaning "the rights of authors," whereas the word "copyright" has through time become associated with the work and disassociated from the author. This disassociation has created a certain bias. It can be said that the present common law system places authors' rights in a position which makes them very susceptible to derogation and attack, the rights being easily, and mistakenly, characterized as monopolistic.

Whatever the basis of a law, it is recognized that legal protection is necessary. Therefore, the major concern should not be with the origins of copyright, nor with a particular theory of copyright, but with expressing public policy objectives according to contemporary needs and concerns. The issue is, how does one balance the apparently conflicting objectives that arise in copyright? An obvious example is found in the juxtaposition of the following two quotations taken from the Declaration of Human Rights; the provision that:

> everyone has the right freely to participate in the cultural life of the community, to enjoy the arts and to share in scientific advancement and its benefits[6] [is to be contrasted with]: everyone has the right to the protection of the moral and material interests resulting from any scientific, literary or artistic production of which he is the author.[7]

Everyone can agree with both these concepts; the problem is to reconcile them. As Lord Mansfield said:

> we must take care to guard against two extremes equally prejudicial; the one, that men of ability who have employed their time for the service of the community, may not be deprived of their just merits, and the reward of their ingenuity and labour; the other, that the world may not be deprived of improvements, nor the progress of the arts be retarded.[8]

The central question then is whether it is possible to reach an equitable balance among diverging objectives; where is the point of balance among competing claims for preferential treatment? In reaching this balance one complicating factor may be the applicable domestic constitutional direction. Additionally, national concerns and objectives may dictate choices or impose constraints which differ from recommendations framed according to the imperatives of copyright philosophy. It is generally accepted that for this reason copyright laws vary from country to country.

Canada was created a federal state by an act of the English Parliament: the British North American Act.[9] The act apportioned powers between the federal government and the various provincial governments. Exclusive jurisdiction concerning "copyrights" was given to the federal government.[10] The Copyright Act[11] enacted pursuant to this federal power came into force in 1924.

This act repealed all prior legislation, and copyright in Canada is solely a statutory matter, except that the act does not abrogate "any right or jurisdiction to restrain a breach of trust or confidence."[12]

The British North American Act is silent with respect to the nature or purpose of copyright law in Canada and it gives no direction with respect to any particular approach to be adopted. That is not the case, for instance, in the United States, where the Constitution provides for granting rights to authors for a specified period of time for the social purpose of benefiting the body politic.[13] The United States Constitution has been interpreted to yield, in essence, a doctrine which views copyright law as being primarily for the public benefit. By comparison the present law in Canada regards copyright as a property matter, with the law being primarily one for the benefit of creators. The materials protected are literary, dramatic, musical, and artistic works and these categories are broadly defined in the act.

The rights granted to authors and owners include the right to reproduce a work, or a substantial part of a work. Certain other rights are provided, such as the right to perform a work or any substantial part thereof in public, to make any translation of a work, to broadcast a work, and to authorize the doing of any of the acts reserved exclusively to the copyright owner.[14] It is an infringement to do anything which the author of a work has the sole right to do[15] and the relevant provision provides exceptions and, in particular, the exception of "fair dealing:"

> the following acts do not constitute an infringement of copyright: (a) any fair dealing with any work for the purposes of private study, research, criticism, review or newspaper summary.[16]

The exception of fair dealing has been in the Canadian act since 1924 and has in general, been, strictly construed by the courts. Whereas the provision has been, and is, seen by users as a basis for justifying unauthorized copying of protected materials, its true legal nature appears to be that of a statutory defense to a claim for infringement, and not a statutory permission to do what would be an otherwise illegal act.

In order to determine whether infringement has occurred, the court must first decide whether one of the exclusive rights of the copyright owner has been infringed. As fair dealing is most often mentioned in terms of reproduction by photocopying, one should note that, with respect to copying, it is not an infringement to copy less than "a substantial part" under Canadian law. Only when a substantial part or more has been copied will infringement indeed occur, and only after it has been established that infringement has taken place can the defense of fair dealing arise.[17]

A leading Canadian case[18] decided that the quotation of a work in its entirety is not fair dealing, and that mere acknowledgment of authorship and the source from which it is obtained does not afford a defense.

By the same token, the possibility of competition between the extract or quotation and the original work will always be an element in the consideration of what amounts to fair dealing. What constitutes a "substantial part" is not determinable by quantitative or qualitative tests, but rests in the discretion of the court. What constitutes fair dealing depends upon the facts. One test is whether the taking competes with the original work. The degree of substantiality, i.e., the quantity and value of what is taken, is also a factor in deciding whether there has been fair dealing. Only published works can be so dealt with[19] and solely for the purposes stipulated under the act. Fair dealing is therefore a defense to an action, and not a broad umbrella under which it is permissible to do certain acts.

At the present time the use of materials by critics, reviewers, and scholars is subject to the law as just stated. The use of machinery, such as videotape and photocopiers, to copy in excess of fair dealing, is infringement. To exceed minimal limits, fair dealing users must obtain permission at whatever fee may be negotiated. As a consequence, authors or owners, in granting permission, may impose whatever conditions they deem necessary, including the right to review the context and use of the material.

The concept of fair dealing as currently expressed in the law has been characterized as being concerned with "news reporting and private study"[20] and as "the most important"[21] of the exceptions from copyright. The Economic Council of Canada held that the complexity of the rules regarding fair dealing "has caused a great amount of confusion in specific cases," particularly with respect to the problems created by the expanded use of photocopies and tape recorders. It was thought that an "unreasonable burden is being thrown on the consciences and amateur legal expertise of such people as librarians and copying-machine operators" and that, in terms of enforcement problems and the growth of technology, it was questionable whether the problems could be met by "simply clarifying and amplifying the fair dealing provisions, although this is certainly worth trying."[22] Regarding the "photocopying problem," where it was concluded that the situation was "not primarily a problem of copyright evasion," the "possible clarification of the 'fair dealing' provisions" was in fact recommended.[23]

But, can the scope of fair dealing be defined? This is highly doubtful, as any definition would be, by its nature, arbitrary. Arbitrary statutory provisions may clarify but they do so at the expense of controversial decisions in many instances.

The new United States copyright law is often referred to as defining *fair use*. But a careful reading of the relevant section[24] reveals that it only codifies cases to provide criteria to be applied by the court *in addition to whatever other relevant criteria are taken into account* in defining, in the particular case, whether the use has been fair. Thus, no material change has taken place. Indeed, the House report says the law is in no way changed.[25] Having wrestled with the problem, the legislators found it impossible to provide an advance means of determining what constitutes "fair use." It is questionable, therefore, whether fair dealing can be usefully defined to provide certainty in determining what can or cannot be done in particular cases.

Although relevant, perhaps, to the print technology it sought to deal with, the doctrine of fair dealing may not be the appropriate concept to apply to technological developments. If it is not, should it be changed to encompass new materials, such as films, tapes, and other new methods of exploiting copyright material? One alternative is that fair dealing be left to deal with its aged realities, and a more useful and relevant tool found to deal with the new technological modes of exploitation of copyright material.

The answer can be found only by examining the need for such a mechanism. The questions arising are almost always posed within the context of seeking to enlarge the scope of fair dealing so that academic and scholarly freedom may not be restricted or impeded, that is, to provide a free marketplace of ideas and scholarly practices.

If one proceeds from the previously stated bias it follows that copyright owners are, by definition, restricting the dissemination process by their demands for royalties, apart from asserting that they alone should have the choice to decide whether their work is to be made available.

Whether academics, for example, ought to be provided with an exception should be decided in the light of whatever argument can be advanced that a special situation exists which extends to enabling them to do what is, absent the exception, against the law. Those who favor maintaining and extending the fair dealing exception are primarily educational institutions and librarians. In general, they cite the inconvenience and difficulties they face in securing the necessary authorizations from owners of copyright.

Education claims a special status, based on its role of disseminating and utilizing present knowledge, thereby generating new knowledge. Also cited are the costs of operating the educational system, with particular emphasis on the limited availability of public funds. It is claimed that use of protected material is essential to the educational process. The solutions proposed range from free access and use, to a single payment for unlimited educational use, including freedom to copy broadcast programs off the air, with appropriate regulation by the government.

Librarians similarly take a position that technology has made it possible for them to provide their traditional services in alternative ways and with greater efficiency. Those services are already defined as including the making of single copies. Indeed, certain users contemplate complete freedom to reproduce material, provided that it is done for noncommercial purposes. The sheer impact of technology is a major factor accounting for demands for further expansion of the fair dealing provision.

In considering general policy, the Economic Council, charged in

1966 with reviewing the law and making recommendations for change, stated:

> While the interests and views of authors, publishers and others who are closely involved with the copyright system should continue to be treated with attention and respect, it must also be recognized that technological and other developments are rapidly increasing the *general* public interest in the total information system and everything associated with it, including copyright. This general interest, embracing such matters as the desirability of maintaining ready, low-cost public access to information and minimal interference with the many complex processes by which human beings exchange ideas and other information with each other, should be adequately reflected in federal government policy-making.[26]

The council also said:

> Subject to two important qualifications, compensation should be in proportion to use and each user should pay his fair share. The two qualifications are that the system must make room for the effective operation of such institutions as libraries, which like the copyright system are a vital part of the broad, publicly sanctioned information policy of society, and the system should be so designed as to be practicably enforceable.[27]

Speaking however of the possible negative effects of any radical change, the council emphasized the economic risks taken by authors and publishers, warning that, if copying techniques permit other persons to copy the work and make no contribution to the original costs of the author and first publisher, "the latter may not consider the game worth the candle."[28]

Indeed, creators and owners of copyright are opposed to the granting of any exceptions to their exclusive rights. That technological progress has made it easier to infringe copyright is not regarded by authors and owners as a justifiable reason for making exceptions.

There is no logic, for example, in exempting from payment the use of protected works because a photocopying machine is used. Authors are also concerned over the use of recorders to record off-air for the purpose of making home collections. It has been suggested that manufacturers of blank tapes be taxed, as a means of providing revenue to authors and composers, who are complaining of increasing encroachments on their rights, and consequential loss of revenue.

In the final analysis, those granted increased exceptions would have to consider the possibility of higher initial purchase fees, as owners would seek to pass on to buyers the costs of having their works subjected to exceptions. Owners would seek to increase the unit selling price to compensate for any reduction in total sales due to increased exceptions. If unit prices could not be increased to compensate for this reduction, then entrepreneurs might ultimately be forced to cease producing material.

Fair dealing is the extent to which copyright material may be used without license or authority of the author and, in this context, is the permitted copying of copyrighted material. There is no universal agreement as to the exact nature of the doctrine but, broadly, it can be seen as a limitation on the statutory rights of the author, or as in Canada, a defense to an act of infringement. It is the doctrine of fair dealing which draws the line between the rights of authors and the legitimate interests of users. Generally, the drawing of the line is left to the courts either by following statutory directions or by developing their own doctrine. Probably, judicial elaboration of such a doctrine leads to more elastic and perhaps just decisions, whereas statutory provisions may have the effect of restricting the doctrine fairly narrowly.

Given that fair dealing is regarded as defense to an infringement action, it follows that the defense does not confer a "right" of access to a copyright work. The defense only makes legal what would otherwise be illegal; it does not result in creating what are loosely described as *rights of users*, or a *right of access*. If access by means of exceptions to rights of creators is deemed socially desirable, then the necessary provisions can be made in the relevant law. But, are such provisions fair? The question of what is to be done about fair dealing in Canada is of immediate concern.

Given the age of the present Canadian copyright law, technological developments and increasing social awareness of the issues, the Canadian government has embarked on a program of revision of intellectual property laws—patents, trademarks, copyright, and industrial design. Working papers in the areas of patents and trademarks have been published; in April 1977, a consultants' paper[29] was published. The paper was not a statement of government policy in the area but was rather the work of two consultants. That approach enabled the adopting of positions and the making of recommendations which accentuated the polarization evidenced by the conflicting views of copyright interests in Canada. The paper's purpose was provoking reaction and insuring the widest possible public discussion of the issues involved with the general aim of seeking an equitable balance of interests.

The government, while engaged in the process of revising its copyright law, has not adopted policy decisions with respect to particular issues, including those created by the fair dealing exception. The answer to the general question of the importance, place, and scope of exceptions to the rights of creators, will depend upon the basic philosophy adopted and the public policy objectives to be achieved in revising the law.

In the revision process it has been possible to identify three major issues of central concern:

1. The confrontation between those who wish to have higher and longer protection and those who wish to have increased, easier, and perhaps free, access to copyright material.

2. The effects of the advance of technology which have created new uses for old copyright works and new rights, e.g., cable television, computer storage, public lending right, performers' rights.

3. The necessity of striking a balance among conflicting interests and the extent to which it may be necessary to regulate and control the exercise of copyright in Canada.

Two general directions seemed possible: (a) *the introduction or extension of compulsory access,* where access to copyright works is based on compulsion, and an author has no choice but to make his work available to whoever wishes to have it. That system does away with authors' exclusive rights to permit access to, or use of, their material and substitutes the right of equitable renumeration; (b) *negotiated access:* this system preserves authors' rights, as they may choose to make their works available or not, leaving authors free to negotiate a price; if the price is not met, they can refuse to make their works available.

The consultants' proposals for the revision of the Canadian law opted for the "negotiated access" solution which insures the maintenance of authors' rights—leaving the way open to free bargaining, rather than compulsory use without bargaining. This included the phenomenon of photocopying, it being recommended that no specific changes be made in the law. It was emphasized that owners of rights should pursue their rights, possibly by using collective agencies to license those photocopying.

The choice was consistent with the basic approach of the consultants which emphasized the primacy of creators' interests, but in the context of seeking an equitable balance. This brings one back to the creator-user equation. The public interest in relation to copyright is difficult to define, but it can be broadly construed to take into account the social and economic pressures resulting from technological development. Indeed, there is increased social awareness of the importance that copyright plays in the everyday lives of people. More importantly, the cultural implications of copyright law are coming to be more fully understood. The public interest may best be served by recommending changes which, on one hand, define with certainty the rights of creators, and on the other, also insure the interests of consumers and users.

If the *public interest* is defined as the reaching of an equitable balance between creators' rights and the interests of users of protected material, exceptions to protection can be regarded as derogations to the norm of the protection of creators. On this basis the consultants' report did not propose to enlarge the scope of exceptions beyond present limits, except to adapt them to modern methods of use and to make technical adjustments.

A major solution to the problems of access to protected material is the urging that rights granted by copyright can be exercised collectively in order to provide a means of securing remuneration to authors and readier permission for potential users to use material. If collective mechanisms are formed, their control and regulation will be necessary to insure equity between owners and users, thereby protecting the public interest—perhaps by means of a tribunal to act as arbiter.

If the mechanism of licensing photocopying, by negotiation, is adopted, users will not need to preoccupy themselves with asking—is what I'm doing fair dealing? Present practices which are, or are not, fair dealing, would be subsumed within the license. The principles of such a solution here received support from users in Canada, for example by the Canadian Library Association.

In any event, to stretch the doctrine of fair dealing in several directions to accommodate conflicting demands is manifestly impossible. It is submitted that, in Canada, the present law of fair dealing should be left unchanged and in the discretion of the courts. On balance, providing a general statement of principles and allowing case law to develop from these principles is the most equitable approach. If exemptions for libraries, educational institutions, and other interests are necessary, those should be made by means of specific provisions.

The problems of revising the law are such that increasing government involvement in regulating the exercise of copyright may be necessary, since revision must be considered in relation to the societal context within which a revised law will operate. New and changing perceptions concerning the needs of society for information, culture, and entertainment, and the implications of the evolution of communications technology and services, make a new law necessary. It is in this double perspective that the issue of the adequacy of social concepts and legislation in the copyright field will finally be regarded, consistent with equitable treatment of authors' rights.

The rights of authors must be determined by a delicate balance between two socially useful but opposed interests: sufficient protection to encourage the production of works vital to the cultural needs of society; but not such extensive protection as to frustrate reasonable access. Reasonable access varies, it appears, according to one's point of view and the particular machinery available.

Revolutionary changes have been brought about by technology, and electronic gadgetry affects the quality of human life. In today's communication age we are faced, for example, with TV, cable and pay-TV, computers, satellites, microreprography, laser beams, and the new home do-it-yourself copyright infringement kit: the home video machine capable of copying programs off-air for later use. This technological development is creating shock waves and has galvanized copyright owners into seeking solutions and bringing actions.

Machinery is used with messianic vigor to provide greater and faster access to more information, and to fertilize bigger, better, and faster machines. In the words of the main architect of the new United States copyright law:

> If the users of . . . technology insist on using authors' works without giving some appropriate compensation in return, they will find that sooner or later there will be no authors worth reading and no works worth reproducing.[30]

NOTES

[1]8 Anne, c. 19, (1710).

[2]Finman v. Columba, AD 561.

[3]Reuben Gold Thwaites (Ed.), *Jesuit Relations & Allied Documents: Travels and Explorations of the Jesuits in New France, 1610-1791* (New York:Pageant, 1959), V. 7, p. 16.

[4]Jeremiah 23:30.

[5]There are ten identifiable theories of copyright. See Francis J. Kase, *Copyright Thought in Continental Europe: Its Development, Legal Theories, and Philosophy; a Selected and Annotated Bibliography* (South Hackensack, NJ: F.B. Rothman, 1967).

[6]Article 27, para. 1.

[7]*Idem.* para. 2.

[8]Sayre v. Moore (1785) 1 East 361 n.

[9]30 Vict. c. 3.

[10]Section 91 (23).

[11]Copyright Act, RSC 1970, C30.

[12]Section 45.

[13]Constitution, Art. 1, sec. 8, cl. 8. "The Congress shall have power . . . to promote the Progress of Science and Useful Arts, by securing for limited times to authors . . . the exclusive right to their respective writings."

[14]Section 3.

[15]Section 17 (1).

[16]Section 17 (2).

[17]Johnstone v. Bernard Jones Publication, Ltd. (1938) Ch. 599.

[18]Zamacois v. Douville et al., 3 Fox Pat. C. 44; C.P.R. 270; (1943) 2 D.L.R. 257.

[19]British Oxygen Co. v. Liquid Air Co. (1925) i. Ch. 383.

[20]Economic Council of Canada, *Report on Intellectual and Industrial Property*, Information Canada, Ottawa, Cat. EC 22-1370, January, 1971, p. 133.

[21]*Ibid.*, p. 41.

[22]*Ibid.*, p. 133.

[23]*Ibid.*, p. 160.

[24]Section 107.

[25]H.R. *Report* No. 94-1476, pp. 65-74.

[26]Economic Council *Report*, p. 143.

[27]*Ibid.*, p. 141.

[28]*Ibid.*, p. 34.

[29]Consumer and Corporate Affairs, Canada, *Copyright in Canada: Proposals for a Revision of the Law*, A.A. Keyes and C. Brunet, Minister of Supply and Services, Cat. RG 43-15/1977.

[30]Barbara Ringer, *Copyright and the Future of Authorship*, Copyright, WIPO, June 1976, p. 158.

France

Marie-Laure Arié is a lawyer who works at the Centrales des Revues, Départment de Gestion des Périodiques. Her report focuses on the status of audiovisual imagery under French copyright law. In its law of 1957, France has a statutory definition of *l'usage loyal,* the equivalent of "fair use." The protection status of broadcast imagery has in recent times been vigorously debated. The debate she reports indicates a polarization between several author-producer groups who advocate strict contractual definition and regulation of authors' rights on the one hand and, on the other, persons like Xavier Desjeux who have argued for unremunerated, unlicensed access to broadcast material on the basis of public interest.

17

AUTHOR'S RIGHTS (LE DROIT D'AUTEUR) AND CONTEMPORARY AUDIOVISUAL TECHNIQUES IN FRANCE

MARIE-LAURE ARIÉ

The fundamental principles underlying author's rights are protection of the creator's work and development of equitable conditions for its use. Several current practices are raising problems for the producers and owners of protected material—the rapidly spreading tools for recording and reproduction of sounds and images in the service of contemporary teaching methods, the television transmission of films, and the practice of nonauthorized videocopying "for private use" and subsequent circulation.

Creators of audiovisual works, because their works express their personality and thereby possess an original character, deserve protection under the Law of March 11, 1957, on Literary and Artistic Property. It guarantees "rights of the author in all intellectual works, whatever their type, form of expression, merit or destination" (Article 2).

This law affirms that an author has exclusive rights to authorize or to forbid exploitations (reproduction, performance, etc.) by a third party. Some exceptions are also stipulated, so as to prevent authors from exercising their rights in a socially irresponsible manner. In particular, authors must allow a derogation of their monopoly on reproduction: fair use (*l'usage loyal*). French law and jurisprudence have established that a third party may copy a protected work for "private use," on condition that the copy not be destined for a collective use (Art. 41, §1, Law of 1957). And §3 of the same article permits a broad class of public uses:

> Analyses and brief quotations justified by the critical, polemical, pedagogical, scientific, or informational character of the work in which they are incorporated.

223

Taking then the principle of fair use stated in the law, how can one apply that to audiovisual creations? How, in practice, can one balance the author's interest with those of the public for whom the works are created?

EDUCATIONAL RECORDING

In practices related to educational recording of audiovisual creations, we must distinguish two circumstances.

(a) The recording of specifically educational programs used during a school year in progress.

(b) The recording of television programs of all types (including entertainment) by educational institutions.

Taking the implicit purposes here into consideration, we might ask whether rigid adherence to the author's exclusive rights would be just as dangerous as a lax application that would fail to protect the author's property rights?

Precisely these questions have been addressed in a forceful manner recently by Mr. Xavier Desjeux, who spoke to the Comité d'Experts Internationaux at a meeting organized by l'Institut National de l'Audiovisuel (INA):

> The film and magnetic tape lend themselves to a variety of uses—including new intellectual creation. In this area, we can justifiably reject the proposition that in considering "created materials," we need not consider the question of merit. And given the magnitude of audiovisual production today, it is really conjectural to affirm that all of them are "original creations" and must therefore benefit from the legislation protecting literary and artistic property.

> Moreover, audiovisual production has assumed a primary social function in informing and educating the masses. It is thus difficult to see why the "creator" of an audiovisual work should be permitted to oppose the diffusion of his work because of his interests. He can certainly claim an intangible property in his work, but social interest can rebut him with the notion of "expropriation for the sake of public benefit"; this juridical technique is applied daily in the capitalist countries (the socialists would doubtless speak more willingly of "nationalization"). To arbitrate the conflict between property and public interest, one must appeal to moderation and prudence. It is not a question of equity, since this notion presupposes not "exclusive rights" but "remuneration" instead. . . . Audiovisual production should be classified primarily as contemporary cultural phenomenon, even when taken from the commercial circuits. It does not seem sensible that the author's right—in the name of individual property—should impede the circulation of an audiovisual product; were this allowed, the law would be attacking education itself. These problems will become proportionately easier to resolve in the measure that we demystify the world of authors' rights. Of importance is that the intellectual worker—authors included—be no less well treated than the manual worker or the small businessman. This is a problem of elementary fairness.[1]

Mr. Desjeux forcefully reminds us that in using modern technologies which reduce opportunities for author exploitation, it is undeniably necessary to assure him a position that is—if not in all respects the best—at least the fairest.

Crucial to the question of fairness are the purposes of audiovisual productions. Audiovisual transmissions, though privileged, are but one among the instruments of communication and education. In current French practice, the audiovisual creation is sponsored either (a) by a state agency with responsibilities for scholastic programs or by a private group with an identical objective, or (b) by a private group that wishes to capture public attention for the purpose of entertainment. Authors customarily sign contracts with such agencies.

In such a contract, the author's rights are expressly retained, or they are assigned to the agency that has commissioned the work. In the latter case, the business or public agency becomes the copyright owner; the work is then used for the purpose leading to its creation, and conflict is no longer possible between the author and the user. Where authors' rights are not assigned, however, it is more difficult to establish permissible exceptions to authors' control. In considering educational uses, exclusive rights should constrain neither creativity in teaching activities nor conditions of normal use in teaching.

These conditions for acceptable instructional use have not, however, been defined. Here we can mention only the recommendations of the Groupe de Travail de l'Ompi and of UNESCO, which were debated in their Paris meetings of September 13-22, 1978:

> School recording of academic programs must be facilitated for those programs used during the school year in progress. However, recordings of nonacademic programs and their use by educational institutions should be governed by the exclusive rights of authors and should remain subject to control by copyright holders, unless the national legislature opts for compulsory licensing that would grant remuneration to those possessing the relevant authors' rights.

The notion of fair use, as defined above, or of compulsory licensing, in effect specifies rather limited conditions for educational uses of recorded materials.

A relevant consideration for the proposed compulsory licensing system is the character of the original transmission. Mr. Xavier Desjeux, who is opposed to such licensing, argues, "It is difficult to see why a free transmission possessing educational purposes and detached from commercial channels could allow anyone to require a remuneration."[2]

Issues of this kind compel us to ask whether we should continue to talk about the moral and exclusive rights of authors. It seems likely that traditional notions will have to adapt to the new realities of communication, information, and education in the audiovisual field. The necessity for assuring a flow of information will have to be balanced against the legitimate rights of authors.

CONTRACTUAL EXPERIMENTS

In concern about such problems, professional organizations representing authors and producers have studied legal problems associated with audiovisual transmissions. Their efforts have resulted in contractual solutions that establish norms for the production and use of video material. Their special objectives have been the retention of authors' rights and the protection of those to whom authors' rights have been assigned.

Two sample contracts have been concluded between the S.N.E.P.A. (Syndicat National de l'Édition Phonographique et Audiovisuelle) and groups of authors. The contract designated *Production,* concluded between producer and author, constitutes a matrix for the second, labeled *Exploitation.*

Simultaneously, groups of authors have established policies for handling their materials. This was achieved through the S.D.R.M. (Société pour l'Administration de Droit de Reproduction Méchanique). The S.N.E.P.A. Exploitation (use) contract is concluded between the producer and the S.D.R.M., which represents authors in the control of mechanical reproduction of their work. The Production and Exploitation contracts of S.N.E.P.A. constitute a coherent and comprehensive arrangement, which is currently without equivalent abroad. It has been in force since June 1978; an experimental two-year period is anticipated for its Exploitation component.

It should be noted that the S.N.V.C. (Syndicat National de la Video-communication) exploitation contract—limited to videograms for institutional use—has existed on an experimental basis for two years. It has been revised and rescheduled for an additional two-year experimental period.

S.N.E.P.A. sample contracts for production and exploitation introduce original notions and requirements. According to their terms, the producer is construed either as an exploiter or as an editor of videographic works, a status conferred upon him by the production contract. Moreover he has a right of review or inspection for use of the videoprograms; terms specified by authors' groups are contingent upon his agreement; subsequent uses in other forms are also subject to his review.

The S.N.E.P.A. exploitation contract concerns videoprograms destined for public or private use. It embraces all works (original or preexisting, reproduced, adapted, or composite) susceptible to uses by the authors' groups, composers, literary editors. It includes even scientific or pedagogical works by the member editors of the Syndicat National de l'Edition, subject to their consent.[3]

ASSOCIATIONS FOR AUTHORS' RIGHTS

In addition to the groups mentioned above we should list other organizations working to protect authors' rights and foster satisfactory relations between producers and users of audiovisual material.

(1) G.A.V.E. (Le Groupe Audiovisuel de l'Edition), which includes the G.P.A.V. (Groupement des Professionels de l'Audiovisuel) and the S.N.E. (Syndicat National de l'Édition). This group coordinates relations between the professions and public authorities and also seeks to establish ethical norms for audiovisual programming.

(2) G.I.C.A. (Le Groupement Intersyndical de la Communication Audiovisuelle), which is an organization of professional unions. It joins eight separate organizations with the following objectives:

(a) study of all problems related to production, editing, and distribution of audiovisual creations

(b) information and documentation regarding such problems

(c) defense of the moral and material interests of the organizations and their members

(d) presentation of these interests to all relevant public and private groups

(e) implementation of group-controlled policies relative to aural and visual communication.

Fifty companies have already joined G.A.V.E., and it is likely that these groups will obtain the support of all editors and producers of audiovisual material. They will thereby secure better protection for their rights and assurance that more uniform solutions can be provided for future conflicts.

NOTES

[1]The speech of Mr. Desjeux has appeared as an essay, "La culture est-elle combattue par la loi?" *La Semaine Juridique*, No. 42, Oct. 20, 1977.

[2]*Ibid.*

[3]Terms of the sample contracts regarding scope of application, distribution of rights, and royalties have been analyzed by Clement Pillerault and published in *Le Journal de l'Audio-visuel*, No. 6, October 78 (71 Boulevard Richard-Lenoir, 75011, Paris).

Germany

The selection representing Germany is taken from an important, internationally comparative fair use commentary by Demetrius Oekonomidis, *Die Zitierfreiheit im Recht Deutschlands, Frankreichs, Grossbritaniens und der Vereinigten Staaten* (The Freedom to Quote in German, French, British, and American Law). This commentary was published by the Internationale Gesellschaft für Urheberrecht (International Society for Copyright Law). (Berlin and Frankfurt: Vahlen, 1970). It is reprinted here by permission of the author, who is a lawyer at the High Court in Athens and also a research associate at the Max Planck Institute (Munich) for the study of foreign copyright.

Rather than being a current report, it provides a statement of some interesting distinctions that have developed in the legal scholarship and case histories related to *Zitierfreiheit*, or freedom to quote, the German equivalent to the fair use principle. In the interpretation developed here, materials of the new media are encompassed within the scope of the freedom to quote. Sections of the commentary, however, suggest the delicacy and difficulty of decisions that relate to works in the visual domain.

Most of the footnotes—references to commentaries and case decisions—have been deleted from these selections. Editor's (JSL) footnotes have been added to clarify the translation of some important terms.

18

THE FREEDOM TO QUOTE ACCORDING TO GERMAN LAW

DEMETRIUS OEKONOMIDIS

According to German legal standards, the freedom of quotation entails the right, under certain conditions, to employ the creative works of third parties wholly or in part, and to copy, distribute, and publicly reproduce them within a new work.

Quotations are especially provided for "in the interest of free scholarly research, the further development of literature, and the education and edification of the people."[1] Naturally, it cannot be assumed that the limits of permissible use can be extended to such a degree that the financial and moral rights of the original author would be substantially infringed upon. The protection of these rights in the context of quotation is also explicitly guaranteed by the law.[2] The pertinent regulation of the *Urheberrechtsgesetz* (URG) § 51 reads as follows:

> Copying, distribution, and public reproduction [of copyrighted works] is permissible to the extent required for a particular purpose,
> 1. if such individual works are, following their publication, incorporated in an independent scholarly creation that elucidates the contents of the copyrighted work,
> 2. if passages of a work, after its publication, are cited in an independent literary work,
> 3. if individual passages of a published work of music are cited in an independent work of music. . . .

With regard to the new law of 1965 . . . one of the important, generally binding rules . . . stipulates that the extent of the quotation must be justified by its purpose. . . . This rule lends itself to limiting freedom of quotation as well as to extending it. . . . The new regulations

229

explain that quotations may not only be copied and distributed, but . . . may also appear in lectures, performances, productions, broadcasts, and the remaining forms of public reproduction.

EXTENT AND PURPOSE OF QUOTATIONS

According to the law, a quotation may not exceed the extent required by its purpose. . . . [And the intended purposes are themselves subject to legally defined conditions.] The rule of the URG, § 51, no. 1, stipulates as the single defined purpose of the quotation that it elucidate[3] the contents of the quoted work. . . .

Basically one can conclude that the purpose of the quotation cannot be merely its promulgation, but its use in reference to the quoted work. The required referential function is established by the use of the quotation as evidence or proof. Typical examples are use of a quotation to elucidate or illustrate one's own statements or those of another, or to criticize another person's views, or to explain or corroborate a thesis, or the use of a quotation for the sake of its striking formulation, or its introduction to establish a conceptual relationship. The quotation also fulfills a related function when used to illustrate the historical or cultural background or to portray the social milieu. In contrast, the function of the quotation as proof has been rejected both by court decisions and legal scholarship when the material employed serves merely to amplify or enlarge[4] the contents of the more recent work.

Especially with respect to the purpose of the quotation in the fine arts area, a court has recently arrived at a rather controversial conclusion. In opposition to previous holdings, the *Oberlandesgericht* (OLG) of Munich, in its decision (March 24, 1966) on the Kandinsky case, permitted quotations for the sake of enhancing the text. The justification for this ruling was that when dealing with works of art—as opposed to a biography, for example—no exact line can be drawn between elucidation and enhancement or embellishment[5] of the text. That the quotations possess not only an elucidating relationship to the text but also an amplifying purpose seemed necessary in a book like *Der blaue Reiter und die neue Künstlervereinigung München,* a scholarly work in the field of art history.

In any case, one must abide by the principle that the quotation may not be the goal in itself, but must remain an accessory means; the inner relationship between the quoted material and the quoting text must be recognizable. Given this assumption, an adaptation in the sense of adjusting and linking the quotation to the work that incorporates it is permissible.

THE RULE AGAINST CHANGING QUOTATIONS

The right of the author alone to determine the form and content of a work is guaranteed in the relevant § 62 of the URG, just as this is also established in the general rules of § 14 and § 39 of the URG. The rule against changing quotations essentially corresponds to the previous law but contains an additional prerequisite regarding the permissibility of quotation that takes into consideration the moral rights[6] of the author. Legally permissible use does not allow changes to be made in the quoted material. Its use, and consequently the quotation as well, can occur only as reproduction of the unaltered original or of its parts. A change in the cited material constitutes an infringement and invites the applicable sanctions. Note that the moral rights of an author are not violated by changes introduced in good faith or changes which, for the purpose of quotation, are unquestionably necessary.

INDICATION OF SOURCES

A prime prerequisite for the admissibility of quotations and for borrowing material in general is a clear indication of sources. An examination of the conditions that necessitate an indication of sources reveals that it fulfills several functions: it serves, first, to preserve the integrity of the author, and to verify the correctness of the material reproduced. In addition, an indication of sources will direct the reader to the origin of the material introduced and his interest in that work should be awakened. This may represent a certain compensation for a reproduction otherwise unremunerated.

REPRODUCTIONS OF WORKS OF FINE ART

With respect to freedom of reproducing works of the fine arts, § 51, No. 1 of the URG maintains that individual works, after their publication, can be used in independent scholarly works for the purpose of elucidating the contents. An application of §51, no. 2 of the URG is not impossible, but difficult. If one allows the reproduction of works (or sections of works) of fine arts in commentaries without placing special restrictions on these, the danger of exploiting the artistic achievements of others increases. As regards instances of the so-called minimal quotation,[7] it cannot even be maintained that the minimal usage would limit the possible damage to the author to a negligible proportion. Here we are dealing with a genuine threat to the property rights of the author.

Therefore it hardly seems justifiable to allow selections from the work of an artist to appear as quotations in biographies or light, popular treatments of their lives, in which images are reproduced merely with reference to the period and circumstances of their creation.

A crucial consideration in the fine arts area, too, is that room must be left for discussions and criticism of individual works. Here it must also be permissible to make visible the object of the presentation.

For quotations in scholarly works, the general prerequisites are binding. The quoted work, that is the entire work, must already have been published; its use must serve to elucidate the contents of the new, independent scholarly work. In this instance, reproduction should be intended to clarify further the ideas in the text of the quoting work; it is not required that the reproductions should function as a scholarly illustration of these ideas. The permissible purpose of quotations is attained when the illustrations in the form of examples contribute to a better understanding of the text or toward delineating the concept of a direction in art. When this elucidation occurs through the use of a fine art work, a privileged character will frequently inhere in such use. Therefore the work quoting the material must primarily fulfill its purpose without such quoted illustrations. . . . These are the essential directions that the law has followed in the majority of cases up to the present time.

If conditions for the use of quoted material in a scholarly work have been met, it is immaterial to which branch of learning the quoting work belongs. According to this principle, it is requisite that critical treatises like reviews and critiques be considered scholarly works. In such instances, scholarship is expressed through its analytical method of presentation. Consequently, a critical catalogue can likewise be regarded as a scholarly work.

The general provisions against change and requiring indication of sources apply also for quotations from works of art. In regard to works in the fine arts those changes are permissible that are necessitated by the process of reproduction. Thus, changes made on a proportionately reduced or enlarged scale as well as alterations in the means of presentation (as, for example, changes in color, among others), may be introduced. . . . On the other hand, it is not permissible to exclude from the reproduction objects that are presented in the original work, or to add others that the original work does not contain. Such abuse of a quotation would doubtless represent a mutilation of the work. This objection has frequently been made against the fragmentary reproduction of works in the fine arts. In the context of scholarly works, however, where there is a close connection between quotation and text, the danger of mutilation can be effectively obviated by an indication of sources and an additional notice that one is dealing with the reproduction of a mere section.

The question whether quotations from works of the fine arts may occur in works of the same genre will have to be answered negatively in the majority of cases. The law is silent on this—with good reason—since opposing arguments already lie in the nature of fine art works themselves (as opposed to works in language and music) and in the goals determined by law. As a very remote possibility one might consider a work of the fine arts employed in the creation of a new, similar work to characterize a certain atmosphere (cf. Pop Art).

QUOTATIONS FROM RECORDINGS

The rights of the manufacturers of recordings set down in §§ 85 ff. of the URG are defined by the rights of usage and therefore also by the freedom to quote. . . . The freedom to quote cannot be obstructed by protective measures regulating competition between manufacturers of recordings. Generally it must be assumed that quotations from recordings are covered by the general regulations. The rules prohibiting changes and those requiring indication of sources apply here, even though they serve as a mere condition for the admissibility of the quotation. The law does not grant the manufacturer of recordings any authority derived from the notion of moral rights. Yet, it may be assumed that the manufacturer can demand protection against a mutilating reproduction of his recording according to the general law of torts.

The recording material under discussion primarily concerns literary works, music, and achievements of practicing artists that may also be quoted within the framework of the law.

QUOTATIONS FROM FILMS AND BROADCASTS

For the quotation from films and moving pictures (series of pictures) the applicable portions of the URG are § 51, § 94, Sec. 4, and § 95. They also cover films lacking the characteristics of a completed work. Accordingly, the use of films or moving pictures in their entirety as well as in part is permissible as a quotation. Thus, in a scholarly lecture, individual filmworks and films may be used to elucidate the contents. Partial use of such works would be necessary and justified, for example, in a documentary film dedicated to a famous director in order to illustrate the development of his art.

Not only the films and moving pictures themselves are subject to the rules governing the freedom of quotation, but also the contributions upon which they are based. This concerns not only works existing independent of the film, such as literary works, music or musical-dramatical works, and others, but also works that are created only for a specific film, such as scripts, film music, illustrations, and sets, also noncreative accomplishments of practicing artists, and finally, photographs. When such works are quoted, one is dealing in each individual case with quotations from individual works protected by copyright or performances of actors, film musicians, and others for which the pertinent rules should be applied. . . .

The general requirements apply to the possibilities of quoting from films and moving pictures and their contributions as just outlined. In view of the organic fusion of individual contributions to films, the extent of the quotation as defined by its purpose should not depend on whether the quotation accidentally encompasses one of the contributions to the filmwork in its entirety. . . .

Live television broadcasts, where the picture sequence represents a creative accomplishment, are also protected by copyright, as are television films of such broadcasts (telefilms) and films on videotape or other material intended for broadcasting. However, the mere reproduction of events—cultural, sport, pictures of nature, broadcasts of opera performances and the like, usually lacks copyright protection. . . . As filmworks, however, in contrast to the events recorded, they are construed as "moving pictures," the protection of which is defined in § 95 of the URG.

Like creative filmworks, the television broadcast can also encompass photographs and performances which are protected either by copyright or the rights protecting artistic achievements. According to § 51 of the URG, in connection with § 87, Sec. 3, the television broadcast, in whole or in part, may be considered a subject for quotation. If, for example, the tendency of a politically committed broadcasting enterprise is to be analyzed either through film, television, or oral lecture, it is conceivable that it would not be adequately portrayed by a reproduction consisting only of segments; it may then seem necessary to discuss individual broadcasts in their entirety. This will hardly ever occur in practice, however, since the work using the quotations must comply completely with the standards of scholarship. The use of segments from television broadcasts is conceivable for the purpose of illustration and documentation. . . .

In regard to radio broadcasts it should also be noted that the quotation can refer to entire broadcasts protected by the rights concerning performances or to individual contributions such as literary works, music, or accomplishments of practicing artists, sound technicians, and others. . . . With respect to the extent of the quotation it is rather unimportant, as with films, if the quotation of segments from broadcasts as such refers to one of the contributions in its entirety; any judgment in this case must consider the complete work as the point of departure.

Quotations from films and broadcasts will most frequently occur in similar works in the context of comments on contemporary or scholarly topics, for the discussion of current problems, and the criticism and analysis of cultural events that are given prominence in television and radio programming.

The regulations against changing a quotation and requiring indication of sources in § 62 and § 63 remain valid as conditions for the permissibility of quotations from broadcasts. In this context it is irrelevant that the law does not provide protection for the moral rights of the broadcasting enterprise. Like the producer of recordings, the broadcasting enterprise cannot be denied protection against misrepresentation of its products according to the rules of the general law of torts.

Borrowed Materials for Collections Used in Churches, Schools, and General Instruction

Borrowings[8] in collections for use by churches, schools, and general instruction must be interpreted as an expression of the general public right to use the works of third parties for the moral and intellectual education of the young, as emphasized in the rationale for this regulation. According to the definitions arrived at in this study a *borrowing* can only be the use of works in their entirety or of parts for the benefit of collections as just mentioned. Unlike quotations, however, borrowings are not used for the purpose of verification or support and explanation of a new independent work, a purpose that implies creative activity in the area of literature, scholarship, and art. Therefore borrowed materials lack one of the most important conditions of a quotation according to the law. In such collections, the creative accomplishment in taking material from others is manifest solely in the selection and arrangement of existing material, not in the creation of a new independent work.

NOTES

[1]§ 51, *Urheberrechtsgesetz* (1965).

[2]According to Dambach, *Gesetzgebung des Norddeutschen Bundes*, p. 78; cf. Müller, *Urheber- und Verlagsrecht*, Bd. I, § 19 Ziff. 1, p. 77.

[3]The word "elucidate" has been used here for *erlaütern*, which also has the meaning of clarification or explanation.

[4]The words "amplify or enlarge" have been used for *vervollständigen*.

[5]The words "enhancement or embellishment" have been used for *Vervollkomnung*.

[6]"Moral rights" is a translation of *Persönlichkeitsrechten*.

[7]"Minimal quotation" is a translation of *Kleinzitat*, a technical term in German copyright law corresponding to *de minimis* in American law; the *Grosszitat* is a quotation of substantial dimensions.

[8]"Borrowing" is a translation of *Entlehnung*.

Japan

Hiroshi Minami is a professor of social psychology at Seijo University and President of the Japan Society of Image Arts and Sciences. Japan has a "fair practice" statute in its most recent copyright legislation (1970). The statute appears to be construed liberally as regards reproduction of materials for scholarly purposes. In other uses of an educational sort, school recordings and textbook reproductions are reported on here, compulsory royalty payments are provided for by law. Probably the least familiar feature of Japanese practice by Western standards is the provision for a copyright mediation committee that channels copyright disputes outside the court system.

19

COPYRIGHT IN JAPAN

Hiroshi Minami

A copyright law was prepared in Japan for the first time in 1899. In 1970, however, this law was rescinded and an entirely new law has been in force since January 1, 1971. In addition to its national law, Japan is a signatory of the Berne Treaty and of the Universal Copyright Convention.

The following essay attempts to outline the existing copyright law of Japan and such portions of it as are pertinent to the fair use of copyrighted materials.[1]

It should be noted, incidentally, that the fundamental difference between the Japanese copyright law and that of the United States is that the Japanese law is a statute containing elaborate stipulations. In contrast, the United States has a system affording dual protection through its federal statute and through its strong common law tradition. Some Japanese specialists think that the common law is preferable. As regards Japan, they believe that the more elaborate the provisions, the more numerous and dexterous are the evasions that infringe upon copyrights.

In the following, an attempt will be made to cite main provisions of the Copyright Law of Japan in order to cast light on the problems that are posed for each of the provisions.

Purpose

Article 1—The purpose of this Law is, by providing for the rights of authors with respect to their works as well as for the rights of performers, producers of phonograms and broadcasting organizations with respect to their performances, phonograms and broadcasts, to secure the protection of the rights of authors, etc. having regard to a just and fair exploitation of these cultural products, and thereby to contribute to the development of culture.

The expression *just and fair exploitation* as used in this article sig-
nifies that since the works are cultural assets which may be commonly
enjoyed by the people, the people are empowered to make free use of
them within a certain scope of limitation. On the basis of this principle,
exploitation of works is authorized to a great extent under the copyright
law of Japan, as will be elucidated in the following.

Reproduction for private use

Article 30—It shall be permissible for a user to reproduce by himself a work
forming the subject matter of a copyright (hereinafter in this Subsection
referred to as a "work") for the purpose of his personal use, family use or
other similar uses within a limited circle.

Thus, users may be able to make free use of otherwise inaccessible
works, such as books, motion pictures, and opera scores, in limited numbers and within a limited circle. The publication or selling of these works
to a large number of people will, however, be an infringement on the
copyright.

Also falling in the category of copying as stipulated in this article is
a research worker's having his or her assistant copy necessary data. By no
means can copying be commissioned to any persons engaged in copying
of the kind that intends to make profits.

Experts in Japan are also of the opinion that a videotape library, in
which television programs are videotaped and a number of television
images are edited in packages, is not permissible.

Next, the *purpose of his personal use,* as referred to in this article,
represents cases where works are copied and read. The word "use" as
employed in this article is different from the "exploitation" of works and
represents the use of reproduced matter.

In a similar vein, libraries and nonprofit organizations are authorized to copy works.

The following articles concern "quotations."

Quotations

Article 32—(1) It shall be permissible to make quotations from a work already
made public, provided that their making is compatible with fair practice and
their extent does not exceed that justified by purposes such as news reporting, criticism or research.

(2) It shall also be permissible for the press or other periodicals to reproduce informatory, investigatory or statistical data, reports and other works of
similar character which have been prepared by organs of the State or local
public entities for the purpose of public information and which have been
made public under their authorship, provided that the reproduction thereof
is not expressly prohibited.

With respect to the expression "their making is compatible
with . . . ," some experts in Japan believe that the reproduction of paintings for a history of art is compatible with fair practice but that if the
reproductions turn out to be something that viewers may actually ap-

preciate independently, this act can in no way be regarded as compatible with fair practice. Here a delicate question arises as to where a line should be drawn between an art history book and a collection of paintings with lengthy commentaries.

Next, the expression "their extent does not exceed that justified by purposes . . ." means that with printed material, a new text cannot consist entirely of quotations from previous texts. Acceptable proportions between new texts and quoted texts have not been defined. In the case of visual material, every part of it, naturally must be quoted, in contrast to cases where sentences are quoted.

Next, the following provisions prevail with respect to reproduction in school textbooks, etc.

Reproduction in school textbooks, etc.

Article 33—(1) It shall be permissible to reproduce in school textbooks ("school textbooks" mean textbooks authorized by the Minister of Education or those compiled under the authorship of the Ministry of Education for the use of children or pupils in their education in primary schools, junior and senior high schools or other similar schools) works already made public, to the extent deemed necessary for the purpose of school education.

(2) A person who makes such reproduction shall be bound to inform the author thereof and to pay to the copyright owner compensation, the amount of which is fixed each year by the Commissioner of the Agency for Cultural Affairs, by taking into account the purpose of the provision of the preceding paragraph, the nature and the purpose of the work, the ordinary rate of royalty, and other conditions.

(3) The Commissioner of the Agency for Cultural Affairs shall announce in the Official Gazette the amount of compensation fixed under the provision of the preceding paragraph.

(4) The preceding three paragraphs shall apply *mutatis mutandis* with respect to the reproduction of works in textbooks intended for senior high school correspondence courses and in guidance books of school textbooks mentioned in paragraph (1) intended for teachers (these said guidance books shall be limited to those published by the same publisher of the textbooks).

In this case, paintings, photographs, and other materials may be reproduced in school text books, etc.

Next, the following provisions prevail with respect to the use of broadcasting programs in school education.

Broadcasting in school education programs

Article 34—It shall be permissible to broadcast a work already made public in broadcasting programs which conform to the curriculum standards provided for in regulations on school education and to reproduce it in teaching materials for these programs, to the extent deemed necessary for the purpose of school education.

(2) A person who makes such a broadcast or reproduction shall be bound to inform the author thereof and to pay to the copyright owner a reasonable amount of compensation.

The use of works in this case represents broadcasting and reproduction. Reproductions are usable only in the textbooks to accompany broadcasting programs. The compensation in this case is primarily left to the discretion of the broadcasting station.

Next, the following provisions prevail with respect to reproduction by educational institutions.

> Reproduction in schools and other educational institutions
>
> Article 35—A person who is in charge of teaching in a school or other educational institution established not for profitmaking may reproduce a work already made public if and to the extent deemed necessary for the purpose of use in the course of teaching, provided that such reproduction does not unreasonably prejudice the interests of the copyright owner in the light of the nature and the purpose of the work as well as the number of copies and the character of reproduction.

In this case, distribution teachers may distribute material in their classes, but they cannot do so for the benefit of all students in their school. Similarly, videotaping an educational broadcasting program for dissemination to all students in a school may be done only by the person who has direct responsibility for audiovisual education of all students.

At the schools, paintings for appreciation by viewers cannot be reproduced. And 8mm cine movies cannot be sold for audiovisual teaching aids, nor can videotapes be reproduced for permanent record in an audiovisual library.

In regard to disputes on copyright, the following provisions prevail.

> Mediators for the settlement of disputes concerning copyright
>
> Article 105—(1) In order to settle, through mediation, disputes concerning the rights provided in this Law, the Agency for Cultural Affairs shall provide mediators for the settlement of disputes concerning copyright (hereinafter in this Chapter referred to as "mediators").
>
> (2) Whenever an affair may arise, mediators, not exceeding three in number, shall be appointed by the Commissioner of the Agency for Cultural Affairs from among persons of learning and experience in the field of copyright or neighboring rights.

The nature of copyright disputes in Japan is such that heavy penalties are not normally produced, but the factors involved in any judgment are so intricate that a system of mediation is established to dispense with the need for the parties to go to court. The mediation committee is made up of a professor in copyright law or the Civil Code, a lawyer specializing in this field, and a person engaged in some business associated with copyright. A check with the Copyright Division of the Agency for Cultural Affairs indicates that thus far there have been no disputes between copyright owners and research workers, suggesting that, broadly speaking, Japanese research workers are placed in a more favorable position than those in other countries.

Incidentally, it is a Japanese practice for the publishing house to secure approval from the copyright owner when the author of a research paper is to make a quotation or reproduction. Hence it is not the practice for the research worker and the copyright owner to engage in direct negotiation and for the research worker to pay a compensation.

As elucidated in the foregoing, research workers are authorized to make fair use of visual material, and copyright owners would not go so far as to impede the freedom of research work and commentary.

NOTE

[1]See also Moriyuki Kato, *Kaitei Chosakukenho Chikujo Kogi* [Seriatim Lecturer on Revised Copyright Law] (Tokyo: Chosakuken Shiryokai, 1974). (In Japanese)

APPENDIX: Survey Questionnaire
Circulated Among Foreign Scholars

Through the circulation of the following questionnaire, the editors of this book sought to obtain fair use data on a large number of countries. Sufficient responses were not received to merit tabulation. The questionnaire was also distributed to the authors writing for the international section. Since some of their information is presented as a response to the concerns of the questionnaire, we produce it here.

SURVEY QUESTIONNAIRE:
VISUAL IMAGES, COPYRIGHT LAW, AND SCHOLARSHIP

Explanatory Note: Bernard Timberg and John Lawrence are editing a volume titled *Fair Use and Free Inquiry: Copyright Law and the New Media.* It is to be published in the Communication and Information Science Series of Ablex Publishing Company in 1979. It will contain an international section that surveys practice in the reproduction of film, video, and comic book images. You can greatly assist us in creating an accurate and comprehensive picture by answering the following questions and sending them to us in the accompanying envelope. Your help is greatly appreciated.

1. Name of country _____ .
2. Are there laws that protect through copyright the status of visual imagery in comics, magazines, advertising, film, and television?

3. Have conflicts arisen between copyright holders (media producers) and users (scholars, teachers, book publishers)?

4. Have there been significant litigations in the courts regarding such conflicts?

5. Has the government of your country attempted to balance the interests of producers and users through legislation?

6. What clearance procedures are used for scholars and critics who wish to reproduce copyrighted images in their histories and critical commentaries?

7. Is there a tradition of "fair use" (fair dealing, *Zitierfreiheit,* etc.) that permits scholars and publishers to reproduce images without obtaining permission? What term is used to designate such a right, if it exists?

8. If it is necessary for scholars to obtain permission, are they required to pay fees to the copyright owners?

9. Do such fees, if they are necessary, represent a significant obstacle for scholars and publishers?

10. If it is necessary to obtain permission, do copyright owners review the text of the manuscript?

11. If the text of the manuscript is unfavorable to the creation of the copyright owner, do the owners exercise the privilege of withholding permission to reproduce the image?

12. Are schools and universities using videotaped material in their instructional programs?

13. If the answer to 12 is yes, is it necessary for the schools and universities to secure permission from the owner of the copyright?

14. *Additional observations:*

Name of scholar _____
    and address: _____

The questions listed above reflect some important controversies that are taking place in the United States and in other media-producing and consuming countries. Answers to some or all of them would permit comparisons and conclusions about international trends. If you would like to write us a letter, in which you elaborate on the particulars of your situation, we would be glad to hear from you. You may write in any language that you feel comfortable with.

VI

STATUTORY LAW, CONSTITUTIONAL LAW, AND THE RIGHTS OF SCHOLARSHIP

New Forms of Media Discourse

In this essay, Bernard Timberg provides a detailed description of the growing presence of film both in social interactions generally and as an important component in formal educational settings. Concurrently, novel forms of film discourse have emerged without any specific statutory rationale or court sanction. Among them are

— use of off-air taped material for historical or analytic purposes,
— use of film discourse as an academic language—including the media dissertation as an example of discourse with documentary requirements for "quoting" from copyrighted audiovisual creations,
— montage or collage creation, which combines copyrighted fragments for analysis or parody.

It is argued that these uses are "fair," but as yet unrecognized by a law that has been too bound by print conventions. (In related fashion, Sigmund Timberg, in Chapter 23, develops the notion of the "Laocöon shortfall.")

The author of this essay is a film maker and radio producer as well as a film and popular culture theorist. He has made montage and collage analyses from copyrighted materials; their circulation has been subsequently constrained by copyright restrictions.

20

NEW FORMS OF MEDIA AND
THE CHALLENGE TO COPYRIGHT LAW

BERNARD TIMBERG

In an article ("Five Dollar 'Movies' Prophesied") written in 1915, D.W. Griffith, the master film maker of cinema's early days, made these predictions:

> The time will come, and in less than ten years . . . where the children in public schools will be taught practically everything by moving pictures. Certainly they will never be obligated to read history again.

> Imagine a public library of the near future, for instance. There will be long rows of boxes or pillars, properly classified and indexed, of course. At each box a push button and before each box a seat. Suppose you wish to "read up" on a certain episode in Napoleon's life. You will merely seat yourself at a properly adjusted window, in a scientifically prepared room, press the button, and actually see what happened.[1]

Griffith's prediction of sixty years ago is daily coming closer to reality. In fact, Richard Sorensen, writing in *Current Anthropology*,[2] outlines a film archive and videotape retrieval system for the National Anthropological Film Center at the Smithsonian Institution that is very close to Griffith's visionary conception of pushbutton learning. If an anthropological scholar wishes to punch "mourning" or "death rituals" on the computer, then punches "Pitt River Indians," he will obtain instant video retrieval of that visual information from within the archive or from any other archive hooked to its terminal.

Such uses of audiovisual materials become increasingly desirable as the environment of contemporary experience becomes "mediated." A significant part of children's early experience comes from television: programs like "Mister Rogers' Neighborhood" and "Sesame Street" are functioning as arenas of education and socialization; "adult" programs

248

may have an equally important effect on their ideas of the world. Social scientists and educators have become increasingly interested in television as an agent of "secondary socialization,"[3] and at least one investigator[4] has argued that only a mother has more influence on a child's early years, fathers coming third.

The learning environment in educational institutions is becoming increasingly audiovisual. Many college libraries have acquired superb television series, such as Alistair Cooke's "America," Jacob Bronowski's "The Ascent of Man," and Kenneth Clark's "Civilization." Home recording machines, such as Sony Betamax and Panasonic VistaVision, make it possible for teachers to videotape programs at home for use in their teaching. And large video screens have become available for home and educational use. We have indeed entered, though more slowly than Griffith wanted, the visual age.

In some ways we have gone beyond Griffith's forecast. Consider, for instance, the information technologies B.G. Herring describes in Chapter 12. Microform and computer technologies are hooking up with cable, fiber optic, and satellite delivery systems in novel ways. New media archives spring up yearly.[5] The impact of media is hotly debated in the press and in popular books;[6] educational theorists discuss the "hidden curriculum" that emanates from the nation's television sets[7] and the relationship of television to what has been perceived as a "literacy crisis."[8] Serious media studies are now on the agenda of institutions of higher education.

One index of increasing academic interest in film and other broadcast media is the number of new courses and academic departments on the university level devoted to these subjects. In the 1940s and 50s there were, for instance, only a handful of college level sequences in film. That changed dramatically in the 1960s; by 1967 an American Film Institute survey cited some 200 colleges and universities that offered courses in film.[9] By 1971 that number had more than doubled,[10] and the most recent AFI survey, published in 1978, lists over a thousand colleges and universities with film offerings.[11]

On the graduate level the 1978 AFI study found 11 schools in the United States offering doctoral programs in film, 45 with masters' programs, and 123 offering bachelor's degrees.[12] The number of graduate level programs in broadcasting and instructional technology[13] is even higher; the use of broadcast media in other departments (English, sociology, political science, anthropology, psychology, education), though harder to document, appears to be substantial. Radio, television, and film have arrived as fundamental components of a modern university education.

And the phenomenon is international. Canada has long been ahead of the United States in supporting the development of filmmaking programs and in training young film makers. Such national film schools as the Academy of Arts in Prague (founded in 1945), the Polish School of Cinema in Lodz (founded in 1948), the Instituto de Investigaciones y Esperiencias Cinematograficas in Madrid and the Centro Sperimentale di Cinematografia in Rome (founded in 1935 and reorganized under the direction of Roberto Rossellini in 1948), are already training a second generation of film makers and film scholars.[14] (The Center for Advanced Film Studies established by the American Film Institute in Los Angeles in 1968 is a relative latecomer.) The 1978 *Educational Media Yearbook* devotes 24 pages to 183 media-related organizations in 48 countries;[15] the United States has over 600 such organizations, many related to institutions of higher education.[16]

It is not surprising then that participants at the Airlie House Conference on Video Recording for Educational Uses in Airlie, Virginia, July 19-22, 1977, determined that much of the off-air videotaping being done in the U.S. educational system was being done at the higher levels of education. There were, in addition, reports of significant unauthorized uses of copyrighted material at the elementary school levels as well. Popular television programs with important educational implications, like "Roots," or informational programs like the PBS documentary series "Nova," were the principal kinds of material being taped for school use.

On occasion straight commercial entertainment was used for educational purposes. One Airlie House participant, William Singer, president of an organization called Prime Time School Television,[17] which distributes information on educationally valuable television programs to approximately 60,000 teachers and educational institutions around the country, described a curriculum unit his organization has written on "Television, Police, and the Law." This unit attempts to describe the "life style of police, and whether Constitutional protections are violated,"[18] and teachers who have used it have also taped segments of "Kojak," "Baretta," and "Starsky and Hutch" to document particular points. In one episode of "Starsky and Hutch," for instance, there is an unusually explicit shakedown scene. Singer, who is a lawyer himself, saw "no problem" with this kind of "limited and partial reproduction of a television program," since it was in accord with his interpretation of the fair use section (Section 107) of the copyright law.[19]

Industry and guild representatives at the Airlie Conference, although generally conceding the need for some kind of fair use policy for off-air taping, were very concerned about systematic off-air taping by school systems (in this connection see BOCES Preliminary Injunction, Chapter 13).

Not only are students from the lowest levels of elementary school on consuming media images; they are producing them as well. "WDUF

News" in Washington, D.C., broadcast on the school system's closed circuit television, is anchored by an eleven-year-old sixth-grader at Dufief Elementary School in Montgomery County. He is one of thousands of elementary and junior high school students in the Washington metropolitan area who use sophisticated electronic equipment on a regular basis during school hours to write, produce, direct, and air their own television programs.[20] Guides to media production for kindergarten through twelfth grade have been published,[21] and teachers have begun to assign "videopapers" in place of traditional written assignments.[22] Even such traditional bastions of the written word as freshman composition programs in college English departments have begun to experiment with classes in "media composition" or courses that compare the communication advantages of video or audiotape with those of the written word.[23]

Taken together, these new uses of media constitute a gradual revolution in the forms of discourse that modern society relies upon for education, public discussion, and the conduct of its daily business.

THE AUTONOMY OF THE PHOTOGRAPHIC, FILM, AND TELEVISION IMAGE

Scholars, academic administrators, and lawyers trained within print-oriented traditions need to understand that new forms of media are not merely supplementary to, or illustrative of, print. These media have distinct, independent, coequal status with print in the transmission of information and opinion in our society. Since they accomplish their purposes in unique ways, translation or paraphrase into other forms can blunt their communicative impact or alter it drastically: the best way to deaden a film's statement is to reduce it to words.

Scholars and critics have for some time grappled with the untranslatable nature of the visual image. As early as 1915 Vachel Lindsay discussed the "tableau logic" of the silent film—a picture-sequence logic distinct from, and irreproduceable by, a sequence of words.[24] More recently, such scholars as Walter Ong and Marshall McLuhan have distinguished between the effects of the "linear" discourse of the printed word and the audiovisual discourse of film and television that comes to us as an integrated series of images.[25] Extending the characterization of communication through imagery, Richard Sorensen makes the following distinction:

> Visual information possesses a complex, multilayered character unlike that of the written word. Because of this, it lends itself to more subtle and complex kinds of examination than allowed by rules of language and [verbal] logic. Like art, it involves such intellectually creative processes as the appreciation and recognition of pattern, significance, and meaning.[26]

Concerning the unique "logic" of visual images, Edmund Carpenter has argued that an "amplification principle" accompanies mass screenings or broadcasts. Using the term *angelization* seriously, he suggests that "electricity has made angels of us all." A television camera trained on us would put us, like the President on national television, everywhere at once, exemplifying the neoplatonic definition of God: a Being whose center is everywhere, whose borders are nowhere.[27] Other theorists, including McLuhan, have emphasized radical differences between reflected images on a screen in a darkened theater and the blue electronic "tattoo" that beams at us from our television sets. Although they disagree on many things, all the theorists agree that visual images present us with a qualitatively *different* style of discourse.

Apart from the question of its distinctiveness, what is the relative power of this imagistic communication? Do the new media have vital, rather than supplementary, functions to serve in teaching and scholarship?

Given the work of such film artists as Ingmar Bergman, few would deny that media discourse has, in some cases at least, attained the stature of the best printed literature. Nor can it be said, as some have maintained, that media imagery belongs in a purely affective realm. In the hands of a Bergman, or a documentary maker like Frederick Wiseman, a film can become an effective tool of cognitive analysis, visually dissecting extremely complex psychological and sociological phenomena. Two of the most important studies of modern marriage have been Bergman's *Scenes from a Marriage* and John Cassavetes' *Woman Under the Influence*. It is not absurd to argue, then, that film or video may be *the* most effective descriptive discourse form for certain areas of psychological and personal interaction. Film and video have become important in the physical sciences as well. Microscopic lenses, lens "implants" and other film and photographic developments have moved the field of biomedical communications into areas of study and research where it has never been before.[28]

We have, then, abundant evidence of the communicative power that accompanies new forms of media in our society. The law, however, fails to meet the challenges these new forms of media present. It is true that the law has developed substantially beyond the view expressed in the Supreme Court's *Mutual Film Corporation v. Ohio* decision in 1915 that motion pictures be regarded as "a business pure and simple," not as a fundamental expression of ideas;[29] but the law still exists, conceptually, within the shadow of that decision.

Some of the problems for contemporary law as it confronts the new media are:

1. Does the traditional distinction between an idea and its form of

expression represent an "acceptable definitional balance"[30] between copyright and free speech when applied to graphic or photographic images?

2. What constitutes an adequate "amount or substantiality of use" in respect to "quoting" films or television programs?

3. What constitutes critical discourse in our society? Has media discourse itself become a valid form of such discourse?

AN IDEA AND ITS FORM OF EXPRESSION

Some legal authorities believe court decisions that distinguish an idea from its fixed form of expression help accommodate competing copyright and First Amendment interests.[31] No one has a monopoly on ideas, the courts have said repeatedly,[32] but one can have a monopoly with respect to particular forms of expression.

The courts have in the past generally been concerned with word sequences. The idea-expression dichotomy does not work very well, however, when it comes to works of criticism, since a critic would be seriously hampered if he were barred from direct quotation of the work under consideration. If a line like Patrick Henry's "Give me liberty or give me death!" had to be rendered in paraphrase ("I would prefer to die rather than to continue in an unfree state"), it would certainly blunt the vividness of the statement, an intrinsic part of its importance and effectiveness. The courts have recognized this problem when it has arisen in connection with the critique of print media, and the right of fairly extensive print quotation is well-established under the fair use principle.

Discussions of photographic imagery raise new problems. The subject of a piece of writing has already gone through one major symbolic transformation into the letters, words, and sentences that make up our print symbol system; the subject and its fixed form of expression are already at one symbolic remove from each other. A photograph is closer to its subject—its transformation (to black and white or color forms on a piece of paper or on a transparency) relates it directly[33] to the physical subject it represents. The idea (the subject) and its fixed form of expression are much closer together in a photograph, and although a manipulation of photographic codes (lighting, composition, the speed of the film) can alter significantly how we perceive a photographic subject, there are unbreachable limits to how far we may "slant" a viewer's perception of the subject by these means. If the photograph crosses a certain line, we accuse it of being subjective, distorted, or "unrealistic." The photographic idea and its fixed form, then, are necessarily linked. It is especially important to have the fixed form of a photographic idea present to the scholar, educator, or social commentator for the kind of comprehensive, careful analysis that distinguishes good criticism.

The problem becomes even more complicated when one approaches film or other forms of video discourse that exist simultaneously in space and time. Video/film discourse is characterized by what Erwin Panofsky calls the "dynamization of space" and the simultaneous "spatialization of time";[34] a principle of "coexpressibility" applies to this kind of discourse, and terms we use in print to discuss film—when we call it an *audio-visual* medium, for instance—may be inadequate because they hyphenate what is essentially a unitary phenomenon.[35]

In a work of analysis or criticism, "freezing" the time-space process by isolating its flow at a single frame, in effect spatializing it, allows us to study more effectively the spatial characteristics of film (composition, lighting, camera angle, the "blocking" of the set). Similarly, temporal aspects can be emphasized by playing back the soundtrack in isolation from the picture. But the combined spatio-temporal qualities of a film sequence can be adequately shown only in a full picture-sound playback. In what has been termed an effect of "synaesthesia,"[36] we "see" sound and "hear" picture.

It would be nonsense for a teacher to present an in-depth analysis of a work of fiction or challenge students to develop their own interpretations of the work if he and they had no text of that work present or had read it only once a few days before. The particular qualities that make up a work of fiction—whether it be short story, play, novel, libretto, or film—must be examined in the work itself. This is true for any medium. And for media in which space and time coalesce, it is even more important for the teacher or critic to have the "fixed form of tangible expression" to refer to.

THE AMOUNT AND SUBSTANTIALITY OF USE

It has been argued that to use an entire still photograph, even if the purpose is clearly scholarly or educational, is to "consume" the photographic work in its entirety and thus a fair use defense for this practice is impossible. But photographs are designed to be consumed in this manner (see Sigmund Timberg on the "Laocöon shortfall" and the doctrine of qualitative substantiality developed by the courts in relation to spatial media); they cannot be analyzed adequately in part or in a verbal "translation" of their content.[37] The more one looks at a photograph, the more one discovers. If the photograph is necessary for critical analysis, as in the cases of Professors Stott and Sproule cited in Chapter 5, it must be used in its entirety.

As regards film material it has been argued that an arbitrary, rule-of-thumb limit be placed on the amount of time an educational film or video program can quote from another copyrighted audiovisual work.[38] This maximum amount of time has been variously pegged at 15 seconds, 20 seconds—or even as much as a minute. Anything below that amount of time would be fair use; anything above would not.

This would indeed solve a lot of problems for broadcasters and administrators, but the principle—derived from the minimum guideline limits Congress suggested for the number of words one could take in a single-print quotation—will not work well with film and television. Arbitrary limits do not make sense in the "flow" of a film or television presentation. Twenty seconds of real time in one film sequence may appear as a mere flash in "film time"; conversely, 20 seconds of real time may, in the viewer's experience of the film, seem to drag on forever. If there is a good deal of rapid action in close-up, 20 seconds may be entirely inadequate; if the frame is frozen or the action quite still, it may be more than enough to study what is in the sequence.

A second, more fundamental objection to an arbitrary time limit is that a reader can pore over a quotation fixed in print. For analysis, this kind of close reading and rereading is essential. A film often allows only one "reading"; unless freeze frame or other analytic techniques are used, the material needs an adequate amount of time to make an impression on the viewer. I have found in my own experience that 2 to 3 minutes is often the length of time needed to follow the cinematic development of a sequence in a feature-length film. Here, of course, we are talking about a single broadcast or one-time classroom use. When it comes to in-depth individual study of a film, radio, or television program, one often needs to examine the entire work in its fixed form.

Gerald Mast (Chapter 6) argues cogently for a solution to this problem that would entail each school's buying prints of film classics it wants to use (the works of the early American and Russian pioneers in film, for instance, or representative works of the German expressionists of the 1920s and 30s). Mast is presently engaged in such a film-buying program at the University of Chicago. The harder case, however, is that of the teacher at a school that simply cannot afford to buy such a collection. And there is a fundamental pedagogic problem associated with this approach. In buying a collection—which will in most cases be restricted to a limited number of prints—a canon of favored works is created. D.W. Griffith comes to "represent" early film, and equally important film makers (Maurice Tourneur, for instance, or George Loane Tucker) may be neglected.[39] Furthermore, buying films would not solve the problems of popular culture scholars who need access to television productions. The fair use of copyrighted works may be the only means by which serious students of film and television can discuss and study the wide spectrum of works available in theaters and on public and commercial networks.

NEW FORMS OF CRITICAL DISCOURSE

Accepting the premise that film and video possess substantial informational and analytic value in a variety of inquiries, what is their value as a means of scholarly presentation in and of themselves?

Scholarly presentations have in fact been made in media discourse forms, and some university departments have created options at the master's thesis level that permit the presentation of imagery. Audio tapes, videocassette productions, slide shows, and film are common at scholarly conferences.[40] And audiovisual montage has become a particularly effective tool of artistic and social critique.

The audiotape radio collages of new journalist and radio artist Scoop Nisker in the San Francisco Bay area, the photographic collages of commercial artist Stuart Bay in Minneapolis-St. Paul, and the film collages of constructivist film artist Bruce Conner (from *A Movie* in 1957 through his most recent work, *Mongoloid*, 1978) are examples of such work. So too is the half-hour film montage of Arthur Seidel and his film associates at Baltimore.[41] After rebuffs of requests for information from several major advertising agencies, Seidel and associates went ahead on a fair use basis to use scores of juxtaposed television commercials in a film, *The 30-Second Dream*, which analyzed the imagery and emotional appeals Madison Avenue directs toward the average consumer. The film identifies four major areas of concern to most Americans: *intimacy, vitality, family*, and *success*, and is designed as a viewing guide to the ways television advertising exploits these concerns.

In a series of movies that use compilation techniques, film critic and historian Richard Schickel has produced fourteen major *auteur* and theme studies on the American cinema. Although at times material was withheld from the producers by copyright owners,[42] with the aid of commercial sponsors Schickel was able to obtain copyright clearances from the major studios for all the scenes he used. Schickel's *Men Who Made the Movies* and *Life Goes to the Movies* series make their most telling points in film-clip montage sequences characterized by careful editing and juxtaposition of quoted image structures. Through such juxtapositions and sudden contrasts Schickel attempts in his own words, to " 'write' history and criticism."[43]

In the examples cited, the film editor takes on the function of a literary narrator or point-of-view essayist in print. In a 20-minute film or slide-tape presentation comprised entirely of intercut quotations, there is, with or without a narrative voice as such, a continuous editorial presence that informs and shapes the thesis, fusing its component parts. The montage of the type just cited, consisting entirely of interwoven visual citations, becomes a newly created structure.

DIALECTICAL AND ADDITIVE MONTAGE

The montage idea can apply to print as well as audio, film, and video discourse, and as Alan Spiegel points out in *Fiction and the Camera Eye*,[44] the montage approach to the exposition of ideas has a distinguished lineage in nineteenth- and twentiety-century literature. Spiegel distinguishes two kinds of montage: The first is *dialectical montage*, popularized by Russian director and film theorist Sergei Eisenstein in the 1920s; this refers to the dialectical confrontation of one image (image A) with another (image B) to produce a third composite perception (a mental image, which we may call *C*). Eisenstein called this a montage of *conflict*, where the jarring, discordant quality of the juxtaposed images (for instance, shots of the medals and uniforms of Kerensky's soldiers cut against shots of wine glasses and tin soldiers to elicit notions of decadence and puppetry) forced the viewer to experience certain kinds of explicit associations. This kind of montage is, as Spiegel points out, at its worst a blunt and not always effective form of agitprop; at its best, however, it establishes a new film form—the cinematic equivalent of the essay.[45]

What is even more intriguing about dialectical montage is its print analogues in the works of such modern literary artists as James Joyce and William Faulkner. Spiegel cites passages from Joyce's *Ulysses* and *Portrait of an Artist as a Young Man* to prove his point ("He halted before Dlugacz's window, staring at the hanks of sausages, polonies, black and white. Fifty multiplied by. The figures whitened in his mind unsolved. . ."[46]), and he characterizes Joyce's montage style as "a way of *abstracting* from his concretized form without ever really departing from it, of creating an atmosphere of intellection and symbolic resonance while working in and through a series of concretized actions."[47] In this way, "Joyce can inject his thought without interjecting his voice."[48]

Spiegel discusses another form of montage—*additive montage*—in the literary works of John Dos Passos and William Burroughs.[49] In his *USA* trilogy (completed 1937), Dos Passos intercuts four different accounts: the straight narrative (the individual view), "Newsreel" (the topical view), biography (the public view), and "Camera Eye" (the private view) in a multi-perspective narrative of epic proportions. Dos Passos himself acknowledged his debt to Joyce and the cinematic montage of Eisenstein[50] but built his composite by arranging "disparate perspectives in an additive manner to create—or at least move toward—a sense of assonance, to make them accumulate steadily and, as it were, flesh out his general attitutde."[51] Spiegel sees Dos Passos' work as coming in a direct line of descent from the epic cataloguers and list makers of American literature, Walt Whitman foremost among them. He characterizes the modern experimental novelist William Burroughs (*Naked Lunch*, 1959) as a writer who employs an extreme form of additive montage,[52] assembling literary fragments in startling ways. Thus the montage idea in print has developed into a serious twentieth-century art form.

Montage has also been used in burlesque, parody, or satire. Since dialectical montage juxtaposes incongruities and additive montage shows surprising repetitive relationships, the results of both techniques are often quite funny. Nisker's audio collages, Bay's photo collages, Schickel's structural film critiques, and Conner's absurdist film collages all take advantage of these humorous possibilities.

If creators feel that the artistic integrity of their works is impaired when a teacher takes a part of their work and "quotes" it out of context in a classroom, how much more so when bits and pieces of their work are held up to public ridicule in contexts that have nothing to do with their original purposes.[53] The guild representatives who attended the Airlie Conference indicated that this kind of fragmented use out of context was one of their principal concerns. As Sigmund Timberg points out in Chapter 23, the copyright law in countries other than the United States is more protective of the artist in this regard than American copyright law is.

A rather simple case of the dialectical montage principle in parody (this time where picture and words are juxtaposed) can be found in any of the numerous books that take photographic images (of former President Richard Nixon, for instance) and put words in the mouths of the photographic subjects in white cartoon balloon spaces. The words are either totally incongruous or used to reveal inner motives not apparent in surface rhetoric. In this case, the photographic artist's work has been taken and used for a purpose entirely alien to his original purpose, and the subject of the photograph is given over to obvious public ridicule.

Yet the right to parody ideas and public figures is an important one in the United States; in literary form such parody falls under the fair use section of the copyright law and also under First Amendment protections of freedom of speech. Do these protections apply to pictures and recorded words as well? What if the teacher or social critic's *educational* purpose is served by the use of humor or the satirical implications of dialectical montage? What if the educator relies on humor not only to elicit the attention of an audience but to force that audience to think about the incongruities under discussion? In such cases educational and entertainment values blend; the one works with the other to catalyze thought and active discussion on the part of those participating in the educational experience.[54] Here even blatant and gross distortions of the original meaning of copyrighted works may be defensible on fair use as well as First Amendment grounds.

But doesn't this use of a work disregard the rights of the creator? Several comments were addressed to this point at the Airlie Conference on off-air recording. A representative of the Library of Congress pointed out to guild representatives that "there comes a time, when you put something out, especially over the air, or in public form, when you can no longer control it."[55] Another conference participant pointed out that the same principle applies to books, where an author always runs the risk that his work will be quoted out of context.[56] And one of the teachers present stressed the point that teachers have their own "integrity" and rights to protect, among them the right to use the best material available for instruction.[57]

We come back, then, to the conflict upon which the entire fair use controversy is predicated—a conflict that does not involve in ethical terms a right and a wrong, but two rights.[58]

ANTHOLOGY, COMPILATION, MONTAGE

Ivan Bender, then counsel to the American Media Producers Association, spoke for himself, the association he represented, and the copyright law itself when he said at the Airlie Conference that the law in general is opposed to the unauthorized preparation of compilations, derivative works, or anthologies.[59]

An *anthology* is a collection of excerpted works, organized by theme or topic, origin or point of view, but otherwise unaltered. A *compilation* is defined in the 1976 copyright act as "a work formed by the collection and assembling of preexisting materials or of data that are selected, coordinated, or arranged in such a way that the resulting work as a whole constitutes an original work of authorship" (Section 101, "Definitions"). Such a work may be independently copyrighted under the new law, but "protection for a work employing preexisting material in which copyright subsists does not extend to any part of the work in which such material has been used unlawfully" (Section 103:a). In other words, compilations that use copyrighted work must use the copyrighted material "lawfully."

A *derivative work* is a work "based upon one or more preexisting works, such as a translation, musical arrangement, dramatization, fictionalization, motion picture version, sound recording, art reproduction, abridgment, condensation, or any other form in which a work may be recast, transformed, or adapted" (Section 101). A copyright for such a work extends only to "the material contributed by the author of such a work" and "does not imply any exclusive right in the preexisting material. The copyright in such a work is independent of, and does not affect or enlarge the scope, duration, ownership, or subsistence of, any copyright protection in the preexisting materials" (Section 103:b).

A montage of the kind discussed here (whether additive, dialectic, or a combination of both) is not an anthology wherein copyrighted materials are copied *in toto* and placed side by side. It is also not a derivative work, since it is not based upon works whose purposes it attempts to "recast, transform, or adapt" in the way, for instance, that the television version of *Little Women* attempts to recast the themes and characters of the novel. It seems to fall most adequately under the definition of a compilation, since it is a "collection and assembling of preexisting materials" that "constitutes an original work of authorship."

Can the special type of compilation that a montage represents lawfully use "preexisting" copyrighted material without requesting specific copyright clearance from the copyright owners? The answer—as it has emerged from numerous workshops, discussion groups, and conference panels attended by the author at which examples of audio, film, and video montage have been presented,[60] is an equivocal "yes"— *if* the use of the copyrighted material meets the four general criteria for fair use under Section 107 of the new law.

It may be in the interests of artists, communications lawyers, and others concerned with the problem of montage to set aside this special category of compilation and give it special treatment. For the fragments that are worked together in the new whole of a montage are not merely "selected, coordinated, or arranged" (the words used in the definition of a compilation) but "fused" into the new unitary creation. What one gets by the dialectical juxtaposition of A and B in Eisensteinian montage, or in the structural echoing effect of additive montage (an inductive process, which creates a general "idea" from a series of particulars) is an entirely new object, not a reworked, expanded, or distilled A and B, but a C. This C is of the nature of an idea—an idea derived from the juxtaposed images used—and as such has preferential treatment under the idea-fixed expression dichotomy which, although not of great value in analyzing a single image, for reasons previously explained, comes to life with new force in the examination of the succession of images that constitute a montage.

The clearest solution under the present copyright law would be to consider not three but four categories of work—anthology, compilation, derivative work—and montage: a work created in mosaic fashion from the fusion of decontextualized pieces of prior works. Anthologies should, as is now the case, generally have copyrighted clearance for all copyrighted materials used. Compilations and derivative works may qualify as "fair use" if the use meets the general criteria of Section 107 of the copyright law. Assuming the purpose and character of their use is satiric or educational, works of montage, which present their ideas through the clash and association of disparate images, should have full fair use and First Amendment protection.

QUOTATION FROM SCHOLARLY MEDIA PRESENTATIONS

Whatever their legal status today, audiovisual montage and other kinds of film or videotape presentation may in the future provide significant tools of exposition and structural analysis in fields as diverse as anthropology, sociology, popular culture, and film, and in scientific presentations in the physical sciences as well. As scholars and artist-critics wed sophistication in their field with sophistication in media production, we may expect to see an increasing number of such presentations.

Given this trend, how will professional scholarship handle the traditional practice of quotation? Can one scholar's media presentation quote from another's? Can a scholar quote from a copyrighted work to illustrate his thesis?

Some professional organizations, such as the National Association of Educational Broadcasters, have recognized this problem. The NAEB has drafted guidelines for the acceptance of media presentations as scholarly "publication."[61] Many institutions of higher education are recognizing media "publication" as valid evidence of scholarship in their promotion and tenure decisions. Despite traditional print-bound attitudes and modes of thought, the academic as well as legal profession will have to come to terms with these important media developments.

VIDEODISCS AND THE FUTURE

No longer on the horizon but already at the test-marketing stage is a development in communications technology that threatens to alter radically the social and economic framework within which fair use issues are being pursued today. After years of promotional announcements, the videodisc playback unit has finally come on the market— Magnavision is test-marketing a videodisc player in Atlanta that uses a high-quality MCA-Phillips optical laser-beam system.[62] The player sold for $700 in 1978, with Disco-Vision records selling for $15 or $16. Heading the list of videodiscs available are such movies as *National Lampoon's Animal House, Jaws, American Graffiti, The Sting,* and the American Film Theater's productions of *The Man in the Glass Booth* and *Luther.* Other videodiscs will contain popular television series like "Kojak," documentaries, concerts, and self-help and self-improvement programs, and will sell for $2.95 to $9.95.[63] With videodiscs, the cost of video entertainment (and information) becomes competitive with the cost of books, and one can assemble one's own videodisc library alongside a book and record collection.

A videodisc can be stamped out in mass production for a labor and material cost of as little as 40 cents,[64] and playback machine costs may drop to the original MCA-Phillips projection of $500.[65] With videodisc prices undercutting videotape costs, it seems likely that few people will want to tape programs off the air when they can be obtained more cheaply, and with better reproduction quality, on disc.

Whatever happens on the home market, it appears to be only a matter of time before videodiscs invade industrial and educational markets.[66] Special versions can be coordinated with minicomputers to access immediately any frame (there are some 54,000 video frames on each half-hour side of a disc).[67] This extremely dense storage capacity, allowing a massive photographic or art collection to be stored on a single disc, is especially attractive to libraries and data centers.

With the development of videodisc and increasing sophistication and availability of videotape recording and playback machines,[68] forms of participant and interactive video will become more and more a part of the average person's daily life. Small format videotape has already had important uses in prisons,[69] in courtroom procedure,[70] in situations of delicate negotiation where face-to-face meeting is not necessarily the best first step (adoption agencies have found videotape the best means of introducing adoptees to prospective parents[71]); even such ephemeral pastimes as videogames have encouraged people to become active users of video, rather than passive spectators. The next generation of students will come to school possessing new levels of "visual literacy,"[72] and the analytic devices of instant replay, slow motion, and stop action will be a familiar part of the conceptual apparatus they bring to the "new languages"[73] of television and film.

The law will have to respond to these changes. The overview statements that follow present, as far as the coeditors of this volume are aware, the first comprehensive attempt by legal scholars to come to grips with the problems presented by the new media and the forms of intellectual inquiry that derive from them.

NOTES

[1]Cited in Harry M. Geduld, ed., *Focus on D.W. Griffith* (Englewood Cliffs, N.J.: Prentice-Hall, 1971), p. 34.

[2]Richard Sorensen, *Current Anthropology*, 16 (June 1975):267-69.

[3]David G. Geulette of the Education Department at Northern Illinois University has summarized recent opinion on television's role in second socialization: "Television: The Hidden Curriculum of Lifelong Learning and 'Lenguaje Total,' " presented at Adult Education Research Conference, San Antonio, Texas, April, 1978.

[4]Charles Corder-Belz, in a research report of the Office of Education, cited by mass communications scholar Timothy Meyer of the University of Texas Radio-Television-Film Department in *Images* magazine of *The Daily Texan* (Dec. 11, 1978), p. 7. Cf. Marie Winn, *TV: The Plug-In Drug* (New York:Viking, 1977) for a comprehensive review of mediated childhood patterns.

[5]See list of film and television archives in Appendix A Chap. 8. *Videography* 3:1 (November 1977): 16-19, is a good summary article on video archives, Jody McMahon, "Keeping History Alive: Videotape Archives, Collections and Museums," cf. Don Kowet, "Let's watch 'Omnibus' and 'The Goldbergs': Visitors to the Museum of Broadcasting can rerun three decades of TV," *TV Guide* 26:4 (Jan. 28, 1978), 32-33.

[6]See, for instance, *Newsweek's* special issue on the "TV of Tomorrow" (July 3, 1978), pp. 62-84. Other recent books that debate the importance and influence of the new media, especially television, are Edwin Diamond, *The Tin Kazoo: Television, Politics, and the News* (Cambridge, Mass.: MIT, 1975); Rose K. Goldsen, *The Show and Tell Machine: How Television Works and Works You Over* (New York: Delta, 1978); Jeff Greenfield, *Television: The First Fifty Years* (New York: Abrams Publishing Company, 1977); Jerry Mander, *Four Arguments for the Elimination of Television* (New York: Morrow Quill Paperbacks, 1978); Frank Mankiewicz and Joel Swerdlow, *Remote Control: Television and the Manipulation of American Life* (New York: Ballantine, 1979); James Monaco, *How to Read a Film: The Art, Technology, Language, History, and Theory of Film and Television* (New York: Oxford, 1977); Horace Newcomb, *TV: The Most Popular Art* (Garden City, N.Y.: Anchor, 1974); Thomas E. Patterson and Robert D. McClure, *The Unseeing Eye: The Myth of Television Power in American Politics* (New York: Putnam, 1976); Michael Real, *Mass-Mediated Culture* (Englewood Cliffs, N.J.: Prentice-Hall, 1977); Tony Schwartz, *The Responsive Chord* (Garden City, N.Y.: Anchor, 1973); Bob Shanks, *The Cool Fire: How to Make It in Television* (New York: Vintage, 1977); Susan Sontag, *On Photography* (New York: Farrar, Straus, Giroux, 1977); Gaye Tuchman, ed., *The TV Establishment: Programming for Power and Profit* (Englewood Cliffs, N.J.: Prentice-Hall, 1974); Raymond Williams, *Television: Technology and Cultural Forms* (New York: Schocken Books, 1975).

[7]See Geulette.

[8]Dennis R. Hall, Department of English, University of Louisville (Louisville, Ky.), "A Semiotic Approach to the Relationship of Television to the Literacy Crisis" (unpublished paper).

[9]Dennis R. Bohnenkamp and Sam L. Grogg, Jr., eds., *The American Film Institute Guide to College Courses in Film and Television* (Princeton, N.J.: A Peterson's Guides Publication, 1978), p. 5.

[10]*The Education of the Film-maker: An International View* (Paris and Washington, D.C.: Unesco Press and the American Film Institute, 1975), p. 154.

[11]Bohnenkamp and Grogg, p. 5.

[12]*Ibid.*, p. 12.

[13]Instructional technology designs strategies for the use of media to accomplish general and specific instructional goals.

[14]*The Education of the Film-maker*, p. 10.

[15]James W. Brown, ed., *Educational Media Yearbook 1978* (New York and London: R.R. Bowker, 1978), pp. 392-432.

[16]*Ibid.*, pp. 291-391.

[17]A more detailed account of the services offered by Prime Time School Television and other educational services that use television can be found in Maya Pines, "Does 'Roots' Make Good Homework?" *TV Guide* 26:50 (Dec. 16, 1978):7-10.

[18]Transcript of proceedings and *Report*, Conference on Video Recording for Educational Uses, Airlie, Virginia, July 19-22, 1977, p. 36.

[19]*Ibid.*

[20]Robert Meyers, "Metropolitan Area Schools Deep into Television Age," *Washington Post*, Mar. 19, 1978.

[21]Center for Understanding Media, *Doing the Media: A Portfolio of Activities, Ideas and Resources* (New York: McGraw-Hill, 1978).

[22]L. George Van Soon, "The Videopaper," *Audiovisual Instruction* 23:8 (November 1978):36-38.

[23]W. Ross Winterowd, Professor of English at the University of Southern California, describes this new interest in media in the introduction to a collection of articles on new approaches to rhetoric published in 1975:

McLuhan is already old hat. Nonetheless, he was the first prophet of a continuing trend in compositional pedagogy, that is, contact, or media, orientation. McLuhanism can have two related manifestations in the composition course. First is the course that uses the media (television, cinema) as its subject matter, and second is the course that turns to composing in the media (making films and television tapes). For instance, an unstartling but extremely successful innovation at the University of Southern California is a cluster of freshman classes in which film is the subject matter for expository writing. More innovative is the course that interprets the word "composing" broadly and allows students to make their statements in writing, film, television, and other media. (*Contemporary Rhetoric: A Conceptual Background with Readings*, New York: Harcourt Brace Jovanovich, 1975, p. 9).

[24]Vachel Lindsay, *The Art of the Moving Picture* (New York: Macmillan, 1915).

[25]Marshall McLuhan, *Understanding Media: The Extensions of Man* (New York: McGraw-Hill, 1965), pp. 7-21.

[26]Sorenson, *Current Anthropology*, 16 (June 1975):268.

[27]Edmund Carpenter, *Oh, What a Blow That Phantom Gave Me!* (Toronto: Bantam Books, 1974), p. 3.

[28]Walter Anderson, "Prescription for Success: How video is making giant strides in the field of medical communications," *Videography* 3:2 (February 1978), 23-27.

[29]Garth Jowett, *Film: The Democratic Art* (Boston-Toronto: Little, Brown, 1976), pp. 119-21.

[30]The wording here is Nimmer's, "Does Copyright Abridge the First Amendment Guarantees of Free Speech and Press?" 17 *UCLA Law Review* 1180, 1192 (1970):

> . . . The idea-expression line represents an acceptable definitional balance as between copyright and free speech interests. In some degree it encroaches upon freedom of speech in that it abridges the right to reproduce the "expression" of others, but this is justified by the greater good in the copyright encouragement of creative works.

[31]*Ibid.*

[32]See discussion of "unity of idea and expression" in *Sid and Marty Krofft v. McDonald's Corp.* 196 USPQ, 105-107. This decision cites *Herbert Rosenthal Jewelry Corp. v. Kalpakian*, 446 F.2d 738, 170 USPQ 557 (9 Cir. 1971), and fifteen other cases where this distinction was significant.

[33]This relation has been described as *indexical* or *iconic* in borrowing from the semiotic categories of C.S. Pierce. See Peter Wollen, *Signs and Meaning in the Cinema* (Bloomington, Ind.: Indiana University Press, 1972); and James Monaco, *How to Read a Film*. The relationship between the photographic image and the object it represents is a very complicated one, much debated by film theorists. My own discussion here is a simplification.

[34]Erwin Panofsky, "Style and Medium in the Motion Picture" (1934; revised 1947), reprinted in David Denby, ed., *Awake in the Dark: Anthology of American Film Criticism, 1915 to the Present* (New York: Vintage, 1977), pp. 3-48.

[35]For the implications of this distinction for legal philosophy, as well as a discussion of the idea-expression dichotomy as it has been applied to cartoon characters in recent court decisions, see Chap. 23.

[36]For a discussion of "synaesthesia," how one sense works integrally with another, see Sergei Eisenstein, *The Film Sense*, Jay Leyda, trans. (New York: Harcourt Brace Jovanovich, 1975), p. 149.

[37]The network-producer-union view presented at the Airlie Conference in one of the discussion groups was stated thus:

> In video, the print concepts of short excerpts, quotations and the like, simply did not and could not apply. An excerpt, it was asserted, might be the crux of an entire presentation. Moreover, it was asserted that the visual and perfor-

mance components are the very inherent and distinguishing values of video production, and not susceptible of isolation into segments or excerpts for fair use. (*Report* of Conference on Video Recording for Educational Uses, Airlie, Virginia, p. 107).

[38]This argument has been made by, among others, Eric Smith of the Public Broadcasting Service in Washington, D.C.

[39]I am indebted to Professor Horace Newcomb of the University of Texas English Department for pointing out this unintended effect of Mast's proposal.

A problem of "internal censorship," as it is called by librarians, has long affected the collections of school and public libraries in this and other countries. It is related to the concept of "prior restraint" in the law, since libraries often steer clear of books or nonprint materials that *might* be controversial. This subtle censorship avoids the more blatant removal of "problematic" works (i.e., bizarre, politically radical, experimental, or other items that confront or shock middle-of-the-road sensibilities). For two discussions of this issue (the first print-oriented, the second nonprint-oriented), see Marjorie Fiske, *Book Selection and Censorship* (Berkeley: California, 1959); Don Roberts, "Report on Past and Present Censorship of Non-Book Media in Public Libraries," a report funded by the Council on Library Resources (Washington, D.C., 1976).

[40]The author himself has made a number of such presentations (see introductory notes to this chapter).

[41]*The Thirty-Second Dream* (color, 16mm, 15 min., 1977) was produced by Lawrence-Brandon-Seidel Film Productions and is distributed by Media Mass Ministries, Baltimore, Md. The film has been shown and has provoked discussion at the Adult Education Association meetings in Detroit, November, 1977, and the National Association of Educational Broadcasters meetings in Washington, D.C., November, 1978.

[42]Richard Schickel, "Clipping the Movie Past," *American Film* 4:5 (March 1979): 57.

[43]*Ibid.*, 58.

[44]Alan Spiegel, *Fiction and the Camera Eye: Visual Consciousness in Film and the Modern Novel* (Charlottesville: University Press of Virginia, 1976).

[45]*Ibid.*, p. 172. The distinctions Spiegel makes between dialectical and additive montage by no means exhaust the subject. Early Soviet film maker and film theoretician V.I. Pudovkin (considered by some the "father" of additive montage) distinguishes five basic types of montage: contrast, parallelism, symbolism, simultaneity, and leitmotif. Contemporary French film theorist Christian Metz constructs a system in which he attempts to show how eight types of montage in filmic editing codes are related to each other. For a summary discussion of theories of montage, see Monaco, *How to Read a Film*, pp. 186-90.

[46]*Ibid.*, p. 168.

[47]*Ibid.*, p. 173.

[48]*Ibid.*

[49]*Ibid.*, pp. 176-81.

[50]*Ibid.*, p. 177, n14.

[51]*Ibid.*, p. 178.

[52]*Ibid.*, pp. 179-81.

[53]The two types of parody distinguished here can be labeled *parody by intent,* direct parody of a work, and *parody by circumstance,* use of the work to parody another idea, personage, or work. In either case what the Europeans call the *moral rights* of the artist are affected.

[54]"The line between the transmission of ideas and mere entertainment is much too elusive for this court to draw, if indeed such a line can be drawn at all." (Stanley v. Georgia 394 U.S. 557, 564, 565-66.)

[55]Conference on Video Recording for Educational Uses, *Report,* p. 176.

[56]*Ibid.*, p. 168.

[57]*Ibid.*, p. 183. In fact, most abuses of artists' moral rights in the United States have come not from users but from producers and distributors who have final say on how the

work is to be presented to the public. See Gilliam v. American Broadcasting Co., 538 F2d 14 (2d Cir.) 1976. See also Hendrick Hertzberg, "Onward and Upward with the Arts: Naughty Bits," *New Yorker,* Mar. 29, 1976. Hertzberg's article discusses the Gilliam case in more detail. (Gilliam was a member of "Monty Python's Flying Circus"; the group as a whole was suing ABC for cuts it made in its "Wide World of Entertainment" broadcast of Monty Python material in 1975.)

[58]*New Outlook* editor Simcha Flapan once made this comment about the Arab-Israeli conflict, and I think it is particularly applicable here.

[59]Conference on Video Recording for Educational Uses, *Report,* p. 181.

[60]These discussions took place 1976-79 at Ames, Iowa; Austin, Texas; Washington, Minneapolis, D.C.; and Minneapolis.

[61]*Evaluation of Scholarly NonPrint Publication:* a statement of the Ad Hoc Committee to Study NonPrint Publication, Thomas O. Olson, Chairman; approved by the Broadcast Education Council of the National Association of Educational Broadcasters, October 26, 1976.

[62]David Lachenbruch, "What Looks Like a Phonograph Record, Works on a Laser Beam and Shows 'Jaws'?" *TV Guide* 26:47 (Nov. 25, 1978): 4-8.

[63]*Ibid.,* p. 5.

[64]*Ibid.,* p. 8.

[65]"Videodiscs: The Expensive Race to Be First," *Business Week* (Sept. 15, 1975), p. 62.

[66]Lachenbruch, p. 8.

[67]See Lachenbruch, p. 5; Richard Koszarski, "Television: The Disco Hustle," *Film Comment* (January-February, 1977), pp. 38-39. See also "The Videodisc: The Impact on AV Technology," *Functional Photography* (January 1976), pp. 17, 32-33.

[68]David Lachenbruch, "Video-Cassette Recorders: Here Comes the Second Generation," *TV Guide* 26:43 (Oct. 28, 1978): 2-11. By the fall of 1978 the home viewer had thirty-three different models to choose from.

[69]Stuart Goldman, "Video Behind Bars," *Videography* 3:1 (January 1978): 16-20.

[70]Walter Wagone, Jr., Carl F. Bianchi, and Howard Polskin, "Video in the Courtroom: Three Different Stories from Around the US," *Videography* 2:10 (October 1977): 21-25.

[71]Paul Stranahan, "In Their Own Image: The Story of One Adoption Center that Uses Videotape to Let Kids Show Themselves to Prospective Parents," *Videography* 3:11 (November 1978), pp. 18-20.

[72]Ralph Hattersley, "What Is Visual Literacy?" *35 MM Photography* (Summer 1976), pp. 6-19, 116-20.

[73]See Edmund Carpenter's "The New Languages," reprinted in Dennis DeNitto, ed., *Media for Our Time: An Anthology* (New York: Holt, Rinehart and Winston, 1971), pp. 3-17. Carpenter has interesting comments on how newspaper formats induce montage perception.

Copyright Law and the Fair Use of Visual Images

Harriet L. Oler, Senior Attorney-Advisor in the United States Office of Copyright, has here given a picture of legislative and case history. Her essay was written without review of the essays written by other contributors to this volume. The characterization provided here is, however, consistent with complaints about the failure of fair use legislation to provide more explicit direction or guidelines in the new media areas of application. In her view, further modifications in legislation or informal agreements among conflicting parties will be necessary to move us beyond the present uncertainties.

The Copyright Office is concerned with how legislation affects its public and regularly gathers information about problems for its reports to Congress. The participation of Ms. Oler in this project is evidence of this responsiveness.

21

COPYRIGHT LAW AND THE FAIR USE OF VISUAL IMAGES

HARRIET L. OLER*

INTRODUCTION AND COPYRIGHT PHILOSOPHY

The concept of copyright is written into the Constitution. To guard against the old English system, under which copyright was a tool of the Crown,[1] Madison, Pinckney, and Noah Webster drafted a constitutional clause[2] to vest literary property rights in authors. Article I, Section 8 empowers Congress

> To promote the Progress of Science and useful Arts, by securing for limited Times to Authors and Inventors the exclusive Right to their respective Writings.[3]

The Constitution embodies the fundamental principle that the cultural history and welfare of our country will be preserved and nurtured by protecting authors' intellectual property rights in their creative expressions once they are fixed in the form of literary, artistic, or musical works.

Within the strictures of authorship, limited times, and "fixed" writings,[4] Congress has a fairly free hand in drafting copyright legislation. Against author's rights in his or her literary property, Congress may balance the important public interest in the wide dissemination of information, the user's rights. This balancing becomes a difficult task in the face of new technology. On March 3, 1909, when the previous fed-

---

*Ms. Oler is the Senior Attorney-Advisor on the General Counsel's staff of the Copyright Office. The views expressed here are those of the author, and do not necessarily reflect official positions of the Copyright Office or the Library of Congress.

eral copyright law[5] became effective, Congress could fairly easily legislate to protect the author's control of his or her printed word or painted picture. But in the past sixty-nine years, the United States has experienced an unparalleled explosion of new techniques for communication. Television, sound recordings, photocopying, videotaping, computer uses, satellite communications, and a plethora of other technologies for exploiting creative writings have been developed.

As each new industry sprang up and became sufficiently strong to threaten the author's market for his or her work, that industry also became strong enough to defend its right to use the author's work without paying copyright fees. In some cases, such as movies and sound recordings, Congress faced up to the need to amend the 1909 law by enacting piecemeal legislation to protect authors.[6] In others, courts stretched the 1909 law to encompass new uses of copyrighted material.[7] In still other cases, such as cable television and photocopying, courts refrained from action and shifted the burden to Congress to enact omnibus copyright revision.[8]

And, authors typically lost control of even those works which were clearly protected by the 1909 statute. Largely because that law wedded federal protection to the concept of publication,[9] producers and publishers, the exploiters of copyrighted material, enjoyed far greater control over copyright markets than the individual author.

Finally, in 1976, after more than a decade of prolonged wrestling with copyright revision bills,[10] and an even longer period of discussion with interested parties of all persuasions,[11] Congress enacted a new copyright law.[12] It was signed by President Ford at the twelfth hour; and it became effective, for the most part, on January 1, 1978.[13]

The law is a compromise between the complex needs and wishes of authors and users. The spirit is clear. The letter is usually clear. But the law's practical application is frequently equivocal. And, in some cases, the law and its accompanying legislative reports acknowledge that Congress' copyright concerns are ongoing.[14] Congress has not finished with copyright. In the areas of "unfinished business," authors, owners, and users of copyrighted property have a continuing obligation and opportunity to keep Congress apprised of issues and answers which warrant further congressional consideration.[15]

I shall outline briefly Congress' new copyright legislation, especially with respect to authors' rights and the public's fair use rights in printed and screen visual images. I shall also examine some possible resolutions to problems raised by others in this book, particularly the alleged problem of "censorship through copyright," or the power of copyright owners to restrict scholars and educators from using copyrighted visual materials for purposes that the owners find unacceptable.

I should note, however, that my remarks are limited and that they are purely personal opinions. The Copyright Office has very restricted regulatory powers, particularly in the areas of fair use and library photocopying.[16] Obviously there are many problems and issues to be ironed out. The office does not know how the law will work, and on some issues, the office must prepare objective reports for Congress in the near future;[17] thus, it cannot give legal advice nor offer *ex parte* solutions. Congress wrote the law; it will legislate any further amendments. And courts will interpret the legislative provisions. The Copyright Office merely administers those provisions entrusted to it by Congress; it has no power to legislate nor to offer views which could be construed as legislating in unsettled areas. Nongovernmental parties must put the law into practice and, where appropriate, advise Congress what needs to be done.

THE 1976 COPYRIGHT LAW

The new copyright law attempts to redress past wrongs, to shift the balance of copyright protection from publishers and producers to individual authors, and to codify the rights of both authors and users to materials communicated by all media, including new technologies. It tries to maintain a judicious balance between specific provisions, lending predictability, and general principles, permitting flexibility. In effect, it hopes to bring United States copyright law gracefully into the twenty-first century.

Federal copyright law now applies across the board to all copyrightable subject matter, regardless of its format, whether or not a work has been published.[18] The individual, independent author now enjoys a federal copyright from the moment that he or she fixes a creative expression in tangible form. All rights in the work inure to the author,[19] endure for a term based on the author's lifetime,[20] and must be traced back to that author.[21]

The rights embraced by copyright are established initially in the law. They are set out without limitation and include

1. The right to reproduce the work in copies or phonorecords;
2. The right to distribute those copies or records;
3. The right to prepare derivative works (such as translations and dramatizations) based upon the copyrighted work;
4. The right to perform the work publicly (excepting copyrighted sound recordings); and
5. The right to display the work publicly.[22]

Subsequent sections of the law[23] limit these exclusive rights by a number of qualifications, exceptions, and exemptions designed to safeguard the public's interest in guaranteed access to, and use of, certain modes of information. These limitations try to insure widespread availability of copyrighted materials at reasonable prices, to guard against monopolistic price suppression or censorship, and to avoid unfair restraints on legitimate uses of copyrighted works within the established philosophical and legal framework of authors' rights. Thus, where certain technologies might preclude user access were the author to retain absolute control of his or her work, the law creates compulsory licensing giving the public guaranteed access (provided certain procedures are observed) and assuring the author remuneration for the use. The law creates compulsory licenses for the performances of recorded nondramatic music on jukeboxes,[24] the production of phonorecords of previously published and recorded nondramatic music,[25] the cable retransmission of broadcast radio and television programs,[26] and the use by public broadcasters of published nondramatic music and published pictorial, graphic, and sculptural works.[27] The latter provision has a significant impact on educational uses of visual works.[28]

Another exemption relates to the performance and display of copyrighted materials, including visual images, for educational and other nonprofit purposes.[29] It allows an educator to perform or display a lawfully made copy of any copyrighted work in a face-to-face teaching situation.[30] And schools may perform a nondramatic literary or musical work or display any work in the course of instructional broadcasts.[31]

The law further specifies limited photocopying which may be done by certain libraries and archives for replacement, for preservation, and (under further restrictions) for individual users' private study, scholarship, or research, without paying the copyright owner.[32]

Finally, the limitation on a copyright owner's exclusive rights most addressed by contributors to this book is that found in the fair use provision of Section 107. That section is the principal focus of this chapter.

FAIR USE: LEGISLATIVE HISTORY AND CASE LAW

From a user's vantage point, fair use is one of the most important limitations on the rights of the copyright owner. It is not an exemption from the owner's exclusive rights, but a defense to an infringement action. The distinction is subtle, but important. It means that a use of a copyrighted work which would otherwise constitute a literal copyright infringement may be adjudged a fair or free one, and that a user may successfully defend such a use in a copyright infringement action. Fair use is a well-established judicial "rule of reason" in American copyright law.[33] It applies to all types of copyrighted works and to all uses of those works. In effect, it allows courts to avoid the injustice which would result if a copyright owner's rights were absolute and rigidly enforced.

The fair use doctrine, which developed through case law over more than a century,[34] has been codified in the new copyright law. Section 107 says that

> the fair use of a copyrighted work, including such use by reproduction in copies or phonorecords or by any other means specified [by Section 106], for purposes such as criticism, comment, news reporting, teaching (including multiple copies for classroom use), scholarship, or research, is not an infringement of copyright.[35]

It also sets forth criteria, synthesized from past case law, to guide courts in deciding questions of fair use. These include the purpose and commercial character of the use; the nature of the copyrighted work; the amount or quantity of the work used in relation to the whole copyrighted work; and the effect of the use upon the potential market for the copyrighted work.[36]

The section appears to be vague and to add little to extant case law. Both characteristics were intended by Congress. The House report accompanying the Revision bill in 1976 confirms this intention.

> The statement of the fair use doctrine in section 107 offers some guidance to users in determining when the principles of the doctrine apply. However, the endless variety of situations and combinations of circumstances that can rise in particular cases precludes the formulation of exact rules in the statute. The bill endorses the purpose and general scope of the judicial doctrine of fair use, but there is no disposition to freeze the doctrine in the statute, especially during a period of rapid technological change. Beyond a very broad statutory explanation of what fair use is and some of the criteria applicable to it, the courts must be free to adapt the doctrine to particular situations on a case-by-case basis. Section 107 is intended to restate the present judicial doctrine of fair use, not to change, narrow, or enlarge it in any way.[37]

The statutory vagueness is arguably a boon to users, for it permits the fair use doctrine to be applied to new uses and thereby allows users' rights to keep pace with their evolving needs. Again, the legislative history of Section 107 affirms this principle:

> Although the courts have considered and ruled upon the fair use doctrine over and over again, no real definition has ever emerged. Indeed, since the doctrine is an equitable rule of reason, no generally applicable definition is possible, and each case raising the question must be decided on its own facts.[38]

Predictions in the fair use area are extremely hazardous because case law tends to be limited strictly to particular fact situations. It is clear that the principle applies to visual images. It is equally certain that new media uses of images are under the aegis of fair use. Fair use applies to reproduction in copies,[39] to photocopying, and to taping.[40] More particularly, the criteria involved through case law and codified in the new law (the kind of use, the nature of the copyrighted work, the relative quantity of material used, and the economic effect of the use on the copyrighted work) may be examined with respect to five types of uses of visual images to give a clearer picture of the present status of the doctrine and of how courts weigh and dovetail the general criteria in particular situations.

The first type of use, of commercial printed materials by nonprofit educational institutions, was the subject of two recent private party agreements which were approved by Congress and reprinted in the 1976 House *Report*. The other four uses were involved in recent or ongoing federal case law and include nonprofit uses of printed scholarly works for private study or research, off-air taping by public schools for classroom uses, and off-air taping of commercial programs by individuals for their private use.

Classroom Copying of Printed Materials by Nonprofit Educational Institutions

Classroom photocopying was perhaps the most hotly debated aspect of the fair use provision.[41] Although Congress declined to include a specific exemption for reproductions of copyrighted works for educational and scholarly purposes[42] it consistently recognized a "need for greater certainty and protection for teachers."[43] The legislative history does not define the bounds of this need, but Section 504(c)(2) of the law protects teachers and certain other nonprofit users of copyrighted material by mandating a court to remit all statutory damages in an infringement suit where a user reasonably believed a given use was "fair" within the meaning of Section 107 and the user was acting in the scope of his or her employment in a nonprofit educational institution, library, or archive.[44]

Moreover, the 1976 House *Report* approved, within the context of Section 107, two private party agreements encouraged by the House Judiciary Subcommittee on permissible educational uses of printed copyrighted materials. The agreements cover classroom photocopying by nonprofit educational institutions from books, periodicals, and published music, and set forth minimal standards of fair use.

The guidelines for classroom copying of books and periodicals[45] were formulated by representatives of the Ad Hoc Committee of Educational Institutions and Organizations on Copyright Law Revision, the Authors League of America, and the Association of American Publishers, Inc. They assume that certain uses will be deemed fair within Section 107, without excluding the possibility of extended fair uses.

The guidelines permit a single copy to be made by or for a teacher, at his or her request, for research or classroom preparation, of a single book chapter, an article, a short story, essay, or poem, or a chart, graph, diagram, cartoon, or picture from a book, periodical, or newspaper. Multiple copies (not exceeding one copy per pupil) may be made for classroom use of poetry, prose, an illustration or a special work combining language with illustrations, provided that the relative length of each copy and the amount of total copying do not exceed stated quantitative limits and provided that the copyright notice is reproduced. A special allowance is recognized for current news items. Guideline copying must always be at the inspiration of an individual teacher who has insufficient time to request permission from the copyright owner. Copying must not be repeated in excess of the guideline standards and must not be from consumable materials (such as workbooks or standardized tests). Copied materials must not be used as a substitute for the purchase of anthologies, compilations, collective works, books, publishers' reprints, or periodicals.

Similar guidelines for educational uses of published music were prepared by representatives of the Music Publishers' Association of the United States, Inc., the National Music Publishers' Association, Inc., the Music Teachers National Association, the Music Educators National Conference, the National Association of Schools of Music, and the Ad Hoc Committee on Copyright Law Revision.[46] Again, they state minimum fair use standards, and they permit emergency copying for works which will be replaced by purchased copies and multiple copying of less than 10 percent of works for study if the copy does not constitute a performable unit of music. Single copies are allowed for study if the works are out of print. Editing of purchased copies is permitted if the fundamental character of the work is not altered. A single copy of a student performance may be made for evaluation and retained by the school. And a single copy of recorded music may be made for examination if the school owns the sound recording.[47] No music copying under these guidelines may be of consumable materials, and no copying may substitute for anthologies, compilations, or collective works. The guidelines allow copies to be used for performances only if the copies replace unavailable purchase copies. All copies must include the copyright notice from the printed work.

These guidelines are significant for several reasons. First, they were drafted late in the day, in 1975-76, at the instance of the House Judiciary Subcommittee, by representatives of educators on all levels, authors, and publishers. The parties had the benefit of witnessing and participating in the long legislative discussions of fair use. They were also aware of judicial attitudes and opinions on fair use. The guidelines represent the parties' evaluations of the weight of projected judicial sympathies toward educational uses balanced against commercial considerations. They reflect an application of the statutory criteria. The uses are of nonprofit character: educational copying for classroom uses. The nature of the copyrighted work is typically commercial, but not necessarily restricted to generally marketable works. Copies may be made of textual and other works published for classroom markets as well as of works intended for the wider public market. The amount of permissible copying, particularly of visual images, is severely limited; and except for very short works, or replacements of purchased copies, it is generally limited to 10 percent of the copyrighted material. Finally, the guidelines incorporate assurances, generally expressed as prohibitions on copying to substitute for subscriptions or purchases and on copying of consumables, that copying will not deleteriously affect the potential market for, or value of, the copyrighted work.

The agreements were approved by Congress, and although they do not bind courts, Congress, or users, they do establish minimum uses which are fair for the time being. They offer objective, quantitative standards for fair uses which educators may rely upon in the context of Section 107. They clearly do not give educators a free ride. They are limited, both in quantity and in scope: they do not cover audiovisual classroom copying.[48] At the same time, when coupled with the liberalized infringement provisions of Section 504, they provide the individual teacher a substantial new measure of security for certain classroom photocopying. And, they do point out that copyright compromises, at least in limited areas, and perhaps in the face of mutual desperation, are possible.

Nonprofit Uses of Printed Scholarly Works for Private Study or Research

The remaining areas discussed in this section have developed in large part through recent case law. Perhaps the most renowned fair use decision in modern judicial memory is the Williams and Wilkins case,[49] first, because it dealt with widespread photocopying and therefore catalyzed the conflict of copyright and new technology; and second, because it reached the highest United States court of law.

Williams and Wilkins arose as a suit for copyright infringement by a publisher of medical journals and books against the National Institutes of Health and the National Library of Medicine, two nonprofit organizations of the federal government. The suit alleged that the NIH technical library subscribed to two copies of each of the four medical journals named in the case, that one copy was typically retained in the library reading room, and that the other copy was circulated among NIH personnel. Researchers could obtain photocopies of any journal article without question and could retain such copies for their personal files. The library would provide a single copy of an article per request and would usually limit each request to a single article of no more than fifty photocopied pages from a journal issue. Exceptions to these limits were granted, provided that the copying was of less than half of an entire journal; and the library did not inquire about the reason or need for requested photocopies. Testimony showed that the library made about 93,000 photocopies of articles in 1970.

The National Library of Medicine allegedly loaned photocopies of its journal materials to other libraries free of charge on a no-return basis. The library typically did not lend articles published within the preceding five years in journals on its "widely-available" list to anyone other than government libraries. Other articles were freely photocopied for all libraries, but the NLM usually filled no more than twenty interlibrary requests from an individual or thirty from an institution per month.

Testimony alleged that the copies made by both defendants were at the request of researchers and medical personnel for their professional work. Within the pertinent accounting period, NIH and NLM made at least one photocopy of each of eight articles from one or more of the four journals in litigation, but plaintiff was unable to prove any specific damages.

The United States Court of Claims reversed the trial judge's finding of infringement and based its opinion on fair use and plaintiff's failure to prove actual damages.

Plaintiff argued that the pre-1909 Copyright Act did not prohibit the copying of books and periodicals, and that the legislative history of the 1909 Act, which included an exclusive right to copy, did not alter the protection with respect to journal articles. The court considered this argument (without fully endorsing it) along with the reported Library of Congress practice of providing photo-duplicates of copyrighted works.

But the main thrust of the court's rationale was the fair use defense. The court considered the public interest served by supporting medical research through the wide dissemination of journal articles; the previously mentioned page, issue, number of requests, and recent article photocopying limitations; the nature of the articles copied; and the dearth of evidence on the economic effect of this photocopying on the copyright proprietor's subscription sales or royalty revenues;[50] and concluded that defendants' photocopying activities were "fair" within the meaning of the 1909 Copyright Statute. The court emphasized the law's leniency toward nonprofit copying for scientific and research purposes, an emphasis which unquestionably weighed heavily in influencing its opinion.[51]

Finally, the court averred that issues involving copyright and photocopying were more properly resolved by Congress than by the courts. Since Congress was concurrently considering omnibus copyright revision, the court deferred to the legislature on the photocopying controversy.

The United States Supreme Court affirmed the Court of Claims' opinion by an equally divided Court without a written opinion.

Congress responded in a limited way to the library photocopying problem when it revised the copyright law in 1976. Section 108 of the revised law creates a separate statutory exemption from the copyright owner's exclusive rights and permits library and archival photocopying of materials under rather broad restrictions as to purpose and quantity. But that statutory section at the same time provides that it in no way abrogates the doctrine of fair use:

> Nothing in this section—
> (4) in any way affects the right of fair use as provided by section 107, or any contractual obligations assumed at any time by the library or archives when it obtained a copy or phonorecord of a work in its collection.[52]

What insight, then, does *Williams and Wilkins* offer on the fair use doctrine? Most important, it seems, was the Court of Claims' balance of the four fair use criteria now incorporated in the copyright statute. The case highlights a judicial predilection to find a fair use where nonprofit photocopying is done for purposes of private research at least in the absence of proof of actual economic detriment.[53] Whether a similar judicial sentiment would prevail if the purpose of the use were commercial, such as the reproduction and incorporation of the copy in a second publication, even a scholarly treatise or critique, is uncertain.

Off-Air Videotaping by Nonprofit Educational Institutions

A more recent fair use decision involved copying of visual images off the air by a nonprofit educational institution for subsequent unlimited classroom use. This time, the copyright owner prevailed. *Encyclopedia Britannica v. Crooks*,[54] commonly called the BOCES case, has been adjudged only on a preliminary motion,[55] yet it is certain to be important in the development of the fair use doctrine, especially with respect to new media uses of visual images.

Plaintiffs in the case are three corporations who produce, acquire, and license motion picture films for the educational market. Defendant, BOCES, is a Board of Cooperative Educational Services of Erie County, New York, a nonprofit corporation organized to provide educational services, including instructional support, to the county's public schools. BOCES admitted that it videotaped both commercial and public television programs of educational value and published a catalog of available videotapes for teachers in the twenty-one school districts it services. The catalog described the programs and directed school districts to supply blank tapes for programs they wished BOCES to copy from its master videotape. BOCES made the requested copies and delivered them to the requesting schools at cost. Copies may or may not have been returned to BOCES, and BOCES did not monitor their use. Copies were viewed by students in the classroom and could be kept in the requesting school's videotape library. All performances of the copies were nonprofit and for educational purposes. Testimony showed that BOCES duplicated approximately 10,000 videotapes during the 1976-77 school year.

On a motion for a preliminary injunction, plaintiffs claimed that their exclusive copyright rights were infringed by BOCES each time it videotaped a film off the air and again each time it distributed a copy of a tape to a requesting school for a classroom performance. Defendant responded, in part, that delayed performances were essential to coincide with classroom hours and activities, that public education would be harmed by the discontinuance of this BOCES service, and that the "noncommercial videotaping of television programs off the air for purposes of delayed viewing in the classroom was not a copyright infringement,"[56] but a fair use.

On a finding of a *prima facie* case of infringement and probable success on the merits, Judge John Curtin granted a preliminary injunction without ordering destruction of the extant tapes and advised BOCES that it could continue its videotaping practice at its own risk.[57]

The judge based his opinion on a discussion of fair use, applying the criteria now incorporated in Section 107 of the Copyright Act.[58] He distinguished the Williams and Wilkins case, on which defendants relied to justify their noncommercial copying, from the one at hand. *Williams and Wilkins,* the court said, involved a use that was fair because of plaintiff's inadequate proof of substantial harm, defendants' need to use the articles for medical research, and Congress' (then) pending consideration of photocopying and copyright revision. The BOCES court found a similar noncommercial use for an equally laudable purpose: public education. Thus, the statutory criteria of the purpose and character of the use were similarly met in *Williams and Wilkins* and *BOCES.*

But, said the court, *Williams and Wilkins* was distinguishable on the criteria of the substantiality of copying and the effect on the owner's market. The earlier case principally involved restricted copying of single articles from a journal; the present case concerned the reproduction of entire copyrighted films. In the BOCES case, unlike *Williams and Wilkins,* the court was willing to assume a substantial effect on the copyright owner's market "because the reproduction is interchangeable with the original."[59] The BOCES court said the question of economic damage should at least be put to a full trial on the merits, where defendant would bear the burden of defending its use as a fair one.

Finally, the court found that defendant could avoid disrupting classroom services by entering into licensing agreements with plaintiffs pending resolution of the case. At this state of litigation, the court did not order destruction of existing tapes and found that BOCES could license the tapes or continue to distribute them at its own risk. BOCES was directed to implement a plan to monitor school use of the copies and to require their return and erasure within a specified time period.

The case is significant although the outcome may be altered after trial. At present, it shows a strong disposition by the New York District Court to enforce a copyright owner's exclusive rights where complete films are taped off-air, even if the copies are used for eleemosynary purposes. At the same time, the court found the educational purpose of the use to be so much in the public interest that it did not order destruction of existing tapes. Rather, it felt the balance of interests to be such that although a *prima facie* case of copyright infringement existed, the case should be tried in full on its facts.

Off-Air Videotaping of Commercial Programs for Private Home Use

If the educational and research purposes of the copying was a deciding factor in *Williams and Wilkins,* and the assumed economic damage from taping complete films tipped the balance in *BOCES,* the ongoing Sony-Betamax litigation should further refine the doctrine of fair use. *Universal City Studios, Inc. v. Sony Corp. of America*[60] (the Sony case) was filed in 1976, and the pre-trial hearing postponed to November 1978.[61] In the complaints, MCA subsidiary Universal Studios and Walt Disney Productions attacked the long accepted, though legally uncertain, right of the individual to record copyrighted televised films off the air for delayed home viewing.[62] Sony Corporation, four retailers, an advertising agency, and an individual user of the machine are defendants. Defendant Sony produced the Betamax system which enables a viewer to videotape at home, and allegedly encouraged home taping through advertising and public promotions.[63]

Neither the 1909 Copyright Law nor the revised law specifically mentions home taping of any sort; but the House Judiciary Committee report on the 1971 sound recording bill[64] says, with respect to sound recordings,

> Specifically, it is not the intention of the Committee to restrain the home recording, from broadcasts or from tapes or records, of recorded performances, where the home recording is for private use and with no purpose of reproducing or otherwise capitalizing commercially on it.[65]

The Sony case for the first time raised the question of a similar fair use of copyrighted televised films.

Earlier opinions suggest a right of users to record audio from program sources including records, tapes, and radio for home and limited noncommercial performances.[66] But *Sony* for the first time, raises the issue regarding the scope of fair use's applicability to copying entire video works for personal, noncommercial performances. It is also unique in raising the question of the possible copyright liability of home video equipment manufacturers for the sale, distribution and use of their product.[67]

If the fair use issue is litigated, the noncommercial use of home videotapes and its benefit to the general viewing public will be weighed against the potential (or proved) economic damage to the copyright owners' markets resulting from free replacement of their films and possible diminished film lease potential. The tip of the scales will be interesting, particularly because the viewing public's particular convenience and edification from delayed viewing and its general interest in advanced communications technology must be evaluated in the Sony case's commercial context of battling corporate giants: movie producers and broadcasters versus hardware manufacturers.

Commercial Use Considerations and First Amendment Rights

The foregoing fair use cases highlight the increasing importance that courts accord to the economic criteria of fair use. In effect, all the standards set forth in Section 107 incorporate a large measure of economic concern, expressly, in the consideration of the purpose and character of a use and its potential market effect on a copyrighted work; implicitly, in the nature of the work and the relative portion used.

Commercial uses were excluded from fair use in a recent federal case, *Triangle Publications, Inc.* v. *Knight-Ridder Newspapers, Inc.*[68] That case held that a newspaper's display of the cover of plaintiff's publication in a televised advertisement to promote sales of a competing publication by comparative advertising was not a fair use.

> The use of a copyrighted work by a commercial enterprise for commercial advantage was not the primary concern in the development of the fair use doctrine.[69]

Thus, the commercial character of the use seems to have been determinative on the fair use issue, even though the defendant displayed only the cover of the publication for a few seconds during a 30-second television commercial. The court found that this use was not for purposes of "criticism," but was rather to enhance the marketability of defendant's publication.[70] That was not the purpose for which plaintiff's publication was created and was not a fair use of the work.

The court found, however, that defendant's use of plaintiff's work in the comparative advertising televised commercial was protected by the First Amendment and could not constitutionally be enjoined.

> Such comparative advertising, when undertaken in the serious manner that defendant did herein, represents an important source of information for the education of consumers in a free enterprise system. . . . Hence, there is a conflict between the First Amendment and the Copyright Act, if as the plaintiff contends, the Act should be applied in the case *sub judice* to strike down defendant's activity. This court believes that plaintiff is seeking to impose too literal an interpretation of 17 U.S.C. Section 106.
>
> The purpose of the Copyright Act . . . would not be served by the invocation of Section 106 in the present situation. In so finding, this court is construing the Copyright Act in a fashion which preserves its constitutionality and its statutory purpose. To extend it to the activities at issue would be a disservice to its goals and would place it in jeopardy of unconstitutionality.[71]

Thus, the court favored defendant's First Amendment rights[72] and the public's interest in comparative television advertising over plaintiff's exclusive copyright rights, which embraced protection against the televised use of a small portion of a copyrighted work for comparative advertising purposes.

CONCLUSION

One must conclude that a copyright owner's exclusive rights in visual and other artistic and literary works, which are paramount under the copyright law, are tempered not only by limited fair use defenses, but also by First Amendment guarantees of free speech and press and the correlative public interest in access to information. To determine whether a given use of a copyrighted visual work is "fair," so as to excuse the user's unauthorized use from copyright liability, each use is evaluated retrospectively by a court in its particular factual context. Statutory guidelines or criteria, legislative history, and past case law highlight the salient weight accorded the potential economic effect on the copyright owner's market from a given use. This is as it should be, for copyright is essentially an economic property: a monopoly of literary property rights. The law's vagueness is essential, because the potential economic effect of particular uses cannot accurately be predicted, especially in an era of rapidly advancing communications technology. The law must be flexible if it is to remain contemporary.

At the same time, users' rights are preserved both by the established applicability of fair uses of visual works and by acknowledged First Amendment rights. Permissible free uses are difficult to predict, but they are undeniably preserved and strengthened in all media where a recognizable public interest in scholarship, knowledge, research, education, or general public information can be isolated. In those instances, courts may submerge the countervailing public interest in encouraging creative authorship and advancing the arts by protecting authors' copyright rights. To the extent that fair uses are predictable, those factors are crucial.

The meaning of *fair use*, in a sense, is anyone's guess. But a new dimension is added because these predictions are no longer mere guesses. When a prospective user intends to use his or her copy publicly, professional, business, and market realities in today's complex society may dictate, or be used to calculate the user's risk. Because fair use is a legal copyright defense, rather than an initial right, and because every legally protected copy or performance of a copyrighted work is at least a technical violation of the copyright owner's exclusive rights, the legal risk of that use is usually borne by someone other than the user. The retailer or the user's employer decides whether to assume the risk.

Thus, the school district that employs a teacher or librarian should be apprised of the employee's copying and use activities and should, in fairness to itself and its employee, provide specific guidelines for permissible uses that it reasonably believes to be "fair." Likewise, publishers must assume responsibility for permitting their authors to use visual as well as literary material where that use can predictably be considered fair. Until and unless further private agreements are reached in the fair use areas,[73] or Congress gives more specific legislative direction, the user—and ultimately the public—is disserved by continued reluctance to predict and document prospective fair uses. Carefully monitored and documented written standards, arrived at and administered with good will, and an understanding of the universal benefit engendered by the copyright scheme, are the best hope at this point for practical resolution of the raging fair use controversy.

NOTES

[1] L. Patterson, *Copyright in Historical Perspective* (1968).

[2] Fenning, *The Origin of the Patent and Copyright Clause of the Constitution*, 17 Geo. L.J. 109 (1929); B. Bugbee, *The Genesis of American Patent and Copyright Law* (Washington, D.C.: Public Affairs Press, 1967); N. Webster, *A Collection of Papers on Political, Literary and Moral Subjects*, chap. VII (NY: Webster and Clark, 1843).

[3] *U.S. Const.* Art. I, §8.

[4] Ideas, principles, and concepts are not subject to copyright protection. Copyright extends only to the fixed expressions of an author. M. Nimmer, *Cases and Materials on Copyright* (1976), §§143.11, p. 166.

[5] Copyright Act of Mar. 4, 1909, as amended, 17 U.S.C. §§1–236 (1970 and Supp. V. 1975).

[6] Motion pictures were expressly added to the subject matter of copyright by the Act of Aug. 24, 1912, c. 356, 37 Stat. 488. Dubbing rights in sound recordings were enacted October 15, 1971 (Pub. L. No. 92–140, 85 Stat. 391) and made permanent December 31, 1974 (Pub. L. No. 93–573, §101, 88 Stat. 1873).

[7]See, e.g., Jerome H. Remick & Co. v. American Automobile Accessories Co., 5 F.2d. 411 (6th Cir. 1925); (1909 Copyright Act held to cover commercial radio broadcasts not contemplated when the statute was enacted).

[8]See, e.g., Teleprompter Corp. v. CBS, Inc., 415 U.S. 394 (1974); Williams & Wilkins Co. v. U.S., 487 F.2d 1345 (Ct. Cl. 1973), aff'd per curiam, 420 U.S. 376 (1975).

[9]Common law copyright ceased at the moment of publication, and a work then became subject to federal copyright protection. Nimmer n.4, §§46–59.

[10]The recent spate of copyright revision bills dates back to 1964; see S. 3008, H.R. 11947, 88th Cong., 2d Sess. (1964).

[11]Between 1961 and 1964, meetings and discussions among a wide range of interested parties were conducted under the auspices of the Copyright Office, preliminary to drafting the bill for general revision of the copyright law that was introduced in both Houses of Congress in 1964.

[12]Pub. L. No. 94-553, 90 Stat. 2541, Oct. 19, 1976.

[13]Pub. L. No. 94-553, §301.

[14]See B. Ringer, "The Unfinished Business of Copyright Revision," 24 *U.C.L.A. L. Rev.* 951 (1977).

[15]For example, on the question of fair use and off-air videotaping, the House subcommittee acknowledged the need for interested parties to attempt a workable solution, and it pledged willingness to "undertake further consideration of the problem in a future Congress." H.R. *Report* No. 1476, 94th Cong., 2d Sess., 1976: 72.

[16]The Copyright Office has no regulatory authority under Section 107. Under Section 108, the office is authorized to issue regulations governing the warning of copyright on library photocopying forms and at the place where copying orders are accepted. Pub. L. No. 94-553, §108d(2) and e(2).

[17]For example, Section 108(h)(i) of the Copyright Act requires the Register of Copyrights to consult with representatives of authors, book and periodical publishers, and other copyright owners, and with representatives of library users and librarians and to submit a report to Congress in 1983 "setting forth the extent to which this section has achieved the intended statutory balancing of the rights of creators, and the needs of users." The report must describe problems which have arisen and present legislative and other recommendations, if warranted. Pub. L. No. 94-553, §108(h)(i).

On the question of fair use and off-air taping, the 1976 House *Report* commentary on Section 107 directed the Register of Copyrights to lead active and constructive discussions among the various interests to resolve the emerging legal problems. H.R. *Report* No. 1476, n.15, p. 72.

[18]Section 301(a) preempts, after January 1, 1978, all legal or equitable rights that are equivalent to any of the exclusive copyright rights within Section 106, in fixed works of authorship within the subject matter of copyright, whether created before or after 1978 and whether published or unpublished. Common law and state statutory remedies for sound recordings fixed prior to February 15, 1972, are preserved for seventy-five years. Pub. L. No. 94-553, §301(c).

[19]Pub. L. No. 94-553, §201(a).

[20]Copyright in works created by an individual after January 1, 1978, lasts for the life of an author plus fifty years. Pub. L. No. 94-553, §302(a). The term for anonymous and pseudonymous works and works made for hire is seventy-five years from publication or one hundred years from the year of creation, whichever is less. Pub. L. No. 94-553, §302(c).

[21]Pub. L. No. 94-553, §203; §304(c).

[22]Pub. L. No. 94-553, §106.

[23]Pub. L. No. 94-553, §§107–118.

[24]Pub. L. No. 94-553, §116.

[25]Pub. L. No. 94-553, §115.

[26]Pub. L. No. 94-553, §111.

[27]Pub. L. No. 94-553, §118.

[28]For example, Section 118(d)(3) permits governmental bodies and nonprofit institutions to tape materials broadcast by public broadcasting entities under the terms of Section 118, and to perform those tapes in the course of face-to-face classroom teaching

activities for a period of seven days from the public broadcast transmission. Pub. L. No. 94-553, §118(d)(3).

[29]Pub. L. No. 94-553, §110.

[30]Pub. L. No. 94-553, §110(1).

[31]Pub. L. No. 94-553, §110(2).

[32]Pub. L. No. 94-553, §108.

[33]See, A. Latman, Study No. 14, "Fair Use of Copyrighted Works," 2 *Studies on Copyright* (Arthur Fisher Memorial Edition) 781 (1963).

[34]Nimmer, *n*.4, §§111, 145.

[35]Pub. L. No. 94-553, §107.

[36]Pub. L. No. 94-553, §107.

[37]H.R. *Report* No. 1476, *n*.15, p. 66.

[38]H.R. *Report* No. 1476, *n*.15, p. 65.

[39]Pub. L. No. 94-553, §107.

[40]The House *Report* says ". . . the doctrine [of fair use] has as much application to photocopying and taping as to older forms of use. . . ." (H.R. *Report* No. 1476, *n*.15, p. 66).

[41]For a summary of arguments, see H. R. *Report* No. 83, 90th Cong., 1st Sess., 30–31 (1967).

[42]*Report* No. 1476, *n*.15, pp. 66–67.

[43]*Ibid.*, p. 67; *Report No.* 93, *n*.41, pp. 30–31.

[44]Pub. L. No. 94-553, §504(c)(2).

[45]H.R. *Report* No. 1476, *n*.15, pp. 68–70.

[46]*Ibid.*, pp. 70–71.

[47]This guideline refers only to permission to copy the underlying music and does not confer express permission to copy a separately copyrighted sound recording (*Ibid.*, p. 71).

[48]The parties discussed fair use standards for educational copying of audiovisual materials, but no agreement was reached.

[49]Williams & Wilkins Co. v. U.S., 487 F.2d. 1345 (Ct. Cl. 1973), *aff'd per curiam*, 420 U.S. 376 (1975).

[50]The court found evidence that:

    (a) between 1958 and 1969, annual subscriptions to the four journals increased substantially;

    (b) between 1959 and 1966, plaintiff's annual taxable income increased, but it decreased in 1967 and 1968;

    (c) the four journals in litigation constituted a small percentage of plaintiff's business;

    (d) plaintiff's assumed economic detriment was not proved by the record.

[51]The court noted that finding infringement would enable copyright proprietors to enjoin nongovernmental libraries from making any photocopies. The court could not compel compulsory licensing where it is not available by statute, and governmental libraries cannot be enjoined. 28 U.S.C. §1498.

[52]Pub. L. No. 94-553, §108(f)(4).

[53]Note that the copies were made for members of the limited market for which the copyrighted work was originally produced.

[54]Encyclopaedia Britannica v. Crooks, 3 Med. Law Rptr. 1945 (W.D.N.Y. 1978).

[55]The case is expected to go to trial in the near future.

[56]BOCES slip op. at 8–9.

[57]BOCES reportedly ceased distribution of the previously taped programs, and discontinued new filming pending a trial of the case on the merits. See *The Video Publisher*, Apr. 24, 1978, p. 5.

[58]The action was brought under the 1909 Copyright Law. Pub. L. No. 94-553, Transitional and Supplementary Provisions, §109.

[59]BOCES slip op. at 20.

[60]Universal City Studios, Inc. v. Sony Corp. of America, No. Cv. 76-3520 F (C.D. Cal., filed Nov. 11, 1976).

[61]District Judge Ferguson has reportedly denied all motions by film producers and distributors for permission to file *amicus curiae* briefs on grounds that interested parties will have an opportunity to testify at the trial. *Variety*, Apr. 26, 1978, p. 2.

[62]Plaintiffs also seek reparation for department store videotaping by Betamax systems.

[63]The Betamax videorecorder tapes color television programs off the air on reusable tape cartridges for later viewing on a conventional television set.

[64]The bill enacted in 1971, Act of Oct. 15, 1971, Pub. L. No. 92-140, 85 Stat. 391, added a dubbing right for owners of copyright in sound recordings, protecting them against the unauthorized reproduction and public distribution of the actual sounds fixed on the recording. The provisions of the Act were scheduled to expire on January 1, 1975, but they were extended and made permanent by the Act of Dec. 31, 1974, Pub. L. No. 93-573, §101, 88 Stat. 1873.

[65]R.H. *Report* No. 487, 92d Cong., 1st Sess., 1971:7. Other countries solicit copyright payments for home taping of sound recordings. For example, West Germany taxes the sale of home recording equipment to offset copyright royalty losses. The United Kingdom's Mechanical Copyright Protection Society issues a home recording licensing for which consumers pay a fee that is shared by copyright owners.

[66]See, e.g., congressional discussion of the home recording and private performance exception to the exclusive rights of copyright owners of sound recordings. *Hearings on H.R. 6927*, 92d Cong., 1st Sess., 1971: 22–23; *H.R. Report No.* 487, 92d Cong., 1st Sess., 1971: 7. Cf., Elektra Records Co. v. Gem Electronic Distributors, Inc., 360 F.Supp. 821, 824 (E.D.N.Y. 1973). For the outer limits of a user's right to perform a licensed broadcast without the copyright owner's permission, see Twentieth Century Music Corp. v. Aiken, 422 U.S. 151 (1975).

[67]Plaintiffs charge defendants with copyright infringement, unfair competition, and undermining contractual relations. They claim that Sony, the retailers, and the advertising agency "have been unjustly enriched" at the expense of the studios and that sale of the Betamax has falsely led the public to believe that recording televised broadcasts does not violate the copyright law. And, they allege that consumer use of the Betamax interfered with studio contractual relations with networks which purchased television film rights.

Plaintiffs seek injunctions against manufacturing, distributing, advertising, and selling the Betamax device or the cassettes it uses for videotaping copyrighted material. (Complaint for Plaintiff, p. 33.) They also ask that material already copied be impounded.

These allegations and requested remedies may affect the public's right to benefit from new technologies of communication. See R. Smith, "The Fight to Ban Video Recorders," *Voice*, Dec. 20, 1976, p. 85.

[68]Triangle Publications, Inc. v. Knight-Ridder Newspapers, Inc., 445 F.Supp. 875 (S.D. Fla. 1978; injunction denied on First Amendment grounds).

[69]*Ibid.*, p. 880.

[70]"When defendant contends that the fluidity of the fair use doctrine would support the advent of comparative advertising as a form of permissible criticism, it misconstrues the purpose of 17 U.S.C. §107." *Ibid.*, citing Lowe's Inc. v. Columbia Broadcasting System, Inc., 131 F.Supp. 165 (S.D. Cal. 1955), and distinguishing Mura v. Columbia Broadcasting System, Inc., 245 F.Supp. 587 (S.D.N.Y. 1965).

[71]445 F.Supp. 875, p. 883.

[72]For a fuller discussion of the emerging issue of First Amendment protection versus copyright protection see Nimmer, "Does Copyright Abridge the First Amendment Guarantees of Free Speech and Press?" 17 *U.C.L.A. L. Rev.* 1180 (1970); Zacchini v. Scripps/Howard Broadcasting Co., 45 U.S.L.W. 4954 (U.S. June 28, 1977; First and Fourteenth Amendments do not immunize the media when they broadcast a performer's act without permission).

[73]A conference at Airlie House, Virginia, in July 1977, under the direction of the Register of Copyrights, discussed possible accommodation of copyright problems raised by off-air videotaping by educators, librarians, archivists, and others. The discussions were constructive and examined possible permissions licensing alternatives including blanket

licenses, per program licenses, a tax levy on blank tapes, a hardware sales tax, compulsory licensing, and the creation of a pre-program clearinghouse with rates set either by statute or through negotiated licenses. No definite solution was agreed to, but the parties pledged continued efforts to reach an accord. See *Transcript of Airlie House Conference, July 22, 1977* (U.S. Copyright Office).

Efforts to schedule a follow-up conference have been made but not concluded at this writing.

The American Constitution . . .

Harry N. Rosenfield's essay treats a subtle and in recent times fiercely debated issue: What relationship exists between the Copyright Clause of the United States Constitution and the First Amendment? Does the First Amendment take primacy over copyright where the two conflict? A related question is whether the First Amendment provides a separate ground, apart from the fair use tradition, permitting the reproduction of copyrighted material. Rosenfield consistently argues for the primacy of the First Amendment and has often done so in the context of printed material. (See his own notes and the Bibliography.) Here he argues the primacy of the First Amendment in relation to the new media and reviews decisions in several recent cases.

22

THE AMERICAN CONSTITUTION, FREE INQUIRY, AND THE LAW

HARRY N. ROSENFIELD

THESIS OF CHAPTER

This chapter espouses the following thesis:

1. Nonprofit educational users of copyrighted material, both written and media or visual, have a constitutional right of *reasonable* access to such materials, as a form of constitutionally protected freedom of inquiry.

2. "Fair use" provides not only a statutory protection to users under the copyright statute but also serves as a legal vehicle for the constitutional primacy of the public interest over the copyright law's protections to copyright proprietors.

3. The user's constitutional right of reasonable access in the pursuit of freedom of inquiry is not limited to the "fair use" doctrine of the copyright law but can also be effectuated by direct application of the First and Ninth Amendments of the Constitution irrespective of "fair use."

THREE CASE STUDIES

Perhaps it is useful at the outset to describe and consider three recent cases in the federal courts to illustrate the basic thesis.

Fair Use as a Protection for Constitutional Rights

Just before the 1978 elections, an issue arose in a New Hampshire case which involved critical copyright questions. The political committee for the reelection of Governor Thomson owned copyright to

a song "Live Free or Die." As part of the election campaign, the governor's committee broadcast a 3-minute advertisement. For the first 60
seconds, the copyrighted song was heard; for the next 60 seconds there
was a campaign message for the governor's reelection; and for the last 60
seconds the song was again heard on the spot.

The challenger's political committee prepared and marketed a
1-minute campaign advertisement on radio. For the first 15 seconds, this
ad used portions of the copyrighted song belonging to the governor's
committee; the remaining 45 seconds carried a campaign message.

The governor's committee sued, claiming infringement, but it lost
the suit. The federal district judge held that the defendant's 15-second
use of the plaintiff's copyrighted song was an infringement, but ruled
against the plaintiff because it was a permissible "fair use." The district
court said:

> In the context of this case, the Court must be aware that it operates in an area
> of the most fundamental First Amendment activities. Discussion of public
> issues and debate on the qualifications of candidates are integral to the opera-
> tion of the system of government established by our Constitution. The First
> Amendment affords the broadest protection to such political expression in
> order to assure the unfettered interchange of ideas for the bringing about of
> political and social changes desired by the people. Although First Amend-
> ment protection is not confined to the exposition of ideas, there is practically
> universal agreement that the major purpose of that Amendment was to pro-
> tect the free discussion of governmental affairs, including discussions of can-
> didates. This is a reflection of our profound commitment to the principle that
> debate on public issues should be uninhibited, robust, and wide open. In a
> republic where the people are sovereign, the ability of the citizenry to make
> informed choices among candidates for office is essential, because the iden-
> tities of those who are elected will inevitably shape the course we follow as a
> nation . . . It does not appear that plaintiff has suffered or will suffer any
> monetary damage, and the mere "possibility" of loss of the election is out-
> weighed by public interest in a full and free discussion of the issues relative to
> the election campaign.[1]

The court discussed the relationship between copyright and the First
Amendment:

> . . . the exclusive right of a copyright holder must be weighed against the
> public interest in dissemination of information affecting areas of universal
> concern . . . Conflicts between interests protected by the First Amendment
> and the copyright law can be resolved by application of the fair use doc-
> trine . . . the Court concludes that there is sufficient evidence upon which to
> base a determination that defendants' use of the plaintiff's political adver-
> tisement, derived from the copyrighted recording, constitutes "fair use." . . .

In denying injunction against defendant, the court specifically mentioned that the use was "noncommercial in nature" and that "the effect
of the use upon the potential market or value of the copyrighted work is
nil. The recordings have sold and are continuing to sell without substantial commercial loss to the plaintiff."

In passing, consider another recent case, also involving a song, that raised but did not settle the constitutional issue. A TV newscast of a well-known and widely attended annual ethnic street fair and float parade included a film clip of a band playing an unidentified copyrighted song. There was no advance notice that the band would play this song. No actual damage was alleged. Defendant network claimed fair use and, as an alternative defense, the First Amendment. The federal district court in New York ruled that it was a fair use and that therefore it was unnecessary to reach the constitutional question. In a footnote, however, the judge said "in the resolution of such claims, the precise office to be performed by the First Amendment is not clear."[2]

Constitutionally Permissible Use Independent of "Fair Use"

The Triangle case arose in Florida. Plaintiff published a TV program guide providing program listings. Defendant was a newspaper publisher that had issued a new supplement to its Sunday edition. In advertising its new supplement, defendant's TV promotional campaign identified plaintiff's publication visually for a few seconds in a 30-second commercial and showed a copy of its past cover on the TV screen. Plaintiff claims that this was a copyright infringement and seeks an injunction, since the cover was part of a copyrighted work and was used without its permission.

Was defendant's visual use of plaintiff's copyrighted cover a fair use under copyright law? The court specifically ruled that it was not. In passing, however, it said the following:

> In this regard, it should be noted that the development of fair use as a judicial doctrine was catalyzed by the importance of permitting non-profit educational institutions to utilize portions of a copyrighted work and the perceived need for the media to be permitted to disseminate criticism, literary or otherwise, of a work submitted for public consumption . . .[3]

The federal court also said something of significance to fair use in the media and visual materials field:

> . . . the open ended quality of the judicial "fair use" doctrine was intentionally preserved by the framers of the new act. However, this was done in order to accommodate the perpetually unsettled quality associated with the *technological* production and dissemination of ideas, products and artistic creations. The fluidity built into the statutory fair use exception is premised on the flux which is endemic to the *means* of transmission—not the substance transmitted. The fluidity built into the statute was designed to diminish the difficulty which arises when an innovation in technology makes possible new techniques of display that could not be contemplated by legislators in the year the statute was framed . . . the fluidity of the statutory exception of "fair use" was oriented toward the unknown—not the known. (880)

Although the defendant's use was not a fair use, ". . . considerations of a constitutional nature compel this court to deny the injunction sought.

This court proceeds beyond a consideration of the fair use doctrine because an interest of greater magnitude is at stake in this case—the interest in preserving the sanctity of free speech, as protected by the First Amendment."

The court ruled:

> When the Copyright Act and the First Amendment both seek the same objective, their future coexistence is easily assured. However, when they operate at cross-purposes, the primacy of the First Amendment mandates that the Copyright Act be deprived of effectuation. Rather than strike down an entire act as overbroad in such a situation, the judiciary prefers to interpret such a statute as narrowly as needed to preserve it for the effectuation of those of its purposes deemed consistent with the Constitution. (882)

The court explained its rationale as follows:

> Such comparative advertising, when undertaken in the serious manner that defendant did herein, represents an important source of information for the education of consumers in a free enterprise system. . . . Hence, there is a conflict between the First Amendment and the Copyright Act, if as the plaintiff contends, the Act should be applied in the case *sub judice* to strike down defendant's activity. This court believes that plaintiff is seeking to impose too literal an interpretation of 17 U.S.C. Section 106 [the exclusive rights provision of the Copyright Act].

In denying the injunction requested by the plaintiff, the court ruled:

> The purposes of the Copyright Act . . . would not be served by the invocation of Section 106 in the present situation. In so finding, this court is construing the Copyright Act in a fashion which preserves its constitutionality and its statutory purpose. To extend it to the activities at issue would be a disservice to its goals and would place it in jeopardy of unconstitutionality. (883)

In commenting on this case, Harriet L. Oler has this to say:

> Thus, the court favored defendant's First Amendment rights and the public's interest in comparative television advertising over plaintiff's exclusive copyright rights, which embraced protection against the televised use of a small portion of a copyrighted work for comparative advertising purposes.

The Triangle case may well be the first American decision which relied expressly and solely on the First Amendment as a defense against copyright proprietor's claim of copyright infringement.[4]

This court said that it "proceeds beyond a consideration of the fair use doctrine" to the constitutional protections of the First Amendment. It specifically ruled that in a conflict between the copyright law and the First Amendment, it was constitutionally necessary that "the Copyright Act be deprived of effectuation," or otherwise be ruled unconstitutional.[5] Under such circumstances, constitutional principles, not copyright doctrine, must be primary in determining the propriety of the contested use of copyrighted materials.

The logic of *Thomson* and *Triangle* is mutually complementary. The

New Hampshire case used constitutional principles to enlarge the concept of "fair use," and found that, as so interpreted, the use there in question was a "fair use." The Florida case, however, held that although the contested use was not a "fair use" under copyright, it was nevertheless a constitutionally permissible use regardless of the copyright law.

These two decisions were rendered by federal district judges, not by appellate courts. The Triangle case (Florida), however, has been appealed to the United States Court of Appeals for the Fifth Circuit. The briefs of both parties strongly downplayed the constitutional issue and both urged that their controversy be settled primarily under the fair use doctrine, and only—if absolutely necessary—under constitutional doctrine. For example, the winning side in the district court told the court of appeals: (1) "This case need not be decided on First Amendment grounds" (Appellee's *Brief*, p. 7). (2) "While the District Court cast its decision ostensibly in First Amendment terms, it need not have reached the constitutional issue, for the court's reasoning may properly be incorporated into an interpretation of the fair use doctrine" (*ibid.*, p. 13). If adopted on appeal, this position would follow the rationale promulgated by the Thomson case. The copyright owner's brief argued that "appellee's infringing conduct is not defensible under the First Amendment" (Appellant's *Brief*, p. 19).

A Supreme Court Colloquy

In the third case, the constitutional issue was briefed and argued, but the Supreme Court did not decide the case substantively because it split 4 to 4 in its views and therefore affirmed the lower court's opinion without any opinion of its own. In *Williams and Wilkins Co.* v. *U.S.* a publisher of medical journals sued the United States for infringement of copyright because federal medical libraries made photocopies of articles from four of its copyrighted magazines and distributed them, on request, to medical researchers and practitioners. Copies were also supplied to other libraries and research institutions as part of an interlibrary loan program. Copying for individual requesters alone involved some 93,000 articles in one year. The copying for individuals was normally restricted to a single reproduction of a single article of fewer than fifty pages; an excessive number of requests from any individual was not honored. The copying was for professional, nonprofit purposes. The trial judge found the defendant guilty of infringement of copyright. But, on appeal, the Court of Claims reversed this, and by a vote of 4–3 held that the copying was a "fair use."

In the Supreme Court, the United States was represented by its top legal officer, the Solicitor General. The following colloquy took place in the argument before the Court:

MR. BORK (Solicitor General): . . . fair use, after all, is basically a constitutional doctrine . . .

QUESTION (MR. JUSTICE REHNQUIST): Are you suggesting that Congress would be constitutionally obligated to incorporate a doctrine of fair use into the copyright law?

MR. BORK: That is debatable. I have seen it debated both ways, Mr. Justice Rehnquist . . .

QUESTION: I thought you said a moment ago that fair use is constitutionally—

MR. BORK: The courts have derived their power to evolve a doctrine of fair use from the constitutional value, the constitutional principle. Whether or not the court could second-guess Congress's decision about what would promote, rather than retard, I don't know. Certainly that's not involved in this case.[6]

The Williams and Wilkins case is not the only one in which the Supreme Court failed to deal directly with the confrontation between the First Amendment and the copyright law. In two more recent cases the parties themselves, and not merely *amicus curiae*, directly posed the constitutional issue and stated that the precise question had never been decided by the Supreme Court. But in both instances the Supreme Court declined to review the decisions of the lower courts.[7] In both instances, the unsuccessful petitioner for review argued that fair use was inadequate to protect freedom of the press. In *Wainright*, the petitioner's brief charged that the lower court had

> shrugged off freedom of press and the public's right to know as if it were a secondary standard limited by the copyright laws rather than the other way around.

And the *Nizer* brief asserted that

> the First Amendment may require a verdict for defendants in a copyright infringement action even where application of the fair use doctrine may result in a contrary conclusion.

This was exactly the court's conclusion in *Triangle*.[8]

The thesis of this chapter is that *Triangle* is the proper answer to the Justice's question.

What Do Case Studies Add Up To?

Thomson and *Triangle* would seem to mean the following:

(1) Fair use in the copyright law must be interpreted to effectuate legitimate First Amendment rights in pursuit of freedom of inquiry, or else the copyright law may be unconstitutional.

(2) Use of copyrighted materials may be legally permissible under the First Amendment even when such use would not be sanctioned by the "fair use" provisions of the copyright law. "Fair use" is not necessarily the maximum permissible use of copyrighted materials.

Under either approach, the developing law seems to be that traditional First Amendment principles prevail in a conflict between First Amendment freedoms and statutory copyright monopoly.

Of course this does not mean that *any and every* desired use of the new media or visual materials by nonprofit educational users is necessarily constitutionally protected. It *will* make a difference that media and material users are planning to make a commercial use of such copyrighted materials without payment to the copyrighted owner. It *will* have significant impact on a court that a use will be noncommercial. Although *Thomson* ruled that there was no commercial harm to the copyright owner, *Triangle* involved a clear-cut commercial and competitive use. Nevertheless, in its recent rulings the Supreme Court seems to be holding that commercial speech has constitutional protection not principally because of its importance to the speaker but principally because of its informational importance and value to society and to the listeners or viewers.[9]

It is, however, important to recognize that constitutional freedom does not necessarily guarantee personal responsibility in the exercise of such freedom. The educational community should and must show responsibile and reasonable restraint in the exercise of its constitutional rights. In this connection it is well to note that Sigmund Timberg (Chapter 23) states, "the First Amendment does not guarantee any user of copyrighted material a free ride on the copyright system." He warns that, with respect to public access, "one should not push this too far." The warning is well taken.

Likewise, Eugene Aleinikoff's "Fair Use and Broadcasting" (Chapter 14) warns that "the commercial stakes in this area are high"; "copyrighted works cannot be used merely for program decoration or augmentation purposes under the aegis of fair use."

The pressure is on the Supreme Court to settle the confrontation between the First Amendment and the copyright law. Sooner or later, the Court can be expected to do so. It is my judgment that in doing so it will, at the least, give an affirmative reply to Mr. Justice Rehnquist's question to the Solicitor General of the United States and, in the appropriate case, will go the whole way as *Triangle* did.

THE PROBLEM

Having stated this chapter's conclusion at the outset and considered three recent cases, let us now return to a broader perspective of the problem itself and to a consideration of some of the major judicial precedents which, together with the case studies, justify the stated conclusions and thesis.

Can copyright owners legally prevent others from using *any* portion of their copyrighted works as they so frequently seek to do by copyright notices in their works? On its face the pre-1976 copyright law seemed to give copyright proprietors absolutely exclusive rights and sought to provide remedies against users who allegedly infringed such monopolistic rights.

Although the first American copyright law was enacted in 1790, not until the one last enacted (1976), did the statute include a "fair use" provision which specifically limited the absolutist conception of the copyright owner's monopoly. Despite the absence of limitations, the courts on their own, without statutory guidance or direction, disregarded the seeming absolutely monopolistic language of the copyright laws and developed their own judge-made exception. This was a doctrine of "fair use," by which a user could, under certain circumstances, ignore the purported monopoly of the copyright owner and make reasonable use of the copyrighted material without the copyright owner's permission or even over his violent objection.[10] As a result of judge-made law, and despite the statutory language of seeming exclusivity, the copyright proprietor had no complete monopoly.[11] As one distinguished scholar (now a jurist) put it, " 'use' is not the same thing as 'infringement,' "[12] despite the traditional, proprietor-sponsored view of the user's rights.[13]

The issue then becomes, in the context here outlined, the nature and scope of the public's right of access to copyrighted works. In the present copyright law (1976),[14] for the very first time in over 185 years of American copyright laws, "fair use" has become a statutory right. Even in its pre-statutory form, the doctrine of fair use was recognized through judicial interpretation, in a very real sense, because without fair use and the resultant freedom of inquiry, the copyright law may not only have been unconstitutional but would in all likelihood have been unenforceable.

THE CONSTITUTIONAL DIMENSION

The Copyright Clause of the Constitution

Article I, Section 8 of the Constitution reads as follows:

The Congress shall have Power . . .

To promote the Progress of Science and useful Arts, by securing for limited Times to Authors and Inventors the exclusive Right to their Respective Writings and Discoveries . . .

This copyright clause "merely empowers Congress to enact legislation and does not in any way confer a substantive right on any individual . . ."[15] It does not mandate that copyright legislation be enacted, nor does it specify what such legislation must include. Did the constitutional clause merely recognize and protect a previously existent right in the copyright holder? "No," said the Supreme Court in the very first case which considered this problem.[16] Today, it is unquestioned law that copyright protection is a purely statutory creature,[17] wholly at the disposal of Congress to grant or withhold.[18]

The First Amendment

The constitutional protection for freedom of the press, in the First Amendment, protects the right of reasonable access to copyrighted materials notwithstanding the copyright law. The statutory copyright privilege cannot oust the constitutional protection of the First Amendment. The Supreme Court has stated that "The First Amendment . . . rests on the assumption that the widest possible dissemination of information from diverse and antagonistic sources is essential to the welfare of the public, that a free press is a condition of a free society."[19] This statement by the Court is a splendid affirmation of freedom of inquiry.

But, isn't freedom of the press limited to the owners of a physical press, and not available to the readers of the press? The answer from the courts is a resounding "NO." Freedom of the press is *not* limited to the publishing business as such. It is the right of the entire American people; the press is merely a trustee for that right.[20] The Supreme Court has recognized that freedom of press and speech are fundamental personal rights and liberties,[21] that the First Amendment's protection of freedom of the press is "not for the benefit of the press so much as for the benefit of us all."[22] *Free press* is simply a shorthand means of saying that the press must be free because of the right of every American to be informed.[23]

The Bill of Rights, including the First Amendment, protects the right of access as a basic prerequisite to freedom of inquiry.[24] The right of *reasonable* access to use copyrighted works through "fair use"—or through direct application of the First Amendment, regardless of fair use—applies as much to the new media or visual material as it does to printed materials. Both vehicles for freedom of inquiry are protected by the First Amendment.

Thus, freedom of the press protects not only the press, but also the public's "right to receive information and ideas"[25] and the user's right to read and hear and see. A recent commentator wrote: "The courts have frequently pointed out that the right to speak implies in the public a right to hear. That in turn implies a right of accessibility."[26] According to the Supreme Court, the constitutionally protected right to know enlarges rather than limits freedom in creative activity. Its basic aim is freedom of inquiry, to unlock all ideas for argument, debate, and dissemination.[27] Such unlocking requires reasonable access to copyrighted materials, and this would apply equally to the new media and visual material and to print works.

That a media user may have other forms of access or inquiry does not vitiate the constitutional right of access and inquiry. The Supreme Court, in holding that the First Amendment guaranteed access to hear, to receive information, to learn, and to know, said the following:

> The Government also suggests that the First Amendment is inapplicable because appellees have free access to Mandel's ideas through his books and speeches . . . While alternative means of access to Mandel's ideas might be a relevant factor were we called upon to balance First Amendment rights against governmental regulatory interests—a balance we find unnecessary here in the light of the discussion that follows . . .—we are loath to hold on this record that existence of other alternatives extinguishes altogether any constitutional interest on the part of the appellees in this particular form of access.[28]

Even the minority opinions in this case agreed and accepted prior decisions concerning the "right to receive information."[29]

The comments of both the majority and the minority in this last cited case as well as the other jurisprudence previously referred to, apply with equal force to the right to see and use the new media and visual material through the constitutional right of access as well as through statutory fair use.

The Ninth Amendment

Customarily, in this context reference is made only to the First Amendment. The Ninth Amendment, however, provides: "The enumeration in the Constitution, of certain rights, shall not be construed to deny or disparage other rights retained by the people." This is the reserved right of the people to all unenumerated rights, the fundamental but unspecified rights which exist side by side with those specified in the first eight amendments. A distinguished scholar has stated that the Ninth Amendment provides for "the right to have access to information."[30] This constitutional provision has been studied elsewhere.[31]

Constitutional Interpretation

Constitutional rights are not self-executing, however; they must be interpreted and enforced by the courts. Like other forms of government regulation and control, copyright can and does conflict with First Amendment rights and freedoms. In such circumstances, the courts are the arbiters of which right prevails. And as in most constitutional conflicts, one is faced with an "iffy" situation, with no certain or preordained result attaching to any particular set of facts and circumstances.[32] Nevertheless, in determining a course of future action from a pragmatic viewpoint, whether it be photocopying, off-air taping, copying from films, etc., it is necessary to consider the basic constitutional situation and to evaluate its relationship to the particular educational activity.

It would be splendid for lawyers to be able to develop a precise chart with clearly defined boxes into which all circumstances can fit. Unfortunately, that's not the way constitutional law works. It will take many suits in the developing shake-down cruise of the conflict between the constitution and the copyright law, perhaps some statutory changes also, before the ultimate pattern will be reasonably easy to predict and understand.

In the meantime, it is important for lawyers to continue to press the constitutional argument in protecting the legal uses by educators, librarians, and scholars.[33] This, for example, was well and successfully done in the Donald Duck case referred to in Chapter 5, in the face of a statement by the copyright owner that "the First Amendment does not protect copyright infringers." (See also Chapter 16.)

A characteristic pattern in constitutional interpretation, especially where conflicting interests are involved, is the balancing of the interests before reaching a final judicial interpretation. How has this worked out in the past?

The universally adopted doctrine is that the public interest has primacy over the copyright owner's interest—Congress, the courts, the Register of Copyrights, and legal commentators have stated this principle, although not always do they arrive at the same application. For example, the House *Report* on the 1909 law (which was replaced by the 1976 act) stated that copyright was established "not primarily for the benefit of the author, but primarily for the benefit of the public."[34] The Supreme Court has often ruled that "the copyright law . . . makes a reward to the owner of secondary consideration."[35] The Register of Copyrights told Congress that "within limits the author's interests coincide with those of the public. Where they conflict the public interest must prevail."[36]

The primacy of public access over the copyright owner's financial interest has also been well stated by legal commentators. Goldstein put it thus:

> [W]hether a use is fair is determined on the basis of a number of factors, predominantly on the strength of the public interest in free access . . . Copyright and trademark law . . . have also experienced a marked shift toward wider public access.[37]

Another, similar comment:

> The primary purpose of the Copyright Act is to give the public maximum access to the author's work; a secondary purpose is to remunerate the copyright owner.[38]

The judicial decisions indicate that in balancing the mere statutory privilege of the copyright owner with the user's constitutional rights, the balance must tilt toward the user.[39] In fact, the courts have begun to rely on constitutional requirements as a justification to interpret "fair use" so as to subordinate the copyright owner's interest to the public interest.[40]

One must face the question whether audiovisual forms of communication are so unique and different from the spoken and printed word that they are deprived of the otherwise applicable constitutional protections afforded to oral and written words. In my judgment, the answer is "NO." Chapter 20, "New Forms of Media Discourse," illustrates that audiovisual discourse or communication has become a basic form of commentary, critique, and basic communication between people. The overriding purpose of the First Amendment guaranty is protection of two-way communication among people. The medium of that communication is purely happenstantial; the First Amendment protects the communication whatever the medium. In constitutional protection, the medium does not replace, displace, or disenfranchise the message.

For example, the New Hampshire case (discussed at the outset of this chapter) dealt with radio communication; the Florida case dealt with TV communication. In both instances, the federal judge applied the constitutional protections of the First Amendment without diminution because the medium was not the printed word.

In an earlier case, the Supreme Court was faced with a somewhat similar situation in the context of what could be copyrighted. There the Copyright Office submitted an *amicus curiae* brief arguing that the method of reproduction does not affect the copyrightability of a work:

> Literary works which in an earlier era would perhaps have been reproduced by hand on illuminated parchment or in other single copies have not become less copyrightable by virtue of their present reproduction in thousands of copies by manufacturing techniques involving the use of movable types, plates, etc. Similarly, painting masterpieces once reproduced on canvas or as murals in single copies are now frequently reproduced in color plates for distribution in thousands of individual copies or in periodical or book form. *Neither the mechanical and manufacturing processes used in this reproduction [nor] the number of copies . . . would appear to affect the copyrightability or essential nature of the work itself.*[41]

Communication, not the medium used by the communicator, is the key to First Amendment rights. Therefore, both "fair use" and First Amendment rights apply—in this author's judgment—to audiovisual communication in the same basic fashion that they apply to oral and written communication.

In summary, I believe that the constitutional dimension derived from the applicable law is as follows:

1. The Copyright Clause of the Constitution gives no property rights to copyright owners. It merely gives Congress the power, but imposes no duty, to enact copyright legislation. Copyright is a statutory privilege, not a constitutional right.

2. The First and Ninth Amendments give users of copyrighted materials, both printed and audiovisual, a direct constitutional right of reasonable access to such materials, a right of free inquiry, which has legal and constitutional priority over the mere statutory privilege accorded by the copyright law to copyright owners.

3. In balancing between the constitutional right of users and the statutory privilege of owners, the courts must tilt in favor of the users' constitutionally protected rights of reasonable access and freedom of inquiry.

4. "Fair use" is both a statutory privilege and a legal vehicle (but by no means the exclusive one) for effectuating the constitutional protection for the primacy of the public interest over the copyright proprietor's interest.

THE VARIOUS LEGAL DOCTRINES

Freedom of inquiry is not static either in life or in the law. The Supreme Court has said that First Amendment rights are protected by the courts "with a jealous eye."[42] It has also stated that

> The modern history of the guarantee of freedom of speech and press mainly has been one of a search for the outer limits of that right.[43]

The gates of interpretation are never closed.[44]

We are here in the midst of a rapidly developing field of constitutional interpretation. The newness of the constitutional doctrine here espoused is shown, for example, by the statement of the federal district judge in the Triangle case (the second of the case studies) that he would not have relied *solely* on the First Amendment "until recently."[45] Law school dean Lyman Ray Patterson wrote in 1975 that "the problem of copyright and free speech has only recently been recognized."[46]

Owing in part to the changing pace of constitutional interpretation and in part to the Supreme Court's inability to reach a majority decision in the appeal in *Williams and Wilkins* (our third case study) and its refusal to entertain appeals raising the issue squarely, there is uncertainty in the applicable law. The last word has not yet been uttered. The result is that at least three legal positions appear in various court decisions.

The Traditional Approach

The traditional position is that the restrictions of the copyright law are *not* mitigated by the First Amendment. As one court put it:

> Defendants' First Amendment argument, in so far as it is distinguishable from their claim to fair use, can be dismissed as flying in the face of established law.[47]

This point of view is customarily advanced by copyright propri-etors. It places copyright users in the defensive position of having to justify their actions in terms of four specific statutory criteria of fair use set forth in Section 107 of the Copyright Act, all of which are econom-ically and commercially oriented, in varying degrees. This position is least sensitive to, or supportive of, freedom of inquiry. And, so far as can be seen from recent cases, it is being slowly eroded as an operative legal position.

The Interpretive Approach

The federal courts have become increasingly uncomfortable with rejecting the First Amendment's constitutional guarantees in copyright infringement cases, but some of them are not yet ready to move to the explicit and full-fledged constitutional position that the copyright law must yield to the First Amendment. Thus such courts seek to combine the copyright law with the First Amendment by ruling that "fair use" must be so interpreted as to include First Amendment consid-eration. This was the position taken in *Thomson* (our first case study)[48] and perhaps was implied in Mr. Justice Rehnquist's question in the oral argument in *Williams and Wilkins* (the third case study).

Why would a court strain in order to impose on the copyright law a consideration which clearly is not explicitly stated there? Courts cus-tomarily are reluctant to resort to constitutional grounds when they can resolve the issues before them through statutory or other interpretation. Therefore, this developing interpretive approach includes constitutional considerations in assessing "fair use," notwithstanding, and even in the face of, the absence of any explicit requirements to that effect either in the copyright statute or its legislative history.

A significant collateral effect of the interpretive approach is that the fair use provision of Section 107 of the copyright law must be en-larged to include considerations—in this instance, First Amendment factors—beyond the four factually oriented "factors" specifically enum-erated in Section 107 for determining the presence or absence of "fair use." Although not stated as one of the four statutory criteria, therefore, the First Amendment becomes an additional and perhaps overriding interpretive criterion under this approach.[49]

The Constitutional Approach

But the next step has already been taken, a clear-cut judicial decision that even where the alleged infringing use is *not* "fair use" under the copyright law, it may still be permissible use under the First Amendment. This was the position taken in 1978 in *Triangle*, the second case study, that "fair use" and the First Amendment are separate and distinguishable protections for users of copyrighted materials.[50]

A leading copyright commentator, Professor Nimmer,[51] put it thus:

> ... the Copyright Clause may not be read as independent of and uncontrolled by the First Amendment. Because Congress is granted authority to legislate in a given field, it does not follow that such a grant immunized Congress from the limitation of the Bill of Rights, including the First Amendment.[52]

He also wrote:

> A grave danger to copyright may lie in the failure to distinguish between the statutory privilege known as fair use, and an emerging constitutional limitation on copyright contained in the First Amendment.[53]
>
> ... This First Amendment principle must, in turn, be distinguished from the doctrine of fair use.[54]

Nimmer also pointed out that there is a major legal and practical difference in these two principles:

> The scope and extent of fair use falls within the discretion of the Congress itself. Fair use, when properly applied, is limited to copying by others which does not materially impair the marketability of the work which is copied. The First Amendment principle, when appropriate, may be invoked despite the fact that the marketability of the copied work is thereby impaired.[55]

Another commentator, Dean Patterson, made an important distinction between commercial and noncommercial access to copyrighted material in warning of the possible total unconstitutionality of the conventional concepts of copyright as related to television:

> Subjecting public communication to protection from the predatory practices of a competitor is one thing; protecting it from use by members of the public is another. Public communication of public information is too important to the welfare of a free and democratic society to be subjected to the private monopoly provided by the current concept of copyright.[56]

Patterson regards copyright as a limited device designed only for the regulation of trade and competition:

> Use by another for profit would constitute infringement, but a nonprofit use would not. Thus copyright would provide protection against competitors, but would not preclude any reasonable use of the work by the public.[57]

And in 1978 the Supreme Court said that so far as "the force of the [First] Amendment's guarantees" is concerned, there is a "commonsense" distinction between commercial and noncommercial speech.[58]

CONCLUSION

As expressed in the thesis in the opening paragraphs of this chapter and throughout, the conclusion reached here is that the provisions and limitations of the copyright law do not limit or proscribe the freedom of inquiry guaranteed by First Amendment rights for reasonable access to copyrighted material. More specifically, it is the thesis and conclusion of this chapter that *both* the interpretive and the constitutional approaches are correct law. This means that reasonable use of copyrighted works (especially by nonprofit education, research and scholarship)[59] is an exercise in freedom of inquiry into the nation's heritage and is protected both by the statutory provisions for "fair use" under the Copyright Act and by the constitutional guarantees of the First and Ninth Amendments to the Constitution.[60]

NOTES

[1] Keep Thomson Governor Committee v. Citizens for Gallen Committee, 401 PTCJ A-2 (Dist. Ct., New Hampshire, Oct. 2, 1978).

[2] Italian Book Corp. v. American Broadcasting Companies, 404 PTCJ A-10, note 14 (S.D.N.Y., Sept. 6, 1978).

[3] Triangle Publications, Inc. v. Knight-Ridder Newspapers, Inc., 445 F.Supp. 875, 880 (S.D.Fla. 1978).

[4] See L. W. Wang, Comment, "The First Amendment Exception to Copyright: A Proposed Test," 1977 *Wisc. L. Rev.* 1158, 1176; Comment, "Photocopying and Fair Use: An Examination of the Economic Factor in Fair Use," 26 *Emory L. Rev.* (1977): 849, 882. See Appellant's Court of Appeals *Brief* in *Triangle*, pp. 11–12, 15, 28.

[5] See also S. G. Plichta, Note, "Constitutional Limitations upon the Congress's Power to Enact Copyright Legislation," 1972 *Utah L. Rev.* 534.

[6] 487 F.2d 1345 (Ct. Cl. 1973); *aff'd by an equally divided Court*, 420 U.S. 376 (1975). The United States' brief was silent on the constitutional issue. Among the many briefs *amicus curiae*, only that filed by the National Education Association dealt with the constitutional issues. The quotation in the text is from the official typed transcript of the oral argument before the Supreme Court, Dec. 7, 1974, pp. 39–40.

[7] The petitioners for writs of certiorari made the constitutional argument in Nizer v. Meeropol, S. Ct. #77-608, 364 PTCJ A-2; and in Wainright Sec. v. Wall Street Transcript Corp., S. Ct., 353 PTCJ A-4 (see note 50 below).

[8] A similar trend may be developing in the relationship between the First Amendment and trademarks. See Universal City Studios, Inc. v. Ideal Pub. Co., 349 PTCJ A-3 (S.D.N.Y. 1977); comment on *Triangle*, 380 PTCJ at 84. *Per contra*: Reddy Communications Inc. v. Environmental Action Foundation, Inc., 359 PTCJ A-1 (App. D.C. 1977).

[9] First National Bank of Boston v. Belotti, 435 U.S. 765, 781–83 (1978), Bates v. State Bar, 433, 364 (1977); Linmark Associates, Inc. v. Township of Willingboro, 431 U.S. 85, 92, 97 (1977); Virginia State Board of Pharmacy v. Virginia Citizens Consumer Council, Inc., 425 U.S. 748, 756–57 (1976); Redish, "The First Amendment in the Marketplace: Commercial Speech and the Values of Free Expression," 39 *Geo. Wash. L. Rev.* 429, 434 (1971); Mimzer and Nickel, "Does the Constitution Mean What It Always Meant?" 77 *Col. L. Rev.* 1029, at 1943 (1977).

[10] 3 Nimmer, *Cases and Materials on Copyright* (1978), Sec. 1305; Rosemont Enterprises, Inc. v. Random House, Inc., 366 F.2d 303 (2d Cir. 1966), *cert. denied*, 385 U.S. 1009 (1967); Time, Inc., v. Bernard Geis Associates, 293 F.Supp. 130 (S.D.N.Y. 1968). See also G. Ball, *Copyright and Literary Property* (1944), 260.

[11] See Fortnightly Corp. v. United Artists TV, Inc., 392 U.S. 390, 393 (1968); Orient Ins. Co. v. Daggs, 172 U.S. 557, 566 (1969); Dennis v. U.S., 341 U.S. 494, 508 (1951).

[12] B. Kaplan, *An Unhurried View of Copyright* (NY: Columbia University Press, 1967), 57.

[13] See 3 Nimmer, Sec. 13.05: *Hearings on S. 1006 before the Subcommittee on Patents, Trademarks and Copyrights of the Senate Committee on the Judiciary*, 89th Cong., 1st Sess. (1965), 118, 122–24.

[14]P.L. 94-553, 17 U.S.C. 107.

[15]Tape Industries Assn. of America v. Younger, 316 F.Supp. 340, 346 (D.C. Cal. 1970), *appeal dismissed* 401 U.S. 902 (1971). Cf.: Deepsouth Packing Co. v. Laitram Corp., 406 U.S. 518, 530 (1972).

[16]Wheaton v. Peters, 33 U.S. 591, 661, 663 (8 Pet.) (1834). To the same effect, see Mazer v. Stein, 347 U.S. 201, 214 (1954); Fox Film Corp. v. Doyal, 286 U.S. 123, 127 (1932); Caliga v. Inter Ocean Newspaper Co., 215 U.S. 182, 188 (1909).

The House Committee's *Report* on the current Copyright Law of 1909 also made the same point:

> The enactment of copyright legislation by Congress under the terms of the Constitution is not based upon any natural right that the author has in his writings, for the Supreme Court has held that such rights as he has are purely statutory rights. . . . The Constitution does not establish copyrights, but provides that Congress shall have the power to grant such rights if it thinks best.

H.R. *Report* No. 2222, 60th Cong., 2d Sess. (1909): 7. See also statement of House floor manager of 1909 bill, 43 *Cong. Rec.* (1909): 3765— "there is no property right in writings."

[17]American Tobacco Co. v. Werckmeister, 207 U.S. 284, 291 (1907); Bobbs-Merrill Co. v. Strauss, 210 U.S. 399, 246 (1939); White-Smith Music Publ. Co. v. Apollo, 147 F.226, 227 (2d Cir.1906), *aff'd* 209 U.S. 1, 15 (1908). See also Loew's Inc. v. C.B.S., 131 F. Supp. 165, 172 (S.D.Cal.1955), *aff'd*, 239 F.2d 532 (9th Cir. 1956), *aff'd by equally divided court*, 356 U.S. 43 (1958); MCA, Inc. v. Wilson, 425 F.Supp. 443 (S.D.N.Y. 1976).

[18]Krafft v. Cohen, 117 F.2d 579, 580 (2d Cir. 1941); Keene v. Wheatley, 14 F. Cas. 180, 185 (No. 7644) (C.C.E.D. Pa. 1861).

[19]Associated Press v. United States, 326 U.S. 1, 20 (1945).

[20]Arthur Hays Sulzberger of the *New York Times* addressed this issue:

> Perhaps we ought to ask ourselves now just what freedom of the press really is . . . Freedom of press—or, to be precise, the *benefit* of freedom of the press—belongs to everyone, to the citizens as well as the publisher. The publisher is not granted the privilege of independence simply to provide him with a more favored position in the community than is accorded to other citizens. He enjoys an explicitly defined independence because it is the only condition under which he can fully perform his role, which is to inform fully, fairly and comprehensively. The crux is *not* the publisher's freedom to print; it is rather the citizen's right to know! What I would point out is that freedom of the press is your right as citizens and not mine as a publisher. Address to Trustees of New York Public Library, Nov. 13, 1956 (privately printed), p. 9.

[21]Schneider v. State, 308 U.S. 147, 161 (1939).

[22]Time, Inc. v. Hill, 385 U.S. 374, 389 (1967). In First National Bank of Boston v. Bellotti, 435 U.S. 765, 782 (1978), the Supreme Court said, "the press does not have a monopoly on either the First Amendment or the ability to enlighten." In his concurring opinion, Chief Justice Burger said that "the First Amendment does not 'belong' to any definable category of persons or entities: It belongs to all who exercise its freedoms," pp. 798–802. In Virginia Pharmacy Board v. Virginia Consumer Council, 425 U.S. 748, 756 (1976), the Court said ". . . the protection afforded by the First Amendment is to the communication, to its source and to its recipients both." And in Young v. American Mini Theatre, 427 U.S. 50, 76–77 (1976), the Supreme Court stated: "Vital to this concern is the corollary that there be a full opportunity for everyone to receive the message . . . But the central First Amendment concern remains the need to maintain free access of the public to the expression."

[23]In Bellotti, n.22, p. 783, the Supreme Court said that its recent cases on the First Amendment and commercial speech "illustrate that the First Amendment goes beyond protection of the press and the self-expression of individuals to prohibit government from limiting the stock of information from which members may draw." In National Commission on Egg Nutrition v. FTC, 570 F.2d 157, 162 (7th Cir. 1977), the Court said: "The First Amendment interest is twofold: it embraces the interests of both the speaker and the prospective audience."

[24]These rights of access include: the right of "suitable access to social, political, aesthetic, moral and other ideas and experiences," Red Lion Broadcasting Co. v. FCC, 395 U.S. 367, 390 (1969); the right to "receive information and ideas," Kleindienst v. Mandel, 408 U.S. 753, 760, 762–65 (1972); Stanley v. Georgia, 394 U.S. 557, 564 (1969); the right to receive printed matter, Lamont v. Postmaster General, 381 U.S. 301 (1965); the right of access to certain religious publications, Cruz v. Beto, 405 U.S. 319 (1972); the right of access to the courts, California Motor Transport Co. v. Trucking Unlimited, 404 U.S. 508, 513 (1972); the right of addressees of letters to read the letters without censorship, Procunier v. Martinez, 416 U.S. 396 (1974); the right to know, Minancini v. Strongsville City School District, 541 F.2d 577, 583 (6th Cir. 1976). See also Note, "Trial Secrecy and the First Amendment Right of Public Access to Judicial Proceedings," 91 Harv. L. Rev. 1899 (1978): 1903–1904.

[25]Kleindienst v. Mandel, 408 U.S. 753 (1972); Stanley v. Georgia 394 U.S. 557, 564 (1964); Red Lion Broadcasting Co. v. FCC, 395 U.S. 367, 390 (1969); Griswold v. Connecticut, 381 U.S. 479, 482 (1965); Lamont v. Postmaster General, 381 U.S. 301, 307–08 (1965) (Brennan, J., concurring). See also New York Times Co. v. United States, 403 U.S. 713 (1971).

[26]G. T. Hunt, "The Right of Accessibility," District Lawyer, No. 3 (1978), 31, 33.

[27]Times Film Corp. v. Chicago, 365 U.S. 43, 81 (1961). See also Kleindienst v. Mandel, 408 U.S. 753, 771 (1972) (Douglas, J., dissenting). A similar protection for the right to learn emanates from the Fourteenth Amendment. Meyer v. Nebraska, 262 U.S. 390 (1923). See also Serrano v. Priest, 5 Cal. 3d 584, 96 Cal. Rptr. 601, 487 P.2d 1241 (1971). See also Hobson v. Hanson, 269 F.Supp. 401, 480, 488, 492, 512–13 (D. D.C. 1967), appeal dismissed, 393 U.S. 801 (1969), where the Court struck down a school board's "track system" of assigning pupils as being contrary to their right to learn. The decision was based on the equal protection clause.

[28]Kleindienst v. Mandel, 408 U.S. 753, 765 (1972). See also Minancini v. Strongsville City School District 541 F.2d 577, 582 (6th Cir. 1976).

[29]Mr. Justice Douglas wrote: "The First Amendment involves not only the right to speak and publish but also the right to hear, to learn, to know." Martin v. City of Struthers, 319 U.S. 141, 143; Stanley v. Georgia, 394 U.S. 557, 564; Kleindienst v. Mandel, 408 U.S. 771 (1972). Mr. Justice Marshall's dissenting opinion, in which Mr. Justice Brennan joined, stated:

> As the majority correctly demonstrates, in a variety of contexts this Court has held that the First Amendment protects the right to receive information and ideas, the freedom to hear as well as the freedom to speak . . . the right to speak and hear—including the right to inform others and be informed about public issues—are inextricably part of that process. The freedom to speak and the freedom to hear are inseparable; they are two sides of the same coin. (Ibid., 775.)

See also Bloustein, "The First Amendment and Privacy: The Supreme Court Justice and the Philosopher," 28 Ruters L. Rev. (1974): 41, 42.

[30]Kutner, "The Neglected Ninth Amendment: The 'Other Rights' Retained by the People," 51 Marq. L. Rev. (1967): 121, 139. The author noted that "(r)elated to this right to information is the right to know as encompassed in academic and cultural freedom. A college professor or school teacher has the right to pursue knowledge."

[31]H.N. Rosenfield, "The Constitutional Dimension of Fair Use in Copyright Law," 50 Notre Dame Lawyer (1975): 790, 799–800.

[32]See Phoenix (Ariz.) Gazette, Sept. 29, 1978, p. A-4; Oct. 10, 1978, p. A-3 (FBI investigation off-air videotaping of TV programs for school use).

[33]In Encyclopaedia Britannica v. Crooks, 447 F.S. 243 (W.D.N.Y., Feb. 27, 1978), a federal court granted an injunction against future (but not past) videotaping of entire copyrighted films for nonprofit school uses and did not even mention the constitutional dimension. Another court agreed it to be only in "certain rare instances when first amendment considerations will operate to limit copyright protection for graphic expressions of newsworthy events," Sid and Marty Krofft TV v. McDonald's Corporation,

562 F.2d 1157, 1171 (9th Cir. 1977). See Nimmer, "Does Copyright Abridge the First Amendment Guarantees of Free Speech and Press?" 17 *U.C.L.A. L. Rev.* (1970): 1180, 1199. (First Amendment does not limit copyright protection. But see note 7.)

[34]H.R. *Report* No. 2222, 60th Cong., 2d Sess. (1909): 9.

[35]Mazer v. Stein, 347 U.S. 201, 219 (1954). *Accord,* United States v. Paramount Pictures, Inc., 334 U.S. 131, 158 (1948); United States v. Loew's Inc. 371 U.S. 38, 46 (1962).

[36]*Copyright Law Revision,* Report of the Register of Copyrights, House Committee Print, 87th Cong., 1st Sess. (1961): 6.

[37]Goldstein, "The Competitive Mandate: From Sears to Lear," 59 *Calif. L. Rev.* (1971): 873, 890, 893. See also Goldstein, "Copyright and the First Amendment," 70 *Col. L. Rev.* (1970): 983 (Supreme Court's tilt toward public interest in libel and privacy cases).

[38]Note, "Cable Television and Copyright Royalties," 83 *Yale L. J.* (1974): 554, 557, cited with approval in Twentieth Century Music Corp. v. Aiken, 500 F.2d 127, 130 (*n.*6) (3rd Cir. 1974), *aff'd* 422 U.S. 151 (1975).

[39]Fortnightly Corp. v. United Artists Television, Inc., 392 U.S. 390 (1968). See also Rosemont Enterprises, Inc. v. Random House, Inc., 366 F.2d 303, 309 (2d Cir. 1966); Time, Inc. v. Bernard Geis Associates, 293 F.Supp. 130, 146 (S.D.N.Y. 1968).

[40]See two cases at outset of this chapter. See also note 39; see further Berlin v. E. C. Publications, Inc. 329 F.2d 541, 543–44 (2d Cir. 1961), *cert. denied,* 379 U.S. 822 (1964); Rosemont Enterprises, Inc. v. Random House, Inc., 366 F.2d 303, 309 (2d Cir. 1966); Greenbie v. Noble, 151 F.Supp. 45, 67 (S.D.N.Y. 1957).

[41]Mazer v. Stein, 347 U.S. 201 (1954), quoted from Copyright Office brief, pp. 30–31 (emphasis supplied).

[42]AFL v. Swing, 312 U.S. 321, 325 (1941). Cf. Brennan, "The Supreme Court and the Meikelejohn Interpretation of the First Amendment," 79 *Harv. L. Rev.* 1, (1965): 1–2.

[43]Curtis Pub. Co. v. Butts, 388 U.S. 130, 148 (1967).

[44]Maimonides, *The Guide to the Perplexed,* ed. S. Pines (Chicago: University of Chicago, 1963): 327–28.

[45]445 F.Supp. 882.

[46]Lyman Ray Patterson, "Private Copyright and Public Communication: Free Speech Endangered," 28 *Vand. L. Rev.* (1975): 1161, 1163 n.4. He refers to law review articles in 1970 by Goldstein and Nimmer and in 1975 by Rosenfield. He makes the interesting comment: "The thirty-four studies on copyright, prefaced [by the copyright office] for Congress, consisting of almost 1,500 closely printed pages, contain no reference to the problem of copyright and free speech."

[47]McGraw-Hill, Inc. v. Worth Publishers, Inc., 335 F.Supp. 415, 422 (S.D.N.Y. 1971). See also Robert Stigwood Group, Ltd. v. O'Reilly, 364 F.Supp. 376, 383 (D. Conn. 1972), *cert. den.* 429 U.S. 848 (1976); Jondora Music Publishing Co. v. Melody Recordings, Inc., 362 F.Supp. 494, 499 (D.N.J. 1973), *cert. den.* 421 U.S. 1012 (1975); U.S. v. Bodin, 375 F.Supp. 1265, 1267 (W.D. Okla. 1971); L. S. Sobel, "Copyright and the First Amendment: A Gathering Storm," 19 *Copyright Law Symposium* (1971): 43, 79–80; cf.: Walt Disney Productions v. Air Pirates, 345 F.Supp. 108, 115–16 (N.D. Calif. 1972).

[48]A somewhat earlier and groping rationale was expressed by another federal judge in 1976:

> The tension between the First Amendment and the copyright statute . . . does not exist . . . because the doctrine of fair use . . . has been precisely contoured by the courts to assure simultaneously the public's access to knowledge of general import and the right of an author to protection of his intellectual creation.

H.C. Wainright and Co. v. Wall Street Transcript Corp., 417 F.Supp. 620, 624 (S.D.N.Y. 1976), *aff'd* 558 F.2d, 91 (2d. Cir. 1977), *cert. den.* 54 L. Ed. 759 (1978). (See note 50.)

[49]On its face this approach is consistent with Section 107 of the Copyright Act ("In determining whether the use made of a work in any particular case is fair use the factors to be considered shall include . . ." the four specified "factors.") But see a statement in the House Committee's report explaining these four factors:

... The courts have evolved a set of criteria which ... provide some gauge for balancing the equities. These criteria have been stated in various ways, but essentially they can all be reduced to the four standards which have been adopted in section 107. . . . House Judiciary Committee, *Copyright Law Revision*, 94th Cong., 2d Sess., *Report* No. 94-1476 (Sept. 3, 1976), p. 65.

[50]But even in 1977, a federal circuit court judge said:

The question of the first amendment protection due to a news report of a copyrighted research report is a provocative one. Conflicts between interests protected by the First Amendment and the copyright laws thus far have been resolved by application of the fair use doctrine ... Someday, legitimate in-depth news coverage of copyrighted, small circulation articles dealing with areas of general concern may require courts to distinguish between the doctrine of fair use and "an emerging constitutional limitation on copyright contained in the first amendment." [Nimmer] . . . But, this is not the case.

Wainright Sec. v. Wall Street Transcript Corp., 558 F.2d 91, 95 (2d Cir. 1977), *cert. den.* 54 L. Ed. 2d 759 (1978). In Time, Inc. v. Bernard Geis Associates., 293 F.Supp. 130, 132 (S.D.N.Y. 1968) (the Kennedy assassination film case), the defendant relied on the First Amendment.

[51]Professor Nimmer was coauthor of the appellant's brief on appeal in *Triangle*.

[52]Nimmer *Cases and Materials on Copyright* (1978), Section 1.10 A, pp. 1–64.

[53]*Ibid.*, Section 1.10 D, pp. 1–85.

[54]*Ibid.*, pp. 1–89.

[55]*Ibid.*, pp. 1–85.

[56]Patterson, p. 1211.

[57]*Ibid.*, p. 1210.

[58] Ohralik v. Ohio State Bar Association, 436 U.S. 447, 456 (1978)

[59]There is a long-established precedent *within* the present copyright law for a separate system by means of an exemption from copyright for nonprofit uses of copyrighted materials. Under 17 Sec. 1(c), pre-1976 law, certain nonprofit uses and reproduction of lectures, sermons, addresses, or similar productions, or other nondramatic literary works were exempted from copyright coverage. And 17 U.S.C. Sec. 1(e) gave the copyright owner of a musical composition only the right, in this connection, "to perform the copyrighted work publicly for profit." The 1909 law thus provided an "outright exemption" for such nonprofit uses of copyrighted materials, House Comm. on the Judiciary, 90th Cong., 1st Sess., *Report on Copyright Law Revision* to accompany H.R. 2512 (Mar. 8, 1967): 26; Sen. Comm. on the Judiciary, 93rd Cong., 2d Sess., *Report on Copyright Law Revision*, to accompany S. 1361 (July 3, 1974): 112.

An Ad Hoc Committee (of Educational Institutions and Organizations) on Copyright Law Revision proposed a limited educational exemption (to include restricted copying) for nonprofit educational purposes, as a reasonable means of retention and effectuation of the "not-for-profit concept of the current law." See *Hearings on S. 1006 Before the Subcommittee on Patents, Trademarks, and Copyrights* of the Senate Committee on the Judiciary, 89th Cong., 1st Sess., pp. 120, 129.

[60]In Smith v. California, 375 U.S. 259 (1963), the *Brief* for the City of Los Angeles argued that a person cannot avail himself of both copyright and First Amendment rights, but the issue was not decided because the Supreme Court vacated the judgment and remanded the case on other grounds.

Late Addendum: *Bruzzone v. Miller Brewing Co.,*
U.S. Dist. Ct., No. Dist. of Calif., 7C-78-2055 SC, May 25, 1979, 439 PTCJ 4-6 (Aug. 2, 1979)

In a decision that became available too late for inclusion in the text, the plaintiff brought and won a suit for a declaratory judgment. The plaintiff was a commercial market research company that tested prime time TV commercials through questionnaires that included five or six isolated TV frames from a commercial, together with text or dialogue, all placed on a "photo board." Brand names were not indicated, nor was color or action included. The questionnaire contained a series of questions about the commercial and also sought to obtain, anonymously, background information about the 1,000 households to whom the questionnaire was sent for response.

The multipurpose nature of the resulting data included analysis of the strengths and weaknesses of different advertising concepts and of specific commercials. The results were sold to advertisers and were used in plaintiff's commercially sold newsletter.

Defendant owned the copyright for the commercials in question and had threatened legal action against plaintiff. In its declaratory judgment the Federal District Court, in California, ruled that plaintiff's use of portions of defendant's copyrighted commercials "in market research and advertisement testing is a fair use of copyrighted materials." Judge Conti said: "Where the assertion of a copyright interest conflicts with the free flow of information in an open society, and so impairs the dissemination of research and intellectual works, the copyright owner's interest should yield to the public welfare lest the very nature of the Copyright Act be frustrated." He also said: "Useful, reliable market research results have value for the public, assist in keeping the competitive market place free of disturbances and confusion, and in general is an essential aspect of a healthy consumer economy . . . Plaintiff's use of defendant's commercials is for the purpose of criticism, comment, news reporting, teaching, scholarship and research" under §107 of the Copyright Act.

In reaching his decision, the Federal Judge made the following statements, among others: (1) "There is no credible evidence that the standard practice of monitoring and evaluating competitor's advertisements impairs the value of said advertisements." (2) "Photo board testing does not impair the value an advertisement would otherwise possess. Plaintiff's advertisement testing does not in any way impair the value of defendant's commercials to defendant or limit defendant's use of its commercials." (3) ". . . the copying done by plaintiff is extremely fragmentary," some five to six frames out of the usual 720 in a TV commercial. (4) Plaintiff does not compete with defendant, and "there is no 'market' for the copyrighted commercial in question." (5) "Although the plaintiff's work contains materials from defendant's commercials, it performs a completely different function than that of defendant's work. Therefore . . . there is no evidence that it has an effect on defendant's (Miller Brewing) potential market. . . . The scope of the fair use is expanded when the use of the copyrighted work does not fulfill the same function in terms of consumer demand, or compete for the same consumer as the original. . . . Deriving a profit from a subsequent use does not render said use unfair. . . . Criticism, comment and review are well-recognized areas of fair use, even if a profit is derived thereby."

Bruzzone v. *Miller Brewing Co.*, U.S. Dist. Ct.,
No. Dist. of Calif., #C-78-2055 SC, May 25, 1979,
439 PTCJ 4-6 (Aug. 2, 1979)

Depending, in part, on public policy without specific reference to Constitutional principles, *Bruzzone* could have important impact in validating *reasonable* uses of copyrighted material for education, scholarship and research. Of special importance is the combination in the Court's opinion of the two legal concepts: (1) "conflicts with the free flow of information in an open society" which impair "the dissemination of research and intellectual works . . . should yield to the public welfare lest the very nature of the Copyright Act be frustrated," and (2) if the use of copyrighted material "performs a completely different function" from that to which the copyright owner put that material, or "does not fulfill the same functions in terms of consumer demand or compete for the same consumer as the original . . . the scope of the fair use is expanded." If the District Court's decision is not reversed, the combination of these two legal concepts could be significantly helpful for "expanded" fair use of copyrighted material for classroom, scholarly and research purposes.

Harry N. Rosenfield
September, 1979

Modernized Fair Use Code

Sigmund Timberg's essay suggests several points of departure for the exploration of fair use issues. The *Laocöon shortfall* in the title is his notion that legal theory has datably lagged behind aesthetic theory—in particular, Lessing's insight that different types of art employ means of expression that are irreducibly different. Yet statutory law and numerous case decisions seem to remain under the sway of conceptions deriving from early forms of literary expression, such as the novel or essay.

Among the most important suggestions in this essay is a modernized fair use code sensitive both to the aesthetics of the new media and to the requirements of the First Amendment. A series of questions is proposed as a substitute for the wrongly canonical criteria of Section 107. The questions would, among other things, identify classes of users and their purposes with more discrimination. They would also separate the issue of the right to quote from the issue of payment.

Although proposing a revised fair use statute, the author believes that mere legislation will not effect an understanding between the conflicting groups, who must work out practical resolutions in nonadversarial discussions.

23

A MODERNIZED FAIR USE CODE FOR VISUAL, AUDITORY, AND AUDIOVISUAL COPYRIGHTS: ECONOMIC CONTEXT, LEGAL ISSUES, AND THE LAOCÖON SHORTFALL

SIGMUND TIMBERG

1. THE ECONOMIC, HISTORICAL, AND LEGAL FRAMEWORK OF FAIR USE

The basic legal focus of this book is on the extent to which the "fair use" defense will protect researchers, teachers, and librarians (and their institutions) from copyright infringement proceedings when they use copyrighted literary, visual, audio, or audiovisual materials in carrying on their work. But this question cannot be answered unless one examines the broader economic, historical, technical, and legal context in which the copyrighted work was created, and the specific use to which the copyrighted work will be put.

The beginning of wisdom in this area is recognition that the copyright concept is not a unitary phenomenon, but a bundle of separate economic interests and specific individual rights, each of which is responsive to revolutionary technological developments in the field of communications and each of which has given rise to large industries in the educational and entertainment sectors of our economy. These technologies, and the industries they have created, have made completely obsolete the concept of copyright that was in the minds of the Founding Fathers when they provided for a federal copyright law in the Constitution. Likewise, Congressional efforts to adapt the Copyright Code to new economic, social, and technical needs have consistently lagged far behind the problems created by the new communication technologies and the industries they have engendered. Thus, the

Copyright Revision Law of 1909 was not amended until 1976, although the sixty-seven years intervening had seen the advent of the silent motion picture, Tin Pan Alley, radio, the sound motion picture, television, videotape, the juke box, cable TV, photocopying, microfilm, and other large industries.

The courts of this country have made a significant contribution to filling some gaps in the law of the use of literary copyright, but their approach has been necessarily selective and leisurely. In any event, the court decisions dealing with literary copyright are inadequate as guidelines for the researcher, teacher, or librarian who is bewildered and feels menaced by the application of copyright law to audiovisual materials, where there is a dearth of relevant court decisions. Hence the occasion and the need for this book.

The divisibility of the copyright concept into a bundle of specific economic interests and legal rights may not have been apparent to the authors of Article I, Section 8 of the Constitution, which gave Congress the power "to Promote the Progress of Science and useful Arts, by securing for limited Times to Authors and Inventors the exclusive Right to their respective Writings and Discoveries." The first federal Copyright Law of May 11, 1790, provided protection for only books, maps, and charts—the two latter could, by some judicial departure from the literal, be classified as "writings." But Congress added musical compositions to the list of works protected by copyright in 1831, dramatic performances in 1856, and photographs in 1865, thereby stretching the definition of *writings* still further and enlarging the beneficiaries of the copyright system to include song writers, playwrights, and photographers.

When Congress adopted the Copyright Revision Law of 1909, the burning issue was the recent emergence of the phonograph and record industry, for whose benefit Congress enacted a unique provision authorizing a compulsory license for the sound recording of copyrighted musical compositions. The inadequacy of literary copyright law to cope with a newer auditory medium of communication is well illustrated by the way in which the federal courts have clumsily attempted to cope with the problem of whether the mechanical reproduction of records and their subsequent sale and distribution constituted the "copying" or "publication" of the records. Some courts held that reproduction of a record did not constitute "copying," with the consequence that the copyright owner could not hold a reproducer of the record liable for infringement.[1] Other courts took the view that the distribution and sale of phonograph records was a "publication," with the consequence that the copyright owner lost whatever rights he had under the common law of copyrights, which protects only unpublished works.[2] The dispute was finally settled in a well-reasoned opinion by District Judge Gurfein in *Rosette* v. *Rainbo Record*, which was affirmed by the Second Circuit.[3]

Judge Gurfein's resolution of this confused area was a decision that the making and sale of a phonograph record was neither a "copying" nor a "publication," thereby preserving the common law rights of the copyright owner.[4] He also held that those common law rights could be lost (at least temporarily) unless the copyright owner filed a notice of use as required by the Federal Copyright Act. Not until 1972 did Congress provide copyright protection for the records themselves, with a court confirming that sound recording firms meet the constitutional requirement of authorship.[5]

In 1954, the Supreme Court, by another exercise of semantic tolerance, held that pictorial, graphic, or sculptured works, even where employed in a design of a useful article, were an appropriate subject for copyright protection,[6] thereby recognizing that there was no distinction between the fine and the useful arts.

The demise of the Gutenberg Era was also signalized by the advent of the radio and TV broadcasting industries, with their insatiable demand for the live performances of audio and audiovisual works, including silent and sound pictures, musical works, background music and, to a lesser extent, pantomime and choreographic works. The end of the Gutenberg Era has also witnessed a trend, on the part of both the creators and the users of copyrighted works, toward forming increasingly large enterprises, some of which have become parts of large industrial conglomerates. The licensing of performing rights in American songs is now handled by a large cooperative, the American Society of Composers, Authors, and Publishers—with 16,000 composer and author and 6,000 music publisher members, with a repertory of three million compositions—and by Broadcast Music, Inc., an affiliate of the broadcasting industry, with one million compositions in its repertory.[8] ASCAP and BMI are currently locked in antitrust litigation with the CBS television network, which is part of an industrial complex that owns television stations in five major cities and radio stations in fourteen major cities, produces TV programs for some 200 local TV stations, and owns CBS Records, reputedly the largest manufacturer and seller of records and tapes in the world.[9]

The degree of concentration in the various media industries, all of which are affected by copyright, is extremely high. CBS, together with the two other large networks, ABC and NBC, accounts for 69 percent of total television revenues; the three have affiliations with 85 percent of United States television stations. In 1976, Warner Communications (also heavily involved in motion picture films) and CBS earned 65 percent of all United States record and tape revenues. In 1976, Warner, United Artists, and Twentieth Century Fox grossed 48 percent of the total United States film revenues; in 1975, Universal, Twentieth Century Fox and Columbia accounted for 52 percent of total film revenues. In any one year, six media companies, ABC, CBS, NBC, Warner, and any two other film companies will hold more than 50 percent of the nonprint media markets.[10] Nor is this economic concentration limited to the electronic media. Don Glassman, author of a crisp and informative commentary on the Copyright Act of 1976, focused somewhat more on literary than on audiovisual copyright, depicts similar concentration trends in book publishing.[11]

Such trends toward concentration on the part of both the creators and distributors of copyrighted materials and of the copyright users have produced a decline in the immediacy of contact and personal relationship between individual copyright creators and users that characterized an earlier America. And as the lawyers representing copyright owners focus on their relationships with broadcasters, motion picture exhibitors, and the other users who account for most of their revenues, they may tend to be somewhat indifferent to the needs and the financial position of the scholarly community, which accounts for a relatively small part of the royalty revenues accruing to copyright owners.

2. AUDIOVISUAL MATERIALS: THE COPYRIGHT AS A BUNDLE OF LEGAL RIGHTS

The relevant law of copyright only further complicates an already complicated picture. One needs, first, some explanation about the bundle of legal rights that enter into the copyright package, and the significance of those rights in connection with visual, auditory, and audiovisual technologies. The copyright owner has the exclusive right to reproduce, adapt, publish, perform, and display the copyrighted work himself, or to subdivide, sell, or license any such right, either *in toto* or for any field of commercial use he pleases.

The basic right to copy or reproduce a musical composition is known as the *recording right*, and is the legal foundation stone of the record, phonograph, and juke-box industries. Where copyrighted music is part of a sound motion picture, this right is referred to as a *synchronization right*. Synchronization rights are also important where TV, videotape, or like audiovisual works are created which involve the use of prior copyrighted music.

Whenever audiovisual works are performed for profit, the copyright owner is entitled to compensation for his right of "public performance." This right is commercially very important to the song publishing, motion picture, radio, and TV production industries and to the radio and TV broadcasting industry. The performing rights relevant to these industries are called *small* performing rights. This distinguishes them from *grand* or so-called *dramatic* performing rights, which relate to the performance of plays, operas, musical comedies, and other works to audiences in theaters and opera houses.

The right to adapt existing copyrighted material for a new derivative work (*e.g.*, a translation of a literary work, an arrangement of a musical work, the motion picture adaptation of a novel) is related to the right to reproduce and copy. It applies to any audiovisualization or sound recording of a copyrighted work, and therefore is important for those industries, referred to in the preceding paragraph, that make use of public performance rights.

The right to publish or distribute a copyrighted work is an old and important one. It relates to the general subject of this book when the educator or librarian goes beyond his basic teaching and research functions and embarks on the commercial distribution of literary or audiovisual materials embodying parts of an existing copyrighted work. In thus embarking on commercial distribution, he may interfere with the copyright owner's legally protected right to undertake such distribution himself or to be compensated for it.

The author's right to public display of his copyrighted work is a right conferred for the first time by the 1976 Copyright Revision Act, which went into effect on January 1, 1978, and is therefore currently indeterminate in scope. To *publicly display* a work means to show a copy of it publicly, "either directly or by means of a film, slide, television image, or any other device or process." Phono records are almost the only kind of copyrighted work that cannot be publicly displayed. The *display right* applies to the projection of images from a motion picture or other audiovisual work; it is differentiated from the *performing right* for such works in that the latter requires the showing of images in sequence, whereas a display right is limited to the individual images of the audiovisual work.

3. FAIR USE: THE PROBLEM FOR THE RESEARCHER, TEACHER, OR LIBRARIAN

A researcher, educator, or librarian, in order to understand the specific "fair use" situation confronting him, must first identify the economic interests and the specific legal rights of the copyright owner that his contemplated use of copyrighted material may affect or infringe. Next he must consider the nature and relative amount of his proposed use, and how much such proposed use would adversely affect the potential market or value of the copyrighted materials, the copyright owner's economic interests, and the copyright owner's general licensing and distribution program. Finally, he must reckon on the normal tendency of the owners of intellectual property rights to secure the maximum financial return from them.

As a matter of law, the "fair use" doctrine permits the researcher, teacher, and librarian to bring up certain countervailing considerations: that the proposed use of the copyrighted material is in the public interest; that the use is for nonprofit educational rather than commercial purposes (if this be the case); that the nature and relative amount of the use does not substantially impair the economic interests and legal rights of the copyright owner; and that the copyright owner's financial return is subordinate to the demands of the public interest.

The mix of relevant factors discussed in the last two paragraphs as needing to be considered in handling the "fair use" situation would seem to involve the hapless researcher, teacher, and librarian in a large number of individual case assessments, with no general rules to guide him. What is the *public interest* in the concrete situation where he is involved? Are there several public interests? Who is to mediate the inevitable differences between the copyright owner and copyright user in assessing the relevant factors that enter into the determination of "fair use?"

How can the few court decisions on "fair use," almost all of which concern the printed materials of the Gutenberg Age, be applied to that vastly different complex of technologies, economic interests, and individual rights that are involved in the creation, protection and use of visual, audio, and audiovisual materials of the Electronic Age? Are the four criteria of Section 107—purportedly a restatement of the common law of fair use long accepted by the courts[12]—appropriate to the media forms that dominate the twentieth-century education and entertainment world? They are

1. The purpose and character of the use, including whether it is commercial or for nonprofit educational purposes;
2. The nature of the copyrighted work;
3. The amount and substantiality of the portion used in relation to the copyrighted work as a whole;
4. The effect of the use upon the potential market or value of the copyrighted work.

In answering the broad questions raised in the preceding paragraph, let us look first at what should be the most important of the four criteria of Section 107, the nature of the copyrighted work.

4. THE NATURE OF THE COPYRIGHTED WORK

The principles of copyright and fair use law were originally developed during the Gutenberg Era, when print was the basic medium employed to create and express ideas, emotions, and aesthetic values. In applying these principles to the twentieth-century Electronic Age, with its proliferation of visual, audio, and audiovisual media, the key is the nature of the medium employed. It is necessary to have a concept of the space-time coordinates within which the author or creator of the copyrighted work manipulates the medium, and within which the viewing and listening audience sees and hears the copyrighted work. Only after this is done, can one effectively apply, to the protection and use of the copyrighted work, the principles expressed in the copyright law and the social policies implicit in the Copyright Clause of the Constitution and the First Amendment.

An excellent starting point for the analysis of the space-time limitations of the individual media of creative expression and communication is *Laocöon*, a revolutionary work on aesthetics written in 1766 by the German philosopher, Gotthold Ephraim Lessing, himself an outstanding dramatist, dramatic critic, and student of Greek literature and sculpture. This work established the principle that each art is limited by the nature of the medium in which the artist works, and that these limitations in turn condition the descriptive, aesthetic, and emotional effects of the artist's work on its viewers and readers. More specifically, *Laocöon* made that most seminal of aesthetic distinctions, that between the spatial (plastic) arts and the temporal arts (poetry and music). *Laocöon*, that great masterpiece of Hellenistic sculpture showing the agonized looks and stretched sinews of the high priest of Troy and his two sons enveloped in the coils of a monster serpent, was the symbol of the utmost that a spatial work could accomplish by way of showing emotion and movement, because it was limited to a single moment of time.[13]

The law of copyright and fair use has been relatively serviceable in dealing with the protection and uses of literary materials, both creative and critical, which in Lessing's time consisted mainly of epics, romances, novels, plays, and more extended poetic and prose works. But fair use law and practice have not been able to strike a balance between the protection and the fair use of audiovisual materials or of very short literary works. This inadequacy is due to the slowness of the law in casting off its verbal and literary moorings and consequently failing to adapt to the physical and artistic requirements of the nonverbal and nonliterary media. This inability will be referred to hereafter as the *Laocöon shortfall*.

We can see the law's defective understanding and the resultant litigation in several of the cases discussed in this volume. Consider the following:

1. Carl Belz's history of rock music that had to be rewritten because the owners of the copyright on rock songs asked such high fees for permission to use a body of those songs that the cost of publishing the history would have been prohibitive (discussed in Chapter 3).

2. The situation involved in *Time, Inc.* v. *Bernard Geis Associates*,[14] where *Life* Magazine sued a historian for copying frames of the Zapruder films of the John F. Kennedy assassination. In this case, the Court, without specifically invoking the First Amendment, upheld the defendant's right to copy the frames on the ground of the "public interest in having the fullest information available on the murder of President Kennedy."

3. The photographs of the Mylai massacres, of which Professor Nimmer has said:

> Consider the photographs of the My Lai massacre. Here is an instance where the visual impact of a graphic work made a unique contribution to an enlightened democratic dialogue. No amount of words describing the "idea" of the massacre could substitute for the public insight gained through the photographs. The photographic expression, not merely the idea, became essential if the public was to fully understand what occurred in that tragic episode. It would be intolerable if the public's comprehension of the full meaning of My Lai could be censored by the copyright owner of the photographs.[15]

4. The request of scholars Stott and Sproule to reproduce copyrighted advertisements in their published studies. In both cases, copyright holders refused permission (see Chapter 5).

5. The recent New Hampshire case of *Keep Thomson Governor Committee* v. *Citizens for Gallen Committee*,[16] decided by the federal district court on October 2, 1978. There the court held that a contender for political office could, on First Amendment grounds, copy one-quarter of his opponent's copyrighted song (see Harry Rosenfield's discussion in Chapter 22).

6. *Triangle Publications, Inc.* v. *Knight-Ridder Newspapers, Inc.*,[17] where the Court refused to enjoin a newspaper publisher from using the copyrighted cover page of the plaintiff's television program guide as part of a television commercial advertising the newspaper publisher's competing TV guide (see Chapters 21 and 22 by Harriet Oler and Harry Rosenfield for detailed accounts).

Were the decisions reached in these six cases by the courts or the copyright owners correct applications of "fair use" principles? Were they sustainable under First Amendment principles? First, let us turn to the fair use problem.

5. THE INAPPLICABILITY OF THE "SUBSTANTIAL USE" CRITERION OF "FAIR USE" TO SHORT, OR INSTANTANEOUSLY PRODUCED OR PERFORMED, PRINTED OR VISUAL WORKS

All six cases just listed have one feature in common—they involve works of art that are capable of being created by the author or artist, and/or performed, and/or viewed or heard by the critic or by the seeing or listening audience, either instantaneously or in a very short span of time.[18] The third, or "substantiality of use," criterion of fair use is "the amount and substantiality of the portion used in relation to the copyrighted work as a whole." This criterion can be easily met by the student of the Homeric epic, or the literary critic reviewing Kazantakis,

John Updike, and Isaac Bashevis Singer; in order to give the flavor of their taste and style, the scholar and critic must of necessity replicate snippets of their works of art. But, by judicial definition, each individual "frame" of the Kennedy assassination, each photo of the Mylai massacre, each lyric of the rock history, each pictorial reproduction of Buffet and Magritte in an art book or art history, is a "work of art." They are aesthetic wholes, incapable of any excerpting or fragmentation. The member of the public interested in information about the Kennedy assassination or the Mylai massacre, the music or art historian, and the critic of seventeen-syllable Japanese haiku must either have access to the entire work or do without it. For copyrighted photographs, prints, paintings, sculptures, and motion picture frames, the "substantiality of use" criterion of fair use appears inapplicable.

6. THE QUESTIONABLE APPLICABILITY OF THE "COMMERCIAL VERSUS EDUCATIONAL" PURPOSE CRITERION OF FAIR USE TO ACADEMIA

Possibly the most frequently applied of the fair use criteria is that the contemplated use is for an educational rather than a commercial purpose. Later in this paper, I develop the thought that the courts' reluctance to apply First Amendment or fair use defenses in specific situations involving mixed educational and commercial purposes does not necessarily reflect a doubt as to the legal right of the alleged infringer to use the work. This reluctance may instead reflect a sense of the unfairness in allowing him to use the work without paying compensation to its creator. For the time being, it is sufficient to note that the court decisions raise grave doubts as to the relevance of the "educational versus commercial" dichotomy as a means of deciding fair use issues.[19]

7. THE INAPPLICABILITY, IN THE CASE OF PHOTOGRAPHS, CARTOONS, AND OTHER VISUAL MATERIALS, OF THE "IDEA-EXPRESSION" DICHOTOMY TO FIRST AMENDMENT DEFENSES AND OF THE "VISUAL IMAGE-TOTAL CONTEXT" DICHOTOMY TO FAIR USE DEFENSES

The conventional way of separating the use of material that is entitled to copyright protection from use which may not be so protected because of First Amendment considerations is to differentiate the "idea," which is noncopyrightable, from its "expression," which may be copyrighted. The basic difficulty with the "idea-expression" dichotomy is that although "ideas" are the building materials of the verbal medium in which authors create literary works, they may be irrelevant to the visual media in which painters and cartoonists create visual works (see Chapter 20). Lessing, quite correctly, had a negative attitude toward critics who made of painting "a silent poem without considering in what measure [it] can express general concepts and not at the same time depart from [its] vocation and become a freakish kind of writing."[20]

One school of thought, to be sure, holds that the expression of "ideas" is outside the field not only of the visual arts but of all the arts; "ideas" belong to the domain of philosophy and related disciplines, rather than to the arts.[21] Another strongly held view asserts that, for the literary and visual arts alike, the creative process is one and the same with the expressive process; there is an identity between "what the artist expresses and what he creates."[22] Therefore, the role of ideas even in the verbal arts is a matter of debate.

Without laboring the issue further, Lessing's insight should be adopted; it should be recognized that the "idea-expression" dichotomy is not an appropriate vehicle "to accommodate the competing interests of copyright and the First Amendment." As Professor Nimmer has said of the Mylai massacre photographs: "No amount of words describing the 'idea' of the massacre could substitute for the public insight gained through the photographs."

8. THE RELATIVE STRENGTH OF THE FIRST AMENDMENT AND FAIR USE DEFENSE

As will be seen later, the current vitality and appeal to the copyright bar of the First Amendment defense to charges of copyright infringement is unmistakable. This writer agrees with the general thrust of Harry Rosenfield's acute and intensive analysis of the First Amendment. The difference is largely one of focus, with this author suggesting solutions to the specific problems of copyright and fair use, rather than directing attention to the more Draconian ultimate solution to the general problem of fair use that Mr. Rosenfield believes hangs, like Damocles' sword, over the heads of those who would resist First Amendment imperatives.

In certain areas, such as those of political expression and of the access of the public to newsworthy information, First Amendment considerations predominate, and fair use considerations are superfluous. This is the area covered by four of the six cases discussed in Section 4 of this chapter—*Bernard Geis Associates*, Mylai, *Citizens for Gallen Committee*, *Triangle Publications*. In these cases, the substantiality of use made of the copyrighted material, whether it be the use by a political opponent of 25 percent of a copyrighted song, the use in a film of parts of the music played in an ethnic parade, the use made of 100 percent of the single Zapruder "frames" of the Kennedy assassination, or the use of 100 percent of a competitor's copyrighted advertisement, was likewise immaterial.

Another case illustrative of the symbiotic relationship between First Amendment and "fair use" considerations is *Walt Disney Productions v. Air Pirates*,[23] a case recently decided by the Ninth Circuit. The defendants in this case were the publishers of two cartoon magazines, *Air Pirates Funnies*, which purported to paraody the Walt Disney cartoons. In the Circuit Court's view, however:

> . . . the themes of defendants' publications differ markedly from those of Disney. While Disney sought only to foster "an image of innocent delightfulness," defendants supposedly sought to convey an allegorical message of significance. Put politely by one commentator, the "Air Pirates" was an "underground" comic book which had placed several well-known Disney cartoon characters in incongruous settings where they engaged in activities clearly antithetical to the accepted Mickey Mouse world of scrubbed faces, bright smiles and happy endings." It centered around "a rather bawdy depiction of the Disney characters as active members of a free thinking, promiscuous, drug ingesting counterculture" (p. 753).

In its opinion, the Ninth Circuit rejected the First Amendment defense, relying on the "idea-expression" dichotomy endorsed by the legal precedents but criticized earlier in this chapter (see Section 7).

The court held, and the Air Pirates defendants did not contend otherwise, that ". . . copying a comic book character's graphic image constitutes copying to an extent sufficient to justify a finding of infringement" (p. 756). Since the infringement was purportedly "a parody of Disney's cartoons," the court turned to the question whether the infringement should be excused through the application of the fair use defense.

Following the premise that fair use involved substantial copying, the court further noted that in the case before it, "verbatim" or "near-verbatim" copying precluded resort to the fair use defense. It is symptomatic of the error inherent in applying literary concepts to the copying of visual images that the court should be referring to the copying of a Walt Disney cartoon as one that might conceivably entail "verbatim" or "near-verbatim" copying. But the court concluded that, whether one defined a copyrighted work as a visual image or as a "total concept and feel,"

> . . . defendants took more than is allowed even under the *Berlin* test as applied to both the conceptual and physical aspects of the characters. In

evaluating how much of a taking was necessary to recall or conjure up the original, it is first important to recognize that given the widespread public recognition of the major characters involved here, such as Mickey Mouse and Donald Duck (see e.g., R. 191–193), in comparison with other characters very little would have been necessary to place Mickey Mouse and his image in the minds of the readers. Second, when the medium involved is a comic book, a recognizable caricature is not difficult to draw, so that an alternative that involves less copying is more likely to be available than if a speech, for instance, is parodied. Also significant is the fact that the essence of this parody did not focus on how the characters looked, but rather parodied their personalities, their wholesomeness and their innocence.[15] [Footnote omitted.] Thus arguably defendants' copying could have been justified as necessary more easily if they had paralleled closely (with a few significant twists) Disney characters and their actions in a manner that conjured up the particular elements of the innocence of the characters that were to be satirized (pp. 757–58).

This effort to substitute, for the "quantitative substantiality" criterion of fair use, what may be called a "qualitative substantiality" standard, is tantamount to judicial censorship of the parodist.[24] There are styles of parody, caricature, and satire that depend for their effectiveness (not for their mere recognizability) on maximum adherence to the original. For a court to impose constraints on cartoonists and parodists to copy only so much as is "necessary to recall or conjure up the original" would cripple their effectiveness and in so doing would impair the exercise of First Amendment rights. One must therefore conclude that the "qualitative substantiality" principle endorsed by the court is still another example of a carryover from the law of literary copyright that cannot rationally be applied to the visual arts. Such a principle would cripple the creative efforts not only of cartoonists, satirists, and parodists, but of sociological and political critics who, under First Amendment principles, should be allowed to present their messages as effectively as the nature of their talents and resources permit.

9. THE CASE FOR A NEW "FAIR USE" STANDARD RESPONSIVE TO THE COPYRIGHT CLAUSE OF THE CONSTITUTION

This paper has attempted to find a satisfactory accommodation between the right of the owner of a copyrighted visual, auditory, or audiovisual work to obtain a proper financial reward from the work, on the one hand, and the right of educators, historians, scientists, and social and political critics to use the work in their own research, teaching, and writing, on the other. We have seen that the "fair use" standard has failed to achieve such an accommodation. For that standard has failed to take account of how the visual, auditory, and audiovisual media differ from the literary media that have thus far generated the judicial decisions on fair use. Further, two of the three other tests of fair use—the "substantiality of the copying" and the "commercial-educational" dichotomy—do not function well for nonliterary media. We have also seen that the First Amendment defense is determinative only where the use made is political, or informational in a political context; that defense does not cover the needs of the educational community in the visual, auditory, or audiovisual fields of expression.

Given the imperfections of the current law of "fair use" and the limited reach of the First Amendment, it is submitted that the fairest and most satisfactory approach to the problem is the one inherent in the Copyright Clause of the Constitution, which states that the purpose of the copyright system is to "Promote the Progress of Science and useful Arts." As stated in *Mazer* v. *Stein*,[25] the economic philosophy underlying the Copyright Clause

> . . . is the conviction that encouragement of individual effort by personal gain is the best way to advance the public welfare through the talents of authors and inventors in "Science and useful Arts."

However, the court made the further comment:

> The copyright law, like the patent statutes, makes reward to the owner a secondary consideration.[26]

Thus, to say that copyright owners are generally entitled to a reward for their labors does not mean that they are entitled to the kind of reward that would frustrate the constitutional purpose to promote the progress of science and the useful arts. As stated in *Berlin* v. *E.C. Publications, Inc.*:

> . . . courts in passing upon particular claims of infringement must occasionally subordinate the copyright holder's interest in a maximum financial return to the greater public interest in the development of art, science and industry.[27]

Nor can reward to the copyright owner be allowed to dominate the equally important objectives served by the First Amendment. Nowhere does this more clearly appear than in *Triangle*, where the court relied heavily upon the Supreme Court's decision in *Bates* v. *Arizona*,[28] stressing the importance of "advertising to the dissemination of ideas in a free society." The *Triangle* court also cited *Mazer* v. *Stein*,[29] for the proposition that "the copyright law, like the patent statutes, makes reward to the owner a secondary consideration" to advancing the public welfare in science and useful arts. Although the court based its decision to deny an injunction against comparative advertising primarily on First Amendment grounds, it also said:

> By denying the requested injunction (against copying) herein, this court cannot envision that the creators of the future will be deterred in any way from investing their efforts in productions beneficial to society as a whole. In fact,

this order should, if anything, provide a stimulus for the creation of products which their progenitors believe to be better than the products currently on the market.

Comparative advertising, as practiced by defendant in the case sub judice, is in harmony with the fundamental objectives of free speech and free enterprise in a free society (p. 884).

The *Triangle* court's reminder that the copyright owner and copyright user function in a free enterprise system is also a reminder that the advancement and development of art, science, and industry contemplated under the Copyright Clause require not only the unhindered utilization of works of art, but also compensation to the creators and promoters of such works. This is the serious deficiency in the First Amendment approach to the problem—it designates certain classes of users as entitled to use the copyrighted works to serve the purposes of "free speech in a free system," but makes no financial provision for the copyright owner and promoter whose work is thus appropriated, even where the user is financially able and should feel morally obligated to pay for the use.

10. A PROPOSED NEW FAIR USE STANDARD

The preceding sections of this essay have demonstrated the unworkability of the four-point "fair use" formula developed at the common law and currently embodied in Section 107 of the 1976 Copyright Revision Act. It is therefore recommended that consideration be given to adopting, in lieu of the present unworkable standard, a new formula adapted to visual, audio, audiovisual, and very short literary works. It would pose the following questions:

I. Does the copier fall within the class of persons engaged in the advancement of the sciences, arts, and industry, or in the dissemination and promotion of information and ideas deserving First Amendment protection? If the answer to this question is yes——

II. Is the nature and amount of the copying consistent with a genuine purpose to advance the sciences, arts, and industry, or to disseminate information and ideas deserving of First Amendment protection, rather than a plagiarizing purpose? If the answer is yes, then the copier has a "fair use" defense against being enjoined from such copying, and the only remaining question is whether he should pay royalties for the copying.

III. Will the use made by the copier of the copyrighted material adversely affect the potential market or value of the copyrighted work? If the answer is yes——

IV. Is the use made of the copyrighted materials such as will result in substantial profits to the copier, and thereby equitably entitle the copyright owner to compensation for such use? If the answer is yes, then appropriate provision should be made for the payment of copyright royalties. If the answer is no, the user should be permitted to copy the copyrighted material royalty-free.

The four-point "fair use" formula just outlined is more consistent than Section 107 of the new Copyright Code with the purpose of the Copyright Clause and the First Amendment of the Constitution—to promote the development of art, science, and industry, to reward copyright creators and promoters by providing them with a financial stimulus, and to promote the dissemination of information and ideas germane to the political and social functioning of our free society.

The modernized "fair use" formula here suggested differs from the currently accepted common law standard and from Section 107 of the 1976 Copyright Revision Act in two important respects: First, it separates the issue whether the court should enjoin a copier from continuing an alleged infringement from the issue whether the court should order the copier to compensate the copyright owner for his use of the copyrighted material. In thus separating the question of injunctive relief from that of compensation for the use of copyrights, the proposed new standard comes down in favor of the proposition that no copyright user is necessarily entitled to a free ride on the copyright system. Moreover, to determine whether compensation is owing the copyright owner for the copier's infringing use, only two questions need be asked—will the infringing use adversely affect the potential market or value of the copyrighted work (point III); will the use of the copyrighted material result in substantial profits to the copier (point IV)?

As noted earlier, the copyright grant should be so used as to promote both the progress of science, art, and industry and the dissemination of information and expression of political thought protected by the First Amendment. It is therefore appropriate that the only questions to be asked in determining whether an injunction should be issued against a copier is whether the copier is a member of a group which engages in, and whether the copier is in fact engaged in the advancement of the sciences, arts, and industry or in the dissemination of information and ideas deserving of First Amendment protection (points I and II).

This new and simplified approach represents a complete change from the judicial philosophy expressed in the leading opinions of the nineteenth century.[30] To appreciate the nature and significance of this change involves recourse to some judicial history, to which we now turn.

The courts, until the 1930s, seem to have been impervious even to the constitutional purpose of the copyright grant to promote the advancement of science, art, and industry, much less the dictates of the First Amendment. The key issues on which the nineteenth-century cases focused have been whether the copying was verbatim, whether the use made of the copyrighted material was substantial, whether the copier had misappropriated the plaintiff's property in the copyrighted artifact and turned it to his own commercial advantage, and whether, as stated by Justice Story in *Folsom* v. *Marsh*, "the value of the original is sensibly diminished or the labors of the original author are substantially appropriated".[31] No one reading the one hundred pages setting forth the briefs and the Supreme Court opinion in *Wheaton v. Peters*,[32] which upheld the copyrightability of reported decisions of the Supreme Court, would ever guess that the First Amendment existed. Nor would a reader of Justice Story's long and scholarly opinion in *Folsom v. Marsh*, upholding the copyrightability of George Washington's letters "copied verbatim and literatim" from the eleven volumes of Jared Sparks' collection of Washington's correspondence (a number of which were official documents) have any notion that a copyright infringement proceeding had any other purpose than to vindicate the property rights and the private equities of the copyright owner. The contested items included (see *Folsom v. Marsh*, 2 Story, 104–105):

> Letters addressed by Washington, as commander-in-chief, to the President of Congress.
>
> Official letters to governors of States and speakers of legislative bodies.
>
> Circular letters.
>
> General orders.
>
> Communications (official) as President to his Cabinet.
>
> Letter accepting the command of the army, on our expected war with France.

Justice Story conceded that

> a reviewer may fairly cite largely from the original work, if his design be really and truly to use the passages for the purposes of fair and reasonable criticism (p. 344).

However, he sharply distinguished the critic's function from that of the historian or biographer, who copied from these eleven volumes not for the purpose of writing a literary review but for the purpose of conveying information to the general public. In Justice Story's words, if the copier

> cites the most important parts of the work, with a view, not to criticise, but to supersede the use of the original work, and substitute the review for it, such a use will be deemed in law a piracy (pp. 344–45).

As is noted by Morris Schnapper in a forthcoming book, *Public Trust, Public Property and Private Property*, Jared Sparks and Justice Story's deceased colleague, the late Chief Justice Marshall, were in effect the literary executors of George Washington's correspondence (the great Chief Justice had written a five-volume biography of George Washington), Jared Sparks' eleven-volume collection (totaling over six thousand pages) constituted the sole practicable source for George Washington's correspondence, yet researchers in the field of American history and biography were precluded from access to, and use of, this treasure trove of data unless they obtained the publisher's consent. Justice Story further cut the ground out from under American historians and biographers by pointing out that Franklin, John Jay, Jefferson, Madison, and other distinguished statesmen held exclusive copyrights in their correspondence and publications, which after their death their literary executors could exercise (pp. 346–47). He recognized that such letters might have been written "upon interesting political and other occasions" (p. 346). He conceded as well that the perpetual injunction he felt constrained to issue enjoining the defendants from publishing or selling any copies of the infringing work "may interfere, in some measure, with the very meritorious labors of the defendants, in their great undertaking of a series of works adapted to school libraries" (p. 349). But, although he hoped "that some means may be found, to produce an amicable settlement of this unhappy controversy," his obligation to issue the injunction was clear: ". . . a judge is entitled in this case, as in others, only to know and to act upon his duty" (p. 349). It is pertinent to note here, as does Mr. Schnapper, that George Washington in 1782, speaking as Commander-in-Chief of the Continental Army, had written a would-be historian of the American Revolution that he considered his documents "a species of public property, sacred in my hands," to which he would be glad to provide access. However, they had to remain secret "until Congress shall . . . say it is proper for the Servants of the public to let them be examined." Jared Sparks, whose publication of these letters Justice Story had actively promoted, stated in a letter to Story (March 26, 1826) that "Washington's public letters and papers are the property of the nation."

More recently the courts in fair use cases have paid some attention to not only the amount, but the nature of the use of the copyrighted material made by the copier, to determine whether such use would further the aims of the copyright clause of the Constitution. They have, however, been conspicuously silent about the rights of the press and other media to use copyrighted material in disseminating news and information to the general public, or about the public's right to information concerning the subjects covered in the copyrighted material. Section 107 of the Copyright Revision Act of 1976, which purports to restate the common law of "fair use," does not refer to the First Amendment even by implication. In fact, not until 1970, in Judge Lasker's opinion in *Marvin Worth Products* v. *Superior Films Corp.*,[33] was a "fair use" formula put forth that included "the public interest in the free dissemination of information:"

(1) Was there a substantial taking, qualitatively or quantitatively? (2) If there

was such a taking, did the taking materially reduce the demand for the original copyrighted property? (3) . . . [D]oes the distribution of the material serve the public interest in the free dissemination of information? And (4) does the preparation of the material require the use of prior materials dealing with the same subject matter?

Judge Lasker's formula, which he repeated in the leading case of *Wainwright & Co.* v. *Wall Street Transcript Corp.*,[34] makes the First Amendment an integral part of the "fair use" standard. It is therefore to be preferred to the existing Section 107 common law standard, which does not refer to the First Amendment even by implication and regards the Amendment merely as an alternative ground for deciding copyright infringement cases.

With this historical background behind us, a few brief comments are in order as to the four component parts of the modernized constitutionally oriented "fair use" standard proposed in this chapter.

I. Is the user one of the intended beneficiaries of the fair use section of the copyright clause and the First Amendment?

In the Wall Street Transcript case the court said:

The classic instances in which courts have permitted authors to use excerpts from a copyrighted work without the consent of the copyright owner are those of literary criticism and parody of the copyrighted work, history and biography.

However, Professor Alan Latman has pointed out that the fair use principle has also been applied to the use of copyrighted information in the fields of science, law, and medicine.[35] For all these fields, accordingly, researchers and teachers who make fair use of copyrighted literary materials should be protected from copyright infringement proceedings. There should be no objection to extending similar protection to teachers and researchers involved in the visual, auditory, and audiovisual fields, such as those concerned with motion picture, radio, and TV production, popular culture, sociology, anthropology, or aesthetic theory.

II. Is the purpose of the user to advance the development of art, science, or industry or promote First Amendment objectives?

This test merely restates the paramount purposes underlying the copyright grant, with considerations of private reward to the copyright owner duly subordinated to the public interest expressed in the Copyright Clause and the First Amendment.

III. Will the use of the copyrighted work by the copier adversely affect the market or potential value of the copied work?

This test is identical with the fourth criterion of the present fair use doctrine, as laid down in Section 107 of the Copyright Code Revision and is as justified for visual, auditory, and audiovisual works as it is for literary works.[36] However, the effect on the market value of the copyrighted work is frequently perceived only in terms of the inroads on the market for the copyrighted work produced by the user's competitive biography, work of fiction, etc. In many cases, consideration is not given to the fact that certain public uses of copyrighted material, such as the broadcast of a popular song or lyric, frequently serve to create increased exposure and consumer demand for the material. This seems to have been the case in the situation discussed in Chapter 3, where the rock music publishers seemingly missed the opportunity to promote their works as having been singled out for special mention in a definitive history of rock music. (The implications of this case history will be discussed in greater detail shortly.)

IV. Is the use by the copier of the copyrighted material sufficiently profitable to the copier to justify his compensating the copyright owner for that use?

The copyright monopoly should not be used to frustrate the constitutional purpose for which it was granted. Therefore, if the teacher or researcher needs to use the copyrighted material for the purpose of carrying on his work and cannot afford to pay for it, he ought, consistently with the purpose of the Copyright Clause, to be allowed to use it gratis. On the other hand, if the use is sufficiently profitable and the copying has been quite substantial, then the copyright owner should in equity be compensated for such use. Admittedly this recommendation will sometimes be difficult to apply: How are reasonable royalties to be determined? When are they to be paid? It is to be hoped that the procedure for implementing this proposal will not involve legislation or judicial intervention, but will be based on industrywide negotiations to establish formulas that will not be onerous to the user and will be fair to the copyright owner.

Throughout this chapter, the assumption has been that both the copyright owner and the copyright user will act in their long-term best economic interests. This may not always be the case. It does not appear to be true of the rock music publishers' actions in frustrating the publication of the rock music history and in causing it to be completely rewritten.

"Fair use" in the literary copyright field originated in that leisurely institution of the Gutenberg Era known as the *book review*. How could a critic give the flavor of the style or the substance of an author's work except by quoting from illustrative portions thereof? Why, from a commercial standpoint, should any publisher object to even long quotations in a book review, since that is still the prime method of creating exposure and consumer demand for books? Can one generalize from this and say that, as a matter of business, the creator or promoter of copyrighted materials, literary, audio, or audiovisual, who gains needed commercial exposure and consequent profits through a use, should permit that use on a free or nominal basis?[37]

11. THE LEGAL VALIDATION OF THE MODERNIZED FAIR USE STANDARD IN ZACCHINI v. SCRIPPS-HOWARD BROADCASTING CO., 97 SUP. CT. 2849 (1977)

There are no cases directly involving copyrights that support the four-pronged "fair use" formula set forth in this chapter. The writer has, however, come across a recent Supreme Court case, *Zacchini* v. *Scripps-Howard Broadcasting Co.*[38] that appears fully to support the modernized standard. This case, which involved a circus performer, Zacchini, who had been shot out of the mouth of a cannon at the Geauga County Fair grounds in Ohio, did not arise in the federal court under the federal copyright law, but in the Ohio state court. The case concerned Zacchini's "right of publicity," a state-created common law right, that gave Zacchini

> "personal control over the commercial display and exploitation of his personality and the exercise of his talents." This right of "exclusive control over the publicity given to his performance" was said to be such a "valuable part of the benefit which may be attained by his talents and efforts" that it was entitled to legal protection.

Zacchini sued Scripps-Howard Broadcasting Company for violating his "right of publicity" by videotaping for a newscast his complete performance of being shot from the mouth of the cannon; the videotape and the performance consumed a total of fifteen seconds. There could be no doubt as to the "substantiality" of the appropriation; Zacchini's "entire act" had been appropriated.

What makes this case pertinent is that, as Mr. Justice White, the writer of the majority opinion, pointed out, the decision of the state of Ohio to protect Zacchini's common law "right of publicity" rested on the same economic consideration as "underlies the patent and copyrights long enforced by this Court:"

> Of course, Ohio's decision to protect petitioner's right of publicity here rests on more than a desire to compensate the performer for the time and effort invested in his act; the protection provides an economic incentive for him to make the investment required to produce a performance of interest to the public.

In stating that the same consideration underlay the state-conferred "right of publicity" and the federally granted copyright, Justice White cited from *Mazer* v. *Stein, United States* v. *Paramount Pictures*, and *Washington Publishing Co.* v. *Pearson*.[39] In the Pearson case, the Supreme Court had stated that copyrights were

> . . . intended definitely to grant valuable, enforceable rights in order to afford greater encouragement to the production of works of benefit to the public.

The issue was whether Scripps-Howard had violated the First Amendment by videotaping and showing Zacchini's performance. Zacchini complained that Scripps-Howard Broadcasting Co. had "filmed his entire act and displayed that film on television for the public to see and enjoy," which was an appropriation of his professional property.

The Ohio Supreme Court held that "Scripps-Howard [was] constitutionally privileged to include in its newscasts matters of public interest that would otherwise be protected by the right of publicity, absent an intent to injure or to appropriate for some nonprivileged purpose." It justified its position by saying that the press

> . . . must be accorded broad latitude in its choice of how much it presents of each story or incident, and of the emphasis to be given to such presentation. No fixed standard which would bar the press from reporting or depicting either an entire occurrence or an entire discrete part of a public performance can be formulated which would not unduly restrict the "breathing room" in reporting which freedom of the press requires.[40]

Justice White's decision was truly Solomonic. On the one hand, he pointed out that there was no dispute but that Zacchini's "state-law right of publicity would not serve to prevent [Scripps-Howard] from reporting the newsworthy facts about [his] act" (p. 2856). On the other hand, he said that the broadcaster's videotaping had gone well beyond its constitutional privilege. Instead of merely reporting that Zacchini was performing at the fair and describing or commenting on his act, with or without showing his picture on television, the broadcaster had gone on to "film and display [Zacchini's] entire act and displayed that film on television for the public to see and enjoy."

Since the broadcaster had broadcast Zacchini's entire act, Mr. Justice White was

> . . . quite sure that the First and Fourteenth Amendments do not immunize the media when they broadcast a performer's entire act without his consent. The Constitution no more prevents a State from requiring respondent to

> compensate petitioner for broadcasting his act on television than it would privilege respondent to film and broadcast a copyrighted dramatic work without liability to the copyright owner . . . or to film and broadcast a prize fight, . . . or a baseball game, . . . where the promoters or the participants had other plans for publicizing the event (p. 2857). [Case citations omitted].

In Mr. Justice White's view, the broadcast of a film containing Zacchini's entire act

> . . . poses a substantial threat to the economic value of that performance. As the Ohio court recognized, this act is the product of petitioners own talents and energy, the end result of much time, effort and expense. Much of its economic value lies in the "right of exclusive control over the publicity given to his performance"; if the public can see the act for free on televisoin, they will be less willing to pay to see it at the fair (p. 2857).

The fair use standard proposed in this chapter is a two-pronged one. If the copier can satisfy the first two tests indicated, i.e., that he falls within the class of persons entitled to invoke the "fair use" defense because he is contributing to the advancement of science, art, and industry or exercising First Amendment rights, and that his purpose in copying is to advance its purposes and not to plagiarize (points I and II), then he cannot be enjoined from the copying. Justice White, however, felt no doubt that the broadcaster's filming of Zacchini's entire performance diminished the value of the performance to Zacchini and the revenues to which Zacchini's performance entitled him. It was crucial that Scripps-Howard had broadcast Zacchini's "entire" performance. According to the Justice:

> The effect of a public broadcast of the performance is similar to preventing petitioner from charging an admission fee. "The rationale for [protecting the right of publicity] is the straightforward one of preventing unjust enrichment by the theft of good will. No social purpose is served by having the defendant get for free some aspect of the plaintiff that would have market value and for which he would normally pay."[41]

No issue arose in this case as to Scripps-Howard's ability to pay and the profitability of its broadcasting operations. Zacchini had not sought an order enjoining Scripps-Howard from copying; he sought only compensation for an infringing use. In Mr. Justice White's view, therefore, there was no inconsistency between the requirements of the First Amendment and the requirement that the broadcaster compensate Zacchini for broadcasting his entire act. His opinion therefore endorses one of the two respects in which the proposed modernized "fair use" standard modifies existing law: where the user's operations are economically profitable and economic harm is done to the owner of the "right of publicity" (or the copyright owner), compensation for the use should be paid.

Justice Powell, in a minority opinion joined in by Justices Brennan and Marshall, dissented on the ground that the majority opinion was not appropriately sensitive to the First Amendment values at stake. Justice Powell felt that

> the First Amendment commands a different analytical starting point from the one selected by the Court. Rather than begin with a quantitative analysis of the performer's behavior—is this or is this not his entire act?—we should direct initial attention to the actions of the news media: what use did the station make of the film footage (p. 2860).

Justice Powell, in addition, thought that the broadcaster's use of its film was "for a routine portion of a regular news program" and he was therefore prepared to hold that

> . . . the First Amendment protects the station from a "right of publicity" or "appropriation" suit, absent a strong showing by the plaintiff that the news broadcast was a subterfuge or cover for private or commercial exploitation (p. 2860).

Justice Powell was at least partially correct. In any "fair use" situation, a major issue is the use made of the film, i.e., was it the reporting of a news event or was it "a subterfuge or cover for private or commercial exploitation?" He parts company from Justice White and the Court's majority, who regard this criterion as relevant only to the issue whether the copyright owner is entitled to an injunction against the alleged infringing use, but as irrelevant to the issue whether the copyright owner may obtain compensation for the infringing use. As already pointed out, the modernized "fair use" formula comes out on the side of Justice White and the Court majority.

In the case of an allegedly infringed copyright, as opposed to a "right of publicity" violation, Justice Powell and his concurring brethren might come to the same conclusion as they did here. However there is some question about this. In the case of a copyright infringement, the right of the copyright owner to compensation is, as it were, written into the Constitution. In the Zacchini case, the legal effect of his "right of publicity" was only to give him the right to control the time and the manner of publicizing his professional activity as performer. Hence the considerations involved in protecting the common law "right of publicity" are quite different from those involved in the protection of copyrights. In the case before the Court, Justice Powell pointed out, Zacchini

> . . . does not complain about the fact of exposure to the public, but rather about its timing or manner. He welcomes some publicity, but seeks to retain control over means and manner as a way to maximize for himself the monetary benefits that flow from such publication. But having made the matter public—having chosen, in essence, to make it newsworthy—he cannot, consistently with the First Amendment, complain of routine news reportage.

Whatever else may be said about this case, it seems to be conclusive as to the inappropriateness and the unworkability of the proposals designed to satisfy the "substantiality" criterion of the current "fair use" standard, that an arbitrary time period, between 15 seconds and a minute, be fixed as the maximum period for which the free use of a copyrighted work will be permitted over a visual, auditory, or audiovisual medium. (See Bernard Timberg, Chapter 20.) Under any sensible "fair use" policy, the educator's or critic's judgment as to what constitutes effective use should not be overturned unless it is completely arbitrary.

12. SUMMARY: RECTIFYING THE LAOCÖON SHORTFALL

This is the proper moment for the author to make an acknowledgment of personal humility that may not have been apparent from the style of the preceding portions of this chapter. Like educators, courtroom lawyers—particularly when confronted with the task of selling a difficult thesis to a jury or a class of students—tend to exaggerate and avoid the necessary qualifications that would appear if the thesis were the subject of quiet library research. Let it be understood, then, that this is more a discussion memorandum than a definitive statement of a new legal code; it is speculation on the *lex ferenda*, the law as it ought to be, and not the *lex lata*, the law as it is.

It may appear presumptuous to suggest, as this chapter has done, that the accumulated judicial wisdom of decades on the law of fair use be largely jettisoned, and that in lieu thereof the law go back to the fundamental insights contained in four lines of a document, the Constitution, published in 1789, and of a book, Lessing's *Laocöon*, published in 1766. But the rationale for this suggestion is clear. The Founding Fathers were political and social realists, with a broad knowledge of human nature and of the needs of society. Hence, although they personally abhorred monopolies, they decided to confer patent and copyright monopolies on authors and inventors in order to stimulate their creative energies through the profit system. The Founding Fathers also knew that the future of the United States rested on the advancement and the dissemination of information and political ideas; hence they stipulated that these monopoly grants were to be subordinate to the public purpose of the advancement of the arts, sciences, and industry. These economic and political insights are as valid today as they were then.

The second basic theme of this chapter has been that the law of copyright and fair use has broken down because of its failure to take proper account of the nature of the copyrighted material. This has led to the uncritical assimilation of judicial rules, that had emerged from cases involving static literary materials, to the far different media of the visual, audio and audiovisual arts. This failure of legal imagination has led to the deficiency in the copyright law already described as the *Laocöon shortfall*, the failure to appreciate the limitations that the differing nature of the media involved in the spatial and temporal arts impose upon the artist working in those media.

13. JUDICIAL, LEGISLATIVE, OR VOLUNTARY IMPLEMENTATION OF THE MODERNIZED CONCEPT OF FAIR USE?

The departure from established legal precedents involved in the proposed modernized concept of fair use is so extensive that it is probably beyond the competence of even the most creative, policy-oriented court. Moreover, litigation is a chancy matter and usually ends in a decision that is geared to the specific facts of the litigated case and does not establish generally operative principles.

The futility of relying on judicial decisions for guidance on "fair use" in situations where the newer electronic technologies have totally changed the research and library patterns of the Gutenberg Era is well reflected in the leading case of *Williams & Wilkins Company* v. *United States*.[43]

Legislation is a more obvious technique for adopting a large-scale overhaul of copyright law such as is suggested here. But legislation, cannot go far beyond mandating the four general guidelines of the modernized code. In *Williams & Wilkins*, the opinion just referred to, Judge Davis repeatedly says that photocopying is "preeminently a problem for Congress" and one that "calls for legislative guidance and legislative treatment."[44] When Congress tackled the problem in the 1976 Copyright Revision Act, it included a Section 106 dealing with photocopying, which clarified old problems and raised new ones. But what did it do with respect to the whole wider area covered in "fair use?" It enacted Section 107, a fourteen-line restatement of the four-point formula that had been applied by the courts in the past to literary works and, as this whole chapter shows, is inapplicable to large and important categories of artistic works. Thus, legislation can sound a general keynote, but there is grave doubt that it is a practicable method of applying the "fair use" concept to the "endless variety of situations and combinations of circumstances that can arise in particular cases."[45]

The most practical forum for resolving controversy and for converting "fair use" ideology into workable rules is the conference table. To obtain such a forum, it is necessary that the lawyers for the copyright creator groups, and their counterparts representing researchers, teachers, and librarians, emerge from their preconceived and fortified legal ramparts, lay aside their adversary and litigation techniques, and industry by industry—photography, motion pictures, TV, videotape, publishing—work out commercially viable rules that will reasonably implement the two rights basic to the copyright system: the right of compensation to the copyright owner and the right of "fair use" to the copyright user.

In this collaborative enterprise, the entertainment and educational industries that depend on the copyright system for their profits should take fuller account of the constitutional mandate "to Promote the Progress of Science and useful Arts." They should recognize the benefits that the teaching, research, and librarian professions confer on the copyright owner by training people to create, produce, and promote the copyrighted radio, motion picture, and TV productions of the future; by exposing current audiovisual productions to the public and thereby stimulating the commercial demand for those productions; and by raising the performance and aesthetic standards of creators and their industry. Those producers of copyrighted and audiovisual materials which derive their revenues primarily from the entertainment world should bear in mind the financial limitations of the educational market, which can make only a modest contribution to their total revenues.

Copyright owners have the right to sue persons who they believe are, under cover of the "fair use" privilege, plagiarizing their works, but they should bear in mind the heavy cost and the uncertainties of such litigation and should engage in it only after they have applied the appropriate cost-benefit ratios. If ever the copyright owner had reason to feel harmed by an allegedly infringing use it was in the Williams and Wilkins case, where the plaintiff copyright owners were four small medical journals, who felt their low margin of profits was being eroded by the large-scale photocopying involved. Yet, the majority of the Court of Claims held that they had not proved economic injury. This holding illustrates the chanciness of litigation.[46]

For their part, the educational users of copyright—the teachers, the researchers, and the librarians—should bear in mind that the First Amendment does not insulate them from the application of the copyright monopoly, except where political matters and news events are involved. Moreover, "fair use" is only a defense to a charge of copyright infringement; it confers no blanket immunity from such charges. Nor should the educational community forget that it, too, is part of the copyright creator world and is therefore the beneficiary of the copyright monopoly.

Educators will appreciate that what is being suggested as a technique for solving the pressing problems of copyright utilization and compensation is that oldest of educational techniques, the dialogue—a dialogue between copyright creators and copyright users that will be based on an enlightened perception of their respective long-term interests. This dialogue should be practical and from it there should emerge rules of fair use that will reflect proper cost-benefit ratios for both the creators and the users of copyright and insure the proper balance between the two constitutional objectives of promoting the progress of science and useful arts and rewarding the authors of the copyrighted works.

NOTES

[1]Corcoran v. Montgomery Ward & Co., 121 F.2d 572 (9 Cir. 1941); cf. White-Smith Music Publishing Co. v. Apollo Co., 209 U.S. 1 (1908).

[2]Shapiro, Bernstein & Co. v. Miracle Record Co., 91 F.Supp. 473 (N.D.Ill. 1950); Mills Music v. Cromwell Music, 126 F.Supp. 54 (S.D.N.Y. 1954); McIntyre v. Double A-Music Corporation, 166 F.Supp. 681 (S.D.Cal. 1958).

[3]Rosette v. Rainbo Record Mfg. Corp., 354 F.Supp. 1183 (S.D.N.Y. 1973), aff'd, 546 F.2d 461 (2d Cir. 1975).

[4]Cf., in accord, Nom Music, Inc. v. Kaslin, 227 F.Supp. 922, 926 (S.D.N.Y. 1964), aff'd on other grounds, 343 F.2d 198 (2d Cir. 1965).

[5]345 F.Supp. 589 (D.D.C. 1972).

[6]See Mazer v. Stein, 347 U.S. 201 (1954).

[7]Noah Webster, the founder of both the American copyright system and the American dictionary, would be astounded to learn that the "writings" of authors referred to in the Constitution now include, in the phraseology of the 1976 Copyright Code Revision,

> original works of authors fixed in any tangible form or medium of expression, now known or later developed, from which they can be perceived, reproduced or otherwise communicated, either directly or indirectly with the aid of a machine or device.

[8]See "Comment, CBS v. ASCAP: Performing Rights Societies and the Per Se Rule," 87 *Yale L.J.* (1978) 873, 876.

[9]See Columbia Broadcasting System, Inc. v. American Society of Composers, Authors and Publishers, 400 F.Supp. 737 (S.D.N.Y. 1975), rev'd in part, 562 F.2d 130 (2d Cir. 1977), reversed,99 S.Ct. 1551 (1979).

[10]James Monaco, *Media Culture: Television, Radio, Records, Books, Magazines, Newspapers, Movies* (N.Y.: Delta, 1978), pp. 13–14.

[11]Don Glassman, *Writers' and Artists' Rights* (Washington, D.C.: Writers Press, 1978), pp. 84–85. He mentions several important acquisitions and consolidations that reduce the number of independent publishers. RCA now owns NBC, Random House, Alfred Knopf, Pantheon Books, and Ballantine Books. CBS controls Fawcett, Popular Library, Holt, Rinehart & Winston, and Praeger Publishing. ITT owns G.K. Hall, Bobbs-Merrill, and Who's Who. Gulf & Western owns Simon & Schuster and Pocket Books. MCA controls G.P. Putnam and Coward, McCann and Geoghehan.

[12]See Meeropol v. Nizer, 560 F.2d 1061, 1069 (2d Cir. 1977).

[13]Lessing stated his distinction as follows: "I maintain that succession of time is the department of the poet, as space is that of the painter." Accordingly, poetry and music make use of "articulated sounds in time" whereas painting employs "form and color in space." Lessing, *Laocöon or the Limit of Painting and Poetry* (Everyman's Library Dutton, 1970). p.p. 54-55.

[14]293 F.Supp. 130, 159 USPQ 773 (S.D.N.Y. 1968).

[15]Nimmer on Copyright, § 9.232, pp. 28.22et seq. (1973).

[16]401 *Patent Trademark and Copyright Journal* (referred to as PTCJ) PTCJ A-2.

[17]445 F.Supp. 875 (S.D.Fla., 1978).

[18]See also the recent New York case of Italian Book Corp. v. American Broadcasting

Co., 404 PTCJ A-10, decided by the federal district court Sept. 6, 1978, where the court held that a TV broadcaster was, on fair use grounds, entitled to perform, in a film clip of an ethnic parade, portions of a copyrighted song.

[19]Thus, in Meeropol v. Nizer (note 12), the Second Circuit held that it was error to hold, *as a matter of law*, that Louis Nizer and his two publishers could rely on the fair use defense for copying, in their book, *The Implosion Conspiracy*, verbatim portions of 28 copyrighted letters, or a total of 1,957 pages. In reversing the District Court so that the case might be tried *on the facts*, the Circuit Court said, "it is relevant whether or not the Rosenberg letters were used primarily for scholarly, historical reasons, or predominantly for commercial exploration" (p. 1069). ". . . Both commercial and artistic elements are involved in almost every work, . . ." "Note," 56 *Columbia L. Rev.* (1956) 585, 597. The Court in the Rosemont case, 366 F.2d. 307 (2d Cir. 1968) cited earlier, concluded that:

> . . . whether an author or publisher has a commercial motive or writes in a popular style is irrelevant to a determination of whether a particular use of copyrighted material in a work which offers some benefit to the public constitutes a fair use (p. 307).

[20]Lessing. see note 10, p. 170.

[21]See 2 *Encyclopaedia Britannica* "Macropaedia" (15th ed. 1974): 47.

[22]See Victorina Tejera, *Art and Human Intelligence* (N.Y.: Appleton-Century-Crofts, 1965), p. 33.

[23]581 F.2d 751 (1978).

[24]The approach taken by the Ninth Circuit in the Air Pirates case may have been attributable to its forced reliance on legal precedents that were irrelevant to the economic and technical situation before the court. Criticism of those precedents and their use carries with it no implication that the court did not reach a just result in the particular case at hand. Sometimes when bad law is involved in a case, the verbal overlay of the court's opinion may conceal its real motivation in deciding the case. It is quite possible that the court's real but unarticulated view was that Air Pirates' efforts to transform figures in "the accepted Mickey Mouse world of scrubbed faces, bright smiles, and happy endings" into denizens of the "porno culture" ranked very low in the scale of First Amendment priorities; that the defendants had engaged in a wholesale appropriation of the Walt Disney work; that the defendants' predominant purpose was not to vindicate political, social, or artistic principle, but to make money, which they did; and that it was unfair to allow the defendants to appropriate the Walt Disney work, without compensating the Walt Disney interests.

[25]347 U.S. 201, 219 (1954).

[26]United States v. Paramount Pictures, 334 U.S. 131, 158; (1948).

[27]329 F.2d 541, 544 (2d Cir. 1964). See, to the same effect, the Rosemont case, n. 19 above.

[28]433 U.S. 350; 97 Sup. Ct. 2691 (1977).

[29]347 U.S. 201, 219 (1954).

[30]Contrary to the position of the courts, for many years both the copyright bar and the academic profession have been commendably vigilant in seeing to it that First Amendment principles are given due weight in "fair use" situations. Thus three persons whose verbal approaches to the First Amendment differ to some extent, Professor Nimmer, Harry Rosenfield, and the author, agree on the uncopyrightability, on First Amendment grounds, of the Mylai massacre photographs.

[31]See Folsom v. Marsh, 9 Fed. Cas. 342, 348, No. 4901, 2 Story 100 (C.C.D. Mass. 1841). Folsom v. Marsh was the judicial mainstay for Attorney General Saxbe's Opinion of September 6, 1974 (Vol. 43, Op. No. 1), ruling the White House papers to be the property of President Nixon. The latest Supreme Court pronouncement on this subject, (Nixon v. Administrator of General Services, 433 U.S. 425, 97 S.Ct. 2777), does not reach the property issues but recognizes the public entitlement for access to such papers.

[32]8 Peters (33 U.S.) 1055 (1834).

[33]319 F.Supp. 1269, 1274 (S.D.N.Y. 1970).

[34]418 F.Supp. 620, 625 (1976).

[35]*Fair Use of Copyrighted Materials*, Study No. 14 prepared for the Senate Judiciary Subcommittee on Patents, Trademarks and Copyrights, 86th Cong., 2d Sess., Committee Print, p. 10.

[36]See Meeropol v. Nizer, 560 F.2d 1061,1070 (2nd Cir. 1977).

[37]See Peterson, "The Production of Cultural Change: The Case of Contemporary Country Music," *Social Research* 45 (1978): 292, 294, 296–97.

[38]97 Sup. Ct. 2849 (1977).

[39]306 U.S. 30, 36 (1939).

[40]47 Ohio St., 235, 351 N.E. 2d, 461.

[41]Kalven, "Privacy in Tort Law—Were Warren and Brandeis Wrong?," 31 *Law and Contemporary Problems* (1966): 326, 331, 2857.

[42]This statement accords fully with what has been said earlier in this chapter concerning the irrelevance and unworkability of the substantiality test of fair use when applied to the visual, auditory, and audiovisual media.

[43]487 F.2d 1345 (Ct. Claims 1973), affirmed by an equally divided Supreme Court, 420 U.S. 376 (1975). The Court of Claims vote on the decision was 4–3, with a report of dissenting opinions. The Supreme Court split 4–4, thereby affirming the decision of the administrative law judge, the low man on the judicial totem pole. Where the judicial vote on the existence of "fair use," in a case involving a detailed record and intensive legal research, is 8 for and 8 against, it can hardly be said that the judiciary is the branch of government best adapted to solving pressing problems of great urgency.

[44]See pp. 1342, 1360, 1362, 1363 of his opinion.

[45]See the Copyright Revision Act, House *Report* No. 1476, 94th Cong., 2d Sess. (1976): 66.

[46]The congressional hearings on the 1976 Copyright Revision Act contained considerable testimony by scientific publishers concerning the impact of photocopying upon the economic health of scientific journals, but it is one thing to present an economic case to a legislative body and another thing to prove it in court. See the testimony of Townsend Hoopes, Association of American Publishers and Robert W. Cairns, American Chemical Society as well as William Koch, "Copyrighting Physics Journals," *Physics Today*, Vol. 24, No. 2. All appear in *Copyright Law Revision: Hearings before the Subcommittee on Courts, Civil Liberties and the Administration of Justice*, Serial No. 36, Pt. 1 (Washington, D.C.: 1976), pp. 229–53.

Addendum

The text of the two federal decisions summarized in this addendum, which bear directly on the issues discussed in this chapter, became available only after the chapter was sent to the printer.

Bruzzone v. Miller Brewing Co., U.S. Dist. Ct., No. Dist. of Calif., No. C-78-2055 SC, May 25, 1979, 439 PTCJ 4–6 (Aug. 2, 1979)

The facts of this case and some of its implications are set forth in the addendum by Harry N. Rosenfield to the preceding chapter (see pp. 308–309), and will not be repeated here.

The "central factor" in the Court's determination that the copying was protected as "fair use" was the absence of any showing that the copying by Bruzzone of Miller's TV advertisements had any effect on the potential market for or the value of the copyrighted material. The Court's findings and legal conclusions with respect to the other three currently accepted criteria of fair use, discussed in Sections 4, 5 and 6 of this chapter, are as follows:

(a) On the "commercial vs. educational use" criterion (see p. 319), the Court found that Bruzzone was engaged in the business of preparing and selling market research studies and reports on television advertisement test results to advertisers, and in publishing an industry newsletter that was distributed to approximately 200 subscribers. The Court dismissed the relevance of this profitable commercial activity in two conclusions of law:

> 6. Deriving a profit from a subsequent use does not render said use unfair.
>
> 7. Criticism, comment and review are well-recognized areas of fair use, even if profit is derived thereby.

(b) The Court ignored the nature of the copyrighted work. Instead, it dealt at length with the nature of, and the purpose underlying, the copying of the work.

(c) As to "the amount and substantiality of the portion of the work copied," the Court found that Bruzzone copied only five or six frames out of a total of 720 in the usual commercial. It also found that, while the words and language accompanying the frame were copied, "there is no color, sight, sound, or action, which elements, images and sound create the totality of the copyrighted material." It further found that:

> ... Plaintiff's use of portions of the original advertisement is the minimum necessary to stimulate recognition of said advertisement, and these portions are only sent in the form of questionnaires to a limited number of households (1,000 throughout the United States).

The writer notes that none of these factors are relevant to the "substantiality" criterion, because from a legal standpoint each of the copied five or six frames is a separate and complete "work of art." Also, the fact that Bruzzone utilized "no color, sight, sound, or action" in the copied frames does not differentiate this case from *Time's* photographs copied from the Zapruder frames of the Kennedy assassination (see the Geis case; p. 317, fn. 14).

While the absence of harm to the copyright owner was the central factor in the Court's decision that Bruzzone's copying was fair use, an equally influential factor was Bruzzone's role as a critic, commentator and researcher. This appears from its Conclusions of Law 6 and 7, just quoted, and the Court's Findings of Fact as to the significance of Bruzzone's research activity, based on the copied TV frames, both for a healthy consumer economy and for contemporary American culture.*

District Judge Conti's opinion reflects the coalescence of Copyright Clause and First Amendment objectives in the determination of fair use (see pp. 322–324). Its Conclusion of Law No. 10 of the court reads:

> 10. Where the assertion of a copyright interest conflicts with the free flow of information in an open society, and so impairs the dissemination of research and intellectual words, the copyright owner's interest should yield to the public welfare lest the very purpose of the Copyright Act be frustrated.

Taking this Conclusion in conjunction wtih Conclusion No. 7 (already cited), and the Court's Findings of Fact Nos. 23, 24 and 25, the basic substantive reason for applying the "fair use" doctrine to Bruzzone's use of Miller's commercials is that the use was "for the purposes of criticism, comment, news reporting, teaching, scholarship, and research" (Finding No. 25) (see Sections 8 and 9 of this chapter).

The "Betamax Case"
Universal City Studios, Inc. and
Walt Disney Productions
v. Sony Corporation of America, et al.,
U.S. Dist. Ct., Central Dist. of Calif., No. CV 76 3520 F
Oct. 2, 1979, 448 PTCJ D-1-D-27 (Oct. 4, 1979)

In this lengthy and well-researched landmark case, District Judge Ferguson held that noncommercial home use recording of copyrighted material broadcast over the public airwaves does not constitute copyright infringement and is a fair use of the broadcast materials. These materials were copyrighted motion pictures owned by the two plaintiffs, Universal Pictures and Walt Disney Productions, and licensed by them for theater and television use. Universal had also recently begun marketing theatrical motion pictures on prerecorded videodiscs.

---

*"23. Useful, reliable market research results have value for the public, assist in keeping the competitive marketplace free of distortion and confusion, and in general is an essential aspect of a healthy consumer economy.

"24. Television programming is an inordinately pervasive force in contemporary American culture, and television advertising is a forceful element of television programming. Television programs and especially television commercials are subjected to constant scrutiny, study, research, comment, and criticism."

The Court's main basis for holding that there was no copyright infringement is the legislative history of the 1976 Copyright Revision Act, which expressed a Congressional intention not to prohibit the home use of sound recordings or the reproduction in the home of televised motion pictures. The Betamax case also marks the first time that a manufacturer of the instrument making possible the alleged infringement has been sued. Sony, the main defendant in the case, manufactures and sells the so-called Betamax videotape recorder, as well as tape cassettes for Betamax models. Besides Sony, the defendants included four retailers of the Betamax recorder, the advertising agency responsible for its promotion, and a home viewer of televised motion pictures using the Betamax recorder.

The Betamax case has limited value as a direct precedent because, as the Court noted, on its facts, it did not involve pay or cable television stations as plaintiffs, organized or informal "tape swapping," tape duplication within the home or outside by individuals, groups or corporations, the home or outside by individuals, groups or corporations, or off-the-air recording for use outside the home (*e.g.*, by teachers for classrooms, corporations for employees).

The Court broaches its discussion of fair use by reference to two general principles. The first is that the doctrine of fair use must, consistently with the Congressional intention, "be flexible to deal with technological change." The second is that "the immediate effect of our copyright law to secure a fair return for an 'author's' creative labor" must yield to "the more fundamental purpose of the protection 'to Promote the Progress of Science and Useful Arts.' " For these propositions, the Court quotes from *Twentieth Century Music Corp.* v. *Aiken,* 422 U.S. 151, 156 (1974); *Fox Film Corp.* v. *Doyal,* 286 U.S. 123, 127; and *Williams & Wilkins* v. *United States,* 487 F.2d 1345, 1352 (Ct. Cl. 1973) (see Section 9 of this chapter).

With respect to the four factors for determining fair use that are codified in Section 107 of the 1976 Copyright Revision Act, the Court concluded:

(a) Home use recording usually involves copying the entire work. In discussing several decisions of the Second Circuit on "fair use," the Court noted that that Circuit was concerned about the "substantiality" criterion only when the copying produced harm to the complaining party.

(b) On the "commercial v. educational" criterion, the Court ruled that home recording and the playback of audiovisual material broadcast free of charge to Betamax owners over the public airwaves was noncommercial. The noncommercial nature of such use supported the Court's conclusion that home recording did not reduce the market for the plaintiff's copyrighted material.

(c) Judge Ferguson noted that the nature of the copyrighted material had not been discussed extensively in "fair use" cases. The Court, speaking of one of the copyrighted films that he had viewed at the trial, the "New Mickey Mouse Club" episode, said that "it cannot, nor would it desire to, pronounce [that material] to be 'mere entertainment,' or 'educational' or 'informational' or 'beneficial.' " It cited the Supreme Court decision in *Stanley* v. *Georgia* for the proposition that the line between the "transmission of ideas" and "mere entertainment" is too elusive for any court to draw (see p. 15).

(d) Judge Ferguson noted a peculiarity with respect to broadcasting and telecasting that rendered any assessment of the harm resulting from an infringement "more speculative." Referring to the Supreme Court decision in

Teleprompter Corp. v. *Columbia Broadcasting System, Inc.*, 415 U.S. 394, 414 n. 15 (1974), he pointed out that the payment process in the television industry differs from that in other copyright-impacted industries:

> ... holders of copyrights for television or their licensees are not paid directly by those who ultimately enjoy the publication of the material—that is, the television viewers—but by advertisers who use the drawing power of the copyrighted material to promote their goods and services.

(e) Another factor that may have influenced the Court's decision as to the absence of copyright infringement and the existence of fair use was the practical difficulty of enforcing the copyright. The Betamax videotape recorder was capable of non-infringing uses in recording noncopyrighted material or material whose owners consented to the copying. Moreover, since the Betamax machines are in private homes, policing their use in connection with the plaintiff's copyrighted materials "would be nearly impossible and in any event highly intrusive."

In the final analysis, in this case, as in the Bruzzone case, the central factor, both as to the absence of copyright infringement and as to the "fair use" of the copying, was the absence of harm to the copyright owner. The Court found that "after seven years of increasing sales of Betamax and several years of sales of its competitors, plaintiffs had experienced no harm" and that the plaintiffs had admitted that "they cannot predict at what date or level of sales the expected harms will occur." After an extensive review of the evidence, the Court concluded that harm to the copyright owners' market potential or the value of its copyrighted materials was speculative and unproven:

> ... More of plaintiffs' predictions of harm hinge on speculation about audience viewing patterns and ratings, a measurement system which Sidney Sheinberg, MCA's president, calls a "black art" because of the significant level of imprecision involved in the calculations. Testimony at trial suggested that Betamax may require adjustments in marketing strategy, but did not establish even a likelihood of harm. Nor did the testimony invoke concern that denial of monopoly power over home use recording would significantly dissuade authors and producers from creating audiovisual material for television.

24

CONCLUSIONS: SCHOLARS, MEDIA, AND THE LAW IN THE 1980s

JOHN SHELTON LAWRENCE AND BERNARD TIMBERG

The issues presented in this book call for a few general comments on the impact of copyright law upon education and scholarship. Proposals about strategies for the educational community are also in order here, for although the history of copyright practice suggests a sluggish pace of change, many of the problems raised in these pages lend themselves to prompt and equitable treatment.

I. GENERALIZATIONS ABOUT COPYRIGHT PRACTICE

Evidence presented in the foregoing chapters represents points of view held by conflicting parties who can be roughly classified as copyright holders (producers, owners, distributors) on the one hand and users, or "fair users," on the other. The former advocate "high protectionism"[1] and draw their most compelling arguments from well-attested stories of piracy, counterfeit, and bootlegging. The fair users favor "low protectionism"—that is, although they accept the basic incentive-reward philosophy of modern copyright, they draw their arguments from cases giving an impression of censorship or prior restraint, both in its direct and indirect forms. A hybrid third group of producer-users is also emerging (see Bernard Timberg, Chapter 20). Some generalizations about the interaction of these groups are warranted.

344

1. The Academic Community Sometimes Harms the Producing Community through Its Activities

Unauthorized copying, especially, damages producers whose markets are specifically educational and who lack capital. We find support for this conclusion in the BOCES case, in the sorts of situations described by R.B. Churchill (Chapter 13), and in the testimony of participants at the Airlie Conference on Video Recording for Educational Uses.[2] No one in the academic community has ventured to call the surreptitious bootleg copying of entire films *fair use*, though some academicians concede that it is a common practice.[3]

In thinking of producer interests, it is, however, a mistake to lump them together and to see them all standing at the door of Parliament with Hogarth's widow, pleading for a few years of copyright extension. Most contemporary media material is produced by corporations whose output is financed independently of any direct service to educational markets. The producers, for example, of the Miss America pageant or the half-time program at the Superbowl, or of daily television game shows, do not market their products to contemporary social anthropology or popular culture courses. Nor do the producers of advertisements market them to instructors of logic or rhetoric. It is difficult to find a valid social or economic reason why the classroom performance of such materials would be harmful. We must therefore, in the traditional spirit of fair use, make important distinctions concerning the sources of copyrighted materials and their usual markets.

2. Fears of Legal Reprisal Are Inhibiting Instructional Media Centers and Preventing Them from Providing Scholar-Teacher Requested Services

Jeanne Masson Douglas's report (Chapter 9), though dating back a few years, still represents the typical frustrating experiences of media centers that are meticulous about securing clearances for off-air taping. When extreme caution is added—prompted by fear of suits against off-air taping—media centers can provide very little service for courses that comment upon contemporary audiovisual material.

3. Some Copyright Holders Are Imposing *de facto* Restrictions on Documentation in Published Scholarly Study, Either Through Prohibitive Fees, Censorious Review, or Threatened Legal Action

Belz's (Chapter 3) and Mast's (Chapter 6) discussions of fees represent experiences reported by numerous scholars working with the new media. The sorts of review discussed in the Alley-"Kojak" episode (Chapter 7), the Stott and Sproule episodes (Chapter 5), and the regular administrative review of material at a major corporation like Walt Disney Productions all remind one of a monarchical exercise of copyright power.

4. Publishers, Whether Because They Fear Litigation or Because They Are Themselves Divisions of Media Conglomerates with High-Protectionist Biases, Are Frequently According the New Media a *de facto* Immunity from Fair Use Privileges and First Amendment Rights

Publishers, even nonprofit university presses, have widely accepted a low-risk policy that dictates permissions clearance and fees as a precondition to almost any use of new media artifacts. It remains to be seen whether Section 107 of the 1976 Copyright Act, as an explicit statutory acknowledgment of the fair use principle, will inspire greater boldness.[4]

5. Courts in the United States, on the Rare Occasions When They Are Asked to Rule on Fair Use Issues Related to Scholarship and Criticism, Have Tended to Reject the *de facto* Restrictions Erected Around Artifacts of the New Media

In a number of landmark cases reviewed in this volume, courts have upheld *both* the notions of fair use and of the constitutional rights of access. *Rosemont, Meeropol* v. *Nizer, Time* v. *Geis, Thomson* v. *Gallen* and *Triangle Publications* v. *Knight-Ridder*[5] are all instructive on the rights of unauthorized use for purposes of criticism and comment. (See especially the essays by Harriet Oler, Harry Rosenfield, and Sigmund Timberg.) Since most media centers and individual scholars do not employ counsel to advise them about case law or to represent them in infringement proceedings, the full value of such precedents is yet to be widely experienced in the academic community.

6. Internationally, Scholars and Copyright Holders Are Experiencing Uncertainties About Fair Use

The legal twilight that prevails in the United States is not the result of unique traits of either the producing or the using communities. Internationally, fair use has similar "equitable rule of reason" status in law and the conflicts related to its application derive from similar technologies, production and ownership arrangements, and similar concerns in the educational communities. Despite the expected conflicts that occur in the fair use field—particularly evident in Marie-Laure Arié's report on the debate in France (Chapter 17)—some countries appear to be achieving amiable and mutually satisfactory relationships between producers and educational users. This is especially clear in the reports on Great Britain (Chapter 15) and on Japan (Chapter 19).

It is apparent then, both nationally and to a more variable extent internationally, that systems basically designed to protect commercial interests are colliding with and frustrating educational systems. To work with the artifacts of the new media and the technologies for capturing them, synthesizing them, and critically commenting upon their significance is to exist in a region of uncertainty, inconsistency, arbitrariness, and concomitant timidity.

II. AREAS FOR ACTION

This conflict lends itself to several types of action. We have chosen to discuss the areas of (1) educating the academic community, (2) politics, (3) litigation, (4) the use of the new technologies.

1. Educating the Academic Community

Understanding copyright law in general, and fair use issues in particular, may seem an arcane calling, as some exhausted readers will now conclude. Describing the law of fair use is not like telling a foreign driver about the local traffic signs and speed limit. Yet, given some patience with ambiguity and conflicting precedents, relatively clear standards can emerge in the effort to define what is reasonable. Our United States authors have repeatedly taken the fair use section of the 1976 Copyright Law and demonstrated how its criteria can be applied in ways compatible with important legal precedents and with a sense of fairness. All answers regarding fair use are essentially contestable (and contested) but they are not arbitrary. And most relevant, they are susceptible to lay understanding.

The educational task for scholars, librarians, and media personnel who have fair use literacy is to share it with associates in media centers, libraries, publishing houses, and other institutions affected by copyright. Some inhibitions can be lessened by the spread of information regarding the law and relevant case precedents. The following simplified principles, which telescope several conclusions reached by contributors in this volume, should be useful in the academic community's processes of self-education. The first three principles show why fair use can and should be extended to the new media; the fourth is a principle of restraint.

(a) *New media channels of expression have a parallel legal status with printed material in the fair use context.* Imagery, whether visual or audio, lacks legal uniqueness in the fair use context. Blanket prohibitions of unauthorized reproduction for purposes of historical writing, criticism, or instruction have not been defined by statute or court precedent. Just as literary and political scholars document their works with quotations that give substance and accuracy to their analyses, scholars working with new media materials are legally free to proceed with the same justifications and liabilities. But the law is here far more generous than current practice.

(b) *Each communication mode is unique; neither its content nor its qualities can be effectively "quoted" through another medium.* It is a literary commonplace that translations from poetry to prose or from one language to another are almost always to some degree inadequate; and these are transformations within the same linguistic mode of communication. Other modalities of communication, such as film, television, comics, recorded music, are even more inaccurately "paraphrased" in print equivalents.

(c) *The right to reproduce and analyze copyrighted material has a dual origin—the fair use tradition and the constitutional rights tradition.* Rights of access to material for purposes of display and discussion have been vindicated on both fair use and First Amendment grounds. These rights have been separately and explicitly distinguished by courts in cases employing multiple lines of defense against the allegation of infringement (see Chapter 22).

(d) *Reproductions that actually compete with or supplant the market for a copyrighted item should result in compensation for the copyright owner, regardless of the degree to which they meet requirements of discussion or criticism.* Numerous commentators, Melville B. Nimmer and Alan Latman among them, have emphasized the crucial importance of "the effect on the owner's market" consideration in the history of judicial decisions (see Sigmund Timberg's separation of fair use considerations from those relating to compensation in Chapter 23). The right to analyze created material is not the right to exploit it as if it were one's own creation. To our knowledge, scholars have not claimed this as a right and are unlikely to get a sympathetic hearing if they do.

Although these capsule formulations perhaps oversimplify, they do help us focus on the issues that will continue to be central to the academic community.

2. Politics: Formulating Equitable Guidelines
and/or Legislation

Scholars need to be politically active in several areas. They should collaborate with professional associations that are working on fair use guidelines. Either directly as individuals or indirectly through their associations, they should also participate in discussions with trade groups representing copyright interests. To some extent, these activities have begun and been carried forward with intelligence and good will. The Airlie Conference on Video Recording for Educational Uses in 1977 has issued a substantial report reflecting a wide range of views and possible solutions.[6] The Information Futures, Critical Issues conference also succeeded in persuading both academic and commercial interests to attend.[7] All such activities are evidence of *bona fides*. If scholars align themselves with the efforts and policies of their associations, it will strengthen their position in negotiations with trade groups and copyright owners—who are perhaps inclined to see the educational community as engaged in conspiracies to amputate their copyrights.

In the negotiations of the 1980s, producers and users will need to approach one another in good faith and to recognize that obviously "correct" answers cannot be reached in some areas. Fair use and free inquiry may for some time be affected by a degree of indeterminacy. As Saul Cohen has said, in commenting on the question of the duration of term in copyright:

> To insist that seventy-five years is right but that seventy years is wrong (or vice versa) or that the life of an author plus twenty-five years is right but life-plus-fifty is wrong (or vice versa) is nonsense. "The" answer lies somewhere along a continuum—in a survey of knowledgeable, concerned persons, we would reach a point at which a substantial majority would agree: *that* is too short and *that* is too long.[8]

Probably the most important aspect of negotiations in this area is that there be a *commitment to limits*.

The political task of working toward satisfactory guidelines should not ignore the antiquity of the fair use criteria in Section 107. Copyright scholars have observed that fair use formulations have been virtually unchanged since their initial appearance in *Folsom* v. *Marsh* (1843);[9] Section 107 merely gives them contemporary statutory garb. Most commentators have been unable to conceive any alternative way of formulating the social imperatives for abridging copyright monopoly. But, as Sigmund Timberg stated in his argument for new fair use criteria (Chapter 23), Justice Story (*Folsom* v. *Marsh*) and the judges and lawyers who succeeded him were unaware of any constitutional conflict in the copyright area. For them, fair use has been primarily, if not entirely, a problem in balancing material equities. (Hence the issue of prior restraint—a common concern in libel and national security cases—has seldom if ever been discussed in a copyright context.) But this book argues that far more than material interests are at stake. The "canonical" fair use text bequeathed by Justice Story may need to yield to a new legislative statement of the limits to copyright powers.

3. The Task of Litigation

Litigation will probably be the last resort for the community of users. The economics of private scholarship, the university, and the academic associations almost assures that they will litigate less often than Walt Disney Productions or other media corporations. There is a danger in such legal passivity. If copyright owners and trade associations are allowed to choose all the important cases for litigation, they may acquire a high rate of success with legal precedents that create a climate of even greater timidity in the academic community. If efforts toward negotiation or legislative revision fail, the academic community may need to litigate actively and to ask for declaratory judgments concerning its rights. It might even be desirable for the American Association of University Professors or other organizations to seek such declaratory judgments for teachers with regard to their own learning centers or publishers—if those agencies refuse to perform the functions that have become crucial to contemporary commentary and education. Such suits naturally would lose good will, but conflict may be the price required to deliver us from the legal twilight zone where so many of us have been working. The universities themselves should heed Vanderbilt's lonely example (Chapter 8) and actively defend the requirements for their instruction and research.

4. Using the New Technologies

Ultimately, we must look beyond legal obstacles to fair use and move toward the endeavors that technology makes possible. Satellite transmission, cablevision, fiber optics, and the computer technology that links them will continue to develop—as will the technologies that "capture" the information and images transmitted: photocopy machines, affordable videorecorders and playback units, audiocassettes, and videodiscs. The discourse of our age will come to us increasingly through these new media. Scholarly discourse can keep pace only if it too uses this technology, not merely to capture the new forms of experience becoming accessible through them but also to "conjure up the originals" at the time it wishes to speak of them.

Universities also have the unrealized potential to be centers for independent creation of new media material, and this could help rectify some of the imbalances that we now see in corporate, global systems of media production and distribution. Don Glassman and James Monaco, authors referred to in this book, remind us that monopolies in information are intensifying in the United States, as all systems of media, old and new, become more tightly woven into a few networks of finance, production, and distribution. The story of *How to Read Donald Duck* (Chapter 4 epitomizes a worldwide problem of cultural dominance in which the United States radiates its messages in one-way fashion to the world's theaters, television sets, and newsstands.

Yet, new technologies of image-making, as tools of independent thought, can work to provide alternatives. Cable television and videodisc distribution could provide national outlets for the creations of university media products, ethnic groups, and new voices of various kinds. At a recent session of the National Association of Educational Broadcasters dealing with fair use, the panel moderator asked those in the audience whether they considered themselves as "producers" or "educators" solely, or as "producer-educators." More than a dozen hands in the latter category went up. These "producer-educators" and their counterparts around the world may foster a significant alternative to the one-way communication that has been a predominant feature of modern mass media systems. Independent media, possessing the freedom to "quote" and to comment upon the hitherto inaccessible imagery of the new media, can fill an important educational and critical gap in the decades to come.

The challenge of the 1980s is to use the new media and their technologies to provide understanding of ourselves and of the symbolic systems that are constantly acting upon us. Thus questions of copyright and fair use that a hundred and fifty years ago were called *metaphysical* and *subtle* have become primary educational issues in our time. Our response to their challenge will affect the rights of free inquiry for years to come.

NOTES

[1]Benjamin Kaplan, *An Unhurried View of Copyright* (N.Y.: Columbia, 1967) used the terms *high protectionism* and *low protectionism*.

[2]See *Conference on Video Recording for Educational Uses*, July 19–22, 1977, Airlie, Virginia. (Transcript distributed by U.S. Office of Copyright.)

[3]Cf. James Monaco, "Stealing the Show: The Piracy Problem," *American Film* III, No. 9 (1978). He writes, "It is now common practice at numerous film schools to tape a movie as soon as it comes in" (p. 66).

[4]The first response of the Association of American University Presses has been to urge its members to increase their vigilance against infringements of their own printed

material. Cf. Sanford Thatcher, *What Publishers Need to Know about the New Copyright Law* (New York: AAUP, 1977), p. 18. The economics of academic publishing justify their concern, particularly as regards the fate of journals, but presses may eventually find in Section 107 an opportunity to expand their scope of publication.

[5]See the citation information for these cases, in the Bibliography of Fair Use Cases

[6]See note 2.

[7]A record of this conference is to be found in Jerome K. Miller, ed., *Copyright and the Teaching Learning Process* (Pullman, Wash.: Information Futures, 1977).

[8]Saul Cohen, "Duration," *UCLA Law Review*, 24,(1977) No. 5, 6, pp. 1230–31.

[9]Alan Latman cites this opinion of Judge Yankwich in his *Study No. 14, Fair Use of Copyrighted Works*, Studies Prepared for the Subcommittee on Patents, Trademarks, and Copyrights (Washington, D.C.: 1960), p. 15.

Bibliography of Fair Use Literature (Selective)

With Assistance from Deborah Lulf

I. Government Documents Related to the U.S. Copyright Act of 1976

The Copyright Act of October 19, 1976, Public Law 94-553 (90 Stat. 2541).

The Senate *Report* (S. Rep. No. 94-473, 94th Cong., 1st Sess., Nov. 20, 1975).

The House *Report* (H.R. Rep. No. 94-1476, 94th Cong., 2d Sess., Sept. 3, 1976).

The Conference Committee *Report* (H.R. Rep. No. 94-1733, 94th Cong., 2d Sess., Sept. 29, 1976).

A General Guide to the Copyright Act of 1976, Sept. 1977. (An extensive summarization of the law prepared by Marybeth Peters, Senior Attorney-Advisor of the United States Office of Copyright. It is not, however, an official interpretation.)

Reproduction of Copyrighted Works by Educators and Librarians: Circular R 21 (April 1978). An edited version of the law and the relevant portions of the Senate, House, and Conference *Reports* that clarify congressional legislative intent on fair use— primarily related to photocopying but a very useful simplification on a number of issues. (Available from U.S. Office of Copyright, Library of Congress, Washington, D.C. 20059.)

Miller, Jerome K., *U.S. Copyright Documents, Selected, Annotated and Indexed for Use by Educators and Librarians*. Littleton, Colo.: Libraries Unlimited, forthcoming).

The Copyright Act of 1976 is, of course, in the public domain and is being reprinted in a variety of sources. Complete or substantial sections are reproduced in Nimmer, Latman (b), and Seltzer listed under Commentaries.

II. Legal Commentaries on Fair Use

Latman, Alan. (a) *Fair Use of Copyrighted Works, Study* No. 14 of the Copyright Revision Studies, Studies Prepared for the Subcommittee on Patents, Trademarks, and Copyrights of the Committee on the Judiciary, U.S. Senate. Washington, D.C., 1960.

    (b) *The Copyright Law: Howell's Copyright Law Revised and the 1976 Act.* Washington, D.C.: BNA, 1979. A commentary for lawyers accessible to the layman; it includes an extensive review of fair use cases, pp. 203–220.

Nimmer, Melville B. *Nimmer on Copyright: A Treatise on the Law of Literary, Musical and Artistic Property, and the Protection of Ideas.* N.Y.: Matthew Bender, 1963–78. The single most extensive and authoritative commentary on copyright. The discussion of fair use in § 13.05 (A) — (F) is accessible to the layman.

Oekonomidis, Demetrius. *Die Zitierfreiheit im Recht Deutschlands, Frankreichs, Grossbritaniens und der USA.* Berlin: Verlag Franz Vahlen, 1970. A comparative study of fair use laws written by a legal scholar. With the exception of Latman (a), this appears to be the only internationally informed systematic study of fair use by a legal scholar.

Seltzer, Leon. *Exemptions and Fair Use in Copyright: The 'Exclusive Rights' Tensions in the New Copyright Act.* Cambridge, Mass.: Harvard, 1978. An acute analysis of the photocopying issue that plausibly alleges obscurity and inconsistency in congressional thinking on fair use.

III. Periodical Articles on Fair Use

The following articles are selected because they confront the general principles of fair use in a comprehensive or provocative fashion.

Cardozo, Michael. "To Copy Or Not To Copy For Teaching and Scholarship: What Shall I Tell My Client," *Journal of College and University Law* IV, No. 2, 1977.

Cohen, Saul. "Fair Use in the Law of Copyright," 6 ASCAP, *Copyright Law Symposium*, No. 6, 1955.

Freid, Stephen. "Fair use and the new act," 'Copyright Symposium Part II,' *New York Law School Law Review* XXII, No. 3, 1977.

Kallal, Edward W. Jr. "Betamax and Infringement of Television Copyright," *Duke Law Journal*, 1977, 1181.

Nimmer, Melville B. "Does Copyright Abridge the First Amendment Guarantees of Free Speech and Free Press," *UCLA Law Review* XVII (1970): 1180.

Rosenfield, Harry N. "The Constitutional Dimension of Fair Use in Copyright Law," *Notre Dame Lawyer*, 50, No. 5, 1975.

Thatcher, Sanford G. "On fair use and library photocopying," *Scholarly Publishing* (University of Toronto Press), July 1978.

Bibliography of Fair Use Cases (Selective)

With Assistance from Deborah Lulf

There are dozens of fair use case decisions and they are comprehensively listed in the treatises of Nimmer and Latman (b). In this volume, relatively comprehensive references are given in the essays by Eugene Aleinikoff, Harriet Oler, Harry Rosenfield, and Sigmund Timberg. Cases listed below relate directly to fair use in the context of teaching, scholarship or publication. (Consult the index for references in this volume.)

Berlin v. E.C. Publications, 329 F.2d 541 (2d Cir. 1964).

Encyclopaedia Britannica Ed. Corp. v. Crooks, No. 77-560 (W.D.N.Y., Feb. 27, 1978).

Folsom v. Marsh, 9 Fed. Cas. 342, No. 4,901 (1841).

Meeropol v. Nizer, 560 F.2d 1061 (2d Cir. 1977).

Public Affairs Associates, Inc. v. Rickover, 284 F.2d 262 (D.C. Cir. 1960).

Rosemont Enterprises, Inc. v. Random House, Inc., 366 F.2d 303 (2d Cir. 1960).

Time, Inc. v. Bernard Geis Associates, 293 F.Supp. 130 (S.D. N.Y. 1968).

Wainright Securities, Inc. v. Wall StreetTranscript Corp., 558 F.2d 91 (2d Cir. 1977), *cert. denied*, 98 S. Ct. 730 (1978).

Wheaton v. Peters, 33 U.S. (8 Pet.) 591 (1834).

Wihtol v. Crow, 309 F.2d 777 (8th Cir. 1962).

Williams & Wilkins v. United States, 487 F.2d 1345 (Ct. Cl. 1973).

Williams & Wilkins v. United States, 420 U.S. 376 (1975), *affirmed*, by an equally divided court, 487 F.2d 1345 (Ct. Cl. 1973).

INDEX